SIAMESE STATE CEREMONIES

[Photo: State Railways Dept.

HIS MAJESTY PRAJADHIPOK, KING OF SIAM, SEATED IN STATE AND ACCOMPANIED BY HIS REGALIA BEARERS.

Frontispiece.]

SIAMESE STATE CEREMONIES

Their History and Function

with

SUPPLEMENTARY NOTES

H. G. Quaritch Wales

Routledge
Taylor & Francis Group
LONDON AND NEW YORK

First published 1992 by Curzon Press Ltd.

Published 2018 by Routledge
2 Park Square, Milton Park, Abingdon, Oxon OX14 4RN
52 Vanderbilt Avenue, New York, NY 10017

First issued in paperback 2018

Routledge is an imprint of the Taylor & Francis Group, an informa business

ISBN 13: 978-1-138-99616-8 (pbk)
ISBN 13: 978-0-7007-0269-5 (hbk)

To my Aunt,

MRS. C. QUARITCH WRENTMORE,

I dedicate this book

in appreciation

of her sympathetic interest

in my work.

PREFACE

TO students of Indian Culture interested in tracing the influence of India in the institutions of her Cultural Colonies, as also to Anthropologists, the Religious Festivals and Court Ceremonies, which still remain the most characteristic features of Siamese social life, offer an important field for research. Yet the subject has been little touched by scholars, and I realize, therefore, that a pioneer work of this nature can only be regarded as an attempt to lay a foundation for further studies, and I hope that other students—particularly those Siamese possessed of an extensive knowledge of their own literature and customs—may be encouraged to endeavour to fill those gaps which remain in our knowledge of most of the Siamese State Ceremonies.

There are two points which I think call for notice here in order to remove possible misconceptions. In the first place, it may be as well to mention that, despite the fact that most of the Royal Ceremonies discussed in this work are Hindu in origin, and retain much Brahmanical ritual, it should, however, be clearly understood that Buddhism is now, and has been for many centuries, the real religion of both the Siamese people and their sovereigns.

The second point concerns the question of transliteration. In the first chapter I quote M. George Coedès' reasons for preferring a scientific system adapted from that used for the transliteration of Sanskrit, and employed by him in transliterating the Siamese stone inscriptions, and I there also express my opinion that this system is equally suitable for use in the present work. I am, however, well aware that my adoption of this system is open to criticism from certain points of view, and hence I take the opportunity of referring to the matter here in some detail. In coming to my decision on the question, I was mainly influenced by the fact that the "Court words" used in connection with many of the Ceremonies are very frequently Indian in origin, and any phonetic system would have rendered them entirely unintelligible to students desirous of tracing the extent of Indian cultural influence in Siam. At the same time, the use of this system, which is purely mechanical, and does not attempt to restore a word to its original Sanskrit or Pāli, avoids the many pitfalls into which in the past certain writers have fallen, owing to their imperfect knowledge of the classical languages of India. The present system, whilst in most cases rendering the Indian origin of a word sufficiently recognizable, allows it to be easily reconstructed in Siamese characters if required. Again, the purely Siamese words, though admittedly often unrecognizable in their transliterated form, are equally easily reconstructed in Siamese characters. It has been suggested to me that two systems, a phonetic and a scientific, might with advantage be used for the Siamese and Indian words respectively, but, quite apart from the inconvenience of using two systems, there would be the sometimes insuperable difficulty of deciding whether a given word is in fact of Indian or purely Siamese origin. If I make a few exceptions to my rule of adhering to one system of transliteration throughout the book, it is only in the case of a few well-known proper names, in deference to established usage.

Much of the material incorporated in this volume was obtained by me while in Siam, and I am especially indebted to H.R.H. Prince Damrong Rājanubhāb, with whom I was privileged to have many illuminating conversations. My thanks are also due to H.H. Prince Dhāni Nivāt, and Braḥyā Prijānuṣāsanā, for valuable information and introductions ; to my friend Professor René Nicolas of Cuḷālaṅkaraṇa University, whose kindly criticism of parts of my manuscript at an early stage was very helpful ; and to Mr. P. S. Sāstrī, the Indian Sanskrit scholar attached to the Royal Institute at Bangkok, who assisted me in the translation of certain Siamese texts.

The present work was accepted by the University of London for the degree of Doctor of Philosophy, and I particularly wish to express my gratitude to Dr. C. O. Blagden, Dean of the School of Oriental Studies, for guiding me in my studies while in England ; also to Dr. L. D. Barnett, whom I often consulted with reference to Indian literature ; and to Dr. B. Malinowski for introducing me to the functional method of social anthropology.

H. G. Q. W.

LONDON,
October, 1931.

CONTENTS

PART I. INTRODUCTORY

CHAP.		PAGE
I.	Scope and Sources	3
II.	An Outline of the History of Siamese Culture	12
III.	Social Organization of the Siamese . .	21

PART II. THE CHIEF FACTORS IN SIAMESE STATE CEREMONIAL

IV.	The Kingship	29
V.	The Court Brahmans	54

PART III. CEREMONIES OF INSTALLATION

VI.	Coronation: The Main Ceremonies	67
VII.	Coronation (*continued*): The Regalia and the State Progresses	92
VIII.	Coronation (*continued*): Installation of the Queen and Assumption of the Royal Residence	116
IX.	Higher Grades in Royal Consecration . .	121
X.	The Tonsure Ceremony	126
XI.	Cremation: The Ceremonies	137
XII.	Cremation (*continued*): History and Function .	155
XIII.	The Worship of Dead Kings	169

PART IV. CEREMONIES CLOSELY CONNECTED WITH KINGSHIP

XIV.	Royal Audiences, and the Reception of Embassies	177
XV.	The Oath of Allegiance	193
XVI.	The Royal Bounty (*Ṭulābhāra* and *Kaṭhina*) .	199
XVII.	Royal Anniversaries (Coronation and Birthday) .	213

PART V. CEREMONIES RELATING TO AGRICULTURE

CHAP.		PAGE
XVIII.	CEREMONIES FOR THE CONTROL OF WIND AND RAIN: Kite-flying, *Baruṇa-Sāṭra*, and the Speeding of the Outflow	221
XIX.	FESTIVALS OF FIRST FRUITS: *Dhānya Daha* and *Sārada*	228
XX.	THE SWINGING FESTIVAL, and the Reception of the Gods	238
XXI.	THE FIRST PLOUGHING	256
XXII.	TEMPORARY KINGS	265

PART VI. MISCELLANEOUS STATE CEREMONIES

XXIII.	THE WHITE ELEPHANT	273
XXIV.	FEASTS OF LAMPS: *Còṅ Pariaṅ*, Kaḥṭikeyā Festival, and *Lòy Braḥ Praḥdīp*	288
XXV.	MINOR BRAHMANICAL CEREMONIES: The Worship of the Sacred Bull, Viṣṇu's Sleep, Śiva's Night, *Snāna*, Top-spinning, New Year	295
XXVI.	THE PROPITIATION OF SPIRITS: Animism, Guardian Spirits of Cities, Guardian Spirits in Great Guns, and Foundation Sacrifices	300
XXVII.	THE EXPULSION OF EVIL: The General Expulsion of Evil at New Year, the Public Scapegoat, the Expulsion of Disease, a Ceremony of Palace Exorcism, and a Royal Exorcism	308

GENERAL CONCLUSIONS

XXVIII.	GENERAL CONCLUSIONS	315
	INDEX	319

LIST OF ABBREVIATIONS

A. Aymonier, *Le Cambodge*, 3 vols., Paris, 1900–4.

BEFEO. *Bulletin de l'École Française d'Extrême-Orient.*

BRB. *Ro̍'aṅ Braḥ Rāja Bidhī Sipsŏṅ Do'an* (Ceremonies of the Twelve Months), by H.M. King Cuḷālaṅkaraṇa, Bangkok.

C. Chatterji, *Indian Cultural Influence in Cambodia*, Calcutta, 1920.

D. Dubois and Beauchamp, *Hindu Manners, Customs and Ceremonies*, 3rd edition, 1905.

ERE. Hastings, *Encyclopædia of Religion and Ethics.*

GB. *The Golden Bough*, by Sir J. G. Frazer, 3rd edition, London, 1915. The eleven vols. are referred to by the following numbers : I, *The Magic Art*, pt. 1 ; II, do, pt. 2 ; III, *Taboo and the Perils of the Soul* ; IV, *The Dying God* ; V, *Adonis, Attis, Osiris*, pt. 1 ; VI, do. pt. 2 ; VII, *Spirits of the Corn and Wild*, pt. 1 ; VIII, do, pt. 2 ; IX, *The Scapegoat* ; X, *Balder the Beautiful*, pt. 1 ; XI, do., pt. 2.

Ge. (1) G. E. Gerini, *Chŭḷăkantamaṅgala*, Bangkok, 1895.

Ge. (2) G. E. Gerini, article on " Festivals and Fasts (Siamese)," in Hastings' *Encyclopædia of Religion and Ethics.*

Gr. Groslier, *Recherches sur les Cambodgiens*, Paris, 1921.

HV. *Gāṁ Ha̲i̲̓ Kāra Khun Hlvaṅ Hā Văt* (Evidence of Khun Hlvaṅ Hā Văt).

JSS. *Journal of the Siam Society.*

KM. *Kaṭa Maṇḍirapāla* (Book of Palace Law).

L. Leclère, *Fêtes Civiles et Religieuses du Cambodge.*

L. L. La Loubère, *Siam*, English edition, London, 1693.

M. *Mahāvaṁsa*, edn. of Geiger and Bode, London, 1912.

NN. *Ro̍'aṅ Nāṅ Nabamāśa* (Story of Lady Nabamāśa).

P. Pallegoix, *Royaume Thai ou Siam*, 2 vols., Paris, 1854.

SBE. *Sacred Books of the East.*

The *Jātakas* (Buddhist Birth Stories) are usually referred to by numbers, the quotations being from Cowell's edition.

LIST OF ILLUSTRATIONS

His Majesty Prajadhipok, King of Siam, seated in State and accompanied by his Regalia Bearers . . . . *Frontispiece*

PLATE		*To face page*
I.	The Altar in the Śiva Temple	54
II.	A *Mantra* entitled "The Worship of the Eight Directions"	55
III.	*Yantra* Diagrams	56
IV.	*Yantra* Diagrams	57
V.	Brahman performing *Homa*	72
VI.	*Pai-Śrī* Trays with Offerings to the Deities .	73
VII.	The King in the Ablution Pavilion receiving Anointment Water from the Prince Patriarch	75
VIII.	The Ceremony on the Octagonal Throne . .	78
IX.	The King seated on the *Brahdrapiṭha* Throne after having received the Regalia . . .	84
X.	Some of the Regalia	92
XI.	The Inscription of the Golden Tablet of Style and Title, and of the Royal Horoscope . .	102
XII.	The Royal Weapons	106
XIII.	The Royal Progress by Land	110
XIV.	The Royal Barge "Subarṇahaṅsa" . . .	111
XV.	The Anointment of the Queen	118
XVI.	The Assumption of the Royal Residence . .	119
XVII.	Mount Kailāsa and the Procession of the Tonsurate	128
XVIII.	Reception of the Tonsurate by Śiva (King Rāma V) on Mount Kailāsa	130
XIX.	The Tonsurate seated in Full State after the Ceremony	131
XX.	The Corpse of King Sisowath of Cambodia dressed for placing in the Urn	139
XXI.	The Lying-in-State in the Tusiṭa Mahā Prāsāda	142
XXII.	Monks Chanting during the Lying-in-State .	143
XXIII.	The Funeral Pyre (Braḥ Meru) of King Rāma VI	145
XXIV.	The Urn being transferred to the Great Funeral Car	148
XXV.	A Royal Funeral Procession	149

Plate		To face page
XXVI.	Bearers of the Royal Gifts to the Monks circumambulating the Meru	154
XXVII.	The Ashes of the late Queen Mother borne in Procession	155
XXVIII.	Statues of the Kings of the Căkrī Dynasty in the Pantheon	170
XXIX.	Royal Relics placed in State on an Altar in the Amarindrā Hall	171
XXX.	The King arriving at a *Văt* on the Occasion of a Land *Kaṭhina*	202
XXXI.	Royal Barge taking part in a *Kaṭhina* Procession	203
XXXII.	"Mixing the Heavenly Rice" in the *Sārada* Ceremony	232
XXXIII.	"Mixing the Heavenly Rice": a Nearer View	233
XXXIV.	The Swinging in Progress	238
XXXV.	The Procession of "Śiva" at the Swinging Ceremony	240
XXXVI.	"Śiva" with his Insignia Bearers watching the Swinging	241
XXXVII.	The Circular Dance of the "*Nāgas*"	242
XXXVIII.	"Śiva" paying Homage to the King	243
XXXIX.	Ceremony in the Śiva Temple	252
XL.	Procession of the "Temporary King" at the Ploughing Festival	256
XLI.	The First Ploughing	257
XLII.	A Siamese Representation of the Miracle of the Jambu-tree	260
XLIII.	The White Elephant of the Present Reign	274
XLIV.	The White Elephant of the Sixth Reign	275
XLV.	The King anointing the White Elephant of the Present Reign	276

Fig.		
1.	The "Rhinoceros", Bearer of the Sacred Fire	150
2.	Arrival of the French Embassy at Ayudhyā	181
3.	The Audience Hall at Ayudhyā	182
4.	(1), Gold Vessel for the King's Letter; (2) Plan of Audience Hall	183
5.	The *Braḥ Mahā Rāja Grū* performing Rites in the Śiva Temple on the First Day of the Waning of the Second Month, at the Point immediately before the Small Images are bathed and placed on the *Bhadrapiṭha* Throne	248

Part I

INTRODUCTORY

CHAPTER I

SCOPE AND SOURCES

This inquiry is limited to a study of the State Ceremonies of Siam, and these are primarily Brahmanical with later Buddhist modifications. The reason for this is twofold: In the first place, the State Religion of those countries from which the Siamese derived their civilization in early days was in the main Hinduism, and kingship, wherever it is found, tends to preserve the usages of former times. Secondly, Hinduism is a religion that lends itself especially to the support of that pomp and circumstance inseparable from Absolute Monarchy, the only form of government the Siamese have ever known. On the other hand, Buddhism is essentially a religion of the people, tolerating kings merely as protectors. Thus, while Siamese kings have always protected Buddhism, and have usually looked to it themselves for spiritual consolation, they have surrounded themselves with the paraphernalia of Hinduism and retained much of its ritual in their Court Ceremonies, the better to support the power of the monarchy. We shall, therefore, make a rather close study of Siamese Brahmanism, but shall only consider Buddhism in so far as it is necessary to enable us to understand the Buddhist additions made by pious kings in later times to many of the State Ceremonies. Only one purely Buddhist festival will be included—the *Kaṭhina*—specially selected as illustrating that aspect of the kingship in which the monarch fills the rôle of protector of the people's faith. To attempt to deal with the popular Buddhist festivals and ceremonies of Siam would be to open up a vast field of research into Siamese Buddhism, far beyond the scope of this work. Nevertheless, though the inquiry revolves mainly around the king and his court, it is more than a study of the kingship; it probes deeply into the whole body of society.

The mode of treatment here employed is an attempt to combine two methods of investigation, namely, the *historical*, or *archæological*; and the *functional method of social anthropology*. The first method is the one which first appealed to me and on the lines of which my former studies of Indian culture had been conducted. In the words of Sir James Frazer :—

> " To sift out the elements of culture which a race has independently evolved and to distinguish them accurately from those which it has derived from other races is a task of extreme difficulty and delicacy, which promises to occupy students of man for a long time to come." [1]

[1] *GB*. x, p. vii.

These words immediately call to mind those two theories of modern anthropology, the diffusionist and that of independent origins. Sir James evidently sees scope for the application of both theories, and I agree with this point of view, with the reservation that the final pronouncement on the question must inevitably await the accumulation of a vastly greater amount of data from all parts of the world than we are in possession of to-day. It is in this connection that I hope that some of the facts that I have brought to light in this book may serve a wider purpose in the hands of comparative ethnographers who may perceive theoretical values of wide application that have escaped me.

In dealing with a people like the Siamese, whose culture is mainly borrowed from India, the diffusionist theory certainly forces itself to the fore ; and within the limited field of the Indian Cultural Colonies there can be no gainsaying the fact that diffusion has played a very prominent part. Indeed Hocart, in his book on *Kingship*,[1] has brought forward interesting evidence in support of there having been much cultural diffusion amongst all those maritime peoples extending from the Mediterranean to Fiji. But this appears to me to be still a long way from establishing the world-wide application of the diffusionist theory from some such source of origin as Egypt.

It will perhaps be as well to define at once in what sense I use the word " origin ". As Dr. Malinowski has pointed out with regard to magic :—

> " Magic never ' originated ', it never has been made or invented. All magic simply ' was ' from the beginning an essential adjunct of all such things and processes as vitally interest man and yet elude his normal rational efforts. The spell, the rite, and the thing which they govern are coeval." [2]

Again, as Hocart remarks :—[3]

> " There are no first beginnings ; there are only beliefs, older beliefs, and yet older beliefs."

I hope, therefore, that it will be understood that I do not use the word " origin " dogmatically, but merely as a term of convenience expressive of that stage, more or less remote, to which we are, in the present state of knowledge, able to trace any given institution.

Turning now to the second method of investigation—the functional method of social anthropology. It was only after reading some of the illuminating writings of Dr. Malinowski that I appreciated the value of this line of approach, and in attempting to apply it to the study

[1] London, 1927.

[2] " Magic, Science and Religion," in *Science, Religion and Reality*, 1925, p. 69.

[3] Op. cit., p. v.

of Siamese State Ceremonies I believe that I am adding much to the value of the work. The object of this method is to show, by functional analysis, the value of any given custom or rite for social integrity and for the continuity of culture. It is eminently practical and is concerned less with the reason that a native priest gives for the performance of a rite, than with the actual sociological value of the rite as evinced in the effect which it has on the life and status of the community. So far, the functional method has been applied almost entirely to primitive peoples, but there seems to be no reason why it should not be also applied to the higher culture, although the increasing complexity of social organization adds to the difficulties, but also to the interest of the work.

Siam to-day is passing through a critical period in her history. She has passed far along the road towards westernization. But a careful observer may note that this change has come about almost entirely in the sphere of the profane. She is indebted to western culture for much that has added to her material well-being ; but here, as elsewhere in the East, western religion has failed to make any appeal. For her spiritual salvation Siam must look to her own cultural inheritance ; and it is fortunate that amongst the masses of the people her religion was perhaps never more influential, and the respect for the monarchy remains undiminished. In the words of Dr. Malinowski :

> " A society which makes its tradition sacred has gained by it an inestimable advantage of power and permanence. Such beliefs and practices, therefore, which put a halo of sanctity round tradition and a supernatural stamp upon it, will have a ' survival value ' for the type of civilization in which they have been evolved. . . . They were bought at an extravagant price, and are to be maintained at any cost." [1]

But there are many Siamese who do not know that. Though the kings of the present dynasty have been, perhaps not unnaturally, staunch upholders of ancient tradition, there are other Siamese in high positions, especially to be found amongst those who have been educated on foreign lines, who fail to distinguish between the facts that whereas it is good for Siam to make material improvements and break down old abuses, it is, on the contrary, suicidal for her to interfere with her religion and cultural inheritance. Since these people have Siam's future in their keeping, it is my hope that the attempt that is made in this book to show to what extent and in exactly what way the various State Ceremonies are of value for the maintenance of social integrity may be of use in guiding them in those modifications which the growth of education may make necessary, keeping that

[1] *Science, Religion and Reality*, p. 40.

which is of lasting good in each ceremony and steadfastly setting their faces against complete abolition, which is almost always both undesirable and unjustifiable.

That the present king is, like his predecessors of the dynasty, alive to the value of tradition, is exemplified by a speech which I recently (12th November, 1930) heard him make to the students of Vajiravudh College on the occasion of their Founder's Day. In the course of this speech he said that school tradition engendered a love of the school and in learning how to love this, their own small world, the students learned to love their country, their world after leaving school, to admire and follow the traditions which their ancestors had carried on down from past ages. Thus, he said, the old traditions lived on to the present and proved a most excellent thing. It taught the people to think of the deeds of their ancestors and to work for their country's progress.

That there is abundant need for such advice as that contained in the royal speech above quoted is at once shown by taking a glance at the less pleasant side of the picture, which may be graphically illustrated by the following extract from a recent issue of a Bangkok newspaper :—

> "Owing to the failure of the public in general to give proper attention and due respect to His Majesty the King when the Siamese National Anthem is being played after performances in the local entertainment halls, H.R.H. the Minister of Interior has issued an order to the police authorities to remedy the situation. It has been noticed that when the band strikes up the National Anthem some persons seem to pay little attention to it, while others walk out of the hall, quite oblivious to the patriotic custom. The police on duty have been instructed to remind the public when the tune is being played, and to take down the names of the offenders in the case of government officials or military men." [1]

In the days of Old Siam there was no National Anthem. But had there been one, or had the people found themselves in the presence of a Royal Letter or any other symbol of royalty, they would have known quite well what to do. They would have immediately thrown themselves flat on their faces. That custom was abolished long ago in accordance with the needs of a new age. But what was left in its place ? Instead of a gradual modification, the schooling of the people in a new etiquette, they were, except for the immediate entourage of the king, left in complete ignorance as to what they should do in such circumstances. Thus, though the people are at present absolutely devoid of evil intent, the door

[1] *Bangkok Daily Mail*, 21st October, 1930.

is left open for the dark teachings of communism, or whatever doctrines may chance to catch the ear of the masses, to step in and hasten the work of social destruction.

I have said that this is an attempt to combine the historical and functional methods of work. In the lower culture the functional method has had to work alone, for the reason that little was definitely known of the past, and it was left to the idle speculations of the "antiquarian", founded on the false evidence of explanatory myths and his own imagination. Very different, however, is that species of archæological work that is founded on the written records and stone inscriptions of a people of the higher culture, carefully documented at every step and corroborated by reference to the histories of neighbouring countries; and it seemed to me that with such a highly developed people as the Siamese much would be gained by a combination of the functional and historical methods. For example, light may sometimes be thrown on the real sociological significance of a custom by a knowledge of its history, when more direct methods of study have failed to afford a clue. Or the historical record of the abolition of a custom several centuries ago may afford valuable evidence as to the present trend of events and the future of the society.

The sources of information of which use has been made in the present study of Siamese Court Ceremonies are as follows:—

1. *Stone Inscriptions.*—Almost the only inscriptions which afford any details concerning Siamese State Ceremonies are those of the first Siamese kingdom of Sukhodaya, especially the famous inscription of King Rāma Gāṁhèṅ, which gives a remarkable amount of interesting information. These have been published by the Vajirañāṇa National Library, with a French translation by M. Coedès.[1] Khmer epigraphy, despite its richness, has proved disappointing, the inscriptions consisting almost invariably of names of kings, dates, records of the founding of temples, and long lists of donations to religion; but practically no ceremonial data whatever.

2. *Siamese Literature.*—This is the main source of information for the study of Siamese Religion and Ceremonial. Unfortunately, the national literature suffered a great blow when it was almost all destroyed at the fall of Ayudhyā in A.D. 1767. Books entirely devoted to a single ceremony (i.e. in the case of Coronation and Cremation) will be considered in the chapters devoted to those ceremonies. Here may be mentioned a few books which are of great general importance in the study of Siamese State Ceremonial. The oldest of such writings

[1] *Recueil des Inscriptions du Siam*, pt. i, "Inscriptions de Sukhodaya," G. Coedès, Bangkok, 1924.

is the *Kaṭa Maṇḍirapāla*, or Book of Palace Law (hereafter referred to as *KM*.), which is known from a manuscript dated A.D. 1805, and is supposed to have existed in almost the same form from about the fifteenth century A.D. The text of this Law was published in Bradley's edition of Siamese *Kaṭhmāy*. It is archaic in style, often ambiguous, and, indeed, the Siamese themselves are uncertain as to the meaning of many passages. A book of which the nucleus is almost certainly as old or even older than the *KM*. is the *Ro'aṅ Nāṅ Nabamāśa*, or Story of Lady Nabamāśa (hereafter referred to as *NN*.). The author is supposed to have been the daughter of a Brahman at the Court of one of the kings of Sukhodaya, and to have become one of the favourite wives of that king. From her father, and from the special opportunities that she enjoyed for personal observation, she acquired a remarkable knowledge of the State Ceremonies which were performed throughout the twelve months at that period, and she has left a short account of each, amongst other material, in the memoirs which purport to have been written by her. From the fact, however, that there is mention of the use of guns at Sukhodaya (about the thirteenth century), and there is also mention of the presence of Europeans and even Americans at the capital, much doubt has been thrown on the authenticity of this book as a whole. However, both Kings Rāma IV and V believed in the authenticity of the greater part of the book, supposing that it had been revised at a recent period by a person whose ignorance made him unsuitable for the task. It seems to me also that the greater part of the book is sound, and I am particularly impressed by the fact that the descriptions of many of the ceremonies imply an earlier stage in their evolution, which is exactly what students would expect to find, but does too much credit to the imagination of the editor, who calmly records the presence of firearms and Americans at Sukhodaya. I therefore attach considerable importance to this book for the study of ceremonial during the period which immediately followed the setting-up of the first free Siamese kingdom. It was printed and published by the National Library in B.E. 2472 (A.D. 1929). Another valuable book of memoirs giving many details about Court Ceremonies in the Ayudhyā period is *Gāṁ Haị̆ Kāra Khun Hlvaṅ Hā Văt*, or Evidence of Khun Hlvaṅ Hā Văt (hereafter referred to as *HV*.), said to have been dictated by King Udumbara, the last king but one of Ayudhyā. It was printed and published by the National Library in B.E. 2459 (A.D. 1916). Both the usual versions of the *Baṅṣāvaḥtāra Kruṅka'u*, or Annals of Ayudhyā, and the version discovered in A.D. 1909 by Hlvaṅ Prasoeṭh, and which bears his name, contain occasional references to State Ceremonies which are of interest. The ceremonial treatises in the possession of the Court Brahmans contain chiefly Sanskrit *mantras* in an Indian character and also short notes in Siamese for the carrying out of the rites. These books will be more fully discussed in Chapter V. All the above books were made use of by King Rāma V in his voluminous *Ro'aṅ Braḥ Rāja Bidhī Sipsòṅ Do'an*, Treatise on the Royal Ceremonies of the Twelve Months (hereafter referred to as *BRB.*). This is a most important work, though obviously intended for Siamese readers, and the author unfortunately died before completing the book, there being no account of the ceremonies for the eleventh month. The book was published by the National Library in B.E. 2463 (A.D. 1920). A historical work which gives valuable information concerning the revival of State Ceremonial at the beginning of the Bangkok Dynasty is the *Braḥ Rāja Baṅṣāvaḥtāra Kruṅ Rățanakosindra Răjakāl Dī Sòṅ*, History of the Second Reign, by H.R.H. Prince Damrong Rājānubhāb, published by the National Library in B.E. 2459 (A.D. 1916). Lastly may be mentioned the Government Gazette, *Rājakiccānupekṣā*, published periodically, since it was first brought out in the last reign; the official programmes for ceremonies which it contains are sometimes useful.

3. *The works of European Authors.*—So far as Siam is concerned, these have, with few exceptions, been found to be almost useless for the purposes of the present study. Most of them devote considerable space to the better known ceremonies, but they are usually superficial and unreliable, or in search of the sensational, and my information has, therefore, been derived wherever possible from Siamese sources. Amongst the exceptions may be mentioned the precious work of La Loubère, ambassador from Louis XIV to the Court of Siam. However, most of the books in European languages, as well as numerous articles scattered throughout various periodical publications, have been carefully perused, and thus a good deal of information which would otherwise have been missed has been brought to light from scattered sources, which will be acknowledged in the body of this book. The only European writer who has given any of the Siamese State Ceremonies the thorough treatment they deserve is G. E. Gerini, whose monograph on the Tonsure Ceremony [1] contains many valuable notes on Siamese Brahman ritual which I have found useful. His derivations and theoretical work are, however, far from being as reliable as his facts. Another work by the same writer which is almost entirely unknown, but which is certainly worthy of notice, is the article on Festivals and Fasts (Siamese) in Hastings' *Encyclopaedia of Religion and Ethics.* Those short notes, based mainly on extracts

[1] *Chūḷākantamaṅgala*, Bangkok, 1895.

from King Rāma V's treatise, form, so far as I know, the only notice on the less well known Ceremonies of the Twelve Months to be found in any European language. For information as to the closely related Cambodian Ceremonies, and the Khmer bas-reliefs of Aṅkor, I am indebted to the labours of the great French scholars. The works of Leclère on the Cambodian State Ceremonies have been especially valuable.[1] In tracing the ceremonies back to India the translations in the *Sacred Books of the East* and Dubois' *Hindu Manners, Customs, and Ceremonies* have been of great help, as has also, from the point of view of comparative ethnography, that mine of information, *The Golden Bough*. A large number of other works on India and the Indian Cultural Colonies have also been found useful, and will be acknowledged in the text.

4. *Personal Observation.*—Although I mention this source of information last, it certainly ranks with the study of Siamese literature as of the first importance. I have personally witnessed most of the public Ceremonies of State on more than one occasion, and was also fortunate in being present in Siam on the occasions of several Royal Cremations, the last Coronation, and the Reception of the White Elephant for the present reign. My official connection with the Lord Chamberlain's Department sometimes gave me special opportunities for observing ceremonial, and also brought me into close connection with the "atmosphere" of the Court, while the special studies which I made of the Brahmanic ritual in connection with the recent Swinging Festival (January, 1931) make the pages dealing with that subject perhaps the most satisfactory in this book. Apart from this, however, my observations have been mainly directed towards endeavouring to understand the functional value of the various ceremonies. Such functional value is almost entirely subconscious, for hardly any Siamese has any answer to make to the question "Why?" other than *pen dharmniam* ("it is the custom"). One is at least not much hampered by explanatory myths now that western influence is beginning to make even the lower classes, at least in Bangkok, despise such things. Nevertheless, one must remember, that so long as a ceremony remains in practice, it must retain some influence over the life of society, however difficult it may be to estimate what is the exact extent of such functional value.

In the same way one can obtain little historical information from the modern Siamese. Priests and officials connected with the carrying out of ceremonies can tell one nothing beyond a bare description

[1] *La Cremation et les rites funeraires du Cambodge*, Hanoi, 1906, and *Fêtes Civiles et Religieuses du Cambodge*.

of the rites and the order in which they must perform them. There are few Siamese scholars in the western sense, the most notable example being H.R.H. Prince Damrong, the author of many important works in connection with the history and culture of Siam, and to conversations with whom I am indebted for much valuable information. But as a general rule Siamese scholarship still suffers much from a failure to apply comparative methods and a bias in favour of everything that may now be called Siamese having originated in Siam. Such an outlook is surely fatal to research in any country which owes nearly every feature of its higher culture to contact with neighbouring civilizations.

After mature consideration I decided to adopt throughout this work the system of transliteration advocated by M. Coedès in his *Recueil des Inscriptions du Siam*, part i, p. 10, in the belief that such a scientific system will be more generally appreciated, and will in time be the one universally accepted.[1] In quoting M. Coedès' words on the subject, I beg to endorse them as equally applicable to the present work:—

> " The transcription into Latin characters adopted in this volume is a scientific one, based on that of Sanskrit. For all alphabets derived from the Sanskrit, there are great advantages in making use of the transcription universally adopted for that language. I recognize, however, the practical utility of transcriptions which endeavour to reproduce the pronunciation. Such are those which M. Finot has employed for the Cambodian or for the Lao, and one might perhaps be able, in this work, to make some concessions to Siamese pronunciation, if it refer to purely Thai texts. But in view of the great number of Sanskrit and Pāli words interpolated in the Siamese inscriptions, and the necessity of employing a single method of transcription, the repugnance which one feels in corrupting the Indian words to their Indo-Chinese pronunciation has resulted in the adoption of the transcription known as ' the Indianists' '. Whatever be the system adopted, the essential is that it permits one to reconstruct the original characters instantaneously. This is precisely the case in this transcription which is purely mechanical and does not attempt to reproduce either the modern pronunciation from which the ancient one differs without doubt on more than one point, or that ancient pronunciation which we do not know and perhaps shall never know."

[1] But I use *ś* instead of *ç* and place the dot above the *m* instead of below it, in accordance with the English method of transliterating Sanskrit.

CHAPTER II

AN OUTLINE OF THE HISTORY OF SIAMESE CULTURE

It will be necessary to devote a chapter to the consideration of Siamese history with special reference to the trend of the various currents of influence which have built up Siamese culture as it is to-day. For a connected account of the obscure portion of the history of the country before the foundation of Ayudhyā we are much indebted to the labours of H.R.H. Prince Damrong, whose work [1] on this period has been followed by W. A. R. Wood.[2] The researches of Prince Damrong are founded on a careful collation of all the available sources for study—the Siamese annals, inscriptions, and the histories of neighbouring countries, including the Chinese chronicles.[3] Despite the fact that the earlier history of Siam is as yet by no means beyond the realms of controversy, it is possible for us to trace the general trend of cultural influences, which is all that is of primary importance to us in the present work. After the foundation of Ayudhyā in A.D. 1350, Siamese tradition had become established and changed little until modern times. We need not, therefore, concern ourselves much with the dates of kings, the fates of dynasties, nor the accounts of battles, which loom so largely in later Siamese history, the adequate material for which has been very satisfactorily treated and attractively presented in Wood's book.

The earliest inhabitants of what is now Siam were (1) Lavā, fragments of which people still exist in the northern hill ranges, and (2) the Môn-Khmer, who stretched from what is now Cambodia through the Mènaṁ valley and the Malay country as far as Pegu.

The first foreign voyagers to disturb these early inhabitants were parties of Indian traders who probably reached Pegu and the west coast of the Peninsula as early as the beginning of the Buddhist era, but the first real settlers probably did not come until the time of Aśoka's invasion of Kalinga, after which refugees reached the Gulf of Siam and traded in Cambodia. Shortly after this, Aśoka sent two missionaries, Sona and Uttara, to Suvarṇabhumi, believed by Rhys Davids to refer to the region from Pegu to the Malay Peninsula; but though Pegu was almost certainly the first to feel this influence,

[1] Translated into English in *JSS.*, vol. xiii.

[2] *History of Siam*, London, 1926.

[3] A full list of these sources is given in *JSS.*, vol. xi.

on account of its geographical position, it is probable that Hīnayānism reached Nagara Paṭhama at a very early period. The form of Buddhism disseminated by the missionaries of Aśoka was, of course, Hīnayānism; and that this was the form first received in Siam is supported by the fact that ancient *cetiya* and *căkra* wheels (which were used by the early Buddhists instead of images), dating from this time, have been found at Nagara Paṭhama. From here Hīnayānism spread further along the shores of the Gulf, and even to Cambodia.

About the end of the first century A.D. King Kaniṣka, under whom rose the Mahāyāna sect of Buddhism in the Punjab, sent missionaries to China, Tibet, and Southern India. From the latter point Mahāyānism spread to the powerful kingdom of Śrīvijaya in Sumatra, which extended its sway over the Malay Peninsula up to about the twelfth century A.D. Thus Mahāyānism found its way to Southern Siam, Central Siam, and Cambodia. Mahāyānistic images "turning the wheel of the law" and dating from the early part of the Christian era have been found at Nagara Paṭhama, while from the third to the seventh century A.D. the Môns formed a kingdom known as Dvāravatī in the Mènăṁ valley, of which remains have been left in the shape of Sanskrit inscriptions and Buddhist images resembling the Sārnāth school in India. Again, although after this time Brahmanism regained its ascendency in India, there were still Buddhist monarchs, and the missions of King Śiladitya about A.D. 656 probably affected Siam and Cambodia.

That the Indian settlers and the natives of Suvarṇabhumi remained Buddhists for a long time is shown by the fact that there are no early Brahmanic ruins in the West. When Śiva and Viṣṇu worship arrived is not definitely known, but no doubt the Indian settlers kept up communications with their motherland and new settlers arrived. These, not liking to dwell amongst the Buddhists of the West, passed on further east to where the early settlers had not been converted to Buddhism. These Brahmanic Indians set up a powerful State in Cambodia, and then extended their rule further west over the Lao country and Suvarṇabhumi, which accounts for later Brahmanic ruins being found nearly all over Siam.

We must now consider the Thai, i.e. the ancestors of the modern Siamese, including their cousins, the so-called Lao, who inhabit the country formerly occupied by the ancient Lavā. They began to move southwards in southern China about 100 B.C., and eventually set up a strong independent State (Nanchao) in the seventh century. From there they moved ever southwards, in response to pressure from the north, and entered the country now known as Siam. Their original religion is not known, but it is probable that they received the teachings of Mahāyānism at a fairly early period. As they arrived within the bounds of the Khmer empire they found that the people of the country were of a religion which was by now a mixture of Brahmanism and Buddhism. They preferred Buddhism, but respected the Brahmans.

The Thai threw off the yoke at Sukhodaya in A.D. 1237. The great King Rāma Gāṁhèṅ succeeded to the throne of the young State in 1276. Under him the kingdom was vastly extended, and almost certainly included both Pegu and Nagara Śrī Dharmarāja within its borders. An occurrence of importance in his reign was the opening up of political relations with China, two embassies having been received from Siam, according to the Chinese chronicles. King Rāma Gāṁhèṅ died in A.D. 1317, and the next king but one was King Dharmarāja I, who succeeded in 1353. From inscriptions we learn that he was versed in the *Tripiṭaka*, in Hindu ritual, skilled in astrology, and able to cast the calendar; that he erected a school for Buddhist and Brahman priests and sent a mission to Ceylon to bring away certain relics. Most important of all, the intercourse which had sprung up with Ceylon since the foundation of the Sukhodaya State culminated in the invitation to the Patriarch of Ceylon to come and teach in Siam where a monastery was built for him. To this period Siam, and also Cambodia, owe their final conversion to Hīnayānism; and this was largely due to the Siamese monarch's respect for and desire to emulate the actions of the great King Parākrama Bāhu of Ceylon, who was almost a contemporary of Rāma Gāṁhèṅ. Towards the end of his life the pious King Dharmarāja I actually became a monk.

After the time of King Rāma Gāṁhèṅ the temporal power of Sukhodaya began to wane. Pegu was lost by Dharmarāja I, and with his successors the territorial extent of the short-lived State further diminished. A rival power sprung up at Ūdòṅ, near the modern town of Suvarṇa, and its prince conquered Labapurī, the old city of Ayudhyā and Căndapurī, parts of the old Khmer empire which had never even fallen under the sway of Rāma Gāṁhèṅ. The prince of Ūdòṅ founded Ayudhyā in A.D. 1350 with the title of Rāmādhipati I. This was the beginning of the present kingdom of Siam, and by about 1400 the remnant of the old kingdom of Sukhodaya had passed under the sway of Ayudhyā.

We need not follow the history of Siam during the next four centuries in any detail. This was the period during which the splendour of the royal city of Ayudhyā was consolidated, and we find little cultural change, even when contact with European civilization was established. Much of its written history is occupied with the fates of dynasties, the bloodthirsty wars against the Burmese on the west, and the less serious ones against the Cambodians on the east. We need only notice the following features :—

Intercourse with Ceylon continued to be on a friendly footing, and mostly concerned with religion, and in response to the request of an embassy from Ceylon a religious mission was dispatched from Ayudhyā in 1753 to bring about the purification of the Buddhist faith which was said to be effete there.

Friendly relations between Siam and China existed in the latter half of the fourteenth and the beginning of the fifteenth centuries. In 1592 the King of Siam offered to send an army to assist China in a war against Japan, but the offer was refused. It seems probable that throughout the whole of the Ayudhyā period there were occasional exchanges of good wishes between the sovereigns of Siam and China, the former no doubt wishing to remain on good terms with their " elder brother ", though never admitting Chinese suzerainty.

Cambodia ceased to trouble Siam seriously after the foundation of Ayudhyā. In fact, it usually occupied the position of a vassal State. It ceased to have any cultural influence on Siam; indeed, the influence was rather the other way.

On the other hand, Burma becomes of primary importance twice in the history of the Ayudhyā period. The Siamese capital was first captured in A.D. 1569, after which Siam was overrun by the Burmese for the space of fifteen years until rescued by the efforts of the hero King Nareśvara. The second and final destruction of Ayudhyā took place in 1767, after a prolonged siege. This was followed by a short period of anarchy but fortunately a strong leader, a man of humble birth and Chinese extraction, appeared on the scene and drove out the Burmese. The name of this leader was Braḥyā Ṭāk, and he established his capital at Dhanapurī, on the river opposite to where Bangkok now stands. He ruled with a firm hand, and completely re-established the country until, in 1782, he became insane, and was deposed by one of his generals, Cău Braḥyā Căkrī, who became the first king of the present dynasty.

The first three kings of the Bangkok period (Căkrī Dynasty) were mainly engaged in endeavouring to restore and imitate the glories of Ayudhyā, and they had little inclination to enter into relations with foreign powers. It was the fourth king (Rāma IV) who was the first to open up modern diplomatic intercourse with European nations, to study English, and to introduce western material improvements.

But he was a great supporter of the cultural institutions of his country, and a deeply religious man who had spent twenty-seven years in the priesthood before being called to the throne. On the whole, therefore, the period ending with his death in 1868 may be rightly referred to as " Old Siam ", and that is the term I shall use throughout this volume, to distinguish it from the new era of rapid material progress which may be said to have really begun with the fifth reign. King Rāma IV is of special interest to us in the present work, because it was due to his staunch faith in Buddhism that many of the State Ceremonies received their Buddhist modifications and additions. The personal religious inclinations of Siamese kings usually left their mark on the State Ceremonies of the time. Thus King Draṅ Dharma (A.D. 1610–28) was a great supporter of Buddhism. On the other hand, King Nārāyaṇa (A.D. 1657–88) is known to have favoured Brahmanism. But perhaps no other Siamese king ever had the knowledge and ability which enabled Rāma IV to interest himself so deeply in the work of religious reform. The later kings of the dynasty have successfully carried on the work of adapting Siam to new conditions, while at the same time maintaining a respect for ancient tradition, King Rāma V having particularly endeared himself to the memory of his subjects by the abolition of slavery and by other wise and good measures.

The following is a list of those kings who, from our point of view, are the most important in the cultural history of Siam, and to most of whom frequent reference will be made in the course of this book :—

Important Kings of Sukhodaya

Name	*Reigned* (A.D.)
Śrī Indrādiṭya	1237–about 1270
Rāma Gāṁhèṅ	1276–1317
Dharmarāja I	1347–about 1370

Important Kings of Ayudhyā

Rāmādhipatī I	1350–1367
Nareśvara	1590–1605
Draṅ Dharma	1610–1628
Prāsāda Dòṅ	1628–1656
Nārāyaṇa	1657–1688
Paramakoṣa	1733–1758
Udumbara	1758–1762

King of Dhanapurī

Ṯāk	1767–1782

Kings of the Căkrī (Bangkok) Dynasty

Braḥ Buddha Yòt F̱ā́ Cuḷālokya (Rāma I)		1782–1809
Braḥ Buddha Lo'ṣ Hlā́ Nabālaya (Rāma II)		1809–1824
Braḥ Nā̀ṅ Kḷau (Rāma III)		1824–1851
Mahāmaṅkuṭ (Rāma IV)		1851–1868
Cuḷālaṅkaraṇa (Rāma V)		1868–1910
Vajiravudh (Rāma VI)		1910–1925
Prajadhipok	Succeeded	1925

The names Rāma I–VI were introduced by King Vajiravudh, and will be used in this volume to denote the first six kings of the dynasty.

I now come to what, for the purposes of the present work, will be the most important part of the historical outline; in it I shall attempt to summarize the cultural influences that have been brought to bear on the Thai in the course of their evolution from a tribe of nomads in southern China to their present position as the rulers of the modern kingdom of Siam. In this summary I shall primarily consider the development of the Thai, other races being considered only in so far as they have influenced the Thai. The foundation on which these influences have been brought to bear was the original stock of primitive culture possessed by the early Thai nomads, and later the independent Thai States in South China. This origina stock, after having undergone centuries of foreign influence, was the heritage of the first independent Thai kingdom in Siam, which was founded at Sukhodaya in A.D. 1237. This heritage was in turn passed on, not without undergoing vital change, to the second great Thai kingdom of Ayudhyā, and after the destruction of this capital in 1767 the early kings of the Căkrī dynasty made every effort to collect and restore all that was known about the culture of Ayudhyā.

While not denying the possibility of other sources of external influence, we may divide the foreign influences, so far as they are known, into two main divisions, Chinese and Indian.

(a) Chinese.

(1) The earliest foreign influence brought to bear on the Thai was almost certainly Chinese. The early Thai must have been animists, but how much of the animism that we see amongst the modern Siamese peasants is of pure Thai origin, and how much was derived from China at an early period and in later times from India, is difficult to determine. The chronicles of the Sui dynasty give interesting details of court life at Nanchao in which we can detect Chinese influence. It is also important to note that, dating from the first contact of the Thai with the Chinese, many words are common to both the Thai and Chinese languages, e.g. most of the Siamese numerals are of Chinese origin.

(2) The influence resulting from the interchange of embassies during the Sukhodaya period and later was probably mainly of a temporal nature, affecting chiefly Court manners and the style in which foreign ambassadors were received, etc. But the door was perhaps never closed against the exchange of cultural ideas between China and Siam.

(3) There was a certain amount of interest in Chinese culture in the early years which followed the fall of Ayudhyā. This was perhaps in the main due to the fact that King Ṯāk was of Chinese extraction. The courtyards of some of the older Bangkok temples are decorated with the figures of Chinese sages. But this contact came too late, and was too limited in duration, to have much, if any, effect on court usages. It seems, therefore, that while the Chinese was the earliest influence on Thai culture, it has in course of time become almost negligible, since it has been swamped to such an extent by superimposed Indian influence that few traces remain of it. The vast numbers of Chinese coolies and merchants who have taken up their abode in Bangkok have had no influence whatever on Siamese culture. They either carry on life according to their own customs and often return to China, or, marrying Siamese women, are easily absorbed by Siam.

(b) Indian.

Indian influence on Siamese culture was partly the result of direct contact with Indian settlers, but mainly it was brought about indirectly via the Indianized kingdoms of Dvāravatī, Śrīvijaya, and Cambodia. We can trace the influence of the Khmers fairly clearly, but the other two kingdoms, especially Śrīvijaya, exerted a strong if undefined influence over the development of Khmer culture, and hence of that of Siam, the extent of which is hardly yet realized.[1] The various streams of Indian influence, direct and indirect, may be classified as follows :—

(1) Indian Mahāyānistic influence originating in the Punjab, and reaching Siam and Cambodia via Southern India, Śrīvijaya, and South Siam. It began about the end of the first century A.D., and probably continued well into the seventh century. It was the means of the conversion of both Thai and Khmers to Mahāyāna Buddhism.

(2) Indian Vaiṣṇava Brahmanism. This reached Cambodia during the early centuries of the Christian era. The Thai people never became Hindus, but the kings of Sukhodaya recruited their Vaiṣṇava Court Brahmans from Cambodia, and assumed much of the Cambodian Vaiṣṇava Court Ceremonial. This intercourse with Cambodia was revived from time to time during the succeeding centuries.

(3) Indian Śaiva Brahmanism. Waves of this cult reached the Peninsula probably between the eighth and twelfth centuries A.D., and streams of later Indian settlers probably introduced modifications. But, although Nagara Śrī Dharmarāja came under the rule of King Rāma Gāṁhèṅ it was at that time under a Buddhist king and, as there were also Śaiva Brahmans in Cambodia, they were probably recruited from that source. Later, during the Ayudhyā period, when Brahmanism was moribund in Cambodia, the Śaiva Brahmans were obtained from the Peninsula. After the destruction of the old capital in A.D. 1767 both Viṣṇu and Śiva Brahmans, or at least those who were able to escape from the Burmese, fled to Nagara Śrī Dharmarāja, whence they were recalled at the foundation of Bangkok.

(4) Sinhalese Hīnayānistic influence. This is of the utmost importance. The Môn inscriptions of Lāṁbūn show that Peguan influences reached Northern Siam about the twelfth century, but it is probable that it was as a result of Sinhalese missions that the mass conversion of both Thai and Khmers to the Hīnayāna form of the faith took place in the thirteenth century. Siamese royal customs were also to some extent affected by the desire of the Siamese monarchs to follow the example set by the great Sinhalese King Parākrama Bāhu. Religious intercourse with Ceylon has been kept up until the present day.

The study of Siamese State Ceremonial which forms the subject of this book will illustrate the nature and extent of these foreign influences on Siamese culture. The omission of any mention of Burmese influence perhaps calls for notice before concluding this

[1] Coedès, *Recueil des Inscriptions du Siam*, part ii, pp. 1–5.

chapter. After much consideration it appears to me that such is negligible because the Siamese and Burmese have almost always been at enmity, a mountain barrier separates the two countries, and intercourse has always taken the form of warlike incursions into each other's territory. The last thing the Siamese would have consciously done would have been to copy any Burmese custom. Cultural resemblances are entirely due to a common origin, both the Burmese and Siamese owing much to the earlier Indian civilization of the Môns. Nevertheless, the very fact of this common origin makes the study of Burmese forms a by no means barren field for research in connection with the present inquiry.

CHAPTER III

SOCIAL ORGANIZATION OF THE SIAMESE

In old Siam the inhabitants of the country were considered only as the goods and chattels of the king, who had absolute power over their lives and property, and could use them as best suited his purpose. Otherwise they were of no importance whatever. Rather different, however, must be the sociologist's point of view, since it is his duty to consider the condition of a society as a whole; and in this work every effort is made to explain each ceremony in the light of its functional value to the society. This being so, it will be necessary to give a short account of the structure of the Siamese society.[1]

We are first considering the conditions in Old Siam, conditions which probably altered little from the early days of Ayudhyā until the time of King Rāma IV, because it was under this régime that the Court Ceremonial of to-day was built up and assumed its mature form. The absolutism of the monarch was accompanied and indeed maintained by the utmost severity, kings of Ayudhyā practising cruelties on their subjects for no other purpose than that of imbuing them with humility and meekness. Indeed, more gentle methods would have been looked upon as signs of weakness, since fear was the only attitude towards the throne which was understood, and tyranny the only means by which the government could be maintained. Despite the fact that all were equally of no account in the presence of the king, a many-graded social organization had been evolved, and the ingrained habit of fear and obedience produced a deep reverence for all forms of authority. The grading of the members of the royal family is a matter of extreme complexity. The *KM*. gives a detailed account of the ranks and privileges of the various princes and princesses, but for our purposes it will be sufficient to note the following: The sons and daughters of the king and queen, or queens, are known as *Čau F̱ā*, while those of the king and ladies who are not queens are *Braḥ Aṅga Čau*. The children of *Čau F̱ā* and *Braḥ Aṅga Čau* are called *Hmòm Čau*. The latter are the lowest in rank to be considered as real princes; for though their children and grandchildren are known respectively as *Hmòm Rāja Vaṅṣa* and *Hmòm Hlvaṅ*, they usually drop their title of royalty on attaining to any civil or military rank. The children

[1] Some of the facts in the earlier part of this chapter are derived from the chapter on "Social Organisation" in Graham's *Siam*, vol. i.

of *Hmòm Hlvaṅ* are commoners; and here we come to a very important point, the disappearance of all title to royalty at the fifth generation. This was the same in Cambodia, and descendants of the fifth generation could not succeed even in the case of complete extinction of the line.[1] Nevertheless, princes of the *Hmòm Càu* rank are sometimes promoted to *Braḥ Aṅga Càu* rank at birth. Princes of the rank of *Càu Fā* and *Braḥ Aṅga Càu*, on attaining manhood, may be appointed to any of the following ranks, in order of increasing importance: *Kram Hmū'n, Kram Khun, Kram Hlvaṅ, Kram Braḥ, Kram Braḥyā,* and *Samtec Kram Braḥyā.* These ranks usually carried with them the control of a *Kram* (government department), or the governorship of a province, but they are now only titles of honour.

The highest officials in the land were the *Mahā Uparāja*, or *Văṅ Nā*, known to Europeans as the Second King, and of whom more will be said in the next chapter; the *Văṅ Hlăṅ*, originally the commander of the rear-guard; and six Ministers whose titles were *Căkrī, Văṅ, Baladeba, Braḥ Glăṅ, Kraḥlāhom,* and *Yamarāja.* The first two of these were always princes; the others were sometimes royal, but usually not, and bore the title of *Òkñā* and, later, *Braḥyā* or *Càu Braḥyā*, the highest of the official ranks still in use. These non-hereditary ranks are as follows, in descending order: *Samtec Càu Braḥyā* (now extinct), *Càu Braḥyā, Braḥyā, Braḥ, Hlvaṅ, Khun,* and *Hmū'n.* Officials, both princes and nobles, received a certain number of marks of dignity called *śăkti nā*, formerly carrying a certain grant of land, but now purely honorary, while princes and the higher nobles are presented with insignia consisting of golden teapots and betel-boxes, which denote their rank. The personal attendants of the king were a body of Royal Pages, known as the *Kram Maḥhātlek* (Lord Chamberlain's Department), the members of which were usually marked out for preferment; but this department was abolished by the present king. All these officials were continually occupied in showing the necessary amount of deference to those above them, and to the king at the top, while mercilessly grinding down those below them in the social scale.

The great mass of the people were divided into a number of departments for public service, called *Lekh*, the members of which were numbered and branded by the noblemen in charge of each department. This system was the relic of an earlier feudal form of government. The *Lekh* were either *Svày*, the members of which were exempted from personal service on payment of part of their

[1] *A.*, vol. i, p. 62.

produce or a tax; or *Brài*, the vast majority of the people, who were collected in rotation as required, obliged to serve as soldiers, sailors, and other public menials, and for whom no escape was possible, the status being hereditary. Occupying the lowest place in the social scale were the slaves, who were either redeemable debt-slaves, or children born in slavery or sold by their parents, and for whom there was no release; but it must be added that Siamese slavery was always of a very mild type.

Anything in the nature of social intercourse or club life amongst the members of the noble and official classes was frowned upon by the monarchy, and social life centred round the Court alone. This state of affairs was strengthened by the fact that royalty died out at the fifth generation, as it still does, and that officials were always known, not by their own names, but by the office which they held. Thus great and influential families were never formed, and the memory of distinguished men died with them.

The reforms of King Rāma V brought about great changes, many of them for the better, in the life of the Siamese masses. One of the most far-reaching of these was the abolition of slavery; another was the abolition of bodily prostration of inferiors in the presence of their superiors. The government and forces of defence were thoroughly reorganized on European lines, ministers being chosen from amongst those of the younger generation who had received a European education. While many old offices passed away and new ones came into being, the old official titles were often retained, but the holders began to be known by their own names. King Rāma VI continued the work of reform and did much to create a healthy social life amongst the middle classes by the introduction of European games and sports. He also endeavoured to institute pride of family by the introduction of surnames. The women of all classes except the upper had always been perfectly free in Siam, and King Rāma VI did much to bring about the education and emancipation of the ladies of the upper class. He set his face against polygamy and made some progress in persuading the nobility to do likewise. Reforms in dress were instituted, and orders were conferred on those who had distinguished themselves in the service of the State. In short, every effort was made to instil into the Siamese the spirit of independence and the pride of nationality.

We must now consider how deeply these reforms really struck their roots into society. That they have been crowned with a considerable measure of success is evident from the present stability of the government and prosperity of the people. Nevertheless, it must be remembered that reform was mainly confined to material needs, the relief of which has added much to the well-being of the people. But every care was taken to see that the cultural tradition of the Siamese should be preserved, especially in regard to religion and respect for the monarchy. To quote the words of Graham:—

> "The absolutism of the monarchy, though outwardly modified by the constitution decreed in 1874, and veiled behind that consideration for his subjects which is His Majesty's chief concern, is as complete in spirit to-day as it was in the darkest period of tyrannical oppression which the nation has ever endured. The monarchy demands now, as it has always done, the most complete submission of the entire people not only to every decree issued by the king but, in theory, to his lightest whim or caprice, and the hereditary instincts of the race prompt it to render such obedience without question and without resentment, no matter what sufferings such obedience might conceivably entail." [1]

So great, it may be added, are these hereditary instincts, that bodily prostration still lingers to some extent although it is, of course, entirely voluntary. Siamese servants often crouch in the presence of their masters, officials lie almost full length when they are offering anything to the King on his throne, and I have seen ladies of the older generation crawling on their hands and knees when in the presence of a prince of high rank with whom they held conversation with their faces parallel to the ground, while the prince was seated in a chair. While the old instincts thus lurk so closely beneath the surface there can be no doubt but that the monarchy still remains the most important factor in the Siamese social organization.

It remains to say a few words about the religion of the Siamese people. We need not consider those religions such as Mahommedanism and Christianity which have been introduced into Siam by foreigners in comparatively recent times. They never had any effect on the Siamese other than to strengthen their faith in Hīnayānistic Buddhism which has been the national religion since the Thai first became independent in the thirteenth century. The Siamese are very devout, but they take their religion light-heartedly, because they are a light-hearted people. The part played in social life by the popular form of the religion professed by the masses is familiar to those who know anything of Siam; so that it is unnecessary to dwell on the importance of the Buddhist festivals frequently held at the numerous *văts*, or monasteries, which still provide almost the only opportunities for social intercourse and exchange of ideas among the country people. The

[1] *Siam*, i, 232.

yellow-robed monks are one of the most characteristic features of every town and village as they go on their begging rounds in the morning or take part in some cremation or housewarming ceremony. Then again most children receive their early education in the monastery schools, and later on it is the custom for every male Siamese to don the yellow robe for at least a few weeks or months. Some stay on and devote their lives to probing the deeper mysteries of Buddhism, and in Bangkok there are monks of great learning and piety, and a renowned school of Pāli.

From our immediate point of view Buddhism is chiefly of importance in that it has instilled into the people the spirit of humility and cheerful forbearance which has, in times past, enabled them to bear the oppression and tyranny of an absolute monarchy, and which, now that conditions have changed for the better, still acts as a powerful force in uniting them in loyalty to the Throne. Thus, Buddhism in its popular form is a religion of the people; in its higher form it is a deeply spiritual religion, the inspiration of those who are tired of the world and the hollowness of its attractions. It is not, therefore, primarily the religion of kings, though it owes its growth to their fostering protection. But, though the more material religion of the Hindus lends itself especially to the support of kingship, and though the Siamese people still to a limited extent respect the Brahmanic deities, there can be no doubt as to the great sociological value of the Buddhist modifications which have been added on to most of the State Ceremonies, in bringing together monarch and people in mutual understanding. This will be more fully appreciated in the course of this book.

Part II

THE CHIEF FACTORS IN SIAMESE STATE CEREMONIAL

CHAPTER IV

THE KINGSHIP

We have seen that the Siamese monarchy is absolute. We must now endeavour to show on what principles this absolutism is based, and why it has maintained such a powerful hold over the minds as well as the bodies of the Siamese people.

The loose expression "divine", which has been popularly applied to the Siamese kingship, requires considerable modification and analysis. As H.R.H. Prince Damrong has pointed out in his *Ṭāṁnān Susān Hlvaṅ Văt Debśirindra*,[1] the Siamese conception of the kingship has always depended on the religious point of view of the people. There may have been an earlier pre-historical pre-religious stage when kings were evolved from magicians, but history only gives us two conceptions —the Hindu and the Buddhist.

According to the Hindu theory, the king is identified with either Śiva or Viṣṇu, and this theory attained its greatest importance in ancient Cambodia.[2] It was introduced into that country by Jayavarman II, who ascended the throne in A.D. 802, and was known as the

> "cult of the Kamrateṅ Jagat ta rājya (the god who is the kingdom) or the Deva-rāja (the Royal God). This deity (which was a Śiva-liṅga) represented the royal essence present in the living king of Kambuja and in all her kings." [3]

The Royal God was not the king of the gods (i.e. Indra), but a god of the king, either Śiva or Viṣṇu, presenting certain peculiarities and identified with a great ancestor or a legendary founder of the kingdom. A similar cult existed in Central Java and in Campā, and all these may have had a common origin in the Kuñjara-Kuñja in South India. In Cambodia the posthumous titles of kings often indicated that they had gone to the heavens of their favourite deities, such as Śivaloka and Viṣṇuloka; and not only kings, but also other distinguished persons, were frequently, from the ninth to the end of the twelfth century, identified, even during their lifetimes, with either Śiva or Durgā, according to their sex. Thus we learn from an inscription that in the Khmer temple of Loley, the two images of Śiva, which bore the names of Indravarmeśvara and Mahāpatīśvara respectively,

[1] Bangkok, 1927.
[2] A., iii, pp. 581–4; C., pp. 103 and 245 sq.
[3] C., p. 245.

represented King Yaśovarman's father and maternal grandfather, Indravarman and Mahāpatīvarman. Such images, though bearing the attributes of the god, had the facial characteristics of the persons they commemorated; and the temples in which they were preserved were also portrait galleries in which ancestor worship was combined with the worship of the god. Such images were also made by the Thai after they became independent, and the modern representative of such a statue hall is the Pantheon in the Grand Palace at Bangkok, where the king and the people pay their respects on certain days to the life-size gold images of the monarchs of the present dynasty. True they are realistic portrait statues, and not, as formerly, idealistic god-like interpretations; but this is only an innovation of the Bangkok period.

No doubt the Khmer cult of the Deva-rāja and the deification of kings was only a highly specialized form of an earlier Indian conception of divine kingship, exemplified by the following passage from Manu :—

> " Even an infant king must not be despised (from an idea) that he is a mere mortal, for he is a great deity in human form." [1]

Again, in Nārada, we have :—

> " How should a king be inferior to a deity, as it is through his word that an offender may become innocent, and an innocent man an offender in due course ? " [2]

Still earlier, we are told that the king

> " is Indra for a twofold reason, namely, because he is a Kṣatriya, and because he is a Sacrificer ".[3]

And, as we shall see later, although the Khmer and Siamese kings were identified with the later Brahmanical gods, such as Śiva and Viṣṇu, there are features that indicate that in Siam we have survivals which support Hocart's theory [4] that in Vedic times or earlier the king was identified with the sun.

The rise of Mahāyānistic Buddhism in Cambodia brought about no great reaction against the cult of the Royal God, although Buddhist deities probably to a great extent supplanted the Brahmanical ones, and we find that Sūryavarman I (A.D. 1002), a Buddhist king, was known by the posthumous title of Nirvāṇapada. The Hīnayānistic

[1] Manu, chap. vii, 8, in *SBE.* xxv.
[2] Nārada, xviii, 52, in *SBE.* xxxiii.
[3] *Śatapatha Brāhmaṇa*, v, 4, 3, 7, in *SBE.* vol. xli, p. 99.
[4] Hocart, *Kingship*, chap. ii.

conversion, however, brought about a definite change, and in Siam to-day we find the only certain relic of the cult of the Royal God in the symbolism of the Coronation Ceremony by which the Brahman priests call down the spirits of Viṣṇu and Śiva to animate the new king; but possibly also in the rôle played by the king as Śiva now or formerly in the Tonsure, Ploughing, and Swinging Ceremonies, and in the Meru and Kailāsa mountains used on certain ceremonial occasions.

With Hīnayānism the Mahāyānistic deities were not recognized, and the Hindu gods were redueed to the rank of spirits ministering to the Buddha, or demi-gods ruling over the inferior heavens. In fact, though they were fitted into the Buddhist scheme of things they were no longer taken seriously; and no Buddhist king would have been flattered to have been told that he was the incarnation of a Hindu deity—and nothing more. The conception of the king under Hīnayānism is obviously that he is a Bodhisattva or incipient Buddha, or else a Cakravartin (Universal Emperor), and this belief, which is still held by all orthodox Siamese Buddhists, is derived proximately from imitation of the great Sinhalese kings and is strengthened in the minds of the people by the evidence of the popular Indian *Jātaka* stories.

Since, according to the tenets of the Hīnayāna form of Buddhism, the accumulation of merit is rewarded by rebirth in happy conditions, just as certainly as beggars and criminals are paying for the demerit piled up by evil deeds in former lives, one might suppose that a Buddhist king would always be particularly careful as to the nature of his actions, and, still being subject to the Wheel of the Law, would probably rule more justly than would a Hindu monarch. Unfortunately, however, history makes it quite clear that the teachings of Buddhism were no more successful in restraining despotic rulers in Siam than were those of other religions elsewhere, and it was always easy for a tyrannical monarch to expiate a life of crime by forcing an army of slaves to build a giant pagoda. Indeed, strangely enough, Buddhism led to what is a world-wide later conception of the Divine Kingship associated with the most overbearing despotism. A Hindu king was regarded as the receptacle of the god, of the divine essence. He was even identified pantheistically with the god; but he was not the god himself. In Buddhism the king is a Bodhisattva or a Cakravartin, a greater being in the eyes of the Buddhists than any Hindu god. When added to this it be remembered that to this day the correct phrase for expressing "I" when addressing the Siamese king means "the Lord Buddha's slave", can one wonder that ambitious monarchs sometimes forgot the humility inculcated by Buddhism, and were tempted to endeavour to accelerate the process of attaining complete enlightenment, to attempt to rid themselves of the galling necessity of showing reverence to the humble yellow-robed monk, even to proclaim themselves the coming Maitreya Buddha ? Such attempts have always met short shrift from the priesthood, it being such an error of judgment that led to the undoing of King Ṯāk ; and at least one similar instance occurs in Burmese history.

It will thus be understood that the condition of the people in Siam has always depended less on the particular conception of the kingship—Brahmanical, Buddhist, or, as it later became, a mixture of the two—than it has on the character of the individual monarch. But, broadly speaking, the functional value of the Divine Kingship, whether from a Brahmanical or Buddhist viewpoint, is obvious to anyone who appreciates the present state of civilization of the Siamese masses. With an education still almost confined to the religious sphere, and bred up on the exploits of the Indian hero Rāma, the conception of a king as a superior being, to be obeyed implicitly, is the only one known to the ordinary Siamese. He has no wish for a share in the government, he does not trouble about politics, and he is as yet unfitted for any other regime than the present. It is certain, therefore, that any conception of the kingship that strengthens his belief in the ruling power is of the highest sociological value. That his belief and loyalty are in the main supported by the pomp and glamour of Royal Ceremonial will be shown in the course of this book ; but the present is a suitable place to consider in some detail those prohibitions or taboos with which Divine Kingship is always hedged around and, in surrounding it with an air of mystery and sanctity, are performing a no less important share in its maintenance than is Royal Ceremonial itself. The following is an attempt to analyse the functional value and arrive at the historical derivation of those royal taboos that have come to my notice.

1. *The King's person was tabooed, more especially the head and hair.*

That the king's person is too sacred to be touched is an idea perhaps universally connected with the divine kingship, and certainly prevalent in all the Indian states, which is probably the direction from which it reached Siam. In the *Mahāvaṁsa* it is recorded that :—

> " Going down even knee-deep into the water the king respectfully gave his right hand to the *thera,* as he came down from the ship." [1]

The point was specially mentioned because in the ordinary way to touch the king's hand was a crime punishable by death. In Siam at

[1] *M.* v, 255.

the present day we have what appears to be a relic of this in the fact that things are always handed to the king through the medium of a golden plate or bowl, never directly by hand.

On board the royal barges there are, or were until recently, bundles of cocoa-nuts intended to be thrown to the king or any member of the royal family in the event of the barge foundering, for it was forbidden on pain of death for any person to lay hands on royalty to save them from drowning. A well known instance of the operation of this taboo is the tragic death of King Rāma V's first queen, who was drowned in full view of numerous bystanders who dared not save her. The rules on this subject are indeed expressly laid down in the *KM.*, from which I translate the following passage:—"If a boat (royal barge) founders, the boatmen must swim away; if they remain near the boat they are to be executed. If the boat founders and the royal person falls into the water and is about to drown let the boatmen stretch out the signal-spear and throw the cocoa-nuts so that he may grasp them if he can. If he cannot, they may let him seize the signal-spear. If they lay hold of him to rescue him they are to be executed. He who throws the cocoa-nuts is to be rewarded with forty ticals of silver and one gold basin. If the barge sinks and someone else sees the cocoa-nuts thrown and goes to save the royal person, the punishment is double and all his family is to be exterminated. If the barge founders and someone throws the cocoa-nuts so that they float towards the shore (i.e. away from the royal person), his throat is to be cut and his home confiscated."

The inhibition against touching the royal head or hair seems to be a specialized development of the general taboo against touching any part of the royal person. Frazer[1] has collected much evidence to show that there is a widespread taboo of head and hair; and Siamese of whatever rank object to anyone touching the head, and used to dislike the idea of anyone walking overhead. This belief seems to be founded to a great extent on the supposed existence of a guardian spirit (*khvăñ*) in the head, who easily takes offence at the slightest indignity of this nature, with disastrous effects on the welfare of the individual; while there is also the supposition that the hair must be the most sacred part of the body by reason of the superior position that it occupies, and it is evidently this belief that has given rise to the use of the word *pham* "hair" for "I" when speaking to superiors, meaning that only the most noble part of the speaker dares to address the superior person spoken to.

There being so much respect for the head amongst even the lowest

[1] *GB.* iii, pp. 252 sqq.

classes of Siamese, it is not remarkable that the king's head should be particularly sacred. As La Loubère remarks :—

> "The most considerable of all (the officers of the Wardrobe) is he that touches his Bonnet, although he be not permitted to put it upon the Head of the King, his Master."[1]

Again, while the Tonsure (Brahmanical Initiation Ceremony) of even the poorest child is carried out with the greatest care not to bring about those calamities which would certainly follow any injury to the *khvăñ*, the Tonsure of a royal prince is attended with those elaborate rites of which some account will be given in Chapter X. But whereas the ordinary Siamese undergoes the usual periodical hair-cutting with no greater ceremony than does the European, the king used not to be allowed the attention of the barber without the due performance of certain magical rites intended to avert the evils which might follow touching the king's head in this manner. On these occasions certain propitiatory verses (*sebhā*) were, and I understand still are, recited during the hair-cutting. *Sebhā* are songs of an amatory nature, and the one recited at the king's hair-cutting is the well-known Khun Jăṅ Khun Phèn, a scurrilous story of the illicit affairs of noblemen and their wives, ending in the assassination of the king by the state sword at the hands of the son of one of the noblemen, these events being supposed to have taken place as long ago as A.D. 185. The reading is intended to act as an admonition against possible dangers from the barber's sharpened tools, and on such occasions it is an old custom to use scissors with blunt points, the use of the razor being proscribed, while to prevent other accidents the barber has to put two charmed rings on his fingers.[2] I understand that cloths are spread around during the hair-cutting in order that the clippings should not touch the ground, and these are afterwards burnt.

It appears to me that this taboo has in times past been the most important of all in maintaining the mystery and air of sanctity essential to the preservation of the idea of Divine Kingship, and that it has also had much practical value in keeping the king's person safe from physical harm, especially the dagger of the assassin.

2. *It was taboo to look upon the face of the King.*

Mrs. Leonowens[3] tells us that even within the precincts of the palace the concubines would turn away their faces at the King's approach. Kaempfer[4] mentions that

[1] L. L., p. 102. [2] Ge. (i), p. 54 fn.
[3] *The English Governess at the Siamese Court*, London, 1870.
[4] Kaempfer's *History of Japan* (1690–2), trans. by Scheuchzer, edn. of 1906, i, p. 21.

> "If one happens to chance to meet the King, or his Wives, or the Princess Royal in the open fields, he must prostrate himself with his face flat to the ground, turning his back to the Company, till they are out of sight."

Until the rule was abolished by King Rāma IV, it was prohibited for any person to watch a royal procession. Lattice fences were erected along the route in front of the houses of the people, and the populace was obliged to keep out of sight behind them. They were not even supposed to peep through the interstices of the fences, although such minor breeches of the law were winked at because they served the valuable purpose of allowing the people to be impressed by the majesty of royalty—from a safe distance. But any loiterers who were so unfortunate as to be caught by the lictors were summarily chastised with bamboos, and Europeans were usually informed well in advance, and advised to take a side street in order to avoid unpleasantness. This taboo no doubt had an eminently practical value for the safety of a tyrannical monarch who could never be sure of the loyalty of his oppressed subjects, and it required a strong king who had endeared himself in the hearts of his people to break through this tradition. Another characteristic of royal processions, which may be attributed to the same lurking fear, and which was very evident down to recent times, was the hustling and disorderly appearance of the mob of courtiers and favourites who crowded round the royal palanquin during the progress.

The taboo by which all subjects had to remain prostrate with eyes averted when in the king's presence may also be mentioned under this heading, but we shall speak of it more fully in the chapter devoted to Royal Audiences.

All the variations of this taboo were common to Cambodia and Burma; probably also to Ceylon, since Knox wrote in 1681:—

> "When they come before him they fall flat down on their faces to the ground three several times, and then they sit with their legs under them upon their knees all the time they are in his presence."

The taboo was also in force in China, but it seems probable that the nations of Indo-China received it from India, the underlying idea being that no ordinary mortal could endure the glory of divine majesty, such idea being expressed in the following passage from Manu:—

> "Because a king has been formed of particles of those lords of the gods, he therefore surpasses all created beings in lustre; and, *like the sun*, he burns eyes and hearts; *nor can anybody on earth even gaze on him.*"[1]

[1] Manu, vii, 5, 6.

Here Manu only goes so far as to compare the king to the sun. His predecessors probably identified the two.

3. *The King was not supposed to touch the ground.*

John Struys in the seventeenth century remarked of the king that " he never sets his foot upon the Earth, but is carried on a Throne of Gold ".[1] Groslier states that the same taboo prevailed in Cambodia [2]; and Knox wrote that the King of Ceylon never went out except in procession, rarely riding on a horse or elephant, usually on a palanquin. We have strong evidence in the *Śatapatha Brāhmaṇa* for the derivation of the taboo from India :—

> " As long as he (i.e. a king) lives, he does not stand on this (earth with bare feet). From the throne-seat he slips into the shoes ; and on shoes (he stands), whatever his vehicle may be, whether a chariot or anything else." [3]

The theory on which this taboo is based is that the king, being divine, should move in a god-like manner, and perhaps it is a relic of the time when the king represented the sun, for the resemblance between a man suspended in the air by the power of *iddhi* and the sun occurred to some Indian minds.[4] And the operation of this taboo must at all times have done much to strengthen the air of mystery surrounding the kingship.

4. *It was taboo to inquire after the King's health.*

This was because one was not allowed to presume that the King could be subject to the ills of the flesh as were ordinary mortals. In the same way it was taboo to allude directly to the death of the King, the term used to express this event being *satec svargagaṭa*, meaning "to migrate to heaven". Illness and death are perhaps the greatest dangers that Divine Kingship had to face ; hence the enormous value of this taboo, the necessity of keeping the people in ignorance of the fact that kings have but mortal frames. As will be shown in a later chapter, the main functional value of the elaborate royal cremation ceremonies hinges upon this taboo, since their effect on the popular imagination is, or was, to produce the impression that the king has merely been translated in full regal state to a nobler plane.

A modification in this taboo has taken place only in very recent times. During the last illness of King Rāma V nothing was known

[1] Struys, chap. iv, p. 30.
[2] Gr., p. 337.
[3] *Śatapatha Brāhmaṇa*, v, 5, 3, 6, and 7, in *SBE*. vol. 41, p. 128.
[4] Hocart, *Kingship*, p. 163.

outside the palace as to the seriousness of his condition, a contrast to that of the late King Rāma VI, during which bulletins, which entered into a surprising amount of medical detail, were issued almost hourly.

5. *Taboos in connection with food.*

> "No one can enter the kitchen of the palace when the food is being prepared; and a confidential officer seals the plates, and accompanies them to the dining room. The king alone can break the seal, but before eating, the officer must taste the dishes ere his Majesty will touch them." [1]

I was informed by the late King's chef that this taboo still remains in force, though in a modified form, the chef being entrusted with breaking the seals when the food is brought into the dining room. These precautions have, of course, a purely practical value, and as such have found favour amongst kings and rulers the world over; but it appears that, quite apart from any instinct for material self-preservation, Siamese kings formerly respected the Indian idea of defilement and used leaf-platters, which are now only used in ritual.[2] The Indian Law Givers, however, laid down very definite rules on the subject of the protection of kings against poison, as the following passage from Manu shows:—

> "There he may eat food (which has been prepared) by faithful incorruptible (servants) who know the (proper) time (for dining), which has been well examined (and hallowed) by sacred texts that may destroy poison. Let him mix all his food with medicines (that are) antidotes against poison, and let him always be careful to wear gems which destroy poison." [3]

6. *It was taboo to spill royal blood.*

When princes were executed by command of the king, as was not uncommon in Old Siam, and when tyrants were deposed and met a like fate, ordinary modes of execution were taboo. It was usual to beat the royal victim on the back of the neck with sandal-wood clubs until he was dead, tie him up in a skin sack loaded with a heavy stone, and throw him into the middle of the river. According to Pallegoix [4] the fate of faithless concubines was the same, except that they were

[1] Bruguière, "Annales de la Propagation de la Foi," trans. in *Chinese Rep.*, xiii, April, 1844.

[2] Gerini, *Impl. and Asiatic Quarterly Review*, x.

[3] Manu, vii, 217, 218.

[4] P. i, p. 271.

not killed before being placed in the sacks, and were thus thrown into the river alive.

This taboo must have had a certain indirect value with regard to the preservation of the kingship, for, though it concerned only a *deposed* king, a disgraced prince or concubine, nevertheless it must have helped to maintain respect for royal blood, or rather the blood of a person who had once been considered as royal, or who had been closely connected with royalty. But the significance of this form of execution, as explained by the Siamese, is Buddhist. The murder of any animal, even an insect, is a terrible sin in the eyes of a strict Buddhist, and much more so is the murder of a man; while to kill a king, a Bodhisattva, under any circumstances, would make the most hardened Siamese criminal shudder with the mere thought of the infinite store of demerit which such action would bring upon the shoulders of the murderer. True, a deposed king is no longer a king especially in Siam, where, at least until very recent times, the conception of the kingship meant everything, the personality of the individual monarch little or nothing; nevertheless the fact that there *was* a certain relationship between the deposed king and the kingship can have hardly escaped the mind of the executioner. Thus the method of executing royalty without actually spilling their blood seems to have been dictated as much by a desire to avoid possible consequences in a future state, as from any feelings of respect. Such a peculiar method of reasoning is supported by the theory that blood is the vehicle of life, and to let the blood escape is the most obvious method of inviting death; which reminds one of the Siamese fisherman's excuse that he does not actually kill the fish, but merely takes them out of the water, after which they proceed to die of their own accord.

7. *The personal name of the King was taboo.*

The King's personal name was considered too sacred for common use; and this had the effect of strengthening the conception of the Divine Kingship. The long string of Sanskrit and Pāli titles[1] which were added to the King's personal name after Coronation were neither known nor understood by the common people; therefore it was usual to refer to the King by some term signifying "Majesty", such as *Braḥ Cǎu Yū̍ Hua* (The Lord over Our Heads), or *Cǎu Jīviṭra* (Lord of Lives), and it may be mentioned here that *Braḥ Cǎu* is also the term used to signify God, whether Hindu or Christian, and Buddha (*Braḥ Buddha Cǎu*). After death, and while awaiting Cremation, the late King was distinguished from the reigning king as *Braḥ Cǎu Yū̍*

[1] For full style and title see p. 105.

Hua nai Paramakoṣa (The Lord within the Urn). This name has gone down to history in the case of one of the later kings of Ayudhyā, who has since been known as King Paramakoṣa (A.D. 1733-68), his real personal name evidently not having been known to the Court chroniclers.

The first three kings of the present dynasty are not known to have had any personal names, each one being known for some time after death as *Braḥ Cau Yū Hua nai Paramakoṣa*, while later they came to be distinguished as *Braḥ Cau Rājakāra dī hnu'n* (Lord of the First Reign), etc. It was King Rāma IV who gave them the posthumous Buddhist names, Braḥ Buddha Yòt Fā, Braḥ Buddha Lo'ṣ Hlā, and Braḥ Nān Klau, by which they are now known, and which signify that they were Bodhisattvas. He also was the first to allow the people to refer to the reigning monarch by the personal name, e.g. Mahāmaṅkuṭ, Cuḷālaṅkaraṇa, etc., but it never was nor has yet been accepted by the masses, who still prefer to refer to past kings of the dynasty by the number of the reign. King Vajiravudh attempted to simplify matters by instituting a method by which all the kings of the dynasty should be referred to as Rāma, a word which occurs in the royal style of every king of the dynasty, the individual monarchs being distinguished as Rāma I–VI. This method has naturally been found convenient by Europeans, but the present King prefers to be known by his personal name, Prajadhipok.

8. *It was taboo to use words of the common language, or common modes of address, when speaking to or about the King and princes.*

As in most Oriental languages, there is a complete set of words, or palace language (*rājāśăpda*), possibly resulting from a desire to create a special vocabulary differing from the one in common use. These Court words are mostly of Sanskrit origin, this language having been freely requisitioned in the effort to escape the vulgar; but when Siamese contains a word of Thai origin and another for the same thing that is of Khmer origin, it is the latter which is considered the polite form, a fact which indicates that during the early years of Thai independence the Khmer was considered more proper for use at Court.[1] The following are the main classes of words which have a special Court form[2]: (*a*) All parts of the body, e.g. Foot, ordinary word *dau*, Court word *braḥpāda*. (*b*) Articles belonging to and used by royal persons, e.g. Clothes, common word *so'a-phā*, Court word

[1] Graham, *Siam*, i, 277.

[2] B. O. Cartwright, *Manual of the Siamese Language*, Appendix H.

chaloṅ-brahaṅga. (*c*) Articles of food and drink, e.g. Tea, common word *nām-jā*, Court word *brah-sudhāraśa-roṅ*. (*d*) Words expressing relationship, e.g. Father, common word *bò*, Court word *brah-janaka.* (*e*) Most verbs of bodily action, e.g. to eat, common word *kin*, Court word *sevay*; to go or come, common word *pai*, *mā*, Court word *sadec.* (*f*) Names of certain animals, fish, fruit, and flowers, e.g. buffalo, common word *gvāy*, Court word *krahpu'ò.*

The modes of address when speaking to royalty are very elaborate, e.g. when speaking to the king the correct pronoun of the 1st person is *khā brah buddha cau*, meaning "I, the slave of the Lord Buddha" (i.e. the king); of the 2nd person, *tai fā lahòṅ dhulī brah pāda*, meaning "the dust beneath the sole of your august feet", and signifying that the speaker does not dare to address the king himself, but only the dust beneath his feet.

The palace language was once an efficient means of maintaining the gulf fixed between the king and his people; an ever present reminder of his superiority to those who came most closely in contact with him, and hence were most likely to forget themselves and become familiar. It is still in use to-day, especially in Royal Proclamations and Official Notices, but the elaborate forms of address when speaking to royalty have lost much of their literal significance and are regarded merely as correct and polite forms of speech.

9. *For male Royal Children of over* 13 *or* 14 *years of age to remain in the palace was taboo.*

This was the case in Siam up to the reign of Rāma IV, as is mentioned by Mrs. Leonowens. The same statement is made by Bruguière [1] and Pallegoix.[2] In Campā

> "the sons, brothers, and more important officials of the king had no immediate access to his person. This was apparently due to fear of being assassinated by them." [3]

This was not, however, the only reason, and probably not even the main reason, at least in Siam. Far more important was the fact that the palace was a city of women, and no males but the King could be tolerated there. No doubt this taboo succeeded to some extent in fulfilling the objects for which it was intended, but it also engendered an atmosphere of suspicion, precluded that degree of filial affection

[1] *Annales de la Propagation de la Foi.*

[2] P. i, 270.

[3] R. C. Majumdar, *Ancient Indian Colonies in the Far East*, vol. i, Champa, 1927, chap. 14.

known to western civilization, and by banishing young princes to outlying provinces provided them with opportunities for rising in rebellion.

10. *Taboos relating to the conduct of persons when near the palace.*

In Siam, archers, whose ammunition consisted of balls of clay, were so placed that they could oblige all, even nobles, to lower their umbrellas, and boatmen to kneel, when passing the royal palace.[1] At Mandalay there was a rule that all must lower their umbrellas as soon as they came in sight of the *prāsāda* spire which surmounts the throne room. In Cambodia,[2] at a distance from the palace, the boatmen must bend over their oars, the horsemen walk, and the pedestrians close their umbrellas. None may enter the palace untidily dressed or overdressed in bright colours, or with a flower or feather behind the ear. Obviously this taboo had the effect not only of inculcating respect, but also of preventing the too close approach of disaffected persons.

It will be concluded from what has been said above that these taboos performed two very important functions, (*a*) they maintained the air of mystery and sanctity surrounding the Divine Kingship, and (*b*) they acted in a strictly practical manner, preserving the lives of individual monarchs. Some of the taboos performed only one of these functions, but most of them combined the two. But though their sociological value was great, we must not take them too literally, for, although some of them are survivals of a very ancient conception of Divine Kingship, Siamese kings in the historical period probably never regarded them seriously except in so far as they afforded them personal safety and strengthened their power as rulers. Indeed, they were good sociologists, and they were also men of considerable common sense. They knew that they had romped about on the ground as children without any ill-effect, that they had gone barefoot during their term in the monastery, and, in a country where the wearing of shoes was not a comfort, no doubt they often did walk about with bare feet, at least in the palace grounds, even after ascending the throne. In modern times the King walks in private life as frequently as most people in this age of motoring, but on state occasions, except when following the Urn at the late king's cremation, he walks only on holy ground, e.g. when he has dismounted from his palanquin and is entering or leaving a temple. Again, in the Coronation Ceremony

[1] P. i, 269. [2] A. i, 59.

the King publicly places the crown on his head with his own hands, but, at the conclusion of the Coronation Audience, after the curtains have been drawn and the King is surrounded only by his pages and chamberlains, he permits his attendants to relieve him of his crown, and in undoing the fastenings they can scarcely avoid touching his head. This I particularly noticed on the occasion of the Coronation Audience of the present King, when, being in my official uniform of the Chamberlain's Department, I was the only European present behind the curtain. The point which I wish to emphasise is, therefore, that it was always of the greatest importance that these taboos should be strictly observed *in public*, since it was then that they were of the greatest sociological value. In private life, when they were in danger of becoming mere useless burdens, they might, and perhaps always were, considerably relaxed. Even at the present day it is of the utmost importance that many of them should continue to be publicly observed since any ill-advised modifications or abolitions are bound to react unfavourably on the popular respect for the kingship.

We will now endeavour to form a picture of the daily life of the divine monarch and for this purpose we will first make use of the details concerning the life of King Rāma IV supplied by Mrs. Leonowens [1] who was probably the only European who was ever in a position to obtain such information. We are not concerned with the personality of this King in particular, nor of any Siamese king, but only with the facts about his mode of life. It need only be said that not only was King Rāma IV the last of the old school, but he was also an extremely learned and pious man, who had spent twenty-seven years in a monastery before being called to the throne. It is probable, therefore, that he reached more closely the ideal, somewhat difficult of attainment, of what a king should be.

> Mrs. Leonowens states that the King, as well as most of the principal members of his household, rose at five in the morning, and immediately partook of a slight repast, served by the ladies who had been in waiting through the night; after which, attended by them and his sisters and elder children, he descended and took his station on a long strip of matting, laid from one of the gates through all the avenues to another. On the king's left were ranged, first his children in the order of rank; then the princesses, his sisters; and lastly his concubines, his maids of honour, and their slaves. Before each was placed a large silver tray containing offerings of boiled rice, fruit, cakes, and the seri leaf; some even had cigars. A little after five, the Pratoo Dharmina (Gate of Merit) was thrown open and the Amazons of the guard drawn up on either side. Then the priests entered, always by that gate—one hundred and ninety-nine of them, escorted on the

[1] *The English Governess at the Siamese Court*, 1870, Chap. xi.

right and left by men armed with swords and clubs--and after humbly receiving the offerings they passed out by the other gate, Pratoo Dinn. After this the king and all his company repaired to the Chapel Royal, where His Majesty alone ascended the steps of the altar, rang a bell to announce the hour of devotion, lighted the consecrated tapers, and offered the white lotus and the roses. Then he spent an hour in prayer, and in reading texts from the Prajna-paramita and the Pratimokṣa. This service over, he retired for another nap, attended by a fresh detail of women—those who had waited the night before being dismissed, not to be recalled for a month, or at least a fortnight, save as a peculiar mark of preference or favour to some one who had had the good fortune to please or amuse him ; but most of that party voluntarily waited upon him every day. The king usually passed his mornings in study. His breakfast, though a repast sufficiently frugal for Oriental royalty, was served with awesome forms. In an antechamber adjoining a noble hall, rich in grotesque carvings and gildings, a throng of females waited, while he sat at a long table, near which knelt twelve women before great silver trays laden with twelve varieties of viands—soups, meats, game, poultry, fish, vegetables, cakes, jellies, preserves, sauces, fruits, and teas. Each tray, in its order, was passed by three ladies to the head wife or concubine, who removed the silver covers, and at least seemed to taste the contents of each dish ; and then, advancing on her knees, she set them on the long table before the king. At two o'clock he bestirred himself, and with the aid of his women bathed and anointed his person. Then he descended to a breakfast-chamber, where he was served with the most substantial meal of the day. There he chatted with his favourites among the wives and concubines, and caressed his children. Then he passed to his Hall of Audience to consider official matters. Twice a week at sunset he appeared at one of the gates of the palace to hear the complaints and petitions of the poorest of his subjects. At nine he retired to his private apartments whence issued immediately peculiar domestic bulletins, in which were named the women whose presence he particularly desired, in addition to those whose turn it was to "wait" that night. Twice a week he held a secret council, or court, at midnight.

For the life of a king of the Ayudhyā period we have the following information concerning the habits of King Nārāyaṇa :—

He always rose at 7 a.m. exactly ; his pages washed and dressed him and he worshipped the Buddha. After breakfast he went into the council chamber and stayed there until noon. He then had his midday meal. He was then undressed and washed and was lulled to sleep by music, to be awakened at 4 p.m. His reader then came and read history to him, sometimes for three or four hours. If he was in the capital [Ayudhyā] he did not go out except for a walk in his gardens unless it was a day of state ceremonial. Sometimes he visited the palace ladies and stayed with them until 8 p.m., when it was time to meet his counsellors again. He deliberated with them until midnight and then had his supper (if he had not taken it previously) and went to bed. When he was in residence at his dry season resort Louvo [Labapurī] his reading usually ended at 5 p.m., and after that he went out for a ride on an elephant. He was also very fond of hunting tigers and elephants.[1]

Naturally a young and active king would prefer to spend a good deal of his time hunting, while an older and more strictly Buddhist monarch would give up more of his time to study; but from the regularity with which both the kings above-mentioned followed a definite daily programme, it is not surprising to find that there is laid down in the *KM.* a time-table which kings were supposed to follow. The following is my translation of the passage:—" At 7 a.m.[2] he goes to the Glorious Throne and the palace ladies attend him; at 8 he partakes of food; at 9 he goes to the place for meeting the monks where the palace ladies offer them royal bounty, attended by lictors; at 10 he calls for food to eat and goes to sleep; he remains inside until 1 p.m., when he goes for a walk. At 2 the royal ladies old and young enter the palace and attend upon him. At 3 the ministers of 10,000 to 800 *śăkti nā* grade confer with the king on matters of State. At 4 he goes for a walk. At 5 he goes to meet the monks. At 6 he goes to the inner palace to discuss internal affairs. At 7 he judges military matters, and at 8 he judges civil matters. At 9 he judges appeals. At 10 he calls for food. At 11 soothsayers (*horā*) and the royal pandits (*rājapăṇḍiṯa*) discuss the law with him. At 12 music is played to him. At 1 a.m. they read history to him. At 2 or 3 he retires to sleep until 7 a.m."

Now it is of great interest to find that in Ancient India kings were also supposed to follow regularly ordered lives, in accordance with rules laid down by the law-givers. Dr. Barnett, summarizing the evidence provided in the *Kauṭilīya-artha-śāstra*, *Mahābhārata*, and other early Indian literature, gives the following time-table for the daily life of an Indian king:—

> " The day and night were each divided into eight *nāḷikās* (about 1½ hours). During the first *nāḷikā* of the day, he was expected to examine accounts of receipts and expenditure and arrangements for defence; during the second, the business or suits of his subjects; during the third he bathed, dined, and studied religious texts; in the fourth he received cash in payment of revenue and attended to the appointment of officials; in the fifth he corresponded with his councillors and considered the report of secret agents; the sixth was given to amusement and prayer; in the seventh he reviewed his troops;

[1] Gervaise, *The Natural and Political History of Siam* (1688), Eng. trans. by H. S. O'Neill, 1929, part iv, chap. 4.

[2] The day was divided into twelve hours (*nāḷikā*), and the night into twelve hours (*dum*).

and in the eighth he discussed military plans with his commander-in-chief. In the first *nāḷikā* of the night he received reports from secret agents; in the second he bathed, supped, and studied; in the third the signal was given for the royal couchée, and the fourth and fifth were spent in sleep; in the sixth he arose, and prepared himself for the day's labour by meditation; in the seventh he considered the working of his administration, and gave his orders to secret agents, and in the eighth he went into court after receiving the blessings of his priests and preceptors, consulting with his astrologer, physician, and head cook, and reverencing with circumambulation a cow, calf, and bull." [1]

The general resemblance between the above and the rules laid down in the *KM.* is very striking, and can leave little room for doubt but that the latter was modelled on Indian principles. But it is all rather formal, and before leaving the subject I should like to quote what Manu has to say on the subject, for his very human document gives a rather fuller picture, and indicates in certain passages that Indian kings were no fonder of obeying the letter of the law laid down for them than were many of those who ruled over Siam. Manu first makes it clear that the main object of the existence of kings was for the protection of their subjects, a fact often sadly forgotten both in India and Siam :—

"2. A Kṣatriya, who has received according to the rule the sacrament prescribed by the Veda, must daily protect this world.

"3. For, when the creatures, being without a king, through fear dispersed in all directions, the Lord created a king for the protection of this whole (creation)."

But of course this protection was to be exercised mainly for the benefit of the Brahmans:—

"79. A king shall offer various (*śrauta*) sacrifices at which liberal fees (are distributed), and in order to acquire merit, he shall give Brāhmaṇas enjoyment and wealth."

Coming then to the daily programme, he lays down as follows :—

"145. Having risen in the last watch of the night, having performed (the rite of) personal purification; having, with a collected mind, offered oblations in the fire, and having worshipped Brāhmaṇas. he shall enter the hall of audience which must possess the marks (considered) auspicious (for a dwelling). 146. Tarrying there, he shall gratify all subjects (who come to see him by a kind reception) and afterwards dismiss them; having dismissed his subjects, he shall take council with his ministers. 147. Ascending the back of a hill or a terrace, (and) retiring (there) in a lonely place, or in a solitary forest, let him consult with them unobserved. 216. Having consulted with his ministers on all these (matters), having taken exercise, and having

[1] *Antiquities of India*, p. 98.

bathed afterwards, the king may enter the harem at midday in order to dine. [Here follow the instructions for eating already quoted.] 219. Well-tried females whose toilet and ornaments have been examined, shall attentively serve him with fans, water and perfumes. 220. In like manner let him be careful about his carriages, bed, seat, bath, toilet, and all his ornaments. 221. When he has dined, he may divert himself with his wives in the harem; but when he has diverted himself, he must, in due time, again think of the affairs of state. 222. Adorned (with his robes of state), let him again inspect his fighting men, all his chariots and beasts of burden, the weapons, and accoutrements. 223. Having performed his twilight-devotions, let him, well armed, hear in an inner apartment the doings of those who make secret reports and of his spies. 224. But going to another secret apartment and dismissing those people, he may enter the harem, surrounded by female (servants), in order to dine again. 225. Having eaten there something for the second time, and having been recreated by the sound of music, let him go to rest and rise again at the proper time free from fatigue. 226. A king who is in good health must observe these rules; but, if he is indisposed, he may entrust all this (business) to his servants."[1]

Making due allowance for the passing of the power of the Brahmans, the rise of Buddhism, and the modifications incidental to changing conditions generally, one cannot but be struck by the remarkable resemblance between the life of an ancient Indian monarch and that of a Siamese king, at least up to the middle of the nineteenth century. In all the above accounts the chief occupations of a king may be classified under three headings: (1) Duties to religion, especially in connection with the State Ceremonies, which form the main subject matter of the present volume; (2) Duties to the secular government, especially in the matter of conferring amongst his ministers and granting audiences, to which a special chapter will be devoted; (3) Recreation, especially in the harem. This institution was of such great importance that it will be necessary here to consider its history and functional value in some detail.

Mrs. Leonowens has given us in her two books[2] a vivid picture of life in the royal harem during the reign of King Rāma IV, but her writings are unfortunately biased by a mid-Victorian viewpoint, and much missionary zeal. With such an outlook the life of many individual members of the harem appeared full of pathos, but that this was to a great extent the product of her European imagination might have dawned on Mrs. Leonowens when she speaks of the wonderful fortitude with which they bore the hardships of their lives. She forgets that this was a time-honoured institution in the country, not only in the

[1] Manu, chap. vii.

[2] *The English Governess at the Siamese Court*, London, 1870; *The Romance of Siamese Harem Life*, London, 1873.

royal, but also in the noble families; that the members of the harem had for the most part known no other conditions, and having but a very limited knowledge of the world were quite contented with their lot, which seemed to them the acme of royal favour. It is true that there was severity, even cruelty, in punishing breaches of discipline, but this was inevitable in the inner life of the harem where it was difficult to preserve much of the atmosphere of mystery surrounding the kingship, and only the strong hand of the man could sustain the dignity and power of the divine monarch.

The harem of King Rāma IV was on a much smaller scale than were those of his predecessors. An interesting note as to its constitution, based on information supplied by that king himself, was published in Bangkok five years before his death:—

> "There have been altogether 27 royal mothers in the king's family: one of them had 7 children, two of them each five, another 4, two of them 3 each, four of them 2 each, and all the others but one each. His Majesty has at the present time 34 concubines. Each of these receives a government salary designed for the support of her own person, not including her children. The most that any one of them receives is 1200 ticals, and the least sum is 120 ticals. The aggregate of their salaries is 12700 ticals. Besides these 34 concubines, there are 74 daughters of noblemen, who have been presented to the king by their fathers, with the view to serve as maids of honour. These receive salaries from government according to their supposed individual merits, amounting to 6440 ticals. When any of them desire to exchange their situation for one out of the palace, with freedom to marry or otherwise, they may obtain the privilege by requesting it of the king. His Majesty has granted many such requests since he began his reign." [1]

There were also elderly women who acted as judges in the case of disciplinary offences, mistresses charged with the education of the younger concubines, and a host of slaves and amazons of the guard. There were no eunuchs and no man except the king ever entered the small town which was reserved within the palace for the harem. In this preserve there were streets with shops, a garden with model houses, and a lake with miniature boats, all intended to be a replica of the outside world, and which for many of the concubines constituted almost their sole idea of its appearance. The concubines were known as *Nāṅ Hǟm*, that is to say "Women Forbidden" (to leave the palace), though in the reign of King Rāma IV it was possible for them to obtain permission to leave the palace on special occasions. It was then usually contrived that they could see without being seen, and there was a strict taboo against any man touching the body of a

[1] *Bangkok Calendar* for 1863, p. 38.

concubine. Not only did a certain amount of amusement and education, among beautiful surroundings within the palace, make the lives of the concubines less burdensome, but regular business was assigned to them which kept them from being idle. Of course, there were petty jealousies and quarrels, as was only to be expected where the main object in life was for one to obtain the position of favourite at the expense of the others. Sometimes there was real affection between the King and his favourite concubines, but, in any case, should a concubine (*cǎu còm*) become the mother of a royal infant (*braḥ aṅga*), she was known as *cǎu còm mārtā*, and her position was assured. Sometimes, indeed, a favourite attained such a position in the estimation of the King that she was able to sway his judgments, and became a powerful influence in the administration of the State; but only after a favourite concubine had lived with the King for a considerable time, and had maintained her place in his affections, could she be elevated to the position of queen. An exception was made in the case of a lady of royal birth, who would be elevated to the queenship without submitting to this period of trial. There were normally four queens at the same time, a greater and a lesser of the right, and a greater and a lesser of the left, and the ceremony of their installation, which has some features in common with marriage, will be dealt with in connection with the Coronation. But there was no religious ceremony of marriage at any time in the life of a concubine, and really no such ceremony is practised by any class of Siamese. Thus Bowring was right when he stated that "no religious rites accompany the marriage, though bonzes are invited to the feast".[1] The tying of the wrists with coloured cords is not peculiar to marriage, and the feast in which the monks participate is a housewarming feast, and not a marriage ceremony. This feast symbolizes the entry upon life in new surroundings, and is performed by the king and his concubines or queen (who may have already been "married" for years) immediately after the coronation at the time of the assumption of the royal residence. Marriage in Siam, for both prince and commoner, is a non-religious civil contract, and is made binding by the handing over of the bride by the parents and the commencement of her common life with the bridegroom. The signing of a register and other formalities are merely the recent introductions of the late king, Rāma VI.

We come now to an important consideration, that of the king's methods of obtaining his concubines, and in this connection will quote from the writings of a Siamese author of the third reign:—

[1] Bowring, *Siam*, London, 1857, vol. i, p. 118.

"When the king would obtain a *Nāṅ Hām* (that is one inferior to a queen) he does not send a delegation to request her from the family of a prince of equal rank with himself; nor does he make a wedding for her, and erect buildings for her abode and pleasure, as the common people do. Sometimes he sees the girl with his own eyes, and sometimes another person brings him a report, that in such a family is a beautiful girl, whose father and mother were formerly connected with noble stock. [Evidently an allusion to the fact that titles of royalty cease at the fifth generation.] The king, if he be taken with the account given of her, sends a messenger to beg that he may be allowed to conduct her to the royal palace, to have her schooled and trained, and then inaugurated as a *Nāṅ Hām*. Sometimes the parents of a girl, thinking it would be a great good to have the king for a family prop as a son-in-law, are pleased to make an offering of their handsomest daughter, or grandchild, or niece, to the prince as the honourable station of a royal concubine. This is quite a common way or mode by which the king obtains his many wives. Again, another prolific source of the royal concubines, is the custom, when a prince has ascended the throne, and become established in his reign, that all his nobles and lords, even down to the *khuns* and *hmu'ns*, present each his most beautiful daughter or niece to the king, for the purpose of having her serve him as a *Nāṅ Hām*. In consequence of this custom, the royal concubines of the kings of Siam have ever been very numerous, numbering many hundreds, and even a thousand and upward to each." [1]

In analysing the functional value of the harem, we must first realize the immense respect in which this time-honoured institution was held by the people in all the States affected by Indian civilization, and that it was held to be one of the chief appanages of royalty from a very early period in history. "Can he be a king, or even a noble, or lord, and not have a multitude of concubines?" inquires the Siamese author from whom we have already quoted, and it is clear from this, which until recently represented the opinion of the Siamese of all classes, that one of the sociological functions of the harem was to maintain the dignity of royalty. In the Siamese *Life of Buddha* we read:—

"Then the Śākya Princes acknowledged his wondrous skill, and presented their daughters to be his wives, and he was invested with the royal dignity, and the beautiful Yaśodharā became his Queen. He passed his days in honour, luxury, and comfort; no cares assailed him, and his beautiful Queen, and the lovely daughters of the Śākyas, unceasingly strove to promote his happiness." [2]

In all this one notices a strong Siamese flavour, an expression of the Siamese traditional opinion as to what should be the ideal of a king's feminine entourage. Conditions were similar in Cambodia

[1] Translated in the *Bangkok Calendar* for 1864, p. 69.

[2] Alabaster, *The Wheel of the Law*, London, 1871, p. 121.

and no doubt represented the ideal which the early Thai kings strove to emulate. Cheou Ta-kouan, the Chinese who travelled in Cambodia in the thirteenth century A.D., remarks that the king had one chief wife, four for the cardinal points, and 3,000–5,000 concubines.[1] On the bas-reliefs of the great temple at Banteai Chhma are represented, amongst other scenes, kings reposing in their palaces amongst women of the harem. The institution was equally well developed in the great Hindu State of Vijayanagar in the Middle Ages; Fernao Nuniz, writing about 1535,[2] noticed the large number of women in the king's harem, and also that women filled most posts in the palace, such as astrologers, musicians, wrestlers, secretaries, cooks, judges, bailiffs, watchmen, and amazons. But, unlike Siam and Cambodia, there were also eunuchs. The Laws of Manu take us a good many centuries further back, and the quotations above made from that source show us the harem as already regarded as a very important royal institution.

We now come to another and perhaps more important function of the harem. We have seen that it was mainly composed of the daughters of noble families, and the result of this was to unite the nobility to the Throne by marriage, and thus to secure their loyalty. The concubines were practically hostages for the good behaviour of their families, and could spy in the king's interests into the intentions of their relatives. This was a two-edged sword, for a girl might be more loyal to her family than to the king, but as a general rule the harem was undoubtedly a powerful instrument for the maintenance of justice and internal peace in the country. The individual might sometimes suffer, but for the good of society as a whole the harem played an important rôle.

One aspect of the harem remains to be dealt with: its effect on the efficiency of the monarch; and whatever this might be it would be bound to affect the well-being of the State. It would really depend almost entirely on the personality of the individual king. A strong-minded ruler like Rāma IV would realize that the harem was a sacred institution of his country, and would be unlikely to lapse into sensuality, but we know from history that such was the temptation to which many a weaker monarch succumbed. Such a possibility was obviously realized and guarded against by the ancient law-givers when they commanded: "He must not take delight in hunting, dice, women, and drinking."[3]

Before concluding this chapter it will be necessary to notice the

[1] A. iii, pp. 645 sq.
[2] Quoted in Sewell's *Vijayanagar*, pp. 382–3.
[3] "Institutes of Vishnu," iii, 50, in *SBE*. vii.

changes in the conception of the kingship and the life and duties of the King that have been brought about by contact with western civilization during the last few decades. As would be expected from the fact that the present King was educated in Europe, his tastes are largely European, and his private life that of any modern European monarch, in fact practically that of any ordinary English gentleman. This also applied to the late King Rāma VI, and the example set by these two modern Kings has been followed by the younger generation of the nobility, and we now have a growing upper class in Bangkok educated on European lines, some of whose members, however, have not been so successful as their royal leaders in knowing what to adopt from western culture and what to discard as unsuitable. In my opinion, however, this change has not as yet had any great effect on the masses, since, whenever the King shows himself to the people on great state occasions, he still appears in procession, riding on a palanquin, surrounded by all the traditional accompaniments of majesty, and this is the picture which still remains indelibly impressed on the minds of the vast majority of his subjects. However, a reform of far-reaching importance which has undoubtedly adversely affected the kingship in the popular opinion, was the abolition of the harem, for this, as we have seen, was far more than an institution of the King's private life. The harem served its purpose as a means of maintaining peace and order in Old Siam, but with the centralization of the government, and the improvement of communications, it became an anachronism. Nevertheless, the reform is not yet complete, and the masses of the people have not yet been educated up to accepting it. Part of the honeycombed city of women still stands within the walls of the Grand Palace, and there still reside a few old ladies, survivors of King Rāma V's harem, with two or three old amazons to guard them from intrusion, though, of course, they are perfectly free to go and come as they please; and, among the older generation of the nobility, the harem still flourishes, though modified by the fact that women of the upper class have now more education and freedom. Indeed, when King Rāma VI attempted to introduce compulsory monogamy and the registration of marriages, he was met by so much passive resistance that he wisely decided not to proceed with the measure. He himself remained entirely celibate until the last year of his life, and his only offspring was a daughter born two days before his death. King Prajadhipok, though married in 1917, is still childless, and this state of affairs, being so contrary to Siamese royal tradition, is a matter of deep concern to his subjects. Indeed, it might not be too much to say that the abolition of the harem is by far the greatest blow that has so far been struck at the traditional conception of the Siamese monarchy. I do not wish, however, to lay undue weight on this unfortunate fact, nor to conclude this chapter on a depressing note, and I therefore desire to emphasize that the present King carries out his other traditional duties with truly remarkable zeal. Despite the increased complexity of the government and the fact that details must often be worked out by subordinates, the King still closely supervises his ministers, and holds frequent cabinet meetings; while in the sphere of religion no king could be more meticulous in carrying out his somewhat arduous duties.

Appendix to Chapter IV

This will be a convenient place to mention a remarkable office, that of the *Mahā Uparāja* or *Văṅ Nā*, commonly known to Europeans as Second King, an office which demands our consideration because the individual who held it was invested with some of the appurtenances of kingship. He was primarily a general who held command of the vanguard, while the *Văṅ Hlăṅ*, the third most important personage in the realm but vastly inferior in status to the *Văṅ Nā*, was the commander of the rearguard. The *Mahā Uparāja* became the chief councillor of the King, and was usually his eldest son. It has frequently been wrongly stated by European writers that the Second King was the brother of the King, but this was only the case when the King's sons were minors. He was, in fact, the Crown Prince. He was entitled to an umbrella of five tiers, had a splendid palace [1] and court of his own, and almost unlimited access to the treasury. His coronation, called *uparājābhiṣeka* and corresponding to the *yauvarājābhiṣeka* of Epic India, was in most respects a copy, on a smaller scale, of that of the King; but the latter performed an important part in it, and himself handed the regalia to the *Uparāja*. Formerly the *Văṅ Nā* did not receive a ceremonial bath at his coronation, nor was there a *Liap Mo'aṅ*, or state progress around the walled city; but this was inaugurated by Rāma IV out of affection and respect for his brother, Braḥ Bin Klău, the *Văṅ Nā* of the fourth reign.[2]

Some interesting information about the *Mahā Uparāja* in the seventeenth century is given by La Loubère,[3] who regarded him as a Viceroy who represented the King and performed the King's functions during his absence, as, for example, when he was at war. He noticed

[1] The palace of the *Uparāja* at Bangkok is now the National Museum.
[2] *Siam Repository*, Oct., 1871.
[3] L. L., p. 95.

that he was the only officer who had the right of sitting in the King's presence. Though it is probable that the office existed in the Sukhodaya period, the earliest specific mention of it in Siamese history is in 1484, but it is also referred to in the *Śăkti Nā* Law of 1454, where it is stated that the *Văṅ Nā* held 40,000 acres of land, ten times as much as the highest officials.[1] The title was common in all the States of Indo-China, including Burma, and is mentioned in the *Mahāvaṁsa*. It originated in India, many examples of the anointing of an heir-apparent being known from Indian literature.[2]

It is easy to understand the functional value of such an office as that of the *Mahā Uparāja* in a State governed by an absolute monarch. The position of an Oriental despot must often have been one of almost insuperable difficulty; and the moral support of one on whom the King could rely for an opinion unbiased by flattery or self-seeking, and with whom he could converse on something approaching an equal footing, must, in a country where the highest official was but as dust, have been not only a great personal comfort to the King, but also a valuable aid to the stability of the government. Then again, the King could send the *Văṅ Nā* on military expeditions with perfect confidence, and when himself absent could leave the Second King in the capital to discharge the affairs of State. Bruguière states that the *Văṅ Nā* remained in the Supreme King's palace, sword in hand, to guard it when he was out.[3] The value of this can be well appreciated in a country where a King could never be certain that on his return from a state progress he would not find an usurper enthroned in his place. It is remarkable that throughout Siamese history the *Uparāja* and the King always seem to have remained on such perfect terms of amity. One may attribute this not only to the careful selection exercised by the King in his choice, but also to the fact that the *Văṅ Nā*, enjoying as he did such a vast measure of power and wealth, would scarcely be likely to think it worth while to risk his all by aiming at the supreme position.

The office of *Mahā Uparāja* was abolished by King Rāma V on the death of the Second King of the fifth reign. With the greater trust that he was able to place on his loyal and better educated ministers who were deeply attached to him by ties of personal affection, and with his desire to model his administration on the methods of western government, he naturally saw that no ends could be served by retaining the institution.

[1] Wood, *History of Siam*, p. 92.
[2] *ERE*. i, p. 20.
[3] "Annales de la Propagation de la Foi," trans. in *Chinese Rep*. xiii, April, 1844.

CHAPTER V

THE COURT BRAHMANS[1]

We will begin our study of the Siamese Court Brahmans by considering them as they are to-day. They are a small body of men whose duties lie mainly in connection with those Ceremonies of State that are not wholly Buddhist. One can discern in their features a trace of Indian Brahman blood but, since no female Brahmans ever accompanied them from India, they intermarried with the people of the country, and so this trace of Indian blood is now but slight. They wear their hair long, in the form of a chignon, and on ceremonial occasions don the Brahmanic cord and wear white (a Siamese lower garment, called *phā̆-nuṅ*, together with a white jacket, embroidered with silver flowers in the case of the head-priest). They represent two sects, the Vaiṣṇavas (*Brāhmaṇa Bṛdhipaśa*) and Śaivas (*Brāhmaṇa Bidhī*), but they have in Bangkok three temples in one enclosure, the larger one (that on the south) being dedicated to Iśvara (Śiva), the middle one to Gaṇeśa, and the northern one to Nārāyaṇa (Viṣṇu), the houses in which the Brahmans live being in the vicinity. The temples are rectangular buildings with Siamese roofs, and with the insides of the walls plainly whitewashed. At the western ends of each of the temples there stands an altar, while in the middle of the Śiva and Viṣṇu temples there stand two upright posts to which a small swing-seat is suspended on certain ceremonial occasions. The altar in the Śiva temple (Pl. I) is the most elaborate, and supports a number of interesting bronze images of Śiva and Umā, sheltered beneath a white canopy, from the four corners of which depend white lace curtains. In front of the altar are several stands for flowers and other offerings, to the right and left of which are situated gilded figures of Śiva astride the sacred bull Nandi. Formerly some images of Harihara were enshrined within this temple, but they have now been removed to the National Museum. Some of the other images were probably brought

[1] As stated in Chapter I, the Buddhist monks now play a very important part in most of the great State Ceremonies, but this is usually in connection with those modifications and additions which have mostly been introduced in later times. The duties of the monks on these occasions consist mainly in the recitation of texts from the scriptures, the study of which could not be adequately dealt with in the present work. I therefore refrain from devoting a special chapter to the consideration of the Siamese Buddhist monks, but shall have something to say as to such rites as they do perform when suitable occasions arise in the body of the work.

PLATE I.

[Photo : Bangkok Times Press, Ltd.

THE ALTAR IN THE ŚIVA TEMPLE.

[To face page 54.

Plate II.

[Photographed from a Manuscript in the National Library, by kind permission of H.R.H. Prince Damrong.

A *Mantra* entitled "The Worship of the Eight Directions".

over from India, but these images of Harihara are certainly the most interesting and the most important historically, because they are definitely of Coḷa period, i.e. they date from about the tenth century A.D. On the altar in the middle temple are some large images of Gaṇeśa, while in the northern temple there is a statue of Viṣṇu, flanked by two modern figures of his *śakti*.

The Court Brahmans speak only Siamese, and do not understand Sanskrit, but they have corrupt Sanskrit texts usually written in an Indian character (Pl. II), which some of them are able to read. They have also one hymn in Tamil, written in an Indian character, but this language they likewise do not understand. It is known, however, that in the Ayudhyā period, there were Brahmans who did understand these Indian languages. The texts which the Siamese Brahmans now possess are the Sanskrit and Tamil *mantras* (hymns) with instructions in Siamese for the preliminary rites intended to be used in daily worship, and as an introduction to the more important ceremonies. A few decades ago they had other manuscripts which gave instructions for all the State Ceremonies, but these were carried off by a certain family of Brahmans who left the royal service. This family was headed by the then head priest, whose name I am told was Um. An attempt was made during his lifetime to recover the books, and to this end his mother was caught and imprisoned. In order to secure her release, the manuscripts of which the National Library has copies (i.e. those dealing with the preliminary rites) were returned; but the others, although almost certainly still in existence, cannot be recovered because the Government does not nowadays like to cause a commotion by attempting to obtain them by force. The Brahmans now use those books that were returned to them for all purposes, and since they do not understand Sanskrit they mumble both instructions and *mantras* indiscriminately. There is now no daily worship in the temples, and the Brahmans perform the State Ceremonies without the aid of written instructions since they or their fathers have seen the rites performed in the days when the other books were extant. Fortunately, King Rāma V had access to these treatises, and made use of them in compiling the *BRB*. Alabaster, who also must have had access to a larger range of Brahmanical literature than we have to-day, remarks that there are frequent references to, and (supposed) quotations from the three *Vedas* (*Ṯrai Beda*) and the *śāstras*. They reject the *Atharva Veda* as did Manu.[1]

I am indebted to Mr. P. S. Sāstrī, the Indian Sanskrit scholar on the staff of the Royal Institute at Bangkok, for the appended list [2] of

[1] *The Wheel of the Law*, p. 176. [2] See p. 63.

the Brahmanical MSS. in the possession of the National Library. As already stated, they refer only to the preliminary rites, now used for all State Ceremonies, the instructions being in Siamese, the *mantras* in corrupt Sanskrit, written usually in the Indian character, but sometimes in Siamese. The only Tamil *mantra* is the "Opening the portals of Kailāsa", which is written in the Indian character. There are also *yantra* diagrams (Pls. IV and V) for use in connection with the ritual, as will be mentioned in later chapters.

I have shown specimens of the Indian script, in which most of the *mantras* are written, to Dr. L. D. Barnett, who is of opinion that they are Pāṇḍyan, and may be ascribed to a period not later than the middle of the thirteenth century A.D. These have not yet been transliterated, but I here give two examples of the corrupt Sanskrit *mantras* which were written in Siamese characters, and which I have transcribed in Roman characters as follows:—

I. Yak utup pot hyai, klāṅ [1]

"*Aḥvănnaḥgaḥsuvănnaḥgănnaḥgănnā vicāvicāraḥnāṁ gaḥṯāgaḥṯāmaḥhaḥvăn nāmamuṯatimutaṯitāṁ saḥraḥnigaḥṯiṯurosaḥraḥnigaḥṯiṯāṁmaḥlāṁ saḥraḥnivaḥnituniyāṁbhăkgā haḥriomavijaivijaiyaḥmāde maḥhākrailăt paḥṯinaḥhākrailăkgaḥnākhoe paḥṯinikgaḥnāsănnăkgaḥnārāyayaḥ paḥriyaḥmāraḥdopaḥṯi. Yāṁmaḥ supaḥrigaḥgănṯumapaḥridaḥrănṯo daḥyebhaḥkumpaḥribhaḥkum paḥritapiṯṯănyāneyānesăṯṯrūnā sāṁnāsāṁbhaiyaḥṯaḥsāṁbhaiyaḥmuhaimuhaiyaḥkănnaḥkănnaḥkinnekinne lāṁbunadaḥretneṯṯeracăṯuvaḥṯera sahjinlaḥmāvasinṯeravaḥṯera mudăṯṯarătdaḥraḥmătdaḥgumdsāṅ săddhāṯera daḥraḥmătasăṯṯrūvinātasāḥnāṁ maḥhāriomasaḥvăṯṯinātapaḥṯināta pòrammaḥrākhāpaḥṯipāṯāpaḥ.*"

II. Yak utup saḥthān braḥ nārāyaṇa [2]

"*Sukaḥrikaḥraḥdugăndosutcāsutcā mikkaḥraḥpaḥṯāṁpraḥsāṁbhāpraḥbhālāṁ praḥsāṁbhādirorakyăksăkpraḥbhammaḥyăk maḥlikkaḥṯānusādocănmoddaḥkoṭdivāso maḥnătjotgaḥṯojogaḥṯā nekgaḥnānācănmaḥdaḥkoṭdaḥvādivā maḥnaḥjotgaḥṯāhiṅgaḥherā dirāmodivisiddhiyā paḥraḥnikumpaḥraḥnik̲h̲ănsăṯṯaḥṯidănbun paḥraḥnigaḥsaḥrănnisaḥnèb bhaḥlaḥcănlaḥdolaḥdăn paḥrināmăndaḥlābhiribramamār năkkhănnăkurāsaḥvāvisaḥvāsasu sunaḥgirisīsăṯṯaḥlaḥsăṯṯaḥnaiyaḥne haḥriombrammāraṯaḥvilailaḥthipāṯaḥparamarājā.*"

[1] This Siamese title means "Making offerings in the large (Śiva) and middle (Gaṇeśa) temples".

[2] This Siamese title means "Making offerings in the Viṣṇu temple".

PLATE III.

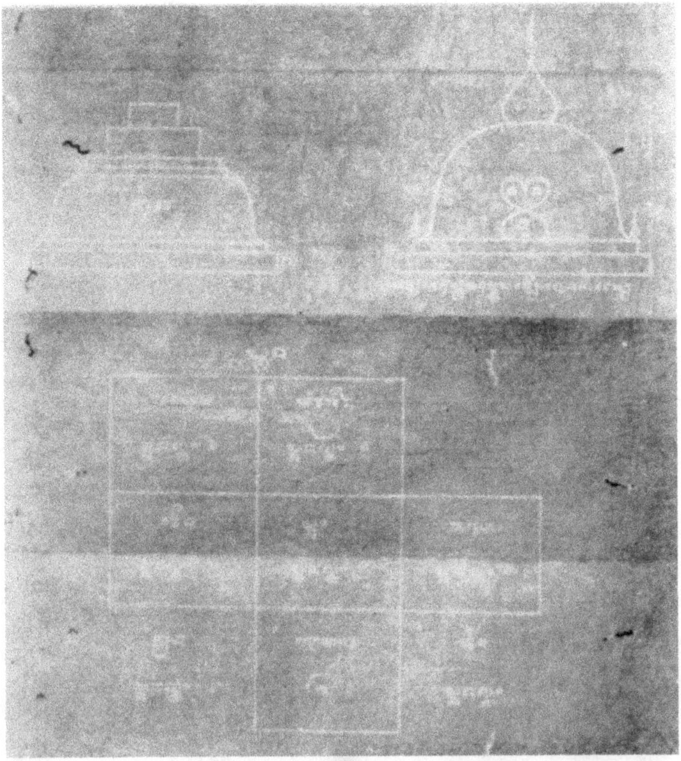

[Photographed from a Manuscript in the National Library, by kind permission of H.R.H. Prince Damrong.

YANTRA DIAGRAMS.

1. *Yantra* representing the stove used in the *homa* rites (see p. 72).
2. *Yantra* representing the mound used in the Kaḥtikeyā Festival (see p. 290).
3. *Yantra* representing *pañcha-gavya* (see p. 252).

[*To face page* 56.

PLATE IV.

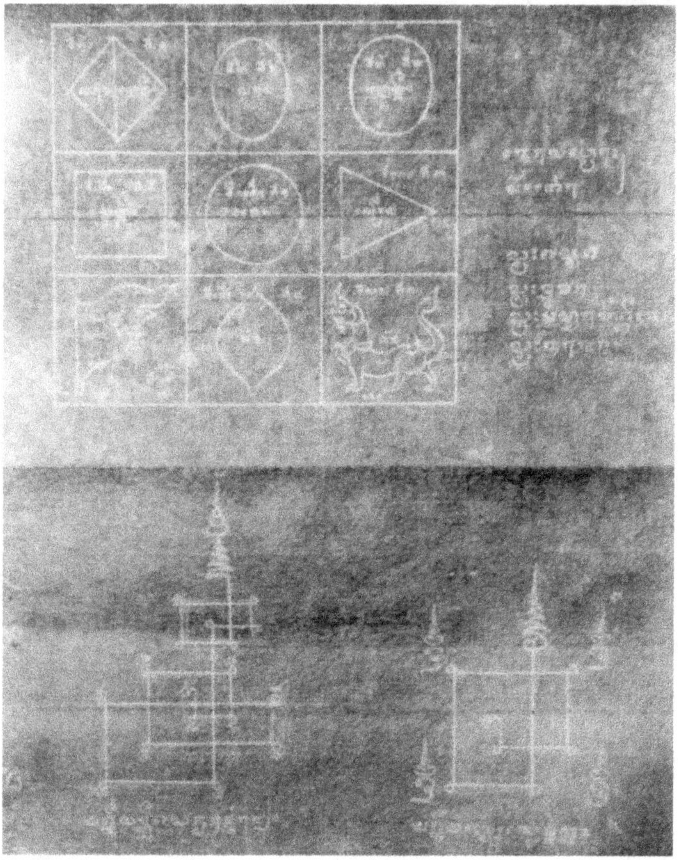

[*Photographed from a Manuscript in the National Library, by kind permission of H.R.H. Prince Damrong.*

YANTRA DIAGRAMS.

1. *Yantra* representing the nine planetary deities.
2. *Yantra* inscribed on the stone mortar (see p. 252).
3. *Yantra* placed in the silver water-pot (see p. 252).

It will be noticed that the above *mantras* retain traces of metrical composition, and here and there we can trace perfectly correct Sanskrit words, e.g. *paramarājā*, which concludes the second *mantra*.

It has already been remarked that most of the State Ceremonies show a blending of the two religions, Buddhism and Hinduism, which was intensified in the reigns of such staunch Buddhist kings as Draṅ Dharma (1610–28), and Rāma IV (1851–68), and it is not surprising, therefore, to find that the Court Brahmans are also Buddhists, and that before they can undergo the ceremony of initiation and wear the Brahman girdle, they must pass through the novitiate as Buddhist monks, and it is also this fact that they are Buddhists as well as Hindus that prevents them from carrying out any animal sacrifices in connection with their rites.

The ceremony of initiation to the Brahman priesthood is still performed, being known as *Pvaj Braṯ*. It consists of two stages, the first of taking the cord of three strings, and the second of taking the cord of six strings. I have had no opportunity of witnessing the ceremony, but was able to photograph in its entirety the manuscript which purports to deal with the subject.

The following is a mention of the ceremony of *Pvaj Braṯ* in Siamese history of the Ayudhyā period :—

> "In 912 Chulasakarat [A.D. 1530], the year of the dog, on the second of the waxing of the eighth month, the King Somdet Phra Mahāchakrapan had the ceremony of Pathamakamma (inauguration of Brahmans) performed at the place Thā Deng. Phra Karmavācā was teacher of unauspicious lore [*sic*]; Phra Bijettha was teacher of the eight requirements ; Phra Indra was judge. In 915 [A.D. 1533], the year of the bull, in the seventh month, the Majjhimakamma (second step in the inauguration of Brahmans) was performed at Jainādburi." [1]

The only other places where Brahmanism is still found in Siam are Nagara Śrī Dharmarāja and Bătaḥluṅ in the Peninsula, where temples of the kind above described still exist; but in times past there were Brahman temples in the ancient capitals and in the main provincial centres. This brings us to a point where we must consider the history of Brahmanism in Siam in order to understand its function at the present day and the low estate to which it has fallen.

In India we know that the Brahmans early achieved ascendancy over the other three castes, that they were the repository of all Hindu learning, and that by this means, although they never attempted openly to take over the business of temporal government, they made themselves to be considered as indispensable to the ruling caste, the

[1] "*Baṅṣāvaḥtāra* of Hlvaṅ Prasoeṭh," in *JSS.*, vol. vi, pt. 3 (1909).

Kṣatriyas. " Let the king in all matters listen to the advice of his astrologers " ordain the Institutes of Viṣṇu [1]; and Manu prescribes as follows :—

> " 78. Let him appoint a domestic priest (*purohita*) and choose officiating priests (*ritvig*) ; they shall perform his domestic rites and sacrifices for which three fires are required. 79. A king shall offer various (*śrauta*) sacrifices at which liberal fees (are distributed), and in order to acquire merit he shall give to Brāhmaṇas enjoyment and wealth." [2]

In the last sentence we notice the emphatic injunction that the officiating Brahmans must be liberally rewarded ; this is characteristic of the Brahmans, who never gave their services for nothing. But in order to make it quite clear that it was not derogatory to their dignity for them to accept such payment, it was necessary for them to admit the divinity of the king. Hence we have the statement from Nārada that,

> " those who being acquainted with the divine nature of a king, endowed with majestic dignity as he is, accept gifts from him, do not in the least disgrace themselves (by doing so)."

But, despite this, no doubt is to be entertained as to the relative positions of the King and the Brahman in the scale of holiness:

> " In this world there are eight sacred objects : a Brahman, a cow, fire, gold, clarified butter, the sun, the waters, and a king as the eighth. These one must always look up to, worship and honour them personally, and turn the right side towards them, in order that one's existence may be prolonged." [3]

The Brahman and the King are, in fact, both offshoots of the same primitive idea, the divinity of the chief. Sometimes the one and sometimes the other obtained the ascendancy, and hence we have to coin the terms priest-king and king-priest. Of the former we shall see many examples in the priestly functions of the King of Siam, for the latter we have to turn to Ancient India, or at least to Ancient Cambodia, where the Brahmans were strong enough to interfere with the temporal government. There were ceremonies of consecration for both kings and priests, but whereas the king identified himself with Indra, the Brahman was Brihaspati, the *purohita* of the gods.[4]

The ascendant position attained by the Brahmans in India was for some time maintained by those who ventured overseas and settled in the States colonized by Indians in Indo-China. In Cambodia the

[1] iii, 75, in *SBE.*, vol. vii. [2] Manu, chap. vii.
[3] Nārada, xviii, 53–5, in *SBE.* xxxiii (Minor Law Books).
[4] Hocart, *Kingship*, London, 1927, chap. x.

Brahmans for many centuries maintained a powerful hierarchy. They were the only one of the four castes that was really organized, this caste having taken form in the fifth century and been constantly augmented by immigrants from India.[1] In the days when Yaśovarman was king (acceded A.D. 889), Śaivism was predominant, and we learn from the following inscription that the Brahmans still enjoyed a position similar to that which was theirs in India:—

> "This king, well-versed (in kingly duties), performed the Koṭi-homa and the Yajñas (Vedic sacrifices), for which he gave the priests magnificent presents of jewels, gold, etc."[2]

The cult of the Royal God, though founded by Jayavarman II (A.D. 802), did not reach the height of its development until some two centuries afterwards, and was especially associated with Vaiṣṇavism and the temple of Aṅkor Văt. This cult led to the Brahmans enjoying an even more exalted position. The Cambodian hierarchy was established by Jayavarman II, and the priesthood became hereditary in the family of Śivakaivalya, who enjoyed immense power; indeed, this sacerdotal dynasty almost threw the royal dynasty into the shade.[3] Brahmans were depicted on the reliefs of Aṅkor Văt and Coedès has identified Droṇa and Viśvāmitra amongst them.[4] In one of the reliefs which illustrates a royal procession, it is interesting to note that the Brahmans are the only onlookers who do not prostrate themselves before the king, as was also the case in India.[5] This is very different from the rule in later times in Siam, for their proximity to the King's person and their dependence on his protection made them the most subservient members of his Court, and in modern ceremonial they still prostrate themselves as in Old Siam. Another point of interest that we learn from the reliefs of Aṅkor Văt and Aṅkor Thom is that not, only the Brahmans, but also the aristocracy wore the chignon, the lower classes having short hair.[6]

One very remarkable sign of the power of the Brahmans during the Aṅkor period is that, contrary to the modern custom, by which princesses of the royal blood rarely marry, formerly alliances were common with the Brahmans[7]; and up to the present day there is a tradition amongst the Bakus, who are the descendants of the ancient Brahmans, that in the event of the royal line failing, a successor would be chosen from amongst them.[8]

[1] A. iii, p. 548. [2] C., p. 114. [3] C., p. 80 sq.
[4] Coedès, *Les Bas Reliefs d'Angkor Vat*, Paris, 1911, plates xii and xiii.
[5] Delaporte, "Cortège Royal chez les Khmers," *Revue de Geog.*, 1878.
[6] Gr., p. 58. [7] A. iii, p. 531.
[8] Aymonier, *Histoire de L'ancien Cambodge*, 1920, p. 178.

As early as the reign of Jayavarman V (A.D. 968) we find evidence of the admixture of Mahāyāna Buddhism with the cult of the Royal God.

> "The *purohita* should be versed in Buddhist learning and rites. He should bathe on the days of the festivals the image of the Buddha and should recite Buddhist prayers." [1]

And the rites and duties of the *purohitas* remained a mixture of Hinduism and Mahāyānism until the introduction of Pāli Buddhism in the thirteenth century,[2] after which this powerful sacerdotal caste degenerated with their religion to the position occupied by the modern Bakus.[3] But the Brahmans of Cambodia perhaps never sank so low as did those of Campā, where "In the Po Nagar Inscription (No. 30) we read that the king's feet were worshipped, even by Brāhmaṇas and priests".[4]

Though the Thai were Buddhists, their kings surrounded themselves with the appurtenances of Khmer royalty, and recruited their Court Brahmans from Cambodia. For centuries, indeed, Brahmanism enjoyed quite an important position; for although Buddhism was the religion of the people, and was protected by the kings, Hinduism was still considered as essential to the monarchy, and so received a great share of royal favour. The famous inscription (about A.D. 1361) of King Dharmarāja I mentions the king's knowledge of the *Vedas* and of astronomy[5]; while the inscription on the Śiva statue found at Kāṁbèṅ Bejra records the desire of King Dharmaśokarāja to exalt both Hinduism and Buddhism. And this is as late as A.D. 1510.[6]

During the Ayudhyā period, as has already been mentioned in Chapter II, Court Brahmans were recruited from time to time, both from Cambodia and from the Peninsula (Śaivas). With the final destruction of Ayudhyā in 1767, those Brahmans who had escaped the clutches of the Burmese fled to Nagara Śrī Dharmarāja, whence King Ṭāk, on the re-establishment of the kingdom, recalled them, and endeavoured to collect all that had survived of their ceremonial lore, a difficult task, since many of their books had been destroyed by fire at the fall of Ayudhyā. But very few of the Court Brahmans who had officiated at Ayudhyā survived, the tradition was broken, and most of those who took service at the Court of Bangkok were the descendants of comparatively recent arrivals. Thus, in comparing the Brahmans of Bangkok with those at Phnompenh, the modern capital of Cambodia, Aymonier rightly says :—

[1] C., p. 163. [2] A. iii, p. 591. [3] A. iii, p. 614.
[4] R. C. Majumdar, *Ancient Indian Colonies in the Far East*, vol. i, Champa, 1927, chap. 14.
[5] Coedès, *Les Inscriptions de Sukhodaya*, 1924, p. 98. [6] Ibid., p. 159.

> "Unlike the Brahmans of Cambodia the Siamese Brahmans are not relics of a once powerful religious caste, but have been brought in later (from Ligor[1] and elsewhere) to conduct the court ceremonies in imitation of other courts with an Indian ceremonial."[2]

Thus it is that we cannot expect to obtain much information concerning the history and significance of the State Ceremonies from that somewhat indolent and unintelligent body of men, the modern Court Brahmans of Bangkok. Nevertheless, though they are so ignorant, we owe them a certain amount of respect for what they represent, and, had they any pride in the tradition of their forefathers, the Siamese Brahmans might take comfort in the words of Manu: "Ignorant or learned the Brahman is a great deity; just as Fire is a great deity whether used sacrificially or not."

Since the tendency after the foundation of the present Siamese capital has continued to be in the direction of the exaltation of Buddhism at the expense of the older religion, many of the purely Hindu ceremonies were discontinued after the fall of Ayudhyā, with consequent diminution in the importance of the Brahmans. But the status of the priests during the Bangkok period itself seems to have changed little; indeed, this would scarcely be possible, short of their complete abolition, and our earliest account of the Bangkok Brahmans, that of Crawfurd, who visited Siam on an embassy in 1821, might almost apply to the present day. One of the Brahmans informed Crawfurd that he was

> "the fifth in descent from his ancestor who had first settled in Siam, and who, according to his statement, came from the sacred Island of Ramiseram, between Ceylon and the Main."[3]

At the present day some of the Brahmans have a tradition that their ancestors came from Benares, and it is quite possible that both these accounts are true, and that there are now in Bangkok descendants of Brahmans from both North and South India. In any case such traditions are certainly interesting as evidence of late immigration from India, whereas the modern Bakus of Cambodia have lost all tradition of such immigration. At least the head priest at Phnompenh recently informed Prince Damrong quite seriously that his ancestor came from Mount Kailāsa (the traditional home of Śiva)!

The duties of the Brahmans of ancient India may be classified under three headings: (1) Those of chief chaplain (*purohita*) to the king, a post held by the head priest; (2) those of the astrologers or

[1] Nagara Śrī Dharmarāja. [2] A. ii, p. 32.
[3] Crawfurd, *Embassy to Siam*, London, 1828, p. 119.

soothsayers (*horā*); and (3) those of the officiating priests (*ritvig*). No doubt at an early period in Siam, as well as in Cambodia, the office of *purohita* was held by a Brahman, but this was not the case during the Bangkok period, since the Brahmans had no longer any power. Under the old regime, however, that is to say prior to the modernization of the government, there was an office of *purohita*, but I understand that it was held by a non-Brahman. On the other hand, the prognostications of the astrologers were considered to be of the greatest importance before contact with western science in the nineteenth century undermined the king's credulity. Siamese history of the Ayudhyā period contains frequent mention of various supernatural omens which had to be interpreted by the Brahmans; and no king would have thought of embarking on any important undertaking such as a military expedition without making sure that his soothsayers considered the day and hour propitious. At the time of the accession of the late king and even of the present one good omens such as the advent of a white elephant were eagerly looked for, while in one State Ceremony at least, the First Ploughing, soothsaying still exists in its ancient form. But these features have been retained on account of their popularity with the uneducated masses; and one cannot imagine a modern Siamese king seriously consulting his Brahmans. Indeed, the rather complicated work of calendar-making and fixing the auspicious dates for the State Ceremonies is really quite beyond the capabilities of the modern Brahmans, and so this duty is now performed by a non-Brahman official who holds the office of royal astrologer (one only), and is known as *Braḥyā Horā*. One cannot help remarking how convenient his appointed times usually are, and, in fixing a propitious date for the King's recent visit to America, one might hazard a guess that he took the steamship schedules into consideration!

The office of *purohita* having long ago been abolished, and that of astrologer having passed into non-Brahman hands, there remain to the present Siamese Brahmans only the duties of officiating priests to be performed. It is obvious that so long as State Ceremonial retains its present form a corps of Court Brahmans will remain essential, and, in making it possible for the King to continue to maintain the pomp and dignity inseparable from absolute monarchy, these priests still perform a very important function for the benefit of the society as a whole.

A List of Contents of the Brahmanical Manuscripts in the National Library, Bangkok

Vol. A. " The Worship of the Eight Directions."
" Jǎ Klòm Haṅṣa."
" Khap Mulagni Yakṣa."
" Opening of the portals of Kailāsa " (" P̱o't braḥṯū Śivalai̱ ").

Vol. B. " Pūjā klāṅ."
" Pañca gavya."
" Vāstu pūjā."
" Kalāsa pūjā."
" Kumbha pūjā."
" Rājahamṣa pūjā."
" Mahāgaṇapāti pūjā."
" Consecrating the water of allegiance " (" Jèn nǎṁ braḥ bibarḍha săccā ").

Vol. C. " Hamṣa Pūjā."
" Navagraha pūjā."
" Homakunda."
" Nīrājana pūjā."
" Hanumān manṯra."
" Prājya pūjā."

Vol. D. " Braḥ avisūṯ."
" Pūjā murai̱."
" Pvaj braṯ."
" Closing the portals of Kailāsa " (" P̱it braḥṯū Śivalai̱ ").

Vol. E. " Inviting the gods " (Ǎñjo'ñ braḥ dǎṅ pvaṅ).
" Worship of Braḥ Yambhū " (" Hvǎi̱ braḥ yambhū ").
" Worship of Śiva, Umā, and Vināyaka."
" Candra Namaskaṛa."
" Veda " (" Veda ṯāṅ ṯāṅ ").

Vol. F. " Festival of Elephants " (" Guśatī sǎnveyak lòm jǎṅ ").

Vol. G. " Raising the Utup " (" Yak Utup ").
" Offering flowers at the three temples " (" Thavāy dòk mǎi poth hyai poth klāṅ lè saḥthān braḥ nārāyaṇa ").

Most of the names of the *mantras* are Siamese, and hence are not the original ones; they have, in fact, often been changed, so it is difficult to identify them with those used by King Rāma V in *BRB*.

Part III

CEREMONIES OF INSTALLATION

CHAPTER VI

CORONATION [1]

The Main Ceremonies

1. *The Succession.*

The Succession to the Throne of Siam is, in theory, regulated by the law of A.D. 1360, according to which the eldest son of the queen shall have precedence over all other members of the royal family.[2] Owing to the frequency of its violation throughout Siamese history resulting from usurpation by a powerful noble or the outcome of a struggle for supremacy amongst the surviving sons of a king, the student of Siamese history might hardly suspect the existence of such a law. Again, when the heir apparent was of tender years, it was frequently found necessary to put a stronger man at the head of affairs, and it was then the king's brother that became Heir Presumptive (*Văṅ Nā*). Such was the condition at the end of the seventeenth century which misled Kaempfer into supposing that

> "By virtue of the ancient laws of Siam, upon the demise of the King, the crown devolves on his brother and upon the brother's death, or if there be none, on the eldest son." [3]

[1] The following are the chief Siamese sources for the study of the Coronation, and have been of the greatest value to me in the preparation of this and the following two chapters:—

(1) "*Rāy kāra laḥiat braḥ rāja bidhī paramarājābhiṣeka chalo'm braḥ rāja maṇḍira (braḥ pāda samtec braḥ paramindra mahā prahjādhipak braḥ pak klâu câu yû hua) è sadec liap braḥ nagara.*" (Programme of the Coronation, Assumption of the Royal Residence, and State Progresses of H.M. King Prajadhipok.) Bangkok, B.E. 2468 (A.D. 1926).

(2) "The Coronation of His Majesty Prajadhipok, King of Siam, B.E. 2468," being extracts from the above translated into English with commentary; together with notes on the Installation of the Queen, by H.H. Prince Dhāni Nivāt.

(3) "*Kaṭhmāy heṭu braḥ rāja bidhī paramarājābhiṣeka samtec braḥ rāmādhipatī śrīsindra mahā vajiravudh braḥ maṅkuṭ klâu câu yû hua.*" (Record of the Coronation of King Vajiravudh.) Bangkok, B.E. 2466 (A.D. 1924).

(4) "*Braḥ rāja baṅṣāvaḥtāra kruṅ rāṭanakosindra rājakāl dī sòṅ.*" (History of the Second Reign of the Bangkok Dynasty), by H.R.H. Prince Damrong, Bangkok, B.E. 2459 (A.D. 1917).

To which I may add that I was fortunate in being present in Bangkok at the time of the Coronation of King Prajadhipok, and witnessed most of the more public parts of the ceremony.

[2] *JSS.*, vol. vi (1909), pt. 3, p. 5.

[3] Kaempfer, *History of Japan*, edn. of 1906, i, p. 36.

In the Bangkok period, the succession has gone more in accordance with the law, five of the seven monarchs having succeeded their fathers. Of the other two, one, King Rāma III, was successful in depriving his elder brother of his rights, but the latter ruled after his death as Rāma IV; while the present King succeeded by reason of the fact that his elder brother (Rāma VI) died without male offspring. The *Court Circular* for 25th November, 1926, the date of the death of the late King, made known the accession in the following words:—

> "His Royal Highness the Prince Prajadhipok of Sukhodaya succeeded to the throne in accordance with His late Majesty's commands as confirmed by a meeting of the Royal Family and the Cabinet in special joint session last night."

Thereupon the new King, in accordance with custom, left his own palace and took up his residence in the Grand Palace, though not as yet in the State Apartments.

It has been remarked above that the law prescribes that the successor shall be the eldest son *of the queen* (of the principal queen, if there be more than one), not simply the eldest son of the king. At first sight this certainly suggests the existence of a system of matriarchy, but, whatever may have been the case in the remote past, there is no evidence for such a system having been *recognized* during the historical period. The recognition of matriarchy is quite incompatible with a social system in which, at least by the upper classes, women are considered as being of no account other than as the chattels of their lords. It is true that kings sometimes married their half-sisters, but there was no obligation for them to do so, and indeed, they rather preferred not to do so because of the greater deference with which they had to treat such a queen. They chose whom they liked from among their concubines for promotion to queenship; the queen owed her position solely to the king's favouritism; and it entirely depended on the king's choice whether the successor was the son of a sister or merely the son of a promoted concubine. Again, kings often installed their predecessor's wives in their own harem. This has been regarded as a sign of matriarchy, but in Siam it appears in historical times to be due to the fact that any alternative would be fraught with danger to the king's position.

It is important to note that matriarchy apparently did prevail in some of the more ancient States of Indo-China. In Burma, Furnivall[1] cites a number of supposed relics of a matriarchal system, both in history and modern custom, including marriage of kings

[1] *Journal of the Burma Research Society*, vol. i (1911), pp. 15 sqq.

with half-sisters and inclusion of the late king's concubines in the harem of his successor, but his evidence is not in itself very convincing. Majumdar[1] states with regard to Campā :—

> "In connection with the hereditary succession it is necessary to note the importance of the females. Kings are succeeded not only by their sister's son, but also by their sister's husband and even wife's sister's son. This has been attributed to the system of matriarchy which used to prevail in those parts of the country."

Again, in the case of ancient Cambodia, Groslier[2] quotes from Barth as follows :—

> "The relationship is not direct from father to son, but from uncle to nephew. The mention of the mother in preference to the father (in numerous texts) would explain how alone they could remove from the nephew the suspicion of a less honourable origin from a wife of inferior rank or a concubine. It seems therefore that the family was entirely constituted by the feminine line where the successor is not the son but the son of the sister and so on."

Groslier adds that in a chronicle of the religious foundations of a sacerdotal family from A.D. 802–1052, the right to priesthood went from the son of the sister to the son of the daughter of the sister. But he is not disposed to accept this as certain proof of the existence of matriarchy in Cambodia, and remarks that there is no sign of it in modern times: Sisowath was the brother of Norodom, who was the eldest son of Ang Duong (and Monivongs is the eldest son of Sisowath). Indeed, it appears to me that we could hardly expect to find recognized matriarchy in modern Cambodia if we do not find it so in Siam, for we know that Cambodia, so frequently the vassal of Siam in later times, has come to adopt many of her institutions.

My conclusion, so far as it is possible to come to one on the small amount of evidence at our disposal, is that matriarchy was probably recognized in ancient Cambodia, but it is doubtful if it could have been derived from India which, in the main, is intensely patriarchal. That it may have flourished in Thai States under the suzerainty of the Khmers is possible; but after the Thai attained independence it has existed only subconsciously and involuntarily, the status of women during historical times making its recognition by the Siamese impossible. But this lack of recognition has no bearing on the sociological aspect of the matter. Though unrecognized, matriarchy has undoubtedly continued to exert an important influence on the characteristics of the rulers of Siam up to modern times.

[1] Op. cit. [2] Gr., p. 336.

2. *Preliminary Considerations.*

I shall take as a basis for study the Coronation of King Prajadhipok, which took place in February, 1926. It differed little from those of the three preceding monarchs, and from those of the first three kings of the dynasty mainly by reason of the greater elaboration of the later Buddhist rites which had in course of time been added to and intertwined with what must have been at one time a purely Hindu ceremony. The last Coronation was in accordance with old custom in that it was held as soon as possible after the death of King Vajiravudh, and within the period of mourning, which was suspended during the ceremonies. This custom was the result of the Siamese theory that the heir to the late king rules only as a regent and not as a king, until he is duly anointed and crowned; in other words, until the prescribed rites have been carried out, he is not as yet qualified to perform the divine and priestly functions of a king. King Rāma VI, who wished that his Coronation should be carried out on a very grand scale before a large assemblage of foreign visitors, was obliged to undergo the more important rites immediately after his accession, the full ceremonies being performed at a later date.

King Rāma I, the founder of the Căkrī Dynasty, on victoriously mounting the throne, underwent a summary ceremony of anointment (*prāpṭābhiṣeka*), but two years later, having collected all the available information concerning the coronation ceremonies of the Ayudhyā period, he was anointed and crowned with full rites, which afterwards became the model for all future Coronations.[1] As we shall subsequently see, some of the features of the modern Coronation were known and practised at Sukhodaya, while many of the rites and ideas can be traced back to a very early period in India. The Siamese preserve the ancient term *Rājābhiṣeka* for Coronation, meaning literally royal anointment (*abhiṣeka*), thereby indicating a fact, in support of which we have plenty of other evidence, namely, that the earlier, and originally the essential, part of the ceremony was the anointment, and not the actual crowning, which has now come to symbolize the supreme moment. In ancient India *Rājābhiṣeka* referred to the consecration of ordinary kings, but if the Siamese ever had rites restricted to such a purpose they have now lost them, for the Siamese *Rājābhiṣeka* is rather a *Rājasūya*, or ceremony for the consecration of an emperor, and it is extremely interesting to find that some of its features can be traced back to the Vedic *Rājasūya* described in the *Śatapatha Brāhmaṇa*. But one cannot definitely identify it as a *Rājasūya*, for it also

[1] *History of the Second Reign*, p. 19.

contains ideas belonging to other early ceremonies of consecration (such as the *Vājapeya*, a Vedic *abhiṣeka* not confined to kings), and the later modifications of Epic and Pauranic times are also reflected in the Siamese ceremony.

The Siamese *Rājābhiṣeka* is followed by, and to some extent interwoven with, two closely related ceremonies, the Installation of the Queen, and the Assumption of the Royal Residence. For convenience these two ceremonies will be studied separately and after the Coronation proper. The former, like the Coronation, is now an almost inextricable mixture of Hindu and Buddhist rites; while the latter appears to be, in its present state, a purely Buddhist ceremony.

3. *Scene of the Ceremonies.*

It will be convenient briefly to mention here the group of older buildings, situated within the Grand Palace (*braḥ parama mahā rāja văṅ*) enclosure, where the Coronation ceremonies are held. This group, known as the Mahā Maṇḍira (Chief Residence) is made up of three sections, as follows: (1) The Căkrabartibimān, or residence proper, containing the state bedchamber, on the south; (2) the Baiśāla Dakṣina Hall, an inner hall of audience, in the centre; and (3) the Amarindrā Hall, the outer or public hall of audience, on the north. All these buildings date from the reign of Rāma I, and were actually inhabited by the first three kings of the dynasty. Their architecture is of the traditional Siamese style, no doubt modelled on that of the palaces of earlier capitals. We know little of such ancient palace buildings because they were always built of wood and so have perished, but Aymonier[1] believes that the stone temples of Phimeanakas and Baphuon situated near the palace at Aṅkor Thom were symbolic of Kailāsa and Meru mountains, and were used in connection with Coronations.

There are three other buildings, also within the Grand Palace, which play a less important part in the Coronation. These are (1) the Chapel Royal of the "Emerald" Buddha, commonly known as Văt Braḥ Kèv, but with the official title of Văt Braḥ Śrī Răṯana Sāsatārām ("the temple containing the beautiful jewel of the monastery of the divine teacher"). It is in itself really a group of buildings including the temple proper, the pantheon, library, a tall gilded pagoda, and numerous small shrines of great beauty and interest; (2) the Tusiṯa Mahā P̱rāsāda, which was the scene of the lying-in-state of the late king; (3) the Căkrī Palace, a modern building in European style, but

[1] A. iii, p. 138.

with a purely Siamese roof. The Chapel Royal and the Tusiṭa Mahā Prāsāda are gems of Siamese architecture built in the reign of Rāma I.

4. *Preliminary Rites.*

For three days before the actual Day of Coronation the Court Brahmans performed *homa,* or sacrifices to Fire (Pl. V). The images of the Hindu deities were placed upon three altars in a ceremonial pavilion (*roṅ braḥ rāja bidhī brāhmaṇa*) erected for the purpose near the Tusiṭa Mahā Prāsāda. Before the altars was placed a copper stove inscribed with the appropriate *yantra* (Pl. III), and nine basins of water each containing a small silver coin known as a *fo'aṅ* (no longer current), eight of these basins being arranged around a central one. The Brahmans began their rites at 8 p.m. in accordance with the rule that Brahmanical rites must be performed after dark whenever possible. The *Braḥ Mahā Rāja Grū* [1] performed the usual purificatory rites (see page 249), read the texts offering worship to the eight directions and to the Brahmanic deities. He steeped the leaves of certain trees esteemed for their purificatory and medicinal values in the water hallowed by the above recitations. Some of these he sent to the King, who brushed himself with them in a manner symbolical of purification; others he dipped in honey and oil, and placed them carefully in the fire, at the same time reciting texts. This is in accordance with a rite performed by Hindus in India, accompanied by the following words :—

> " I offer to Śiva the triple leaves of the Aegle Marmalos endowed with the three qualifications, with the three eyes and with the three weapons; and which destroy the sins of the three existences. By seeing the Aegle Marmalos or by touching it one is delivered from all sins. A single leaf of Aegle Marmalos destroys the blackest sin." [2]

At the conclusion of the *homam* the fire was extinguished by some of the hallowed water being poured on it from a chank shell.[3] This *homam* sacrifice used to be performed also in connection with the *Còṅ Pariaṅ* and New Year Festivals. In the former case it was

[1] He is the " High Priest of Śiva " but he is also the Head Brahman who presides over all Siamese Brahmanic ceremonies. The Vaiṣṇavas have really now no separate existence in Siam, and a Brahman takes the part of " High priest of Viṣṇu " only for the Coronation Ceremonies.

[2] *Brahmakarma,* iv, 5.

[3] The chank-shell (*sāṅkha*) is much used in Siamese ceremonies, and, as in India, is especially prized when turned rightwise. Both large and small ones are used for lustral water, and as conch-trumpets are most important sacred musical instruments. Those used for lustral water are often set with gold and jewels. Several Indian legends as to their origin are known in Siam (see Ge. (1), p. 154).

PLATE V.

[Photo: State Railways Dept.

BRAHMAN PERFORMING *HOMA*.

To face page 72.]

PLATE VI.

[*Photo: Narasingh Studio.*

P<u>AI</u> ŚRĪ TRAYS WITH OFFERINGS TO THE DEITIES.

abolished by King Rāma IV, but it still survives in the New Year and Coronation Ceremonies.[1]

At the commencement of the above ceremonies offerings were also placed before the altars of the Hindu deities in the Brahman temples, before the royal white umbrellas to propitiate the spirits thereof, and before the images of the guardian spirits of the city (see Chapter XXVI). These offerings are usually placed on structures known as *paị śrī*, three being used together, i.e. one of gold, one of silver, and one of crystal (Pl. VI). Each *paị śrī*, of whichever material, consists of superimposed trays of decreasing dimensions, so that the whole has an auspicious tapering appearance. Probably the *paị śrī* is an elaborate development of a primitive pile of leaf platters.

During these three days Buddhist services of benediction (*svat brah buddha manṭra*) took place in all three sections of the Chief Residence with the recitation of *paritta suttas*, the protective thread (*sāy siñcana*) being stretched around the buildings.[2] Each evening a monk of high standing delivered a sermon in the Baiśāla Hall, the King himself attending some parts of every service ; and, on the following morning, each day, the King presented food to the monks who had officiated, and also sent some offerings to the Hindu deities. The services were concluded on the morning of the Coronation Day by the extinguishing of the Candle of Victory.[3]

[1] *BRB.*, p. 163, from which source most of the above information concerning the Siamese *homa* is derived.

[2] Gerini (Ge. (1), pp. 49 sqq.) has published a good deal of information concerning the various collections of *paritta suttas*, or Pāli protective stanzas, which make up a great part of the recitations performed by the Buddhist monks in the Siamese State Ceremonies. It will therefore be unnecessary for me to allude to these texts further. The *sāy siñcana* is a thread of unspun cotton which the monks pass round anything that they wish to preserve from evil influences, such as the scene of their rites, a building, or even the whole city. The monks hold one end of the string in their hands while they recite the *paritta suttas*, and the power of their merit is supposed to pass along the *sāy siñcana* by induction, hallowing all within the enclosure. Lustral water is also consecrated by means of the *siñcana* string and the recitation of *paritta* texts, the consecrated water then being known as *nāṁ brah pariṭa*, i.e. *paritta* water (Ge. (1), p. 151).

[3] The Candle of Victory (*dian jaya*) is lighted at the beginning and extinguished at the end of all great Buddhist ceremonies, and is believed to be the equivalent of the Hindu sacred fire. The *dian jayas* are prepared under the direction of the head priest of some royal temple. The wax in each one weighs ten Siamese catties (about 26 lb.) ; the wick contains 108 threads, a Buddhist sacred number ; the length is about five feet, and around it are inscribed magical formulæ and diagrams. The *dian jaya* is usually lighted by means of " celestial fire ", generated by means of a burning glass and kept in a special lamp until ready for use, when it is applied to the *dian jaya* by the King by means of a special taper. The special formulæ recited on the solemn occasions of lighting and extinguishing the Candle of Victory are recorded by Gerini (Ge. (1), p. 161).

5. *The Ceremonial Bath and First Anointment.*

On the morning of the Day of Coronation (25th February), the King proceeded to the Baiśāla Hall, where Princes, Foreign Representatives, and higher Officials of State were assembled. After making profession of the Buddhist faith, at 9.53 a.m., the time being auspicious, the High Priest of Śiva (*Braḥ Mahā Rāja Grū*) invited the King to take a ceremonial bath of purification and anointment, for which purpose the King was clothed in a white robe symbolical of purity.[1] Prior to taking the bath the King paused at an altar erected in the courtyard to light candles and make offerings to the Hindu deities.

The ceremonial bath took place in a specially prepared pavilion (*maṇṭapa braḥ kāyaḥsanāna*) between Baiśāla Hall and Căkrabartibimān. The erection of such a pavilion is evidently in accordance with ancient Indian tradition. A Môn inscription [2] records the building of a great palace at Pagān in the reign of Kyansittha, probably about A.D. 1101–02. It included an "ablution pavilion" probably used in connection with the king's consecration.

The water used in this ceremony originated from (*a*) the five principal rivers of the kingdom, i.e. the Cău Braḥyā, the Săk, the Rājapurī, the Bejrapurī, and the Paṅpaḥkaṅ rivers, in analogy to the famous classical five of ancient India: Gaṅga, Māhi, Yamunā, Sarabhu, and Airāvati; (*b*) water from the four ponds of Subarṇapurī sanctified through constant usage in every State Ceremony where there is a purificatory bath, both in the Ayudhyā and Bangkok periods[3]; and (*c*) some of the water which had been consecrated by the monks[4] at various shrines in the seventeen provinces of Siam, such shrines being chosen either on account of their being the surviving centres of ancient civilizations, or in default of such qualifications, from their being near the present seats of administration. The preparation of the consecrated "water" for the *Rājasūya* is described at length in the *Śatapatha Brāhmaṇa*.[5] It was obtained from rivers, wells, ponds, the sea, etc., but included honey, clarified butter, etc., and these together were considered to be seventeen kinds of water. This number is remarkable in view of water being collected from the seventeen provinces of Siam, but may be only coincidence. From a sociological point of view, however, it certainly seems a point of some importance

[1] And with *matum* (Aegle Marmalos) leaves placed over the right ear, and *phromachan* leaves over the left, according to Ge. (1), p. 129 f.n.

[2] No. ix in *Epigraphia Birmanica*, vol. iii, pt. 1.

[3] *History of the Second Reign*, p. 23.

[4] Water is consecrated by the Buddhist monks either (1) by means of the *paritta* thread (*nǎṁ braḥ pariṭa*) or (2) by the recitation of the *mantras* (*nǎṁ manṭra*).

[5] *Śatapatha Brāhmaṇa*, v, 3, 4, in *SBE*. xli, pp. 73 sqq.

PLATE VII.

[*Photo : State Railways Dept.*

THE KING IN THE ABLUTION PAVILION RECEIVING ANOINTMENT WATER FROM THE PRINCE PATRIARCH.

To face page 75.]

that every province in the land should be given a share in the consecration.

The King having taken his seat in the ceremonial (Pl. VII) pavilion, some of the water was first handed to him by a Brahman in a small golden bowl. The King then dipped his hand into this, and rubbed it on the top of his head. A rope was then pulled, which released a shower of water from the canopy above, through the petals of a golden lotus. The water thus represented a celestial shower. In the Vedic *Rājasūya* the king also rubbed the sprinkled water over himself with the horn of a black antelope, the explanation of this action being, that the

> "collected essence of the waters wherewith he anoints himself means vigour: 'May this vigour of mine spread through my whole self,' thus he thinks, and therefore he rubs it all over himself." [1]

Finally the Siamese king is offered water by ministers and relatives, in the case of the last Coronation, by the late Prince Barṇarăṅṣī, the Prince of Nagara Svarga, and the Prince Patriarch (head of the Buddhist priesthood).

It appears to me probable that this part of the ceremony is primarily a rite of purification, preliminary to the anointment proper, which formed the main part of the consecration, and will be considered in the next section. My reasons for supposing that it was originally only a preliminary rite are as follows:—

(1) Ablutions, as an antidote against defilement, are the daily duty of every high-caste Hindu, and would especially be requisite before embarking on any important ceremonial.[2] If possible, the water used should be from one of the sacred rivers of India, but where this is impossible "he fixes his thoughts on the Ganges, and imagines that he is really bathing in that river".[3] Such a bath of purification as performed by an Indian king is described in the *Antagada Dasao*,[4] in which, although the bathing was not on the occasion of a royal consecration, it is remarkable to note the similarity to the ideal aimed at in the Siamese ceremony, and in the construction of the bathing pavilion:—

> "There in a delightful bath-chamber, entirely covered with lattice-work, and pleasant, and floored with divers gems and jewels, he sat comfortably on a bath-dais figured with patterns in divers jewels, and was bathed with pure waters, with scented waters, with flower waters, and with holy waters again and again, according to the rule of happy and excellent bathing. When the happy and excellent

[1] *Śatapatha Brāhmaṇa*, v, 4, 2, 4, in *SBE*. xli, p. 96.
[2] D., p. 186. [3] D., p. 242.
[4] Oriental Translation Fund, N.S., volume xvii, 1907, p. 20.

bathing had been brought to an end with hundreds of manifold charm wrappings, his body was rubbed with downy soft cloths dyed with fragrant saffron. His limbs were smeared with fresh sweet-scented gosira sandal. A perfect and noble robe of great price was wrapped round him. A pure chaplet and an adorning unguent were put upon him."

(2) The *amount* of water used gives one rather the idea of a bath than of an anointment. The *sprinkling* of kings at their consecration is mentioned in many *Jātakas*; and in the *Jātaka* reliefs in the Ānanda Temple, Pagān, there are coronation anointment scenes in which Brahmans are represented as offering consecrated water *in conches*, i.e. in small quantities suitable for anointment.[1]

(3) In Hastings' *Encyclopædia of Religion and Ethics*,[2] where the general features of the *abhiṣeka* during the Pauranic period are summarized, it is stated that

"prior to the rite (e.g. on the previous day) the king undergoes a purification, consisting of a bath, etc. . . . while, later, in the actual ceremony, the king is sprinkled not only by the *purohita*, but also by other priests, by the ministers and relatives and by the citizens."

In Siam this offering of water by ministers and relatives takes place at the time of the purificatory bath, and so seems to have been transposed from its original place in connection with the anointment proper.

My conclusion, therefore, on the above evidence, is that the Pauranic purificatory bath has in Siam been confused with the earlier idea of anointment, and that the ceremony is now a mixture of the two. I suggest that this confusion might have been brought about by reason of the fact that, since oil is not used for anointment as it was in ancient India (mixed with other ingredients), the main outward distinction between the two rites has been lost and their significance thus confused. But this confusion of the negative rite of lustration with the positive one of unction is not confined to Siam. The earlier idea was that fat or oil (imbued with the sacred essence by means of magical or religious formulæ) was the most suitable medium for transferring power or sanctity to a person or thing, and that water was only purificatory. But, later, water also came to be regarded as a suitable unguent.[3]

During the time that the ceremonial bath was in progress, ancient

[1] *Epigraphia Birmanica*, vol. ii, pt. 2, showing anointment scenes of the following kings: No. 47, Janaka; No. 105, Nimi; No. 206, the son of Vedeha; No. 217, Candakumara; No. 221, Bhuridatta.

[2] Art. "Abhiṣeka".

[3] Crawley, *Studies of Savages and Sex*, chap. viii.

guns were fired within the precincts of the Grand Palace, a fanfare of drums and trumpets was sounded, and the Brahmans played their ceremonial music,[1] while eighty Buddhist monks, assembled in the Baiśāla Hall, chanted stanzas of benediction.

6. *The Ceremony on the Octagonal Throne and Second Anointment.*

After the Ceremonial Bath the King retired, shortly to reappear in full regal robes which included the gold embroidered *phā-nuṅ*, or Siamese national lower garment, not derived from Cambodia, but probably an adaptation of the Indian *dhoti*; and the gold embroidered robe or long tunic. Such a long tunic is mentioned in inscriptions as having been worn by the kings of ancient Campā.[2] In Vedic India the presentation of special garments to the king at *Rājasūya* consecration took place, and the inner and outer garments were regarded as the amnion and chorion, thus symbolizing rebirth.[3]

The King then made his way to the Baiśāla Hall, preceded by Brahmans and Court Pandits, in the following order:—

Left File	*Right File*
1. Brahman priest, bearing an image of Gaṇeśa.	1. Court Pandit (*Rājapăṇḍita*), bearing an image of the Buddha, called Lord of Victory.
2., 3. Brahmans with *păṇḍaḥvaḥ* drums.	2., 3. Brahmans with *păṇḍaḥvaḥ* drums.
4., 5., 6. Brahmans blowing conches.	4., 5., 6. Brahmans blowing conches.
7. High Priest of Viṣṇu, scattering roasted grains.	7. High Priest of Śiva, scattering roasted grains.
8. A Brahman.	8. A Brahman.

The King

[1] Besides the conch-trumpet, the Brahmans have a small flageolet, a bell, a gong, and a drum called *păṇḍaḥvaḥ*, similar instruments being recognizable on the bas-reliefs of Aṅkor (Gr., Figs. 81 and 82). The *păṇḍaḥvaḥ* drum is now, I believe, only used in connection with the Coronation. The Brahmans describe it as a drum used to awaken Śiva in the morning, and one of identical shape is still used by a sect of Śaivites in India, where it is known as the *damaru*. The *păṇḍaḥvaḥ* is a small hour-glass shaped drum, operated by a string and ball attached to a peg projecting from its middle (Ge. (1), p. 153). An outburst of music from these instruments marks the critical moments in most state ceremonies, especially in the Coronation. Such was also the case in ancient India, as, for example, in the Coronation described in the *Antagada Dasao*, where there was "great massed beating of noble drums, with loud pealings of trumpets, gongs, tambours, kettledrums, and other drums great and small."

[2] Majumdar, op. cit., chap. xiv.

[3] *Śatapatha Brāhmaṇa*, v. 3, 5, 20–1, in *SBE*., xli, pp. 85 sq.

It will be noticed that the Buddha, as well as the chief Hindu gods, are represented either by their images or priests in the above procession, thereby symbolizing the participation of both Hinduism and Buddhism in the coming ceremonies. It may also be mentioned that the Court Pandits, who play an important part throughout the Coronation, are not Brahmans, but high Siamese noblemen or even princes who take the part of Wise Men of the Court, just as, until the government was reorganized on modern lines, the post of *purohita* still survived but was held by a Siamese noble, not by a Brahman.

On entering the Baiśāla Hall, the King seated himself on the Octagonal Throne (*Braḥ-ḍī-năṅ Ăṭhadiśa*), of fig-wood (*udumbara*), beneath the seven-tiered White Umbrella of State, there to receive further anointment (Pl. VIII). The throne was spread over with *hyā gā* (corresponding to the Indian *darbha* grass), covered with a white cloth; while opposite each face of the throne was a small table on which was placed the image of the guardian of the quarter (*lokapāla*), and the ceremonial water and conch. The King first sat facing the East, the quarter of the sun, and hence perhaps another indication of the king's early equivalence to the sun. The Pandit for this point advanced to the foot of the throne, and, having made due obeisance (*thavāy paṅgam*), addressed the King in Pāli to the following effect [1]:—

> "May it please your Majesty! May the Sovereign here give me leave to pronounce his victory. May the Sovereign, turning now towards the East, seated upon his royal throne, extend his protection and exercise his royal authority over all those realms situated to (the east) and all beings that therein dwell. May he remain on earth, further protecting this kingdom, as well as her Buddhist Religion and her people. May he remain long in sovereignty, without ills, accomplishing success, and may his years number a hundred. May the Sovereign Guardian of the East, renowned as Dhataratha, gently protect the King and his realms. Whoever create evil in this eastern quarter, may the Sovereign, through his might, triumph over them all in a righteous manner."

The Pandit then handed a conch of anointment water from the Eastern Provinces, while reciting the following stanza:—

> "Through the power of the Triple Gems (the Buddha, the Law, and the Brotherhood), and through this water poured down upon him may the King be awarded success in the way heretofore invoked."

The King answered in Pāli verse as follows:—

> "Your auspicious speech, going right to the heart of kings, I fain accept. May it come to pass as you have said. I shall extend my

[1] The following speeches, translated into English from the Pāli, are from H.H. Prince Dhāni's pamphlet on the Coronation.

Plate VIII.

[Photo : State Railways Dept.

THE CEREMONY ON THE OCTAGONAL THRONE.

[To face page 78.

protection and exercise my royal authority over all those realms to the East and all beings that dwell therein. I shall remain on earth further protecting this kingdom, and her Buddhist religion and her people."

The Pandit then said,

"Good, my Lord."

The King then turned to the south-east, where the same dialogue was repeated with modifications as to names of the quarters and their traditional celestial guardians. Thus the King turned round in order, until, finally having completed the round, he turned again to the Pandit for the East, who summed up the benediction and the King answered in Pāli verse similar to the above.

I shall now analyse, under a number of sub-headings, the derivation and significance of the Ceremony on the Octagonal Throne:—

(1) My first contention is that the anointment on the Octagonal Throne corresponds to what was at an early period the essential *abhiṣeka* of kings, but which has now been overshadowed both by the Ceremonial Bath and by the Actual Coronation, the latter being, I believe, of comparatively late origin.

(2) As already stated, the anointment was undoubtedly formerly performed with oil as in India, but the change to water was brought about by Buddhism in both Siam and Burma; but in Cambodia the custom of anointing with oil was only discontinued at the coronation of Sisowath.

(3) In the Vedic *Rājasūya* the king was anointed by the *purohita*, and in Pauranic times by the *purohita*, other priests, ministers, relatives, and even citizens. Now in Siam the Brahmans have fallen too low and the kingship been elevated too high for any to perform that office but the King himself, and thus, though Brahmans and others hand him water, he actually anoints himself. This is, of course, really rather illogical, since before the King has been anointed, he is not properly qualified to perform divine or priestly functions.

(4) A point of interest in connection with the *abhiṣeka* in ancient India, is that in the Vedic *Rājasūya* the king was anointed "whilst standing with his face turned towards the East",[1] while the Siamese King, although seated, also first anoints himself on the Octagonal Throne when facing the East.

(5) The King's promise to protect his people and the Buddhist Religion may be contrasted with those oaths of fidelity extracted by the Brahmans in ancient India. Though we get no oath in the *Rājasūya* described in the *Śatapatha Brāhmaṇa*, the following

[1] *Śatapatha Brāhmaṇa*, v, 4, 2, 1, in *SBE*. xli, p. 94.

ceremony of passing round the sacrificial sword clearly indicates the ascendency of the Brahmans at the time when the passage was written, but it may be a later interpolation for we know that in early Vedic times the Kṣatriyas and Brahmans lived more or less on equal terms :—

> " A Brāhmaṇa then hands to him (the king) the sacrificial (wooden) sword—either the Adhvaryu, or he who is his (the king's) domestic chaplain—with ' Indra's thunderbolt thou art : therewith serve me ! ' —the sacrificial sword being a thunderbolt, that Brāhmaṇa, by means of that thunderbolt, makes the king to be weaker than himself."[1]

And in the *Indrābhiṣeka* described in the *Aitareya Brāhmaṇa*, the king swore life-long fealty to the *purohita*.[2] In later times, in those States where the power of the Brahmans was absolutely supreme, the coronation ceremony consisted almost entirely of oaths, as shown, for example, by the twelfth century Arakanese ceremony.[3] In the Siamese Coronation we find little surviving trace of an oath, and should hardly expect to do so, considering the relative position of the King and the Brahmans. This abolition of the coronation oath is a late development in the history of kingship :—

> " From the earliest times the consecration was made conditional on a just rule, and it is only when nations reached the phase of excessive centralisation and excessive elevation of the kingship over all other ranks that kings and their courts tried to forget the conditional nature of the royal power." [4]

(6) The use of Pāli, the sacred language of Buddhism, and the Buddhist flavour of the whole dialogue, even when issuing from the mouths of supposed Brahman Pandits, is indicative of its late invention. There appears to me, however, to be an ancient basis to the opening speech of the pandits, " May the Sovereign give me leave to pronounce his victory, etc." It is interesting to compare it to the following passage referring to the coronation of Prince Goyame in the Jain scripture, *Antagada Dasao* :—

> " Victory, victory to thee, O blessed one ! Victory, victory to thee, O happy one ! Happiness to thee ! Conquer the unconquered, preserve the conquered, dwell amidst the conquered . . . Mayst thou preserve thy supreme life free from harm and loss, glad and joyful for many years, many hundreds and thousands and hundreds of thousands of years ! "

Again, there is the shout of victory of the Buddha after he had been handed the symbols of royalty in the Tusita heaven, just before

[1] Ibid., v, 4, 4, 15. [2] *Aitareya Brāhmaṇa*, viii, 15.
[3] *Journal of the Burma Research Society*, vii (1917), pp. 181 sqq.
[4] Hocart, *Kingship*, p. 95.

his last birth, and beginning " I am the chief of the world ".[1] And in the Burmese coronation ceremony these words were repeated aloud by the new king.[2] The Siamese and Cambodian ceremonies of Coronation are replete with references to victory, e.g. Candle of Victory, Gong of Victory, and Crown of Victory. But what kind of victory is referred to ? It was certainly not a physical victory, for the King of Siam quietly succeeded his brother, and the King of Cambodia was appointed by the French government. The early Indian writings mention the same kind of victory, for example, in the *Vājapeya* the sacrificer makes an offering of ghee, thinking that he does thus

> " smite the fiends, the Rakshas, in the quarters, by that thunderbolt, the ghee ; and thus he gains the victory thinking, ' May I be consecrated, when safety and security have been gained ! ' "[3]

In the Vedic *Rājasūya* there was actually a symbolic foray or sham fight in which the king obtained the victory,[4] and the idea of victory is present in the *Punarābhiṣeka.*[5] Hocart [6] has pointed out that this magical victory in a magical contest, where the victory was gained over the demons by the power of sacrifice, was common in Indian literature, and he has also shown that this idea of victory is extremely widespread in coronation ceremonies.

(7) It is interesting to note that the Octagonal Throne is made of figwood (*udumbara* = *ficus glomerata*), and that the throne used in the *abhiṣeka* described in the *Aitareya Brāhmaṇa* [7] was also of figwood, (though in the *Śatapatha Brāhmaṇa* [8] it is said to have been of *khadira* = *acacia catechu*). The *ficus glomerata* has been esteemed as sacred in India since time immemorial, partly because its fruit seemed to appear without a previous flowering stage and partly because this fruit was in early times a staple food in India. Later the Hindus and Buddhists encompassed it with religious myths.

(8) The eightfold ceremony on the Octagonal Throne is evidently the modern representative of a rite which took place in the ancient Vedic *Rājasūya*. In the account given in the *Śatapatha Brāhmaṇa* [9] two such rites are described at different stages in the *Rājasūya*, but, bearing in mind the repetition which is characteristic of Brahmanic literature, it seems certain that they are two versions of one and the same rite. The first is :—

[1] Rhys Davids, *Buddhist Birth Stories*, p. 155.
[2] Harvey, *History of Burma*, p. 325.
[3] *Śatapatha Brāhmaṇa*, v, 2, 4, 7, in *SBE*. xli, p. 49.
[4] Ibid., v, 4, 3, in *SBE*. xli, pp. 98 sqq., and note 1, p. 100.
[5] *Aitareya Brāhmaṇa*, viii, 10.
[6] Hocart, *Kingship*, chap. iii.
[7] *Aitareya Brāhmaṇa*, viii, 5.
[8] v, 4, 4, 1, in *SBE*. xli, p. 105.
[9] v, 4, 1, 3–8, and v, 4, 4, 6, in *SBE*. xli.

> "He then makes him ascend the regions, with 'Ascend thou the East! May the Gāyatrī (metre) protect thee, the Rathanatara-sāman, the threefold stoma, the spring season, the Priesthood, that precious treasure!'"

A similar verse is repeated for each of the other four regions, South, West, North, and the Upper Region, with modification as to season, etc., and concluding with the explanation of the commentator:—

> "And as to why he makes him ascend the quarters—that is a form of the seasons: it is the seasons, the year, that he thereby makes him ascend; and having ascended the seasons, the year, he is high, high above everything here, and everything here is below him."

The second version of the rite is as follows:—

> "He (the *purohita*) then throws the five dice into his (the king's) hand with 'Dominant thou art: may these five regions of thine prosper!' Now that one, the Kali, is indeed dominant over the (other) dice, for that one dominates over all the dice; therefore he says, 'Dominant thou art: may these five regions of thine prosper!' For there are indeed five regions, and all the regions he thereby causes to prosper for him!"

In later times, perhaps as a result of greater geographical knowledge, we get the eight regions substituted for the five, and another late introduction is evidently the Invocation of the Guardians of the Quarters, for they are not those of classical Hindu mythology, but are in accordance with the Siamese Buddhist modification, viz.: Dhataratha (E.), Virulhaka (S.), Virupakkha (W.), and Kuvera (N.), the subsidiary regions being entrusted to the followers of the above four, i.e. Bhūta or genii (S.E.), Deva or celestials (S.W.), Nāga or serpents (N.W.), and Yakkha or giants (N.E.). From a sociological point of view, this anointment facing the eight directions must always have been of great value in emphasizing the Siamese king's protection of all parts of the realm, especially in the days of Old Siam, when the royal power grew weaker in proportion to the distance at which an outlying province was situated from the capital.

7. *The Ceremony of Actual Coronation.*

The Ceremony on the Octagonal Throne having been completed, the King advanced towards the western part of the Baiśāla Hall, preceded by the Brahmans and Pandits in the order already described, and followed by chamberlains and pages bearing the Regalia in the following order:—

Left.			Right.
(a) Royal Regalia and Utensils.			
1. The Great White Umbrella of State (*Braḥ śveta chătra*).	The Brahman Girdle (*Braḥ sănvāl brāhmaṇadhurām*).	The Golden Tablet of Style and Title (*Braḥ subarṇapăṭa*).	The Great Crown of Victory (*Braḥ mahā bijăya mankuṭ*).
2. The Sceptre (*Dhārbraḥkara*).	The Girdle of Brilliants (*Braḥ sănvāl braḥ naba*).	The Girdle of the Nine Gems (*Braḥ sănvāl nabarăṭana rājavarābharaṇa*).	The Sword of Victory (*Braḥ sèn kharga jayaśrī*).
3. The Fan (*Bătvālvijanī*).	The Whisk of the Yak's Tail (*Braḥ sè jāmrī*).	The Whisk of the White Elephant's Tail (*Braḥ sè hăn jăn*).	The Slippers (*Chalòn braḥ pāda*).
4. The Stick (*Dhār braḥkaradevarūp*).	The Diamond Ring (*Braḥ dhāmmaranga vijiaracinta*).	The Ring (*Braḥ dhāmmaranga răṭanavarāvudha*).	The Personal Sword (*Braḥ sèn făkdònkliăn*).
5. The Receptacle (*Braḥ subarṇa śrībŭachèk*).	The Betel Nut Set (*Bān braḥkhān hmāk*).	The Water Urn (*Braḥ maṇḍapa*).	The Libation Vessel (*Braḥ tau dăk ṣiṇodak*).
(b) The Eight Weapons of Sovereignty			
6. The "Hostage Sword" (*Braḥ sèn tābjaley*).	The Discus (*Braḥ sèn căkra*).	The Trident (*Braḥ sèn ṭrī*).	The "Diamond Spear" (*Braḥ sèn hòk bejrarăṭana*).
7. The Long Handled Sword (*Braḥ sèn khò hāv sèn bal bāy*).	The Sword and Buckler (*Braḥ sèn tāb khen*).	The Bow (*Braḥ sèn dhanū*).	The "Gun of the Saṭon" (*Braḥ sèn pū'n khām mènām saṭon*).

The history and significance of the various articles of the Regalia will be fully considered in the next chapter.

The ceremony of Actual Coronation is performed on a throne of gilded figwood called the *Bhadrapiṭha* Throne (Pl. IX), which seems to correspond to a throne of the same name used in coronation ceremonies of Pauranic times.[1] It is covered with *hyā gā* (= *darbha* grass), overlaid with a white cloth upon which again is laid a cloth of gold embroidered with a vermilion figure of a royal lion (*rājasīha*). The latter is a very ancient feature, for both the *Aitareya* and *Śatapatha Brāhmaṇa* mention that the throne was draped with a tiger skin and this persisted with the golden *Bhadrapiṭha* thrones of the Pauranic period.

The King seated himself on the *Bhadrapiṭha* Throne beneath an umbrella of seven tiers, which, after the King was crowned, was replaced by one of nine tiers, emblematic of full sovereignty. The High Priest of Śiva then came before him and, after rendering homage, pronounced the Tamil *mantra*, the Siamese name of which means "Opening the portals of Kailāsa". He then paid homage in the following Pāli speech, at the same time handing to the King the Golden Tablet of Style and Title :—

"May it please Your Majesty to grant me leave to address Your Majesty! Since Your Majesty has received full anointment and

[1] *ERE*. art. "*Abhiṣeka*".

become His Majesty the King of Siam, we therefore beg in unanimity to present to Your Majesty Your full style and title as engraved upon this tablet of gold as also to hand to Your Majesty these regalia befitting Your high dignity. May Your Majesty be known by that style and accept these regalia. Having done so, may Your Majesty take upon Yourself the business of government, and, for the good and happiness of the populace, reign on in righteousness!"

The King replied, also in Pāli, "Be it so, Brahman"; and the dialogue was then repeated in Siamese. This use of the three languages is interesting: The corrupt *mantras*, by reason of their being unintelligible, together with their venerable antiquity, are of sociological value in surrounding the ceremony with an air of mystery. On the other hand the Pāli dialogue seems to be modern; it was made up after the knowledge of Sanskrit was forgotten, and Pāli was used, perhaps not so much out of reverence for Buddhism, but because it was the only alternative sacred language. But it is obvious that no purpose could be served by keeping the officials and people in ignorance of the meaning of this dialogue; hence the repetition in Siamese, which performs the valuable sociological function of impressing on their minds the dignity of the new king.

The High Priest of Śiva then took the Great Crown of Victory from its bearer and handed it to the King, who put it on his head. Although he received the Crown from the hands of a representative of the god Śiva, it is quite natural that a divine or priestly king would not tolerate the idea of actually being crowned by mortal hands—and hence the King crowned himself. In Europe the contrary view prevailed, except in Russia, where

"the Tsar was anointed by the metropolitan, but placed the crown on his head himself. He received the sacrament among the clergy, the priestly theory of his office being recognized." [1]

This is a remarkable parallel to the procedure in Siam.

The King's placing the Crown on his head, now considered the supreme moment of the Coronation, was signalized by the usual Brahmanic music and fanfare within the palace, the firing of salutes without, and the ringing of monastery bells throughout the country. At the same time, Buddhist monks, waiting in the other parts of the Chief Residence, recited a blessing.

The High Priest of Śiva then handed one by one the other regalia to the King, who touched them to signify his acceptance, after which they were placed by attendants on tables ranged on either side of the

[1] *Encyclopædia Britannica*, art. "Coronation". The Kings of Prussia also crowned themselves.

PLATE IX.

[*Photo: State Railways Dept.*

THE KING SEATED ON THE *BHADRAPIṬHA* THRONE AFTER HAVING RECEIVED THE REGALIA.

[*To face page 84.*

throne. The High Priest of Viṣṇu handed the nine-tiered Great White Umbrella to the King, and substituted it for the one of seven tiers above the throne. At the same time he made a speech in Pāli, similar to that delivered by the High Priest of Śiva, to which the King replied as before, with again Siamese repetitions. A Brahman then chanted a *mantra* in praise of Śiva, following which another Brahman chanted a *mantra* in praise of Viṣṇu, and these recitations were accompanied by the usual ceremonial music of the Brahmans. At the conclusion of this, all the Brahmans rendered homage before the King, and the High Priest of Śiva, kneeling in front, thus pronounced a final benediction :—

> "May His Majesty, the Supreme Lord, who now reigns over the kingdom here, triumph over all and everywhere alway."

It has already been remarked that the ceremony of actual crowning together with the presentation of the other regalia, has in Siam come to usurp the place of chief importance held in early times by the *abhiṣeka*. Now it is known from an old manuscript, that survived from the Ayudhyā period, that at the Coronation of King Paramakoṣa (A.D. 1733), Buddhist monks recited the scriptures for three days, following which in the morning the king took a ceremonial bath, mounted the Octagonal Throne, and the Brahmans pronounced his victory and recited *mantras*. There was no ceremony on the *Bhadrapiṭha* Throne nor any presentation of the regalia.[1] I do not, however, think that we can accept this as evidence that there was no ceremony of Actual Coronation on the *Bhadrapiṭha* Throne during the Ayudhyā period, but only that it was then considered less important than the *abhiṣeka* and was likely to be omitted in troublous times. The idea is certainly old, though far younger than that of the *abhiṣeka*, and takes us back at least to Pauranic times. Indeed, so far as Siam is concerned, an inscription of the reign of King Dharmarāja I of Sukhodaya [2] records the *abhiṣeka* of that king, *with the presentation of regalia*, and a new name. The presentation of the regalia to the king, though not the actual crowning, can even be traced back to Vedic times. Then the *purohita* presented the newly consecrated king with a bow and three arrows, accompanying the act with the following words addressed to the bow :—

> "Thou art Indra's Vritra killer . . . May he (the king) slay Vritra by thee,"

[1] *History of the Second Reign*, p. 16.
[2] Coedès, *Inscriptions de Sukhodaya*, Ins. iv, p. 97.

whereby, the commentator explains, he means to say,

"May he slay by thee his spiteful enemy." [1]

The fact that the only regalia presented to the king at the time when this Brāhmaṇa was written, were warlike weapons, and the nature of the words that accompany the presentation, indicate that we are not then far from the time when the king was the actual war-chief. Later other regalia were evolved, the donning of the crown coming in course of the ages to signify the supreme moment in the king's consecration.

To return to the Siamese ceremony, the King, having received the final benediction of the Brahmans, pronounced his first command as a fully anointed and crowned monarch, in the following words:—

> "Brahmans, now that I have assumed the full responsibility of government, I shall reign in righteousness for the good weal of the populace. I extend my royal authority over you and your goods and your chattels, and as your sovereign do hereby provide for your righteous protection, defence and keeping. Trust me and live at ease."

The High Priest of Śiva was the first man formally to receive the King's command, thus: "I do receive the first command of Your Majesty." But though this royal speech is designated as a command, it appears to me to have very much the appearance of a disguised oath of office, a survival from the days when kings had to swear fealty to the Brahmans.

The symbolism all through the ceremony of actual Coronation is, as Prince Dhāni has pointed out, clearly along the lines of an assumption that the chief deities, especially Śiva, are invited down to the earth to become merged in the person of the crowned King. Hence the hymn "Opening the Portals of Kailāsa", by way of invitation; the *mantras* in praise of the two high gods; the presence among the regalia of such articles as the Brahman girdle; Viṣṇu's discus, and Śiva's trident; the epithet, within the full style of the king, of the "Incarnation of Celestial Gods" (*Dibyadebāvaṭara*); and finally the use of the mystic contraction, referring to the Hindu Trinity, in the phrase "*Omkāra*" to denote the command of the crowned King, whereas before Coronation his command never ranks as an *Omkāra*. We therefore seem to have a mild form of identification of the King with the deity, a process which reached its acme in the cult of the Deva-rāja in Cambodia, but which has been weakened by Hīnayāna Buddhism in Siam. We can trace the idea back to Vedic times where,

[1] *Śatapatha Brāhmaṇa*, v, 3, 5, 28, in *SBE*. xli, p. 88.

in the *Rājasūya*, we find the pronouncing of the *āvid* formulæ, after the presentation of regalia, which announce the presence of the deities to witness and approve the consecration. Thus:—

> "'Present are Heaven and Earth the all propitious'; he (the *purohita*) thus announces him (the king) to those two, the heaven and the earth, and they approve of his consecration; and approved by them he is consecrated."[1]

And, later, in the *Rājasūya*, the *purohita* addresses the king, thus:—

> "'Thou art Brahman! Thou art Varuṇa of true power!' He thereby lays vigour into him, and causes Varuṇa to be of true power. . . . 'Thou art Brahman! Thou art Indra, mighty through the people!' He thereby lays vigour into him and causes Indra to be mighty through the people."[2]

Being now fully crowned, the King scattered gold and silver flowers and coins among the Brahmans, an action which he repeated later, on leaving the hall of audience. Prince Dhāni regards this as a symbol of riches and plenty, but I think that the gold flowers are rather more reminiscent of those angelic showers of flowers which were rained from heaven on great occasions, as, for example, frequently mentioned in the Siamese *Life of the Buddha*. The earliest classical reference in Indian literature to a king making such presents at the time of his consecration seems to be supplied by the *Rāmāyaṇa*, in the case of the Coronation of the hero Rāma.

The King next poured out a libation to Nāṅ Dharaṇī, the Goddess of Earth. This, in my opinion, is not in itself an oath or "Vow of his undertaking to take up the reins of government for the good of all", as Prince Dhāni supposes. It is rather the confirmation or ratification of the former promises given by the King in his "first command". The outpouring of water is an ancient Brahmanical ceremony of ratification. It is frequently mentioned in Buddhist works also, as, for example, when the King of Magadha presented his garden Veluvana to the Buddha as a site for a monastery, he ratified the gift by pouring water from a shell upon the earth.[3]

8. *The Buddhist Benediction.*

The King then removed the Crown (a sign of humility in the presence of the Buddhist Chapter he was about to meet), and proceeded to the

[1] *Śatapatha Brāhmaṇa*, v, 3, 5, 36, in *SBE*. xli, p. 90.
[2] Ibid., v, 4, 4, 10–11, in *SBE*. xli, p. 109.
[3] Alabaster, *The Wheel of the Law*, p. 224.

Căkrabartibimān, with chamberlains and pages bearing the regalia after him. Here the King received the first royal blessing from the Prince Patriarch, in full assembly of the clergy who had been officiating since the 22nd February.

9. *The General Audience.*

At 1 p.m. on the Day of Coronation the King received the homage of the Royal Family and the official world in the Amarindrā Hall. Guards of Honour lined the grounds within the Grand Palace, the King's charger was fully caparisoned, and the State Elephant was ready at the mounting platform outside the Hall of Amarindrā, which reminds one of the fact that the choice of an elephant and a white horse (two of the royal *ratnas*) was an essential of coronations in the Pauranic period in India.[1]

The King was in full state robes, wearing the Great Crown of Victory, and seated upon the *Braḥ-dī-nǎṅ Budtān Dòṅ* (Golden Hibiscus Throne). This throne is more highly ornamented than the *Bhadrapiṭha*, and is set on a tall pyramidal tiered base carved with figures of *devatās* and *garuḍas*.[2]

The ceremony, at which I was amongst those present, was in the nature of a Royal Audience, and will be considered in the chapter devoted to Audiences. At the moment I shall speak only of the special features of the Audience, in relation to the Coronation: H.R.H. Prince Barṇarāṅṣī read an address of congratulation and formal avowal of loyalty in the name of the assemblage, to which the King replied, thanking and enjoining all to carry on the government as heretofore, assuring them at the same time of his readiness to see and hear every official so far as opportunity might allow. But this is a modification of ancient custom to suit modern constitutional methods of government. An account of the ceremony as performed in Old Siam is given by Pallegoix:—

> " One of the chief nobles advances crawling, and thus addresses the King: 'Your Majesty's servant is directed, on behalf of all the dignified nobles here present, to offer our united homage, bending our heads at the sacred feet of your glorious Majesty, Somdetch Phra Chom Klau, our refuge, who are mounted on the diamond-adorned throne, invested with the sovereign power; seated under the many-tiered umbrella, the terror of your enemies, whose august name is written on the plate of gold. We ask leave to deposit at the sacred feet of your Majesty everything we possess, and all the treasures of the kingdom.' The King answers: 'All the dignified nobles shall have the privilege of appearing in my presence, as they desire, to

[1] *ERE*. art. " *Abhiṣeka* ".

[2] The history of this throne will be discussed in the chapter on Royal Audiences.

offer their services according to their several functions. So let each, without fear, come and present his service.' Then the Phya Phra Klang (the minister for foreign affairs) prostrates himself, and presents to the King the royal barges, ships of war, arsenals, soldiers, and military appurtenances. The Phya Suphavadi offers the elephants, horses, and the capitals of the provinces of the first, second, third, and fourth order, with all their inhabitants. The master of the palace presents the palace and all its contents. The minister of justice presents the city of Bangkok. The minister of agriculture offers the produce of the fields and the gardens. The treasurer gives the twelve departments of the royal exchequer." [1]

But the king immediately returned all these riches to the guardian-ship of those who had presented them, enjoining all the officials to carry on the government as heretofore.

This ceremony possessed, as it still does in its modern form, an important functional value. It impressed upon the officials and the people at large that they enjoyed their offices and the fruit of the land directly through the munificence of the new ruler, and not as legacies from the past reign. The prototype of this audience first appears in Pauranic times, with the ceremony of presentation of the officials to the king, and in his confirmation of their appointment.[2]

10. *Audience to the Palace Ladies.*

The General Audience having terminated, the King, having doffed the Great Crown and donned the *Kaṭhina* Crown,[3] retired to the Baiśāla Hall for the Ceremony of the Queen's Investiture, which will be described in Chapter VIII. The King then received the congratulations of the ladies, to which he replied thanking all, and again giving the customary permission of access to his person.

11. *Acceptance of the Headship of the Buddhist Religion.*

At 4 p.m. on the same day, the King, seated on a state palanquin, was carried in procession to the Chapel Royal. He wore the Great Crown while seated on the palanquin, but when on foot before mounting the palanquin, after leaving it, and while on his way to enter the temple, he wore a Royal Hat.[3] On entering the Chapel Royal the King made offerings of gold and silver flowers and lit candles before the " Emerald Buddha " and the images of Buddha representing the earlier kings of the dynasty. Then, in full congregation of the higher

[1] P. i, 261–6. Prince Damrong (*History of the Second Reign*, p. 30) gives a similar account of the ceremony at the coronation audience of Rāma II, but states with greater accuracy that it was the *Kraḥlāhom* who offered the royal barges and military appurtenances.

[2] *ERE.* art. " *Abhiṣeka* ".

[3] See p. 98.

clergy of the kingdom, he made a formal declaration of his religion and of his willingness to become "Defender of the Faith" (*braḥparamarājūpathămabhakbraḥbuddhaṣāsanā*), in the following formula:—

> "My Lords! Whereas being a believer and one pleased (with the religion of the Buddha), having taken refuge in the Trinity in due form, and now having been anointed in sovereignty, I therefore give myself up to the Buddha, the Law, and the Brotherhood; I shall provide for the righteous protection, defence and keeping of the Buddhist Religion. If agreeable, my Lords, may the Brotherhood recognize me as 'Defender of the Buddhist Faith'."

The whole clergy then signified their acceptance and the president of the Chapter then pronounced the supreme blessing as follows:—

> "May the Great King Paraminda Mahā Prajadhipok of Siam live to a full century of years in happiness and good health. May all his duties and deeds be crowned with success, may wealth and victory be his for ever!"

We recognize in this purely Buddhist ceremony a late addition of King Rāma IV designed to leave no doubt in the minds of any that Buddhism is supreme, and that the king is above all a Buddhist monarch.

12. *Homage to Ancestors.*

The King, borne on a palanquin and wearing the Great Crown, next proceeded in full state to the Tusiṯa Mahā P̱rāsāda. He removed the Crown and entered the building on foot for the purpose of paying homage to the memory of his predecessors. Here the late King Rāma VI was lying in state, and the urns containing the relics of the other five kings of the dynasty as well as those of the late Queen Mother had also been brought thither in order that the King might pay homage before them. A full consideration of the subject of paying homage to ancestors will be found in Chapter XIII, and need not, therefore, be enlarged upon here.

After leaving the Tusiṯa Mahā P̱rāsāda the King and Queen retired, accompanied by noble ladies, and this completed the ceremony for the day. But the private ceremony of the Assumption of the Residence had yet to be performed. It will be considered in Chapter VIII.

13. *Special Audiences.*

On the 26th February, at 4 p.m., the King received in audience the special envoys (representing foreign powers) and the diplomatic corps, who submitted an address of congratulation in the Cǎkrī

Palace, after which the King repaired to the Hall of Amarindrā, where he handed letters patent to three monks, one each from a chief section of the Buddhists of Siam, namely the Mahānikāya, the Dharmayūtika (reformed sect), and the Peguan, promoting them to the rank of abbot, by way of the first act of grace after his Coronation. He then received traditional offerings of flowers, incense, and candles from members of the Royal Family, and officials of State. Finally, the day's proceedings were terminated by a Lord Abbot delivering a sermon of benediction.

Next day there was a similar reception of offerings from officials of State in the Hall of Amarindrā, where the Supreme Patriarch delivered a sermon on the ten virtues of a king.

Though somewhat modernized, one can discern in these ceremonies traces of very ancient ideas. In promoting the abbots the King is exercising his newly acquired priestly functions, while the offerings made to him on this occasion might be compared to offerings to a deity. Sociologically, however, the promotion of the abbots is now only to be regarded as a first act of grace, which, correlated with the exercise of the royal clemency in releasing a number of prisoners in celebration of the Coronation, is valuable as an indication to the people that the ceremonial promises are not empty ritual.

CHAPTER VII

CORONATION (*continued*)

THE REGALIA AND THE STATE PROGRESSES

The first part of this chapter will be devoted to a detailed study of the Siamese Royal Regalia (Frontispiece and Pl. X). I shall not attempt to speculate along the lines of Sir James Frazer[1] as to whether kings were originally evolved from magicians. History only takes us back to a time when there were gods, and kings, and priests in India, and gives us the early Siamese conception of the king as identical with the deity, a stage when religion had already gone far towards supplanting magic. I shall only state that if, as Sir James Frazer maintains, the evolution of kings from magicians was only *one* of several ways by which the former have been evolved, it seems reasonable to suppose that the evolution of regalia from magicians' implements is not the only means by which regalia have been developed. At any rate there seems to be little magical significance attaching to any of the Siamese regalia at the present time, though in the case of the most ancient among them there probably was in early times; while others seem to belong entirely to the religious stage; and others again appear to have once been of practical value, and never to have been connected with either religion or magic. I shall endeavour to distinguish between these various types when we discuss each article of the regalia in turn.

Whatever the early significance of the regalia, we may be quite sure that it is little understood or for one moment considered by the Siamese people, or even by the officials of the Court, who see in them merely the bright adjuncts of royalty. Their sociological value is indeed, like that of the regalia of European kings of modern times, merely to invest the person of the king with the outward brilliance of majesty and, thereby, like the ceremonial which accompanies them, to impress the people with the respect due to the kingship.

From the list of Siamese regalia one can pick out five that are undoubtedly of great antiquity and can be traced far back in the history of India. These five insignia (*pañcarājakukadhabhaṇḍa*) are mentioned in the *Mahāvaṁsa*,[2] and are to be regarded as the classical quintette of ancient India. They cannot, however, be traced back to Vedic times since there then appear to have been no regalia except the bow, which is to-day represented amongst the royal weapons of Siam.

[1] *GB*. i. [2] *M*. xi, 28.

PLATE X.

[Photo : State Railways Dept.

SOME OF THE REGALIA.

[To face page 92.

But there is also a reference to shoes which were put on after the symbolic foray of the *Rājasūya*. In Cambodia, and also in Burma,[1] the classical quintette were recognized.

We will now proceed to the detailed consideration of each article of the regalia :—

1. *The Great White Umbrella of State.*[2]

I place the White Umbrella first because I believe it to be the most ancient symbol of regal authority, vastly older than the Crown which has now supplanted it as the most important of the regalia. The White Umbrella of State consists of several tiers—five for the *Văṅ Nā*, seven for the King before he is fully crowned, and nine after he has attained full sovereignty. Similar custom prevailed in modern Cambodia and Burma, and, in fact, seems to have been common to all the Indianized States. Parasols are indicated on the reliefs of the Borobodur in Java, they were used by royalty in Campā, and they are represented on the *Jātaka* reliefs of the Ananda temple at Pagān, Burma. In one of those reliefs (No. 6) the Bodhisattva Temiya is reclining on his couch over which is a single-tiered white umbrella from which the goddess is seen issuing in order to give Temiya advice not to become king.[3] But it is in the bas-reliefs of Aṅkor Văt that we find the greatest profusion of umbrellas. Groslier[4] delineates a single and a three-tiered umbrella which seem to show clearly that Cambodia is the proximate source of the Siamese State Umbrella; and parasols are mentioned in the earliest Cambodian inscriptions (seventh century A.D.).[5]

The Pauranic literature of India mentions the White Umbrella as one of the *ratnas* of a king,[6] and in the *Nidāna-kathā* it is referred to as one of the regalia of the Buddha in the Tusita Heaven.[7] In the *Mahāvaṁsa*, among numerous other references to the White Umbrella, we have a euphemistic description of the throne in the Lohapāsāda in the course of which we note :—

> "A white parasol with a coral foot, resting on mountain crystal and having a silver staff, shone forth over the throne."[8]

This, together with a reference in *Jātaka* 415 to "a throne with the white umbrella erected over it", are the earliest specific records known

[1] Harvey, *History of Burma*, p. 325.

[2] The Siamese terms for this and the other articles of the regalia have been given in the table on p. 83.

[3] The idea of a protective genie residing in the State Umbrella is also known in Siam.

[4] Gr., chap. vii, Figs. 48*d* and *f*.

[5] Gr., pp. 41 sq.

[6] *ERE*. art. "*Abhiṣeka*".

[7] Rhys Davids, *Buddhist Birth Stories*, p. 155.

[8] *M*. xxvii, 36.

to me of the State Umbrella being placed over the throne exactly in the same way as it is to-day in Siam. But the following passage, also from the *Mahāvaṁsa*,[1] is of greater importance for our inquiry :—

> " When he had caused the state parasol of his uncles to be brought and purified in a natural pond that is here (i.e. Anurādhapura), Paṇḍukābhaya kept it for himself and with the water of that same pond he solemnized his own consecration."

Here we note the great importance assigned to the Umbrella in the consecration, whereas there is no mention whatever of a crown. Considering this in conjunction with *Jātaka* 539, " Give the royal umbrella up to me or give battle," can there be any doubt that the Umbrella was the pre-eminent symbol of royal authority in ancient India ?

From Ceylon it is an easy matter to trace the Umbrella back to the time of Aśoka in the third century B.C., the umbrella-crowned dagabas of Anurādhapura being obviously copied from those erected in India by the great Buddhist Emperor. And we can trace the Umbrella back to a vastly more remote period according to an interesting article by A. H. Longhurst on " The Influence of the Umbrella in Indian Architecture," [2] from which I make the following extracts :—

> In the earliest times the umbrella was a symbol of authority and power. It first appears in the wall pictures of the Egyptians and later in the bas-reliefs of the Assyrians. The Greeks borrowed from earlier empires this mark of elevated rank. It is most important in Asia where it is not only a symbol of rank but also of religion. This is particularly so in Burma, China, Japan and Siam—the pagoda being derived from it—but the idea originally came to them from India. The primary idea is derived from a shady tree (compare the primitive umbrellas of some modern peasants) and it derived its sanctity from its resemblance to certain sacred trees, the sal and bo tree, which are frequently depicted on the bas-reliefs of Sanchi and Bharhut and are a relic of primitive tree-worship.[3] The idea as an emblem of sovereignty probably came from Persia owing to the similarity of those of the Assyrian and Persian reliefs. Indian stupas of the Aśokan type (3rd century B.C.) were crowned with umbrellas. The earliest may have been the actual umbrella of Aśoka placed on the monument as a symbol of his royal protection and other stupas were doubtless crowned with the umbrellas of other devotees. As these would quickly perish when exposed to the weather the idea arose of crowning the stupas with more permanent materials—wood, stone and bronze. The reduplication of the umbrellas probably arose

[1] *M.* x, 77. [2] *Journal of Indian Art and Industry*, vol. xvi.

[3] This is an unfortunate example to give as it is now generally accepted that the bo trees depicted on Sanchi and Bharhut are merely symbols of the enlightenment of the Buddha. Nevertheless, tree-worship undoubtedly existed in early times, in the sense that the spirits in the trees were propitiated with offerings.

through other chiefs placing their umbrellas on top of those of former protectors. The model stupas on the Sanchi bas-reliefs show examples not only of single umbrellas but also of two and even three apparently on the same handle, as in the modern umbrellas of China and Burma (and Siam).

It seems probable, therefore, that we can explain the multi-tiered umbrellas of Siam on the theory of the accumulation of honour. Just as the greater would be the honour to a relic the larger the number of royal umbrellas that had been placed over it, so in later times a king might seek to augment his dignity by multiplying the tiers of the umbrella above his head. But if the umbrella was originally a tree, it seems to me that it first symbolized spiritual protection (as the tree symbolizes physical protection), and only later came to represent authority. Evidence for this is that to this day whenever the King of Siam goes out in state a single-tiered umbrella is held over his head, the sun's rays being perhaps considered especially dangerous to sacred persons; that the Great White Umbrella is supposed to be inhabited by a protective genie; and possibly in the statement in the *Mahāvaṁsa* [1] that "the thera Indagutta created, to ward off Māra, a parasol of copper that he made great as the universe".

The White Umbrella perhaps stands out alone among the institutions of modern Siam, in that we seem to have definitely enough evidence to enable us to trace it back to ancient Egyptian times; a fact which certainly makes one wonder to what conclusions we should be led could we but have as much evidence as to the origin of many another feature of Siamese culture. It is not for me to attempt to dispute or confirm the evidence adduced by Longhurst; I can only add one interesting point: Neither in the *Aitareya* nor in the *Śatapatha Brāhmaṇa* is there any mention of the umbrella in connection with the *abhiṣeka* therein described, and therefore it seems certain that this article of the regalia was not known in India in Vedic times. It might be about the time of Aśoka that it was introduced from Persia. However that may be, the very fact that the Umbrella can be traced so far back corroborates my contention, based on evidence already adduced from the *Mahāvaṁsa* and the *Jātaka*, that it is the earliest and originally the most important of the classical quintette. But, just as in India it was preceded by the bow, so in other parts of the world the earliest regalia were probably warlike weapons.

2. *The Great Crown of Victory.*

The essential part of the Siamese crown (*maṅkuṭ*) may be described as a cone of several stages terminating in a tapering spire. The whole

[1] *M.* xxxi, 85.

crown is highly ornamented and is surmounted by a small tiered umbrella. The crowns worn by Siamese actresses impersonating kings are similar to the royal crowns, while those worn by Rāvaṇa, Sugrīva, and other important personages in the Siamese drama [1] differ only in matters of detail; and the modern royal crown of Cambodia has the same form as the Siamese.

The feature that strikes one most forcibly about the Siamese crown is its marked difference in shape from the world-wide conception of a crown—the point above the head being its most important part rather than, as is usually the case, the diadem around the brow. My deduction from this is that the crown was originally conceived by the early Thai and the Khmers as a helmet of definitely practical protective value; and a king's helmet would at first only differ from that of an ordinary warrior by reason of its more elaborate ornamentation. The shape of this helmet-crown would largely depend on the method of dressing the hair. Now we know that the Thai, while yet under Khmer domination, arranged their plaited hair in three or four stages piled up on the head and ornamented by five rows of chaplets, as shown by a bas-relief at Aṅkor Văt where a Thai leader and several of his warriors are shown, identified by the inscription: "These are the Syam Kut." [2] For such a mode of hair-dressing a tall spired helmet or crown would be necessary, and would be adopted by the Thai when they obtained their freedom. On the other hand, the reliefs of Aṅkor Văt and Aṅkor Thom show that the Khmer aristocracy, as well as the Brahmans, wore the chignon,[3] the elongate crown being unnecessary. Groslier says of the Khmer crown:—

> "During the six centuries of the classic period the royal crown is conical, *squat*, of from three to seven stages, set on a stiff head-dress, decorated and encircled by a band, and not once does the point, which surmounts the modern crown, appear, added to the three-staged cone on the bas-reliefs. It is necessary, therefore, to look for this modification after the 12th century, which is impossible in Cambodia since stone construction ceases at that period. On the oldest modern wood carvings where one finds *mukuta*, the ancient cone is already transformed. It is therefore between the 13th and 16th–17th centuries that the change occurred. Now we believe the origin to be recent. It has come from Siam because the *mokoth*, such as it is to-day, is modelled in the votive offerings in baked earth found in the ruined monuments of Sukhodaya and Svargaloka (end of 14th century). This *mokoth* is both the Siamese and the modern Cambodian crown to-day." [4]

It appears to me, therefore, that the Thai, on attaining independence, elongated the Khmer crown and increased the distance between

[1] An adaptation of the Indian epic *Rāmāyaṇa*

[2] A. iii, p. 263. [3] Gr., p. 58. [4] Gr., pp. 62, 63.

each stage. This was a purely practical modification, rendered necessary by their mode of dressing the hair, and it does not explain the long tapering spire which completes the crown. Groslier seems reluctant to give the Siamese the credit for the invention of this feature, but he does not make any useful suggestion as to what might be its origin. My opinion is that we must turn to Ceylon for the elucidation of the problem.

We have seen that the votive tablets of the Sukhodaya period prove that the change had come about by the thirteenth century, and as this was the period during which the Siamese kings were actively engaged in imitating the splendour of Parākrama Bāhu, we might expect to find Sinhalese influence in the Siamese crown. Indeed, Prince Damrong recently remarked to me that there is a relief in a certain temple at Sukhodaya which definitely proves this to be the case. I have not seen this relief, nor do I know the exact nature of the evidence. If my hypothesis that the tapering spire has come from Ceylon be correct, we should naturally suspect Buddhist influence, and I believe the modern Siamese crown to be a comparatively late attempt to combine the purely practical helmet-crown with the Buddhist *sirotama*, or flame-shaped glory often represented in Buddhist images and paintings, and mentioned in the *Mahāvaṁsa*.[1] In support of this theory there is the following very interesting passage in the Siamese *Life of Buddha*:—

> " On his head there is a sirorot, like a glorious angelic crown, in imitation of which all the kings of the world have made crowns a sign of royal dignity." [2]

In concluding this historical analysis we may note that the Indo-Javanese art of the Śrīvijaya period, which spread over Cambodia from about the seventh to the ninth centuries A.D., is characterized by images in which the hair is dressed high and the brows are encircled by a diadem. This is also found in some images of the earlier part of the Aṅkor period, and it evidently spread from Java (where we see such forms on the reliefs of the Borobodur) and was originally derived from India, where it first appears in the Epics, being unknown in Vedic times. We thus have the world-wide conception of the crown as a diadem encircling the head in early times in Cambodia, where it was later superseded by the Khmer helmet-crown. From this the Siamese crown was derived in the thirteenth century with the addition of the Buddhist glory.

It will be convenient to mention here two other Siamese royal

[1] *M.* v. 92: The Buddha "adorned with the crown of flames".

[2] Alabaster, *Wheel of the Law*, p. 115.

crowns. These are: (1) the *Kaṭhina* Crown (*Braḥ jaṭā mahā kaṭhina*) used in former days on occasions of the presentation of robes at the royal monasteries, and dating from the reign of Rāma I; and (2) the Personal (or Lesser) *Kaṭhina* Crown (*Braḥ jaṭā mahā kaṭhina nŏy*) made severally for each individual sovereign and worn during his State Progresses through the city and on the river, as well as on certain later occasions during the reign, such as special *Kaṭhina* presentations.

There are also three Royal Hats (*braḥ mālā*) which are for use in going to and from the scene of ceremony. Bruguière,[1] in an account of the coronation procession of Rāma III, mentions the king's wearing a broad-brimmed hat of black felt, similar to those royal hats worn to-day, but to his description may be added the fact that a feather is worn stuck in the side, and the summit is ornamented by a small replica of a Siamese crown. These hats are known to be of European origin, having been derived from the Court of Louis XIV in the seventeenth century.

3. *The Sword of Victory.*

This is considered to be one of the foremost of the Siamese regalia. It was brought from Cambodia in 1783, and is supposed to be an emblem of sovereignty of the ancient Khmer empire, perhaps dating from the tenth century A.D. It is thus similar to the famous *Braḥ Kharga*, so jealously guarded by the modern Bakus of Phnompenh, and which is reputed to have been handed down from Jayavarman II (A.D. 802–69). The stele of Văt Mahādhātu,[2] dating from the reign of Dharmarāja I, records that a similar sword named Jayaśrī was given to the founder of the kingdom of Sukhodaya by a king of Aṅkor Thom; and two later Sukhodaya inscriptions [3] mention this sword among the regalia.

Possibly the idea of the sword as a royal emblem was preceded by the similar use of a more primitive indigenous weapon in Cambodia. This seems to be the opinion of Aymonier [4] who, in the course of his description of a king represented on a relief at Aṅkor Văt, says:—

> "The king, seated on an elephant, is armed with a *phgak* resting on the shoulder, which shows that at this time the *Braḥ Kharga*, now considered as the palladium of the empire, had not yet replaced in esteem the old cutting weapon of Cambodia."

The Khmers must have derived the idea of the Sacred Sword from India, for, as we have seen, it is mentioned in the *Mahāvaṁsa* as one of the classical quintette of India. But though it is not known to have

[1] Loc. cit.
[2] Coedès, *Inscriptions de Sukhodaya*, No. ii, p. 63.
[3] Ibid., Nos. iv and v.
[4] A. iii, pp. 257 sq.

been regarded as a royal emblem in Vedic times, the idea must be extremely ancient, for :—

> "The girding of the new monarch with a sword is a practically universal feature of coronation ceremonies. It is a reminiscence of the days when the king was not merely the titular but the actual war-chief of his people." [1]

4. *The Slippers.*

In Old Siam shoes were not worn by the common people, and those who wore them had to remove them as a sign of respect as soon as they entered the precincts of the palace. They were probably regarded as suitable only for royalty. This was also the case in Cambodia, where shoes were probably of great rarity, and considered as sacred, since, though they are mentioned in early Chinese texts and in inscriptions, they are not figured on the bas-reliefs.[2] The same view was probably current in Ancient India. The earliest reference to shoes in Indian literature is that in the *Śatapatha Brāhmaṇa*, where it is mentioned that they were put on after the symbolic foray of the *Rājasūya* :—

> "He then puts on shoes of boar's skin. Now the gods once put a pot of ghee on the fire. Therefrom a boar was produced : hence the boar is fat, for it was produced from ghee. Hence also cows readily take to a boar ; it is indeed their own essence (life-sap, blood) they are readily taking to. Thus he firmly establishes himself in the essence of the cattle : therefore he puts on shoes of boar's skin." [3]

Though their sanctity is evident from the above, I do not think that the evidence is sufficient for us to regard the shoes as having been considered as regalia in Vedic times. In Epic times, however, there seems to be no doubt of it ; for Rāma, who had retired to a forest life, sent his shoes to represent him and govern in his place, while, in *Jātaka* No. 461, we have the same story with the following interesting addition :—

> "The courtiers placed these straw slippers upon the royal throne when they judged a case. If the cause was decided wrongly, the slippers beat upon each other, and at that time it was examined again ; when the decision was right, the slippers lay quiet."

Here we seem to have traced the slippers back to a time when they had a magical significance, almost to a time when (some) kings were magicians and their regalia magicians' implements.

[1] *ERE.* x, pp. 632-9.

[2] Gr., p. 53 sq.

[3] *Śatapatha Brāhmaṇa*, v, 4, 3, 19, in *SBE.* xli, pp. 102 sq.

5. *The Fan.*

This is the last of the five chief regalia of ancient India. It comes to Siam from Cambodia as is evident from those figured on the bas-reliefs of Aṅkor Văt, and these were obviously made in exactly the same way as the modern Siamese royal fan, i.e. from a palm leaf bent at right angles on its stalk. The fan, as an adjunct of royalty, is associated with the idea of coolness and sublime comfort attributed to divine kings, especially in hot countries.

6. *The Whisk of the Yak's Tail and the Whisk of the White Elephant's Tail.*

The former is an extremely ancient emblem, and seems sometimes to have replaced the fan as one of the primary quintette.[1] As chowries or fly-whisks (Sanskrit, *cāmara*) they are mentioned in Pauranic accounts as one of the royal *ratnas* requisite to a king, and were evidently associated with the same idea of divine comfort, as was the fan.[2] Yak-tail whisks are mentioned in the *Mahāvaṁsa* [3] and in *Jātaka* No. 532 as emblems of sovereignty. Nuniz (about A.D. 1535) mentions that in Vijayanagar yak-tail whisks were the highest marks of distinction conferred by the king on the nobles. These emblems became common in all the Indianized States, and are frequently delineated on the bas-reliefs of Aṅkor and Borobodur, as well as being mentioned in Khmer inscriptions. The material from which these chowries were made seems to have been chosen on account of their supposed auspicious nature. But from the whisks mentioned in the *Mahāvaṁsa*, *Jātaka*, and Cambodian inscriptions being specifically described as of yak's tail, whereas there is, so far as I am aware, no classical mention of the White Elephant's Whisk, it seems to me that the use of the latter is a late, probably Buddhist, modification.

7. *The Sceptre and the Stick.*

These appear to be two forms of the same emblem. The sceptre is present in the regalia of Siam, Burma, and Cambodia; and Knox, who wrote in 1681, may refer to a sceptre of the King of Ceylon in the following passage:—

> "Commonly he holdeth in his hand a small cane, painted of divers colours, and towards the lower end set around about with such stones as he hath and pleaseth, with a head of gold."

But as I can find no specific mention of the Sceptre in ancient Indian literature, I doubt if it were ever regarded by Indian monarchs as such an important article of the regalia as it was in Europe. It may,

[1] Harvey, *History of Burma*, p. 325. [2] *ERE*. art. "*Abhiṣeka*." [3] *M*. xxxi, 78.

however, correspond to the Brahmanic baton or the thunderbolt (*Vajra*) of Indra for

> "the sceptre as a symbol of authority is world-wide. In the form of club, baton or wand its origin may date back to the stone age." [1]

8. *The Personal Sword.*

This sword is borne after the King of Siam on almost every occasion, even prior to Coronation Day, by the Steward of the Household. It may correspond to the golden sword which Cheou Ta-kouan, the Chinese traveller who visited Aṅkor in A.D. 1296, states was worn by the king whenever he went out of his palace. It seems to me that at that late period in the history of the Khmers, the *Braḥ Kharga* had achieved such sanctity as to have lost its practical use. The Personal Sword was probably invented to take its place, and now, in Siam, we see it in turn losing its practical use and passing into the regalia.

9. *The Brahman Girdle.*

This is a traditional Attribute of Śiva, and its presentation to the King symbolizes the merging of the god into the personality of the King.

10. *The other Girdles and the Rings.*

These were no doubt formerly amulets, especially the Girdle of the Nine Gems, symbolizing the planets; but they have now degenerated into ornaments. Similar ornaments were worn by the Khmer kings [2]; and in *Jātakas* 479 and 487 and also in the *Rāmāyaṇa*, signet rings are mentioned as being used as tokens.

11. *The Receptacle, the Betel Nut Set, the Water Urn, and the Libation Vessel.*

These are all articles of personal use which in Indo-China are regarded as insignia of rank, not only by the king himself, but also by officials to whom similar articles were presented by the king on the occasion of their promotion. The regalia of the Alompra dynasty of Burma [3] are remarkable on account of the inclusion of a great variety of these personal utensils such as pickled-tea bowls, betel-boxes, tea-pot, water vessels, water-pot stands, and scent box; and on the reliefs of Aṅkor Văt a number of similar utensils are represented.[4] No doubt the custom of regarding such articles as emblems of rank was derived from ancient India; but perhaps it would be going too far to interpret the Libation Vessel as being the descendant of one

[1] *ERE.* x, pp. 632 sq.
[2] Gr., chap. vii.
[3] *Indian Antiquary*, 1902.
[4] Gr., Fig. 77.

of the golden vessels filled with water, honey, milk, clarified butter, and udumbara shoots, which were regarded as a necessity in the Pauranic *abhiṣeka*.[1]

12. *The Golden Tablet of Style and Title.*

A consideration of this important object of the regalia will necessarily require considerable space, as it will be convenient here not only to describe the special ceremony at which the tablet is inscribed (Pl. XI) but also to discuss the nature of the Style and Title itself.

On the last occasion the preparation for the inscription took place on 3rd February (i.e. twenty-two days before actual coronation), this preparation consisting of the holding of a service of benediction (*svăt braḥ buddha mantra*) by Buddhist priests. Next day the inscription (*caru'k braḥ subarṇa paṭa*) was made on a gold tablet by a royal scribe in the Chapel Royal in the presence of the Buddhist monks who had officiated the previous day, and of a deputy of the King. The ceremony of inscribing the golden plate with the Style and Title was performed as follows:—

The royal scribes were seated at low tables in the Chapel Royal with the sacred *siñcana* thread stretched around them to ward off evil influences. The royal astrologer (*Braḥyā Horā*) beat the Gong of Victory at 10.34 a.m. as a signal that the auspicious moment for commencing the inscription had arrived. One scribe engraved the *Subarṇapaṭa*, while another inscribed the Royal Horoscope (*braḥ jāt braḥ janam barṣā*) on another gold plate. The chapter of monks recited stanzas of victory; the Brahmans blew the conches and played the other ceremonial instruments all the time that the work of inscribing the plates went on. When this was completed, the Brahmans offered lustral water in conches and the *Horā* anointed the gold plates. The Brahmans then rolled up the *Subarṇapaṭa* in red silk tied with a silken thread of five colours. Then they placed it in a gold tube, sealed it up, and placed it in an embroidered bag. Similarly, the *Horā* rolled up the Horoscope and placed it in a gold tube in an embroidered bag. Both were then placed in a golden box embossed with floral designs, which was placed on a gold plate of two tiers, which in turn was placed on a gold stand while the Brahmans and officials performed the *vian dian* [2] rite around it. The golden box was finally

[1] *ERE*. art. "*Abhiṣeka*".

[2] This is the light-waving rite frequently performed in Siamese ceremonies, the Brahmans and others passing from hand to hand tapers, fixed in lenticular holders, around the person or thing it is desired to honour, and fanning the smoke towards that person or thing. It is a form of *pradakṣina* intended to ward off evil influences. It is well known in India, being first mentioned in the *Śatapatha Brāhmaṇa*, i, 2, 2, 13. See p. 107 f.n. and Ge. (1), p. 159.

PLATE XI.

[Photo: State Railways Dept.

THE INSCRIPTION OF THE GOLDEN TABLET OF STYLE AND TITLE, AND OF THE ROYAL HOROSCOPE.

To face page 102.]

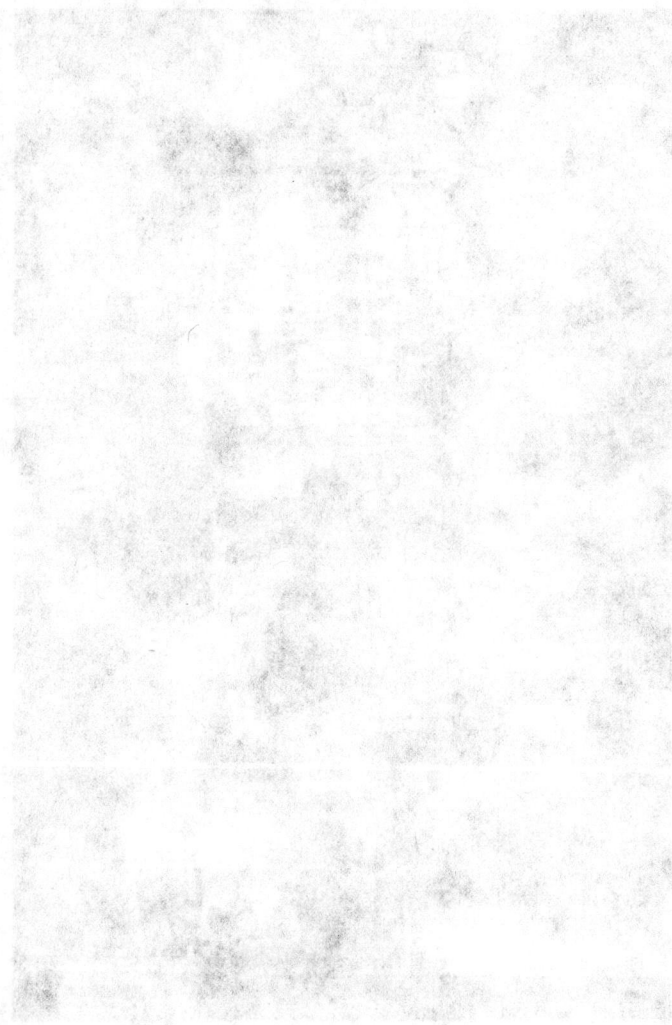

deposited with the other regalia on the altar in the Chapel Royal until 21st February, when it was carried in state on a palanquin to be placed on an altar in the Baiśāla Hall.[1]

Though inscribed gold plates are mentioned in *Jātakas* 440, 482, 491, and others, I am informed by Mr. Sāstrī, of the Royal Institute, Bangkok, that no mention of the term *subarṇapaṭa* occurs in Indian literature, and it is, therefore, very remarkable that it should have been preserved in Siam. But the custom of kings changing their names on accession is a very venerable one in India. Thus in the Vedic *Rājasūya* :—

> "He (the *purohita*) then hails him (the king) as one bearing auspicious names—'Much worker, better worker, more worker'. Whoever bears such names speaks auspiciously even with a human voice." [2]

To this the translator appends a note explaining that the meaning of these titles is "increaser of the prosperity of himself and his people". The changing of the name symbolizes the rebirth of the newly-consecrated king, and his identification with the deity.

The same custom seems to have become established in all the Indianized States. In Ceylon we have the statement in the *Mahāvaṁsa*[3] that :—

> "Suvaṇṇapiṇḍatissa was his name before his reign, but he was named Sūratissa after the beginning of the reign."

Likewise in Campā :—

> "There seems to have been a fairly general practice among kings of Champa to take a new name called Abhiṣekanāma at the time of the coronation. Thus Prasastadharma, son of Rudravarman, took the name Śrī Sambhuvarman at the time of his coronation." [4]

In modern Cambodia the ceremony of inscribing the royal style and title is carried out as in Siam, and that the ancient Khmer kings changed their personal names on accession to one ending in *varman* is exemplified by the following seventh century inscription :—

> "He is the son of Śrī-Viravarman, and who is not inferior in power though the youngest brother of Śrī-Bhavavarman, he, named Śrī-Citrasena, who possesses all the marks of the great, has chosen the name of Śrī-Mahendravarman at his coronation." [5]

[1] Most of the above information concerning the ceremony of inscription is derived from "Programme of the Coronation, B.E. 2468" (i.e. Source No. 1). There is a short account of the inscription of Rāma IV's titles in *Siam Repository*, Oct., 1871; and the *History of the Second Reign* (p. 22) gives a brief description of the ceremony at the coronation of Rāma II. All these accounts are substantially in agreement.

[2] *Śatapatha Brāhmaṇa*, v, 4, 4, 14, in *SBE*. xli, p. 110.

[3] *M.* xxi, 9. [4] Majumdar, op. cit., chap. 14. [5] *BEFEO*., t. iii, p. 445.

In later days the Cambodian kings possessed a string of titles. A modern inscription of Aṅkor Văt refers to a king who reigned in A.D. 1747 as Samtec Braḥ Pāda Paramanaṭha Braḥ Pāda Paramapubitra, " The lord, the sacred feet, Paramanaṭha, the sacred feet, the supreme purification " ; and almost the same titles are used of a king mentioned in a thirteenth century inscription at Aṅkor Văt, and believed to refer to the founder of that temple.[1] Aymonier believes that these multiple royal titles probably originated in the thirteenth century, and mark the commencement of the period of decadence.[2]

We have practically the same story in Burma : In the Môn inscription of Myanpagān, Pagān,[3] on face C, the king is referred to by his usual name as " Śrī Tribhuwanāditiyadhammarāja ", but on side D this is lengthened to " Śrī Tribhuwanādityadhammarājarajādhirājaparamiswarabalacakkrāwar ", meaning " supreme king of kings, overlord, mighty universal monarch ". And the last king of Burma was known as Athet-u-san-paing-than-ashin, " Lord of the life, head and hair of all human beings." [4]

In one of the Siamese inscriptions of the Sukhodaya period,[5] it is stated that the king changed his title on his accession from Brañā Ḷu'daiyarāja to Śrīsūryavāṁśa Mahādharmarājādhirāja, but this is a comparatively modest title to the long string of Sanskrit epithets expressive of divine majesty that was accumulated during the Ayudhyā period, and revived and even extended by the sovereigns of Bangkok. Thus the full style of the first two kings of the present dynasty was as follows :—

" Braḥ pāda samtec braḥ paramarājādhirājarāmādhipatī śrīsindraparamamahăcăkrabartirājādhipatindra dharaṇindrādhirāja rāṯanākāśabhāṣakravaṅṣa aṅgaparamādhipeśra ṯrībhūvaneṯravarnāyaka tilakarāṯanarājjāṯiājāvaśarāyasamudăyataromanṯa sakalacăkravāḷādhipendra suriyendrādhipatindra hariharindrādhātādhipatī śrīsuvipulyaguṇòkniṭha ṛdathirāmeśvaramahānṯa paramadharmikrājādhirājatejojaiya brahmadebātidebanaṛpatindra bhūmindraparamādhipeśra lokjeṭhavisuddhi rāṯanamakuṭapraḥdeśagaṯā mahābuddhāṅkūraparamapabiṯra." [6]

And in the course of the next hundred years the royal style continued to expand until it reached the dimensions of that of the present king, which runs as follows :—

[1] A. ii, p. 258.
[2] A. iii, p. 281.
[3] *Epigraphia Birmanica*, vol. i, pt. 2.
[4] *ERE*. art. " Burma ".
[5] Coedès, *Inscriptions de Sukhodaya*, No. iv, p. 84.
[6] *History of the Second Reign*, p. 21.

" Braḥ pāda samtec braḥ p̱aramindramahāpraḥjādhip̱ak mahănṯatejantilakrāmādhipatī debyap̱arīyamahārājaravivaṅśa asămabhinabaṅśabīraḥkaṣăṯra puruṣarăṯanarājanikarotama căṯurănṯaparamamahăcăkrabartirājasăṅkāśa ubhaṯosujăṯasāṁśuddhagerāhṇī căkrīparamanātha cuḷălaṅkaraṇarājavarăṅkūra mahāmakuṭavaṅśavīrasūrajiṣaṭha rājadharmadaśabidhauṯakaf̱aṣaṭanipuṇa atulyakrṣaṭăbhinīrahāra pūrabădhikărasusădhiṯadhaṁnayalăkṣaṇaviciṯrasauva bhăgyasarbăṅga mahājanoṯamăṅgamăndasandhimaṯasamănṯasamāgam paramarājasambhāra dibyadebăvaṯara baiśălkiaraṯiguṇa agulayaśăktiteja sarbadeveśapriyānurăkṣa maṅgalalăgananemāhvăy sukhodăyadharmarājā abhinauvaśilap̱aśu'kṣātejanāvudha vijăyayuddhaśāsatrakośala vimalanarayabiniṯa sucariṯasamăcāra bhădrabhjiañānapraḥtibhānasundra p̱raḥvaraśāsanop̱asatamabhaka mūlamukhamāṯayavaranāyakamahāsenānī sarājanāvībayūhayodhaboyamacara paramajeṣṭhasodrasamamaṯa ekarājayaśasadhigamaparamarājasampăṯi nabapaṯalaśevaṯachăṯrātichăṯra śrīrăṯanoplăkṣaṇa mahāparamarājābhiṣekābhiṣikṯa sarbadaśadigavijiṯatejojaiya saklamahaiśvara yamahāsvāmindra maheśvaramahindramahārāmădhirājavarotama paramanāthajăṯiăjănyăśrăya buddhădiṯrairăṯnaśraṇārăkṣa viśiṣaṭaśăkaṯòăgranareśvarādhipatī meṯṯākruṇāśīṯlahaṛdăya anop̱amaiyabunayakāra sakalabaiśălamahărăṣṭārădhipatindra p̱aramindṛadharmikamahārājādhirāja parananāthapabiṯra braḥ p̱ak klău cău yū hua."

Our study of the royal style and title has revealed two main underlying ideas which are of considerable sociological interest. In the first place we have the substitution of the king's personal name, which was taboo after accession, by a long string of titles expressive of the king's majesty and of his identification with the deity. These titles were not understood by the common people who used such simple terms as *Cău Jīviṯra* (Lord of Lives), but they probably always knew that some such titles did exist, while the fact that they were appended to all official proclamations performed the valuable function of impressing the dignity of the kingship upon the literate and official classes. That the actual fact of changing the royal appellation meant something in the estimation of the people is borne out by the custom which prevails to this day of even the humblest officials changing their names on promotion.

Secondly, it is to be remarked that the evolution of a long string of euphemistic titles seems to be late, and characteristic of a decadent period, when the real power of the king was on the wane, and it was necessary to support it by the invention of haughty titles. But it must not be forgotten that other factors have been brought to bear on the situation, and that with the rejuvenation of the modern kingdom, such titles are little more than a relic of Old Siam, a shortened form having, in fact, been sanctioned by the late king.

13. *The Eight Weapons of Sovereignty* (*Braḥ sèṅ aṣaṭāvudha*) (Pl. XII).

It is possible that the Bow represents the oldest article of the Indian regalia, antedating the classical quintette and receiving mention in the *Śatapatha Brāhmaṇa*, while the Trident and Discus are, of course, attributes of the gods Śiva and Viṣṇu, and symbolize the king's identification with those gods. On the other hand, many of the other weapons seem to be of purely Siamese historical interest, and supposed to date from some national event, especially in connection with King Nareśvara (A.D. 1590–1610). It was he who killed the Prince of Pegu with the Long Handled Sword in a fight on elephant back, and it was also he who fired the Gun of the Sa̱toṅ across the river of that name at a Burmese pursuing column, killing the leader with the first shot. Actually, however, I am informed that all these weapons are reproductions made in Bangkok, the originals having been lost at the time of the fall of Ayudhyā. But this is not realized by the masses, and the replicas no doubt fulfil their sociological function of inspiring the people with a respect for their historic past and for the glory of kings, just as well as ever did the originals.

* * * * *

This will be a suitable place in which to consider the Coronation State Progresses, because, like the Regalia, many of the features of the processions are of great historical interest. The first State Progress of King Prajadhipok took place on 1st March, 1926, on which occasion he was borne in procession on a palanquin through the streets of the capital, and paid his respects at the principal shrines, namely, the Pavaranivesa and Jetavana monasteries, where the monks were waiting to receive him. On entering these temples the King paid homage before the principal images and before the urns containing the remains of the late Prince Patriarch. He also offered a gorgeous robe to each of the images. The second State Progress took place by water on 3rd March, the procession of state barges making its way to Văt Āruṇ, a monastery on the west bank of the river, where the King paid homage and made religious offerings as before. On both occasions the King wore the Personal *Kaṭhina* Crown, except when entering and leaving a temple on foot, and when embarking in the royal barges, at which times he wore a Royal Hat.

These State Progresses are a modification of a very ancient ritual. Formerly they consisted only of a Progress (known as *Liap Mo'aṅ*)

PLATE XII.

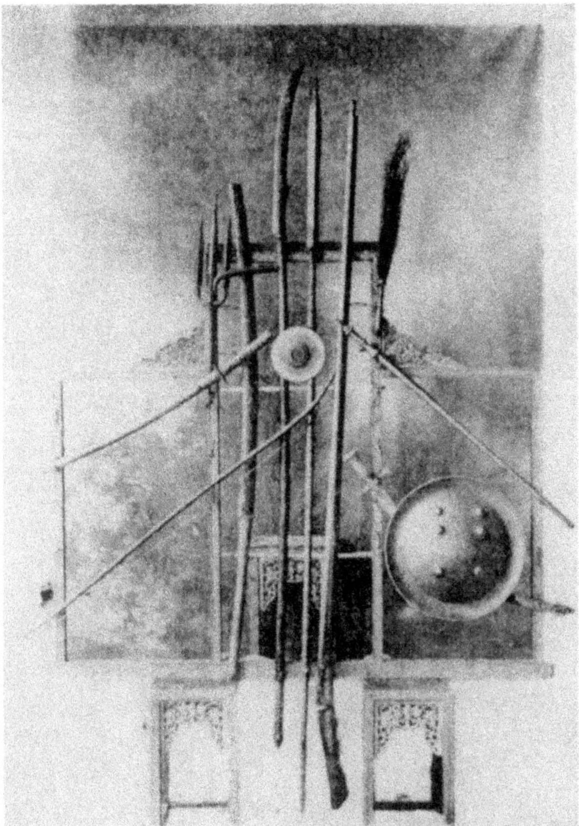

[*Photo : State Railways Dept.*

THE ROYAL WEAPONS.

[*To face page* 106.

around the city, without any visits to the temples. This latter was an innovation introduced by that pious Buddhist monarch, Rāma IV. Formerly the Progress enabled the people to have a view, albeit a limited one on account of the lattice fences, of their new monarch in full regal state. The later modification possessed the additional sociological value of showing the King to the people as a supporter of the national religion. But the *Liap Mo'aṅ* has a far older significance, though perhaps this was long since forgotten by the common people. It was performed rightwise and it was, in fact, the ancient Hindu rite of *pradakṣina*. According to the *Agni Purāṇa* and the *Manasara*, the coronation was concluded by the king riding *pradakṣina*-wise around his city [1]; and *Jātaka* 472 mentions the rightwise procession of a king around his city; but the rite was not known in Vedic times. In Siam to-day the Progress by Land is a true *pradakṣina*, the King keeping his right shoulder to the Grand Palace, but the Progress by Water is not. It seems that this rightwise circumambulation of the King around the city represents the path of the sun, and is important evidence in favour of the solar origin of kings.[2]

[1] *ERE*. art. " *Abhiṣeka* ".

[2] This being our first mention of the rite of circumambulation, which we shall frequently come across in other Siamese ceremonies, it may be convenient to quote here a few extracts from Hastings' *Encyclopædia of Religion and Ethics* (art. " Circumambulation "), in order to explain its significance in ancient India :—" The custom is observed, with a religious or magical signification, among the most diverse peoples, particularly among the Indo-Europeans. In India, the *Śatapatha Brāhmaṇa* enjoins walking round the offering, holding a burning coal in the hand. The *Grhya Sutras* require the young Brahman at the time of his being initiated, to drive three times round the site, sprinkling it with water, and repeating the verse of the *Rig-Veda*, ' O Waters, ye are wholesome.' Among marriage ceremonies the Laws of Manu order the bride to pass three times round the domestic hearth ; it is the seventh step in this walk that makes the union irrevocable. Circumambulation also figured in the funeral ceremonies and the sacrifices to the Pitris. The *Mahā Parinibbāna Sutta* tells that the pyre on which lay the body of Buddha took fire of its own accord when the 500 disciples walked round it three times. Even at the present day, for the Hindus, circumambulation round certain sacred spots has the effect of blotting out sins. It was the same with the Buddhists who, long before our epoch, had constructed round their stupas, or eminences containing relics, circular galleries for the circumambulation of pilgrims. . . . It is a rite intended to ward off sinister influences, in the interest either of those who perform the circumambulation or of the person or thing placed at the centre. . . . It is usually only regarded as bringing good fortune when performed towards the right, which is called by the Brahmans *pradakṣina*. The opposite process (Sanskrit, *prasavya*) is considered of ill omen. . . . *Pradakṣina* represents the daily march of the sun, which in our hemisphere rises in the east, passes thence to the south, and sets in the west. This is what Brahman ritual tells us clearly : ' While the Brahmans perform the *pradakṣina*,' says the *Śatapatha Brāhmaṇa*, ' they think, sunwise this sacred work of ours will be accomplished, and therefore they again walk thrice round sunwise.' It may be asked whether in the same way the treble repetition of the circuit is not connected with the traditional three steps of Viṣṇu."

The royal procession of King Prajadhipok's Progress by Land (Pl. XIII) was constituted as follows:—

MILITARY GUARDS
(*Khapvaranådahårpak*)

A number of units representing the various arms of the modern army, established on European lines.

THE ROYAL PARTY
(*Khapvararåjiśrīyayaśa*)

Left side (vertical): Officers of the Ancient Bodyguard of Gentlemen-at-Arms / Chamberlains / Processional Umbrellas (seven-tiered, small sunshade, five-tiered, and so on) / Eight Representatives of Brahmā, with lances

Right side (vertical): Officers of the Ancient Bodyguard of Gentlemen-at-Arms / Chamberlains / Processional Umbrellas (seven-tiered, small sunshade, five-tiered, and so on) / Eight Representatives of Indra, with lances.

	A Nobleman A Nobleman	
Flags	Metal Drums Metal Drums	Flags
	Silver War Drums	
	Drum Major	
	Gold War Drums	
	Herald Trumpets	
	Small Bugles	
	Master of Ceremonial Instruments	
	Brahmans blowing conch shells	
	Inspector of Instruments	
	Pages bearing Royal Weapons	
	Grand Umbrellas of Ceremony	
	Signal Stick	
	Signal Instrument	
Monkey Standard (*dhaṅ jaya kraḥpī dhuj*)		Garuḍa Standard (*dhaṅ jaya garudha båha*)
Supporters of H.M.:— Seven Lords Lieutenant in single file (aides-de-camp)	* Royal Golden Palanquin	Supporters of H.M.:— Seven Lords Lieutenant in single file (aides-de-camp)
	Sunshade (*pǎṅ braḥ sray*) Fan (*bǎt pok*), and Umbrella (*braḥ klat*)	
Escort of King Cuḷālaṅkaraṇa's Bodyguards	Chamberlains bearing Royal Paraphernalia (*krūaṅ sūṅ*) Reserve Chair of State The Master of the Horse Royal Chargers	Escort of King Cuḷālaṅkaraṇa's Bodyguards

---

Military and Naval Units and Bands

It is the Royal Party that focusses our attention, and we need not give further consideration to the modern military and naval units, except to say that they are sociologically important in that they perhaps impress the ignorant masses with the might of the Government just as much as does the brilliance of the royal party.

The constitution of this central body no doubt follows closely the arrangement in force in the days when Ayudhyā was capital; and that almost every feature in it was derived from the Khmers is evident when one compares it with the coronation procession of King Sisowath (1906),[1] and with those depicted on the bas-reliefs of Aṅkor Văt (eleventh century A.D.).[2] In the modern Cambodian royal procession we find ceremonial instruments, processional umbrellas, state umbrella, sunshade and fan, noblemen supporting the king, and the royal palanquin. We notice, however, a few differences: the presence in the Cambodian procession of an amazon guard from the inner palace, an institution abolished in Siam with the harem; the inclusion of elephants, a mode of royal progression which was never popular in Bangkok, and is used nowadays only when the King visits the North, where the elephant is still the traditional royal mount; and, finally, the presence of a chariot which is a typically Khmer form of royal vehicle. The Cambodian king, indeed, halts three times in his *pradakṣina* circuit of the city. Each of these halts is at one of the cardinal points, and the king, on descending from his vehicle, is presented by a Brahman with holy water with which he bathes his face and pours out a libation to the Goddess of Earth. At each of these halts the king changes his vehicle, thus making use of four in all—palanquin, chariot, horse, and, finally, elephant, the four traditional royal modes of conveyance. But in Siam, although the royal chargers take part in the procession, the King remains on his palanquin throughout. Another point of interest is that the Cambodian king changes his head-dress each time he changes his vehicle. The Hindu gods had each a different vehicle. Can it be that this change of head-dress and vehicle symbolizes the king's representation of several of the gods of the Hindu pantheon?

Thus it appears that Cambodia still preserves certain features which have been lost in Siam. We know from Cheou Ta-kouan's account of the royal procession that he witnessed at the end of the thirteenth century,[3] that the Khmer king rode on an elephant, and held the precious sword; and we find most of the features of the modern Cambodian procession depicted on the bas-reliefs of Aṅkor Văt.

It will be interesting to consider in a little more detail some of the component parts of the Siamese Coronation Procession. The

[1] L.. *Coronation du roi Sisowath.*
[2] Delaporte, *Cortege Royal Chez les Khmers, Revue de Geog.*, 1878.
[3] Pelliot, in *BEFEO.* ii, April, 1902.

picturesque uniforms of the Ancient Bodyguard (*Ṭāṁrvac*), with their old-time tunics, embroidered *phā̌-nuṅ*, and heavy swords, are reminiscent of the fighting men of the Ayudhyā period; but it is important to note that they are evidently intended to guard against evil influences from the spirit world, just as much as against more material foes, for they carry the sacred *siñcana* cord stretched along each side of the procession. None the less remarkable are the uniforms of the umbrella-bearers and of the drummers, who march in two files, those on the right dressed in green, those on the left in red, and presumed to represent *gandharvas* (heavenly minstrels). These, together with the representatives of Indra and Brahmā, symbolize the fact that the King is to be regarded as a deity surrounded by the traditional followers of the gods. In striking contrast to all these are the semi-European uniforms of the chamberlains and pages.

The Monkey and Garuḍa Standards, always carried before the King in state processions, represent the monkey god Hanumān and the sacred bird Garuḍa, the mount of Viṣṇu. In one of the reliefs of Aṅkor Văt the king is preceded by an ensign representing Viṣṇu mounted on Garuḍa [1]; while the indented flags or pennants used in Siamese processions are also shown on the Aṅkor Văt reliefs,[2] and on those of the Borobodur.

The Fan is similar to that which forms one of the regalia, but it is larger, and is put to practical use, during the progress, for the benefit of the King. The large and highly ornamented Sunshade has also its prototype in the Aṅkor Văt reliefs.[3] The Umbrella is large and single-tiered, and is evidently intended both as a practical protection from the rays of the sun and as a symbol of authority, which latter function is also performed by the numerous five- and seven-tiered umbrellas in the procession.

The last feature that calls for special mention is the Royal Palanquin, the only vehicle now used by the King in state processions by land, and frequently used as an alternative to the elephant and the horse in the Ayudhyā period, as mentioned by most seventeenth century European writers. Palanquins are mentioned in the earliest Khmer inscriptions, i.e. those of the seventh century,[4] but in the classical period of Cambodia they appear to have been used only for the transportation of images, *liṅgas*, and the sacred fire. Classical palanquins of this type are shown in the reliefs of Banteai Chhma, Aṅkor Thom, and Aṅkor Văt,[5] from which the modern Cambodian palanquin [6] and that of Siam seem to have been derived. Similarly, royal ladies

[1] A. iii, pp. 257 sq.
[2] Gr., Fig. 49, *a*, *b*, *c*.
[3] Gr., Fig. 48, *m*.
[4] Gr., pp. 41 sq.
[5] Gr., Fig. 66.
[6] Gr., plate vii, *b*, *c*.

PLATE XIII.

[Photo: State Railways Dept.

THE ROYAL PROGRESS BY LAND.

To face page 110.]

Plate XIV.

The Royal Barge "Subarṇahaṅsa".

both in Siam and Cambodia are carried in a type of curtained palanquin of which the prototype is depicted on a relief at Banteai Chhma,[1] and strangely enough, not represented at Aṅkor Thom, Aṅkor Văt, nor in any other relief. It appears, therefore, that although the palanquin was known during the classical period of Cambodia, not until later times did it come into use as a royal vehicle. Persons of quality probably preferred to be carried on hammock-litters, suspended from poles, these being frequently delineated in the bas-reliefs, but having now completely disappeared from Siam and Cambodia. They were, however, until recent times the ordinary mode of conveyance of people of rank in Cochin-China,[2] and may have reached Cambodia from China by that route.

We now turn to the consideration of the State Progress by Water, which took place on 3rd March, 1926, in connection with the Coronation of King Prajadhipok. The King, wearing state robes and a Royal Hat, was borne on a palanquin from the Grand Palace to the Royal Landing (*Dă Rājavaratiṭha*), where, in the Royal Pavilion (*Braḥ-dī-năṅ Rājakicavinicachăy*), accommodation was provided for the Royal Family, while tents were erected on the river front to seat members of the Diplomatic Corps, Officials of State, and the general public. The King and Queen watched the procession of state barges filing past, until the Royal Barge (Pl. XIV) came alongside the landing, when the paddlers, with joined palms, bowed low three times in unison, according to the traditional method of paying homage. The King then embarked, and, donning the Personal *Kaṭhina* Crown, seated himself under the golden canopy (*puṣpaka*) beneath the *prāsāda* spire amidships. He was attended by several nobles of high rank, as well as by chamberlains bearing the regalia, the large fan, the sunshade, the large single-tiered umbrella, and several five-tiered processional umbrellas. The order of the procession of state barges was as follows:—

Left File		Right File
1. Tiger barge		Tiger barge
2–10. Barges of the line	First drum barge	Barges of the line.
11. Gold barge of the line	Inspection barge	Gold barge of the line
12. Monkey barge of the line		Monkey barge of the line
13. Asura barge of the line (drums)		Asura barge of the line (drums)
14. Sugrīva barge (drums)	Inspection barge	Bālī barge (drums)
15. Garuḍa barge (trumpets and conches)		Garuḍa barge (trumpets and conches)

[1] Gr., Fig. 64, *a*.

[2] Crawfurd, *Journal of an Embassy to Siam and Cochinchina*, 1828, plate facing p. 282.

16. Royal Pavilion barge "P̱raḥbhăśarajăya" (fish figure-head) conveying the King's offerings to religion

17. Barge conveying metal drums	Second drum barge	Barge conveying metal drums
18. Escort barge	Royal Throne barge "Subarṇahaṅṣa" (Golden *haṅṣa* figure-head) with the King on board	Escort barge
19. Escort barge	Royal Pavilion barge "Anekajāṯibhujaṅga" conveying the King's state robes	Escort barge

20. Royal Throne Barge "Anănṯanāgarāja" (*nāga* figure-head) in reserve for return journey

21. Royal reserve barge

The procession of royal barges constitutes, without a doubt, the most spectacular of the many brilliant sights that are to be seen in the Kingdom of Siam; and as such they have been justly celebrated by European writers since the seventeenth century.

> "Probably the largest dug-outs in the world are the Siamese royal state barges. These are of *mai yang* [Dipterocarpus spp.] wood and each boat consists of a single tree. They are 150 feet or rather more in length and about eleven feet beam, and are made in exactly the same way as the smallest canoe, the tree being hollowed out with adzes, submerged in water until thoroughly soaked and then opened out over fire. The symmetry of these royal barges, which are without superstructure of any kind, but are simply one piece of timber with prow and stern continuations, is quite perfect. . . . They have a smooth rounded bottom and beautiful lines running up into a graceful curve at the tapering stern. The sides are intricately carved and heavily gilded, and from the bow and stern depend large tassels of Yak hair, two at each end, with a piece of cloth-of-gold brocade hanging between them, charms to keep away evil spirits. A little aft of amidships, a pavilion with cloth-of-gold roof and side-curtains is supported on gilded pillars, and the boat is manned by seventy paddlers seated in pairs forward and aft of the pavilion. At the stern are the two steersmen, and near the bow an individual stands on a small platform, where he controls the stroke and keeps the time by tapping on the deck with the butt-end of a long silver spear. The crew, who are dressed in the crimson uniform of the warriors of ancient Siam, are well drilled and flourish their long paddles in perfect time, raising them high in the air at the end of each stroke." [1]

That the beauty and majesty of the royal barges does not fail to impress the minds of the Siamese people is indicated by the well-

[1] Graham, *Siam*, ii, pp. 83 and 245.

known poem called the " Song of the Procession of Boats ", from which I quote a translation of the first two stanzas :—

" The king embarks upon the water
Using his most magnificent barge
Handsomely ornamented with 'King Keao';
The movement of the pliant paddles is beautiful to see.

Crowded together but preserving order,
Each shaped in the semblance of a curious beast,
The vessels move along with their flags flying,
Making the water to roar and foam." [1]

I have indicated in the table showing the order of procession the function of each type of barge, but may add here that the barges of the line and the escort barges are manned by navy men in modern white uniforms, while marines, armed with rifles, occupy the central pavilions. The barges are mostly distinguished by their figure-heads, these being chiefly representations of characters from the Siamese version of the *Rāmāyaṇa*: Hanumān, Sugrīva, Bālī, and Garuḍa. Since, in times of old, kings of Siam used to embark on warlike expeditions in procession similar to the one we are considering, it seems that the array was intended to represent Rāma and his army, and the figure-heads were far more than mere ornament; they struck terror into the enemy.

It is, of course, the magnificent royal barges proper, those that bear the King and his religious offerings, which primarily claim our attention, and, by comparative methods, I have arrived at what I think is an interesting theory as to their evolution. Barges of the classical period are represented on the reliefs of Banteai Chhma, Aṅkor Thom, and Aṅkor Văt.[2] Cheou Ta-Kouan was wrong in describing them as built of planks; they were obviously hollowed out of a single tree in exactly the same way as are the modern royal barges. Though some of the more primitive barges were of slender form, the later classical ones [3] were of a much heavier and less graceful line than either the early barges or those of the present day, consisting almost entirely of poop, figure-head, and luxurious cabin. The seventeenth century Siamese barges [4] were also of comparatively heavy design. I attribute the sweeping graceful lines of some of the modern barges of Siam and Cambodia to influence from Burma during the latter part of the Ayudhyā period, for it is to the Burmese royal barge that they show the closest resemblance.

[1] Ibid., i, p. 283. [2] Gr., Figs. 72 and 73. [3] Gr., Fig. 73, *b*.

[4] L. L., plate at p. 40; de Chaumont, plates at pp. 34 and 76; Tachard, Figs. 19–22 (Fig. 2 in the present work).

The somewhat superficial resemblance between the modern Siamese and Burmese royal barges is strengthened by evidence concerning the figure-heads. An early text of the southern Tsi (A.D. 479–501) mentions the barges of Funan as having the bow and stern shaped as the head and tail of a fish.[1] In both classical Khmer barges and those of seventeenth century Siam, the prow rose up comparatively abruptly from the hull. Sometimes there was no figure-head, and the poop and prow were formed by plain beams; but when there was a figure-head the most common form was that of a great fish (the stern representing the tail). This was the primitive type, and is still seen in the modern royal barge of Cambodia, and was found in the war barges of Siam up to modern times, the prow of one of which is preserved in the Bangkok museum. A more complicated form of figure-head in classic Khmer times was that in which a seven-headed *nāga* issued from the mouth of the fish, and doubtless the modern "Anănṯa-nāgarāja" was derived from that source. Sometimes the *nāga*-head was replaced by an *apsaras*, while figure-heads of Viṣṇu on Garuḍa were also used, as they were in recent times in Siam, there being one dating from the reign of Rāma IV preserved in the National Museum. But in classical Cambodia there is no trace of the *haṅṣa* figure-head, which, taken in conjunction with the more sweeping lines of the boat on which it is used, gives us the most beautiful royal barge of modern Siam. On the other hand, this figure-head was characteristic of the Burmese royal barges, and was probably derived from the Môns, since the *haṅṣa* was their most popular emblem. There seems no doubt, therefore, that this feature was derived by the Siamese from Burma, probably towards the end of the Ayudhyā period, since the seventeenth century Siamese barges have a rather primitive form of this figure-head.

In classic Khmer times a rectangular curtained cabin was erected amidships, at least in those barges not designed for warfare. In Siam, both in the seventeenth century and to-day, this type of cabin is found in the pavilion barges used by the King only in *Kaṭhina* processions and for the conveyance of royal offerings and formerly for noblemen and ambassadors, while those used by the King on the most important occasions such as the Coronation Progress (and in the seventeenth century used to convey the French king's letter) are known as throne (*braḥ-dī-năṅ*) barges, and have a smaller cabin crowned by a *prāsāda* spire, such as is found on the summit of many Siamese royal and religious buildings. This *prāsāda* spire is also found on the Burmese barges, and is characteristic of Burmese royal buildings, for

[1] Gr., p. 109.

example, the spire crowning the Mandalay palace. On the contrary, nothing of the kind is found in Cambodia, at least until modern times, when it has been copied from the Siamese. That the *prāsāda* spire was evolved in Burma there can be no doubt; a building of the eleventh century at Pagān, the Bidagāt Taik, has been well described as the Mandalay spire in stone.

I conclude, therefore, that though the Siamese received their first idea of a royal barge from the Khmers, as is obvious from the design of the pavilion cabin and most of the figure-heads, yet they were later much influenced by Burmese designs which gave them the *prāsāda*-crowned throne-barge and the *haṅsa* figure-head, and thus their most beautiful royal barge, the " Subarṇahaṅsa ".

There are two other points of interest concerning the royal barges. Firstly, at all periods, both in Cambodia and Siam, the barge was steered by a man standing at the stern with a long paddle. That the rudder was known to the ancient Khmers we know from the fact that a Chinese junk with rudder is depicted on the reliefs of Aṅkor Văt [1]; but neither the Khmers nor the Siamese ever adopted this mode of steering for their state barges. A second point noticeable from a study of the classical reliefs is that the paddles were thrust through holes which would prevent their being raised high out of the water with a flourish at every stroke as in modern Siam. In the seventeenth century barges the holes have disappeared, but none of the pictures show the paddles raised out of the water. Perhaps this was also a modification introduced from Burma.

[1] Gr., Fig. 73, *c*.

CHAPTER VIII

CORONATION (*continued*)

Installation of the Queen and Assumption of the Royal Residence

1. *The Installation of the Queen.*

The Installation of Queen Rāṁbai Barṇī took place immediately after the General Audience on Coronation Day, 25th February, 1926. It took place then because the King desired thus to honour his consort (whom he married in 1917) immediately after his own attainment of the supreme power, but there was no necessity for him to have done so. The late King Rāma VI did not raise his consort Cau̇ Còm Savathana to queenly rank, and she was not, therefore, permitted to sit beside him on state occasions; and in Siamese history we find instances of kings who, though possessed of many wives, did not see fit to raise any of them to the queenship. Nevertheless, there were normally four queens, a greater and a lesser of the right, and a greater and a lesser of the left, the former side being considered the more honourable, as was also the case with the officials of the two divisions. Not only was it important for the king to secure the succession by fathering an heir of the *Cau̇ F̲ā̇* rank, but ancient Indian tradition considered a queen as one of the royal *ratnas* which every king should possess. Thus, says Manu :—

> "Let him wed a consort of equal caste (*varṇa*) who possesses auspicious marks (on her body), and is born in a great family, who is charming and possesses beauty and excellent qualities." [1]

The sprinkling (*abhiṣeka*) of queens is mentioned in the *Cullakalinga Jātaka*; but queens are not mentioned in Vedic literature, and the king's wives were considered of little account in those early times.

Although I have said [2] that there is really no marriage ceremony in Siam, the Installation of the Queen has certain features in common with marriage and Hocart [3] has gone so far as to derive that institution generally from Coronation. A common notion in ancient India was that male = heaven and female = earth. Then the king might be looked upon as a heavenly god, e.g. the Sun, and the queen as the Goddess of Earth. The intercourse between a king and a concubine

[1] Manu, vii, 77. [2] p. 48. [3] Hocart, *Kingship*, chap. viii.

could only be physical; to make it spiritual the concubine had to be raised to the royal status, i.e. she had to be identified with the deity, just as was the king. Hence it seems to me that this Investiture of the Queen may be looked upon as a kind of spiritual marriage.

Queen Rāṁbai Barṇī is a cousin of the King, but under the old regime a Siamese king had three possible choices when he selected a queen. He could promote a favourite concubine, the most usual procedure; he could marry a half-sister or even a full-sister; or he could invite or accept the offer of a foreign princess. The latter is of extremely rare occurrence in Siamese history, but it is believed to have been accompanied by great pomp and circumstance.

I have mentioned elsewhere [1] that the installation of a sister as queen was not particularly popular with Siamese kings, because of the greater amount of deference that had to be shown to them. But apart from any relic of a former system of recognized matriarchy which this custom may or may not represent, and which was certainly not taken into account by any Siamese king, there were two very strong reasons for the installation of sisters as queens. One of these was distinctly practical, the other traditional, and connected with religion. In the first place, if a royal sister were unmarried, it was still necessary to confine her to the inner palace, for it was considered to entail danger to the monarchy to allow her to marry anyone but the king; so it was safer to make her a queen. Secondly, there is the classical Buddhist example of sister-marriage with the object of keeping the royal line pure, which has been followed by later Buddhist kings. The progenitor of the Śākya clan, in which Gautama was born, was King Okākarāja, whose four sons founded the city of Kapilavastu. These four princes,

> "finding that among their followers there were no daughters of the royal race whom they could marry, resolved, in order to keep pure the blood-royal, to marry their four youngest sisters." [2]

Queen Rāṁbai Barṇī, on the occasion of her Installation, wore a diadem and ancient queenly dress, of which it is particularly interesting to note that it included the *sarong*, the classical lower garment of the Khmers, and still worn by modern Cambodian and Siamese dancers. The Siamese lower garment (*phā̉-nuṅ*) is an adaptation of the Indian *dhoti*, and was introduced into Cambodia by Prince Śrī Supanma of Cambodia, who was captured and educated by the Siamese, and then sent back to rule over his own country as a vassal in 1602, and who was the means of introducing many Siamese rites and customs into

[1] p. 68. [2] Bigandet, *The Life and Legend of Buddha*, 3rd ed., p. 11.

Cambodia. The antique *sarong* worn by the Queen is thus a relic of ancient Khmer times, and is not to be confused with the *sinn*, the national skirt of the Laos, the wearing of which has become a fashion amongst upper class Siamese ladies only during the present century.

The ceremony commenced [1] by the Lord Privy Seal (Prince Damrong) reading a proclamation announcing that the King, who was now full crowned and thereby empowered, intended to raise his consort to the rank of Queen (*braḥ paramarājinī*). The King, who was in full state robes and wearing the *Kaṭhina* Crown, then anointed the Queen with consecrated water from a conch (Pl. XV), and invested her with the paraphernalia of rank, including the insignia of the Royal Family Order of Căkrī, while a fanfare of ceremonial music was sounded. The Queen then sat beside the King on a Royal Chair, and, after receiving the congratulations and homage of the ladies, they retired to the Royal Residence scattering riches.

It is interesting to note that although the ceremony is Brahmanical, being in fact a replica on a very small scale of the *abhiṣeka* of a king, the Brahmans do not perform the anointment. Not only is there a taboo against touching a royal lady, but the King, being himself fully consecrated, is in a position to exercise his divine and priestly functions.

The following is a probably not very reliable note on the ceremony of Installation of a Queen as carried out in the reign of King Rāma V :—

> "Three days are usually devoted to the purpose. The chief officers of the palace, the chief scribes, and the chief princes and nobles of the kingdom are present, both Buddhist and Brahman. The princess is copiously bathed in pure water, in which the leaves of a certain kind of tree, supposed to possess purifying and healthful influences, are put. Most of the time is spent in feasting, but on the third day, she is placed on a small throne under a white canopy, where she is bathed with holy water, the priests reciting prayers the while. She is then conducted to a place where the wet clothes are laid aside, and she is arrayed in queenly costume, jewels and diamonds, and then displays herself to those in attendance." [2]

2. *The Assumption of the Royal Residence.*

This ceremony, known as *Chalo'm Braḥ Rājamaṇḍira*, corresponds to the popular one of housewarming commonly taking place after marriage, with which it has been confused by Europeans. In the case of the King it naturally follows the Coronation, when the King is about to take up his official residence in the Grand Palace.

[1] I find no mention of a preliminary ceremonial bath of purification, and if there was such a rite it presumably took place in private.

[2] *Siam Repository*, January, 1873.

PLATE XV.

[*Photo : State Railways Dept.*

THE ANOINTMENT OF THE QUEEN.

[*To face page* 118.

Plate XVI.

[Photo: State Railways Dept.

The Assumption of the Royal Residence.

Housewarming ceremonies are doubtless world-wide, since as Frazer says, "Demons are especially feared by persons who have just entered a new house."[1] There was such a ceremony in China,[2] but the Siamese ceremony is purely Buddhist, though with indications of early magical rites, and was no doubt derived from Ceylon with Hīnayānism. Evidence for this is supplied by the following interesting passage from the *Nidāna-kathā* :—

> "On the next day the festivals of the coronation, and of the housewarming, and of the marriage of Nanda, the king's son, were being celebrated all together."[3]

Here we have the housewarming mentioned in connection with the coronation, exactly as we have it to-day in Siam.

The housewarming ceremonies in connection with the Coronation of King Prajadhipok were as follows: It has already been mentioned[4] that Buddhist monks had for three days prior to Coronation Day been engaged in the recitation of protective stanzas in all three parts of the Chief Residence, especially in the Căkrabartibimān section. At 6 p.m. on the 25th of February the Brahmans also performed a *vian dian* rite, as a protection to the Chief Residence. All this having been accomplished, the King and Queen made their way to the State Bedchamber in the Căkrabartibimān section, attended by young ladies of the Royal Family (Pl. XVI) bearing the following articles of personal and domestic use, and presumably the relics of former magical rites :—The cat (signifying Domesticity), the grinding stone (Firmness), the gherkin (cool, therefore Happiness), and grains, peas, and sesamum (Prosperity and Fertility); and an image of Buddha was first carried into the residence, signifying the nature of the household religion.

The Queen Aunts, Savang Vadhana, and Sukhumāl, as senior relatives of the King, handed to him a whisk of the White Elephant's tail, and a golden bunch of Areca Flowers, and then a senior Dame of the Palace handed a golden key to the King, symbolic of the fact that he was now entrusted with the Royal Residence and the private treasury therein. Finally, the King lay down formally on the royal couch and received blessing from the two Queen Aunts.

The sociological value of this essentially private ceremony seems to be that by it the king would be impressed with the sanctity of his high office, not only as ruler of the country and people at large, but also as guardian and protector of the private institutions of royalty, the welfare of the royal family and the sacred apartments which had

[1] *GB.* iii, p. 63. [2] Mentioned in the *Li Ki*, *SBE.* xxvii, p. 196.
[3] Rhys Davids, *Buddhist Birth Stories*, p. 226. [4] p. 73.

been the residence of his ancestors. The ritual of his being blessed by his relations, especially the senior queens, brings home to him more closely than could any priestly benediction, the anxiety of the royal family for his well-being, as well as his responsibility for theirs. Thus, though there are indications that the ceremony was formerly accompanied by certain magical rites which have now been lost, it remains, in its present form, an institution of considerable sociological importance.

In Cambodia there is practically the same ceremony of Assumption of the Residence as that described above, and it has evidently been introduced into that country from Siam. But a remarkable difference is that the astrologers take part and address prayers to the guardian spirits of the umbrella and of the palace, and pretend to receive satisfactory promises of protection from them.[1] This seems to be a case of the Brahmans, who retained more influence in Cambodia than they did in Siam, interfering in a ceremony that did not concern them originally.

[1] L., *Coronation du roi Sisowath.*

CHAPTER IX

HIGHER GRADES IN ROYAL CONSECRATION

1. *Pusyābhiṣeka.*[1]

In India the idea of the consecration of kings differed from ours in that there was not a single and final " coronation ", but numerous ascending grades of anointment (*abhiṣeka*), spread over a number of years, perhaps throughout the lifetime of the monarch. Correlated with this was the idea that the divinity of a king required a periodical renewing.

In Siam there was such a periodical royal consecration, known as *pusyābhiṣeka*, which used to take place in the second Siamese lunar month (Pauṣa), but it was discontinued after the fall of Ayudhyā.

The object of the ceremony is said to have been the maintenance of the welfare of the kingdom, presumably by means of the reinforcement of the king's divine powers. The king mounted a dais (*maṇṭapa* piled with fresh flowers of seven kinds, changed his attire, and anointed himself. Eight Brahmans were in attendance and offered a blessing. They then performed a dance known as *dèṅvisai* (" the angel tournament "), of Hindu origin, and performed at Siamese state festivals up to modern times.

This ceremony corresponds to the Indian *pusyābhiṣeka*, the special feature of which was that it took place at the conjunction of the moon with the asterism *pusyā*, which feature was retained in Siam. It was at this time that Indra originally conquered the demons,[2] and the coronation of Rāma was also an example of *pusyābhiṣeka* ; but it was not confined to the inauguration of sovereignty.[3]

2. *Indrābhiṣeka.*

We have already seen that the Siamese *Rājābhiṣeka* contains many ideas derived from the Vedic *Rājasūya*, or consecration of emperors. There was also in Vedic India another ceremony for the consecration of emperors, known as the *Indrābhiṣeka*, or anointment with the rites of Indra. It is described in the *Aitareya Brāhmaṇa*, but, though the Siamese have preserved the ancient name, the ceremony with which they connect it seems to have little in common with that of

[1] Sources : *BRB.*, p. 76 ; mentioned in *NN.* (p. 70), *KM.* and *HV.*
[2] *Rāmāyaṇa*, ii, 14, 46. [3] *ERE.* art. " *Abhiṣeka* ".

Vedic times. Indeed, the only recorded instance of it ever having been performed in Siam seems to be the occasion on which King Rāmādhipatī II in A.D. 1510 successfully brought the northern part of what is now Siam under the sway of Ayudhyā, and thus considered himself entitled to the rank of emperor. The *KM*. gives an account of the Siamese ceremony of *Indrābhiṣeka*, but the following is only an approximately correct translation of this peculiarly difficult and ambiguous passage :—

" For the royal ceremony of *Indrābhiṣeka* a Meru, of a height of 1 *sėn* 5 *vā*,[1] is built in the middle of an open space. There Indra sits on the Meru, surrounded by Isindhara and Yugundhara mountains, one *sėn* high ; and there stand Karavika Mountain 15 *vā* high and Mount Kailāsa 10 *vā* high. On the inside are golden umbrellas, in the middle are red gold umbrellas, and those of silver are outside. Outside these again is a *rājavăt* [2] fence with umbrellas of five colours. Within the umbrellas stand figures of *devatā*, and outside them is a *rājavăt* fence. Paper umbrellas and figures of giants (*yăkṣa*, *gandharba*, *rākṣaṣa*) stand at the foot of the Meru, and there are figures of various kinds of lions (*gajasīha*, *rājasīha*, *sinṭo*, *kilen*), goat-antelopes, cows, buffaloes, tigers, bears, and *devatā*. On Kailāsa sits a figure of Śiva and graceful Umā. On the top of Meru is a figure of Indra. Figures of *asuras* are in the middle of the Meru ; Viṣṇu sleeps on the water at the foot of the Meru, and a seven-headed *nāga* encircles the Meru. Outside the open space stand *asuras*, and outside the walls are dancing halls. Lictors are dressed as 100 *asuras*, and pages represent 100 *devatā*. There are Bālī, Sugrīva, Mahājambhū, and a train of 103 monkeys. They pull the ancient *nāga* : the *asuras* pull the head, the *devatā* pull the tail, and the monkeys are at the end of the tail. One side of Meru is gold, one side is red gold, one side crystal, one side silver, the Yugundhara mountain is gold, the Isindhara is red gold, Karavika and Kailāsa are silver. On the surrounding space outside are elephants, horses, and the four divisions of the army. Officials of 10,000 marks of dignity wear precious stones and put on coats and silk *phā̆-nuṅ* of honour. Those of 5,000 grade wear golden hats and put on coats and splendid silk *phā̆-nuṅ*. Those of 3,000 wear hats of foreign silk and coats and silk *phā̆-nuṅ*. Those of 2,400 to 1,200 marks of dignity carry silver and gold flowers according to rank, with flowers and pop-corn to pay homage. Brahmans of various

[1] 1 *vā* = 1 fathom, 1 *sėn* = 20 fathoms.

[2] The *rājavăt* fence is made of lattice, decorated at intervals with small tiered paper umbrellas. It is erected around the area in which ceremonies are performed when these take place in the open air, in order to exclude evil influences.

sects sit within the enclosure. On the first day there is *kārdhibhaṣa* (a discourse ?); on the second day *rāpvăn* (all is quiet ?); on the third day *srāṅvăn* (the building goes on ?); and on the fourth day *capsamīddha* (?); and on the fifth day they pull the ancient *nāga*. On the sixth day they make three pools of angelic water, a three-headed elephant, a white horse, and a king of oxen. They take arms, elephant weapons, and ropes for catching elephants, and steep them in water. They take one hundred figures of Śiva, Viṣṇu, Indra, and Viṣvakarmā, and bear utensils for following the custom of entering to offer a blessing (*thvāy brahbar*). On the seventh day the Brahmans offer a blessing and on the eighth day the king offers a blessing; on the ninth day they offer the elephants and horses and the four divisions of the army; on the tenth day they offer the twelve treasuries; on the eleventh day they offer the taxes; on the twelfth day they offer the city; on the thirteenth day they offer the consecrated water; on the fourteenth day they make offerings to the *devatā*; on the fifteenth day they make offerings to the king; on the sixteenth day they make offerings to the princes; on the seventeenth day the king rewards the Brahmans; on the eighteenth day there are offerings of *kalpavṛkṣa* fruits [1]; on the nineteenth, twentieth, and twenty-first days gold and silver flowers are scattered. For a month theatricals are performed. They build a standing effigy of a giant 1 *sen̐* high. The pages represent monkeys and go out through openings in its ears, nose, eyes, and mouth, and drive in royal cars scattering alms about the city. This is the end of *Indrābhiṣeka*."

One immediately identifies the above as a sort of theatrical representation of the myth of the "Churning of the Ocean", as told in the *Rāmāyaṇa*; and it gives one the impression of being an old-time description of the type of popular festival of which the Siamese have always been so passionately fond. At first sight, however, one might fail to appreciate the connection between this and the idea of an *Indrābhiṣeka*. But since Mount Meru is the home of Indra, it appears that in this ceremony the king is identified with that god, and the "Churning of the Ocean" and the other entertainments are performed in his honour.

3. *A Comparative View of Royal Consecration Ceremonies.*

Before passing on to the consideration of other Ceremonies of Installation, it will be convenient to pause here to note to what extent Siamese Royal Consecration Ceremonies fall into line with those of other countries. In his book on *Kingship* [2], Hocart brings forward what

[1] See page 146. [2] Chapter vii.

appears to me very convincing evidence for the common origin of all coronation ceremonies within a very wide area, stretching from Fiji to Western Europe. No one will deny the probability of common origin within the Indian sphere, and the countries with which Hocart deals have one important feature in common: they were for very many centuries connected by maritime intercourse. But, as I have already mentioned in Chapter I, this very fact precludes our allowing this theory of common origins a world-wide application, at any rate in the present state of our knowledge. And that this is fully realized by Hocart is indicated by the admirable wish with which he concludes his chapter on the subject: "May we hope that the present study will serve as a stimulus to others to seek out other more distant forms and thus widen the basis of our inquiry?"

I fear I cannot be of much assistance in that way, at least so far as Coronation is concerned, because the Cambodian Coronation, which is so similar to that of Siam, is one of the examples which he analyses. However, his study of the Cambodian ceremony is not very detailed or satisfactory, and it may, therefore, be worth while to see what light Siam can contribute. He analyses the complete coronation ceremony into twenty-six parts. Not all these twenty-six components are to be found in the ceremony of any one country in the area with which he deals, because each country seems to have lost one or more factors. Even so, the resemblance between the coronation ceremonies of all the countries in that area is very remarkable.

I will now quote the components as Hocart tabulates them, placing in square brackets those which definitely do not seem to be represented in Siam:—

(*a*) *The theory is that the King* [(1) *dies*]; (2) *is reborn*; (3) *as a god.*—But the idea of death must formerly have existed since it is implied by the rebirth as a god.

(*b*) *By way of preparation* [*he fasts and*] *practises other austerities.*—For three days beforehand the King attends preparatory Buddhist religious services, and keeps the Buddhist precepts.

(*c*) (1) *Persons not admissible to the sacrifice, such as strangers, sinners, women, and children, are kept away, and are not allowed to know anything*; (2) *an armed guard prevents prying eyes.*—In Siam the palace is, of course, strictly guarded, and the more important ceremonies are, or used to be, distinctly private.

(*d*) [*A kind of sabbath is observed*; *the people are silent and lie quiet as at death.*]—One would not expect to find this in Siam, since the idea of death, in connection with Coronation, has been lost.

(*e*) *The King must fight a ritual combat* [(1) *by arms, or*] (2) *by ceremonies, and* (3) *come out victorious.*—In Siam the combat is evidently fought and the victory attained by means of ritual, but note the presence of the Sword of Victory and the other arms.

(*f*) *The King is* (1) *admonished to rule justly, and* (2) *promises to do so.*—But not with the emphatic type of oath used in many countries.

(*g*) [*He receives communion in one or two kinds.*]—Soma drinking has disappeared in all Buddhist countries.

(*h*) *The people indulge at one point in* [(1) *obscenities*] *or,* (2) *buffoonery.*—Except at the last coronation, there were theatrical performances for the benefit of the public.

(*i*) *The King is invested with special garments.*—In Siam the new King wears for the first time the ancient regal garments, including a long tunic.

(*j*) *He is baptized with water*—the purificatory bath in Siam—

(*k*) *and anointed with oil*—but the oil is replaced by water in Siam

(*l*) [*when a human victim is killed*]

(*m*) *and the people rejoice with noise and acclamations.*—In Siam there are the fanfares, firing of cannon, and ringing of bells,

(*n*) *and a feast is given*—especially the feeding of the monks.

(*o*) *The King is crowned,*

(*p*) *puts on shoes,*

(*q*) *and receives other regalia, such as a sword, a ring, etc.,*

(*r*) *and sits upon a throne.*

(*s*) [*He takes three ceremonial steps in imitation of the rising sun.*]—But in the ceremony on the octagonal throne he first faces the direction of the rising sun.

(*t*) *At the conclusion of the ceremonies he goes the round of his dominions and receives the homage of the vassals.*—Circumambulation of the city.

(*u*) *He receives a new name.*

(*v*) *The Queen is consecrated with the King*—but not necessarily, in Siam.

(*w*) *So are the vassals or officials either at the coronation ceremony, or in the course of the King's tour.*—In Siam the King confirms the officials in their offices at the coronation audience.

(*x*) [*Those who take part in the rites are dressed up as gods, sometimes with masks*]

(*y*) [*which may be those of animals, thus identifying the wearer with some kind of beast*].

(*z*) *A King may be consecrated several times, going up each time one step in the scale of kingship,* e.g. *Indrābhiṣeka* in Siam.

CHAPTER X

THE TONSURE CEREMONY

The Tonsure Ceremony in Siam is a rite of initiation of youths, corresponding to the Hindu *Cūḷākănṭaḥ Maṅgala*. It is the most important of the Hindu *samskāras*, or initiation rites, still surviving in Siam, the only others that are to some extent observed being the *Sikjāṭhahpaḥnaḥ Maṅgala* (ceremony of shaving the first hair of the new-born), *Nāma Maṅgala* (ceremony of giving the first name to the child), and *Naḥhānaḥ Ṭiṭha Maṅgala* (auspicious rite of taking a child to water and teaching him to swim), the latter now reserved for princes and princesses of *Cău Fǎ* rank.

It will be readily appreciated that the study of most of these *samskāras* does not fall within the scope of the present work for the reason that they are connected with the childhood of kings (princes and commoners as well), and are private rather than state ceremonies. The Tonsure Ceremony, at least that form of it in which a prince of *Cău Fǎ* rank is the initiate, is, however, an exception, since it throws considerable light on certain aspects of the kingship: Firstly, the reigning king, or his substitute, plays the rôle of the god Śiva, and this, it will be shown, is of great importance in connection with the conception of the kingship and the theory of " temporary kings ". This aspect of the ceremony has, so far as I know, not been elaborated by any European writer, and is not understood by the Siamese. Secondly, a close relationship can easily be traced between the Coronation and the Tonsure Ceremonies. The resemblance between the two series of rites is most apparent in the tonsure of royalty, less so in that of the nobles and commoners. Gerini went so far as to compare the two ceremonies in the words : " The tonsure for a prince of so high a station (*Cău Fǎ*) becomes an imposing State Ceremony which may be ranked as second only to the Coronation of a king " [1]; but it remained for Hocart [2] to trace the parallelism in detail, and advance the theory of the actual derivation of both Initiation and Coronation from some earlier common Ceremony of Installation. He does not, however, include either the Cambodian or the Siamese Tonsure Ceremonies among those which he analyses, and which would strongly support his theory.

The very detailed knowledge which we possess concerning the Siamese Tonsure Ceremony is due to Gerini's scholarly monograph

[1] Ge. (1), p. 94.   [2] *Kingship*, chapter xii.

which remains the only instance of a Siamese Brahmanic ceremony having been made the subject of profound study and research. Though further study might show that Gerini's work is neither infallible nor exhaustive, for the purpose of supporting the above mentioned theories his facts will be adequate, especially as there has now been no opportunity of witnessing the Tonsure of a *Cău Fā* prince for many years, the last occasion being that of the present King. The following is a condensed summary of the facts adduced by Gerini, on which I shall base my conclusions concerning the two aspects of the ceremony with which we are concerned in the present work:—

In Siam, Tonsure takes place either in the eleventh or thirteenth years, whereas it was performed in India between the sixteenth and twenty-fourth years, according to the caste of the candidate. The change to an earlier date in Siam is evidently due to Buddhism, since when a boy enters the novitiate, which event must take place before the fourteenth year (not earlier than the ninth), the Buddhist Tonsure of the whole head is performed unceremoniously; and it is important that the Brahmanic Tonsure, with the rites due to the three privileged castes, should previously have been disposed of with all due ceremony.

The Tonsure of princes is designated *Sokănṭa*, in distinction from that of nobles and commoners, which is known as *kāra kon cuk*. The generic and at the same time classic Pāli term used in Siam is *Cūḷākănṭaḥmaṅgala* (corresponding to the Sanskrit *kesānta*). The *Sokănṭa* differs in the main from the *kāra kon cuk* by reason of the fact that in the former a special artificial mountain (Kailāsa) within the palace grounds is used, whereas in the latter the ceremonies are carried out on an ordinary ceremonial dais with canopy, erected in the private house of the initiate's family. For princes of *Braḥ Aṅga Cău* and *Hmòm Cău* rank, a permanent rocky structure about ten feet high, and situated within the precincts of the palace, is utilized as a Kailāsa; but for *Cău Fā* a special mountain of from 20 to 46 feet in height is built. The reason for the use of a structure symbolizing the Kailāsa is that, following Brahmanical tradition, the *Sokănṭa* is carried out in accordance with the ceremonial which accompanied the mythical tonsure of Śiva's son Gaṇeśa on Mount Kailāsa. The Siamese have a standard text-book of cosmology called *Traibhūmi* (" the three worlds "), which was compiled in A.D. 1776 from ancient Buddhist texts in the Pāli language. Gerini [1] gives a fairly full explanation of this world-system, but for our purpose it is sufficient to note that though the arrangement differs considerably from that of the ancient Hindus, and the Kailāsa has lost its classical position, it nevertheless

[1] Ge. (1), pp. 95 sqq.

retains its significance as the home of the god Śiva. With the necessary modifications due to the smallness of the scale on which the work must be carried out and the necessity of reaching the summit by means of ladders instead of supernatural power, the Kailāsa used at the *Sokănṭa* is an attempt to portray the traditional wonders of the Great God's home (Pl. XVII).

In the case of the Tonsure of the late king, then Cȧu F̱ā Mahā Vajiravudh, which took place in December, 1892, and to which all the following details of the *Sokănṭa* refer, the Kailāsa was forty feet high. It was a hollow structure of plaited bamboos, supported on poles and covered with tinsel of the appearance of gold and silver. On its summit towered a central pavilion which was profusely gilded and decorated. Inside it were placed urns containing sacred relics and hallowed water for the anointment. This pavilion was surrounded by a *rājavăt* fence, decorated with the usual tiered umbrellas and sunshades, with gateways at the four cardinal points. At the four corners stood the guardians of the quarters. On the northern and southern sides of the terrace stood chapels containing images of the Hindu deities. Access to the top of the hill was provided by two ladders leading up in opposite directions, one from the east and one from the west, while at the base of these were landing stages suitable for the approach of palanquins. Half-way up the hill was situated the grotto for the aspersion of the candidate. It was carved in the tinsel rock with a floor representing the Anotatta lake in miniature in front of which was a marble platform on which the candidate was to stand while receiving the aspersion with the hallowed water led through the mouths of four effigies, representing horse, elephant, lion, and bull respectively. A little to the right of the grotto was a small pavilion in which the candidate was to change his apparel after the bathing. All over the Kailāsa were representations of ascetics, bird-men, and the various fabulous animals of the Himālayan fairy-land [1]; while set-pieces illustrating episodes from the Hindu epics and other stories were also to be seen.

The Tusiṭa Mahā P̱rāsāda had been prepared as a "rites hall", and here on the eve of the festival (25th December), Buddhist monks recited *paritta* texts, for in the Tonsure, as in most State Ceremonies, Buddhist modifications have been appended to what was once a purely Hindu observance. At the same time the Court Brahmans performed their preliminary rites in a chapel erected outside the Tusiṭa Mahā P̱rāsāda.

The morning of the first day of the festival (26th December), was

[1] Mentioned in detail on pp. 167 sq.

PLATE XVII.

[From a painting by a Siamese artist.

To face page 128.]

MOUNT KAILĀSA AND THE PROCESSION OF THE TONSURATE.

given up to the recitation of *paritta* texts in the Tusiṯa Mahā P̱rāsāda, and the usual presentation of food to the monks who had officiated. In the afternoon the prince was borne on a palanquin in a royal procession and by a circuitous route to the Tusiṯa Hall, first filing past the King, who then, by a direct route, was also carried on a palanquin to the Tusiṯa Mahā P̱rāsāda. Here he assisted the prince from his palanquin and they both made offerings of tapers and incense before the sacred images. At the same time another of the King's sons of *Čau F̱ā* rank made similar offerings before the images on the Kailāsa, where a chapter of monks was engaged in consecrating the aspersion water. These ceremonies completed, the prince returned by the same route, this time seated on the same palanquin as his father, who again assisted him to alight. Similar ceremonies were performed on the afternoons of the following two days (27th and 28th December).

On these occasions the candidate was dressed in a handsome costume of white, richly embroidered with gold, a small jewelled coronet similar in form to the king's *maṅkuṭ*, and heavy gold bangles on wrists and ankles. The procession was made up in much the same way as is the state progress of a king. First marched military units, then came pages dressed as *devatā*, and groups of boys dressed in the costumes of various countries, but all wearing the toupet which showed that they had not yet reached adolescence; there were red and green drummers of victory, Brahmans scattering parched rice or playing ceremonial instruments, and damsels bearing peacock standards; then came the prince's palanquin accompanied by royal umbrella, sunshade, and fan; officials impersonating *devas* of the Indra and Brahmā heavens, and maids of honour carrying the royal insignia denoting the rank of the prince. Next followed a bevy of young girls wearing the toupet, and lastly, pages leading caparisoned chargers. During the proceedings the usual entertainments, common to all great state festivals, were in progress for the amusement of the public.

On the Day of Tonsure (28th December), the auspicious moment for performing the operation was declared by the *horā* to be between 6.6 a.m. and 6.59 a.m. The young prince was borne in procession to the Tusiṯa Mahā P̱rāsāda by a shorter route than on the previous days. Clad in white garments, and wearing jewelled coronet and bangles, he was led to a Chair of State in front of the officiating monks, who recited the usual *paritta* texts. In the Ayudhyā period the *Čau F̱ā* candidate was actually tonsured on the *Bhadrapīṭha* Throne, on which was laid a lion's skin. After the topknot had been parted into five tufts, the King, as the auspicious time drew near, placed on the candidate's right hand the Ring of the Nine Gems (*braḥ mahā vijiara nabrătana dharmaraṅga*). Then the King poured on to the prince's head a few drops of lustral water from a chank shell, the favourable moment was proclaimed by the sounding of ceremonial instruments, and the King severed three of the tufts with golden shears. The remaining two were severed by the two eldest princes in attendance, after which the head of the Royal Wardrobes Department completed the shaving.

Following the conclusion of the actual Tonsure, the King proceeded to the Kailāsa mountain, where he was to receive the candidate, who was carried thither in state, this time wearing a *mālā* royal hat, which reminds one of the custom of a king when proceeding to and from ceremonial halls at the time of his coronation. On arrival at the Kailāsa the prince was assisted from the palanquin by the King, and led to the Anotatta lake. Seated on the bathing platform, with *matum* leaves placed over his right ear and *phromachan* leaves on the left, and holding tightly a charm called *kraḥpòṅ bejra* ("diamond-cudgel"), the water from the mouths of the symbolical beasts of the cave was showered down upon him. This preliminary bath over, the King advanced and poured the contents of the great chank shell upon the head of the prince. The Queen, and other relatives in order of rank, came forward and poured water from other chank shells on to the prince's head. Finally, the chief Brahman did likewise. The prince was then led to the pavilion, where he changed his white bathing garments for the gorgeous apparel of a prince of the highest rank, with jewelled *mālā* hat.

We now come to a most interesting part of the ceremony, that of the reception on the Mountain by the god Śiva (Pl. XVIII). The King, dressed in full state, wearing the Great Crown of Victory, and holding in his hand the Sword of Victory, impersonated Śiva, and, accompanied by princes and nobles dressed to represent the god's courtiers, he ascended to his palace on the top of Kailāsa. Thence he commanded two of his celestial attendants to descend to the pavilion at the side of the hill where the young prince was waiting. They led him up the mountain by the western approach to where, at the top of the stairs, Śiva was waiting. The latter presented him to the public, who offered homage, and the two then proceeded to the central pavilion on the top of the hill. There the prince, amid the congratulations of all present, received from the King's hand a jewelled coronet larger than the one he had formerly worn, and other insignia of high station. The prince was then led to the western approach, and descended with the help of the god's two attendants.

PLATE XVIII.

RECEPTION OF THE TONSURATE BY ŚIVA (KING RĀMA V) ON MOUNT KAILĀSA.

[To face page 130.

PLATE XIX.

THE TONSURATE SEATED IN FULL STATE AFTER THE CEREMONY.

Since the prince was now deemed to have received his apotheosis, all those who had formed part of the procession, excepting only the Brahmans, changed their white garments for pink ones as a sign that the period of fasting and purification had terminated, and the white garments, required as a symbol of purity when taking the vow of observance of the Buddhist *śīla* precepts, could now be cast aside for the worldly attire used on festive occasions. The companies of youths who took part in the procession changed their coronets for conical hats in an endeavour to conceal their topknots so as to appear that they also had received the tonsure. For the same reason the young girls wearing the toupet were replaced by older ones who had already received the tonsure. The procession, having thus been reconstituted, circumambulated the Kailāsa mountain three times, *pradakṣina*-wise.

Of the remaining rites it will be sufficient to note that in the afternoon of the Day of Tonsure, a golden throne surmounted by a three-tiered umbrella was erected in the centre of the Tusiṯa Hall for the prince, the insignia of rank such as jewelled betel-box, water receptacle, spittoon, etc., being arranged on side tables as in the Coronation (Pl. XIX). A second throne was placed in the eastern apse for the use of the King, the western and northern compartments being reserved for members of the Royal Family and officials respectively. At 5 p.m. the prince, arrayed in robes of state, was escorted to the Tusiṯa Hall, where the King in full regal attire and wearing the Great Crown, received him. *Pa̱i-śrī* trays of food were offered to the spirit (*khvăñ*) of the young prince which, after a period of wandering during his early childhood, now comes to rest finally in the body of the tonsurate. Then the Brahmans performed a *vian dian* rite, wafting the smoke towards the prince. The Brahman head-priest gave the tonsurate three tablespoonfuls of cocoa-nut milk mixed up with food from the *pa̱i-śrīs* (as food for the *khvăñ*). Then he tied round his ankles the usual protective threads (corresponding to the *say siñcana*), and lastly, anointed him in the form of a *unalom* scroll (sign of Śiva) on the left palm, it being forbidden to touch so sacred a part of a prince's body as the forehead. The tonsurate himself, however, after passing the point of his right forefinger across the left palm, described his own unction on the space between his eyebrows. The King completed this final anointment by pouring a few drops on the prince's forehead from the great conch shell. The ceremonies for the day were brought to an end by the presentation to the prince of gifts from the King and members of the Royal Family, but all the ceremonies of the afternoon were repeated on the afternoons of the following two days (30th and 31st December). The last day of the festival (1st January) was devoted to the carrying of the hair in state procession down the river, and ceremoniously casting it into the water.

The above completes our summary of the facts concerning the *Sokănṭa*, and it will now be possible to draw certain conclusions from them. Firstly, as regards the part played by the King in impersonating Śiva, Gerini [1] has shown that in the *Sokănṭas* recorded in the Siamese Annals for the Ayudhyā period, and in the early part of the Bangkok period, the King never filled the rôle of Śiva himself, but appointed some prince of high rank as a substitute. King Rāma IV was the first to perform this part in person, and his example was followed by King Rāma V in the tonsure of Prince (afterwards King) Vajiravudh and of his other sons. But the earliest *Sokănṭa* of which Gerini was able to find a detailed description dates back only to A.D. 1633, although he finds mention of a Tonsure Ceremony as far back as A.D. 1358. It is almost certain that the Brahmanical rites of *Cūḷākănṭaḥmaṅgala* were introduced about the ninth century A.D., and had we fuller details of the rites as performed in the Sukhodaya period, I feel sure that we should find that the King performed the part of Śiva in person. Later we should find the substitution of a prince or high noble when the idea had arisen that it was dangerous for the King to perform his magical and divine functions himself. The substitute was, in fact, a "temporary king" or "temporary god" in this ceremony, just as he was in a number of other State Ceremonies where the chief part was formerly played by the King. Later, in the Bangkok period, the *raison d'être* of the substitute came to be forgotten, as it has been in the other State Ceremonies, and the King resumed his early functions. But the *Sokănṭa*, as performed in the fourth and fifth reigns of the present dynasty, is especially remarkable as showing the extreme form of this return to former conditions, the King not merely being present as a spectator, instead of being confined to his palace, but actually carrying out in detail all the traditional functions of a god. This is as far as I can go with this subject in the present chapter. When we have studied the other ceremonies in which the idea of a substitute for the divine monarch exists, we shall be in a better position to further elaborate and strengthen the theory of "temporary kings".[2]

The second aspect of the Tonsure Ceremony to be considered is its relationship to the Coronation. The resemblance between the two ceremonies may indeed appear sufficiently obvious from the summary

[1] Ge. (1), p. 130 f.n., and pp. 138 sqq.

[2] See Chapter XXII, "Temporary Kings."

of the *Sokănṭa* rites already given, but it will be convenient once more to make use of Hocart's table of analysis in order to show the main corresponding features as clearly as possible, again placing in square brackets those features not represented in Siam :—

(*a*) *The theory is that the King* [(1) *dies*] ; (2) *is reborn* ; (3) *as a god.*— Here again I find no explicit idea of death, but it must be implied, since the tonsurate is definitely reborn, i.e. he is initiated to a new life, that of maturity. This is especially shown in the substitution for the young girls in the procession those who have been tonsured, and by the hats worn by the boys in an endeavour to conceal their topknots. That he is reborn as a god is certain—he becomes Śiva's son Gaṇeśa.

(*b*) *By way of preparation he fasts and practises other austerities.*— This is indicated in the case of the *Sokănṭa* by the dressing in white and the observance of the *śīla* precepts by the candidate and his attendants.

(*c*) (1) *Persons not admissible to the sacrifice, such as strangers, sinners, women, and children, are kept away, and are not allowed to know anything* ; (2) *an armed guard prevents prying eyes.*—This feature is undoubtedly exhibited in a marked degree in the *Sokănṭa*, since the reception on the Kailāsa and the rites performed in the palace of Śiva thereon are essentially secret and mystical.

(*d*) *A kind of sabbath is observed ; the people are silent and lie quiet as death.*—This is distinct in the *Sokănṭa*, though not found in the Coronation. The people rigidly observe the *śīla* precepts, and silence is enjoined by tradition during all tonsure rites.[1]

(*e*) *The King must fight a ritual combat* [(1) *by arms or*] (2) *by ceremonies, and* (3) *come out victorious.*—This is less definite than in the Coronation, but we still have the Brahmanical sacrifices and the presence of the Sword of Victory and the drums of victory.

(*f*) *The King is* (1) *admonished to rule justly,* (2) *promises to do so.*— The whole object of initiation is obviously that the candidate should appreciate that he has now passed to man's estate and will be expected to conduct himself accordingly.

(*g*) *He receives communion in one or two kinds.*—In partaking of the *khvăñ's* food it seems to me that we may have a survival of a Brahmanical form of communion which has disappeared in the Coronation.

(*h*) *The people engage at one point in* [(1) *obscenities*] *and* (2) *buffoonery.*—There are the usual games and entertainments here as at the Coronation.

(*i*) *The King is invested with special garments.*—This is also the

[1] Ge. (1), p. 129.

case with the tonsurate, and the garments are similar to those worn by kings.

(*j*) *He is baptized with water*—the ceremonial bath on the Kailāsa—

(*k*) *and anointed with oil*, but, as in Coronation, the oil is replaced by water in Siam

(*l*) [*when a human victim is killed*]

(*m*) *and the people rejoice with noise and acclamations.*—There is the public homage when the prince is presented to the people on the Kailāsa; but it is not the custom for the people to show their joy on these occasions in a noisy manner when in the presence of royalty,

(*n*) *and a feast is given.*—The officiating monks are fed on this as on the occasion of other important religious festivals.

(*o*) *The King is crowned*—and so is the tonsurate.

(*p*) *Puts on shoes*—special shoes are part of the ceremonial dress of the tonsurate,

(*q*) *and receives other regalia such as a sword, a sceptre, a ring, etc.*—We have seen that the candidate is presented by Śiva with a special ring, and the *kraḥpòṅ bejra* charm, representing the Vajiravudha or adamantine mace of Indra, and corresponding to a sceptre. Other insignia such as betel-box, water-receptacle, etc., are presented to the prince, and he is accompanied when in procession by pages holding state umbrella, sunshade, and fan, while the throne on which the final rites are performed is shaded by a three-tiered white umbrella. The sword does not appear amongst the insignia of the prince, presumably on account of the taboo against carrying weapons in the immediate presence of the King.

(*r*) *and sits upon a throne.*

(*s*) [*He takes three ceremonial steps in imitation of the rising sun.*]

(*t*) *At the conclusion of the ceremonies he goes the round of his dominions, and receives the homage of the vassals.*—We have the circumambulation of the prince, after receiving his apotheosis, around the artificial mountain, symbolical of his father's home Kailāsa.

(*u*) *He receives a new name.*—It is now the custom to change the name and titles of royal children on the occasion of the river bathing ceremony. The account of the Tonsure of Prince In in 1633, as recorded in the Siamese Annals shows, however, that the name and titles were formerly changed at the *Sokănṭa*: "He received from the King's hands a golden plate (*subarṇapăṭa*) on which were engraved his new rank and title." [1]

(*v*) [*The Queen is consecrated with the King.*]

(*w*) [*So are the vassals or officials either at the coronation ceremony*

[1] Ge. (1), p. 138.

or in the course of the King's tour.]—In Siam a *Cău Ḟā* prince was always tonsured in a special festival for himself alone. But the presence of numerous untonsured youths who make believe that they have been tonsured after the ceremony suggests that at one time the prince's youthful followers also received initiation with their royal master.

(*x*) *Those who take part in the rites are dressed up as gods* [*sometimes with masks*].—We have the impersonation of Śiva by the King or his substitute.

(*y*) [*which may be those of animals, thus identifying the wearer with some kind of beast*].—But the presence of the mythical beasts from the Himālayan fairyland is to be noted.

(*z*) *A King may be consecrated several times, going up each time one step in the scale of kingship.* And it seems that Tonsure is to be regarded as the preliminary step.

The Tonsure Ceremony is undoubtedly falling into dis-esteem with the growth of modern Siam. Its greatest enemy has for centuries been the *sāmaṇera,* or Buddhist novice ordination, which fulfils all the functions of a Ceremony of Initiation, besides being a part of the living religion of the people. Thus while the entry to the Buddhist novitiate has a definite meaning in the eyes of the people, and to have a son in the yellow robe is the pride of every Siamese mother, on the other hand the *kāra kon cuk* has little more in its favour than that it is auspicious, and *ṗen dharmniam* (is the custom). The preservation of the topknot through the years of early youth has become too irksome a duty to be expected of the modern Bangkok schoolboy, and consequently, its tradition undermined by Buddhist modifications and Western " education ", it is rare to see a topknot in Bangkok except on the heads of young and pampered scions of nobility. It is, however, still a common sight amongst the unsophisticated people of rural districts.

A *Sokănṭa* of the first order, that of a *Cău Ḟā* prince, not having been performed for many years, little is remembered of it by most Siamese. But it is probable that the festival would be carried out on something approaching its former scale were there the occasion for it; and, since no king of the present dynasty (except the founder) has failed to undergo the *Sokănṭa*, it is important to consider the sociological value of this ceremony in connection with the kingship. The effect which the ceremonies have on the onlookers is not of primary importance, since the Tonsure occurs within the precincts of the Grand Palace, and is witnessed only by a comparatively small number of people. On the other hand, as with all initiation ceremonies, it is the effect upon the initiate himself that is the essential feature, and from this follows the indirect but equally important effect which the initiation has on the welfare of the people as a whole. Indeed, the *Sokănṭa* of a *Cau̇ F̱ā* prince, who is later to be a king, undoubtedly has been an institution of great sociological value in Siam in the past, and will continue to be such so long as the present conception of the monarchy exists. However ignorant of the meaning of the complicated rites the young prince may be, he must at least subconsciously realize that this festival signifies a break with childhood days, that he must begin to take life seriously, and that he is a person of great importance on whom will eventually rest the responsibility for the welfare of the people. Again, I often heard it remarked at the time of the last coronation that the proceedings must have constituted a great ordeal for the King, the speakers evidently thinking that he had experienced nothing like it before. They had evidently forgotten the *Sokănṭa*, than which no finer training for a possible heir to the throne in regal bearing and the duties that might later be required of him could possibly be conceived. Taking place in early youth, the most impressionable period of his life, this first lesson is never likely to be forgotten.

Unfortunately, signs are not wanting that this important institution is not likely forever to escape the undermining influences of the West. Young princes brought up, as they will be in the future, in surroundings bristling with European influences, and having had their first taste of life in one of the modern "public schools" of Bangkok, will look askance at this seemingly incongruous episode. There is, indeed, evidence that Siamese youth never did take very kindly to the ceremony; for example, in the case of the *Sokănṭa* of Prince Issaresra Cudamani in 1821: This young prince was evidently possessed of a mind of his own, for after having fainted at one stage of the long drawn-out proceedings, he next day stubbornly refused to be dressed in the state robes and coiffed in the heavy coronet, exclaiming, "D'ye think you can yet deck and daub me up like a mannikin?"[1]

[1] Ge. (1), p. 144.

CHAPTER XI

CREMATION [1]

The Ceremonies

1. *Preliminary Considerations.*

Cremation is the only means of disposal of the remains of deceased royalty in Siam. It is, in fact, the means by which the vast majority of the Siamese people dispose of their dead, the exceptions being criminals, victims of cholera and smallpox, people who have been struck by lightning, and women who have died in childbirth, whose corpses are buried. These exceptions are explained either by fear of the fatal disease, or by fear of the *phī* (ghosts).

The cremation of a royal person (known as *kāra parama śaba, kāra braḥ meru* or *thavāy braḥ blo'ṅ*) differs from that of a noble or commoner by reason of the extreme length and elaboration of all the ceremonies connected with it; as well as by reason of the fact that whereas the cremation of the ordinary Siamese is almost entirely Buddhist, the cremation of royalty is Buddhist superimposed on a Hindu basis, and accompanied by the survival of much Brahmanical ritual.

In Siam it is usual to store the bodies of deceased princes and princesses until a number are awaiting cremation, when the obsequies are carried out with pomp and circumstance befitting their rank. A king, however, is always honoured with a special cremation, the

[1] Sources: I know of few Siamese texts providing information concerning the Cremation. However, (1) H.R.H. Prince Damrong's *Ṭāṁnān susān hlvaṅ văt debśi-rindra* (History of the Royal Cremation Ground of Văt Debśirindra), Bangkok, 1927, supplies some valuable facts; (2) *Kaṭhmāy heṭu ṅān braḥ meru grăṅ kruṅkǎu* (Treatise on Cremation Buildings in the Ayudhyā period), an eighteenth century MS. (published by the Royal Institute in 1916), would be of greater value in a study of Siamese architecture than in the present work; (3) "Siamese Customs for the Dying and Dead," *Bangkok Calendar*, 1864, has an interesting account of cremation buildings of the early reigns of the present dynasty; (4) Leclère's *La Cremation et les Rites Funeraires du Cambodge* (Hanoi, 1906), has been of great assistance, especially in indicating certain rites which have now disappeared from the Siamese ceremony. Perhaps my most important source of information has been (5) an official who has been intimately connected with the carrying out of royal cremations for many years, and is extremely well versed in the technique, but who prefers that his name should not be divulged. (6) I was fortunate in being in Bangkok on the occasions of the cremation of the late H.R.H. Prince Asdang (heir presumptive, 1924), and of the late King Rāma VI (1926), and was able personally to observe the more public rites I was also present as a guest at a number of ordinary Siamese cremations.

magnificence of which greatly exceeds that of even the highest royal prince. Very rarely a high dignitary of the Buddhist Church has been accorded the honour of a royal cremation of a magnificence equalling that of a king. For example, the *Săṅgharāja* (Patriarch), who died in 1822, at the age of 90,

> "was placed in a great gilded urn, an honour reserved for the king and princes of high rank, and was cremated during the following May, on the site for royal cremations." [1]

A king was usually not cremated until many months after death but in the case of the late King Rāma VI the cremation, which on no account could have taken place until after the hundredth day rite had been performed, was carried out only four months after death. This curtailment of the time devoted to lying-in-state was not the only reduction made in the ceremonies. In fact, both the late King and King Rāma V, had given strict orders that their cremations were to be on a smaller scale than had previously been thought necessary, and they had in view the saving of trouble and expense. This being the case, although I shall make the cremation of the late King Rāma VI the basis for study, I shall be obliged to complete the picture by reference to the proceedings of earlier occasions.

There is one question which I feel sure has already arisen in the mind of the reader, and that is as to why I include "Cremation" under the heading of "Ceremonies of Installation". This is a question which cannot satisfactorily be answered at the present juncture, and I must therefore crave patience until the latter part of the next chapter. I must now proceed with the detailed description of the ceremonies.

2. *Ceremonies performed shortly before the dying King expires.*

When it is seen that the condition of a king is very grave, he is, if possible, removed to a special apartment in the Royal Residence reserved for such occasions. King Rāma VI died there, but his father died in another palace, since he was too ill to be moved to the Grand Palace. In the days of Old Siam certain Buddhist priests of high standing were then charged with the duty of writing scriptural texts in the Pāli language on nine sheets of gold leaf shaped like sacred Bodhi leaves, which were placed on the nine principal parts of the body after death. This evidently corresponds to an ancient Vedic rite in which "the seven apertures of the body (nose, etc.) were covered with gold pieces".[2] The bed used to be draped with white material, and paintings representing scenes in paradise were suspended

[1] *JSS.*, xxiv, Oct., 1930, pt. 1, p. 15. [2] Barnett, *Antiquities of India*, p. 148.

Plate XX.

The Corpse of King Sisowath of Cambodia dressed for placing in the Urn.

To face page 139.]

in order to draw the dying man's attention away from earthly scenes to a contemplation of the future beatified state. The king was watched day and night by members of the royal family and ladies of the palace, the latter preserving the utmost calm until the doctors had pronounced life to be extinct, when they gave themselves up to loud lamentations. I understand on good authority that none of these rites were performed at the death of the late King.

3. *Bathing and adorning the Royal Corpse and placing it in the Urn.*

As soon as the King had breathed his last, the royal princes approached and placed him on his back, closing the eyelids and mouth, and covering the body (*braḥ parama śaba*) with a golden shroud, while two candles were lighted. The princes then immediately gathered in another room in order to confirm the new King's accession. This pressing business of State had to be attended to without any delay, since the welfare of the living is even more important than that of the dead. This meeting concluded, the royal family assembled and bathed the corpse with scented water, afterwards placing it on a beautiful gilded bed.

The next duty was to dress the body and prepare it for the Urn. Silk drawers embroidered with gold, and a cloth-of-gold *phă̌-nuṅ* clothe the lower part of the body, above which is an embroidered vest of yellow silk and an amice (*săṅvian*). Silken gloves and socks are also put on, gold plaques are placed on chest and sides, and baldricks studded with diamonds are crossed over the chest. There are gold shoes and epaulettes (*chalòṅśò*), heavy gold bracelets, anklets, and rings, and a golden mask (*dòṅ pit braḥ bhăkṯra*) covers the face, symbolic of the radiant visage of a god. A pair of gilt candles, a lotus, and a pair of gold horns containing areca nut wrapped in betel leaf are placed in the hands, and a silken *mālā* hat is set upon the head (Pl. XX).

The corpse having been left thus for half an hour, the Urns are brought to the foot of the bed. The inner one (*còṅ ṅo'n*) is of silver, with a lid that can be hermetically sealed. The outer one (*braḥ koṣa dòṅ h̍yai*) is of great magnificence, being of gold ornamented with the nine gems and capped by a tapering pyramidal spire. The height of the inner Urn is about 1.20 metres, and the breadth at the widest part 0.60 metres, while the height of the outer Urn to the top of the spire is 3.00 metres. The outer Urn is octagonal in shape, and the spire has the form of a *maṅkuṭ*. It was used both for the Lying-in-State of King Rāma VI and his father, King Rāma V, and for all *Cǎu F̱ā* princes and princesses who have died in recent years.

In former times it used to be the custom at this stage in the preparations to remove the mask from the face of the dead king and pour a certain quantity of mercury down the throat with the object of expediting the drying of the corpse. This process is still carried out in Cambodia, but according to my informant, and contrary to the common opinion amongst Europeans, this has not been done for very many years in Siam. It is, however, still the custom to place a gold ring in the mouth, which may be the equivalent of the coin that is placed in the mouth of any dead commoner. Graham [1] states that with the common people this coin is intended to pay the toll at the gates of paradise. If the gold ring truly corresponds to the coin it can only be regarded as the survival of a very primitive idea, for such an idea seems curiously incongruous in connection with the death of a divine monarch.

The corpse is next " invited " (*jo'ñ braḥ śaba*) to sit on a small camp-bed. The trunk is lifted, the palms joined opposite the face by means of an iron clamp, a sort of wedge is placed under the chin, and the knees are lifted to the level of the hands and tied in a sitting position. The corpse, thus seated, is placed on sixteen long strips of cotton material, the ends of which are raised and tied over the top of the head. The new King then sets the late King's Personal *Kaṭhina* Crown upon the head of the corpse, and suspends a heavy gold chain studded with diamonds around the neck. In this position the corpse is saluted by all present, then lifted and placed in the inner Urn which in turn is placed within the outer gold one. The term used to express the late King now that he is seated within the Urn is *braḥ cau yū hua nai parama koṣa*.

It will be seen from the above account that the dead king is arrayed in richer attire than he ever wore in his lifetime. That this funeral state has preserved the splendid accoutrements which ancient kings actually wore when they were alive we may be sure, for we see such things on the reliefs of Aṅkor and in the dress of the modern Siamese dancers when impersonating kings and heroes. An interesting feature in the preparation of the corpse is that the hands are joined in an attitude of supplication. This is a late Buddhist modification, adopted to show that the deceased monarch, be he regarded as Bodhisattva or Hindu deity, pays homage to the Buddha.

The above ceremonies of preparation are all carried out by members of the Royal Family in conjunction with officials of the Royal Wardrobes Department. The Court Brahmans take no part in these rites in Siam, though in Cambodia they still assist in the bathing of the corpse.

[1] *Siam*, i, 164.

4. *Transfer to the Tusiṯa Mahā P̱rāsāda, and ceremonies connected with the Lying-in-State.*

All the private ceremonies described above took place, in the case of the late King Rāma VI, on the day of his death, 25th November, 1926, and that same day the corpse within the Urns was transferred to the Tusiṯa Mahā P̱rāsāda to lie in state. In Cambodia, according to Leclère, the preliminary ceremonies were spread over several days, and the *braḥ cǎu yū hua nai parama koṣa* was kept in the royal residence for two months, before being transferred to lie in state.

The procession from the Căkrabartibimān to the Tusiṯa Hall was a short one, since it only had to traverse a few hundred yards through the grounds of the Grand Palace. It consisted of the usual drummers of victory, processional umbrella-bearers, gentlemen-at-arms, and Brahmans playing ceremonial instruments. The great Urn was borne on a gilded palanquin under an immense nine-tiered umbrella of State, and accompanied by large single-tiered umbrella, fan, and sunshade. Behind the palanquin walked King Prajadhipok, also shaded by an umbrella, and accompanied by the princes. It was a small procession, but it was impressive because it was personal, almost a family affair; and it took place in venerable surroundings, with an absence of that display of modern militarism which, however great its sociological value, always seems to strike a jarring note in every State Ceremony where it is present.

In the western apse of the Tusiṯa Mahā P̱rāsāda stood the royal catafalque, on which the Urn was to be placed in state. A special inclined plane was used for placing the Urn in position both on the catafalque and later on the pyre, the Urn being slowly drawn up by means of pulleys, to the accompaniment of the blowing of conches and the firing of guns. This undertaking was known as *jo'n braḥ śaba khu'n braḥ dèn*, i.e. inviting the corpse to be seated. It is a variation of the taboo mentioned on page 36, concerning the King not being supposed to touch the ground, the Urn seeming to glide up the plane and take its position on the catafalque in a god-like manner.

I did not see the Urn on the catafalque until several weeks of the Lying-in-State had passed by. It was on the occasion when the Lord Chamberlain placed a silver wreath at the base of the catafalque on behalf of the Kram Maḥhātlek. The Urn, over which hung from the ceiling a great nine-tiered white umbrella, presented an impressive spectacle on the summit of the pyramidal catafalque (*ṯhanvèn fǎ*) of graduated stages, decorated with flowers and candles, and illuminated by means of electricity (Pl. XXI). It is the opinion of Prince Damrong that this catafalque is modelled on the shrine called Baksai Chamkrong at Aṅkor Thom.[1] Before it were placed offerings of food and flowers, renewed daily, and to right and left were glass cases containing the late monarch's uniforms and personal possessions, while his decorations were laid on cushions. At each of the four corners of the catafalque stood a sentinel, and the Urn was never for one instant left without this military guard during the period of Lying-in-State. From the base of the Urn there depended on the east, north, and south sides a long embroidered ribbon (*braḥ bhūṣāyoṅ*) about 6 inches wide. The lower ends of each of these ribbons rested on a gold tray at the base of the catafalque. Their significance is in connection with the *Satăpakaraṇa* rite, as will shortly be explained.

The daily ceremonies, carried out during the Lying-in-State were as follows: Day and night four Buddhist monks, who were relieved every few hours, kept up an almost incessant chanting in a kind of choir-stall some distance from the catafalque (Pl. XXII). They ceased only to have a smoke and a cup of tea or to renew their quids of betel. At the Lying-in-State of former monarchs they also ceased when the wailing palace women came to lament before the Urn, to the accompaniment of the blowing of conches. This they used to do five times a day, each period lasting about half an hour, but this rite was omitted in the case of King Rāma VI. The food which was daily placed before the late King's Urn was, so I was informed by his chef, in accordance with his favourite menus, and was served at his customary mealtimes.

On certain days the Tusiṯa Mahā P̱rāsāda was open for the various government departments and for the general public to pay their respects before the Urn. Wreaths were placed by high officials and members of the Diplomatic Corps at the base of the catafalque, and every Siamese present crawled up to a position in front of the catafalque and about 20 feet from it, and saluted in the traditional manner by lowering the head and raising the joined palms three times, then crawling away. The utmost awe was noticeable in the behaviour of the officials in the presence of the Urn. None would have thought of standing while paying his respects, and thus we see the old custom of prostration surviving in the presence of the dead King long after it has disappeared in the presence of the living one.

From the day of King Rāma VI's death until some time after the actual cremation, the whole nation was in mourning. The mourning colour in Siam is white; but officials of high rank also wear a gold sash. Up to the fourth reign it was compulsory for every Siamese, male and female, to shave the head during the period of mourning. The only exceptions were in favour of the new King and princes

[1] *Ṯāṁnān Susān hlvaṅ*, p. 2, n. 1.

PLATE XXI.

[Photo : Narasingh Studio.

THE LYING-IN-STATE IN THE TUSITA MAHĀ PRĀSĀDA.

[To face page 142.

PLATE XXII.

[Photo : Narasingh Studio.

MONKS CHANTING DURING THE LYING-IN-STATE.

older than the deceased monarch, but this custom has now been completely abolished. The Coronation of King Prajadhipok took place during the period of mourning, and this led to the strange procedure of suspending the mourning regulations for a time, so that the people might duly celebrate the Coronation, but the ceremonies around the Urn continued as usual.

On certain days during the four months of the Lying-in-State, there were special religious services in the Tusiṯa Hall. Of greatest importance were the seventh, fiftieth, and hundredth day rites, the latter being the earliest day after which Cremation of a royal person can be performed. Then there were special services on the *Văn Braḥ*, or Buddhist Sabbaths, i.e. the eighth day of the waxing moon, the full moon, and the eighth and fifteenth days of the waning. There were also special services on the 23rd February, the day before cremation, and on the 24th, in the morning, immediately before removal from the Tusiṯa Mahā P̱rāsāda.

The King visited the Tusiṯa Hall every day up to the hundredth day after which his place was taken by other princes. On these visits he lit candles in front of the image of the Buddha on the altar at the east end of the Hall, and then lit candles in front of the Urn. On the special days a high dignitary of the Church and a chapter of thirty Lords Abbot chanted stanzas suitable for the occasion, usually from the Abhidharma. The King then laid down cloths and robes for the *Satăpakaraṇa* Rite, in which the monks chant the *paṅsakula* verse [1] and hold the ends of the pendant ribbons above mentioned, thereby transferring to the robes offered by the King the special merits supposed to belong to cloths found in graveyards, which merit accrues to the deceased king.

On the special days above mentioned, Chinese and Annamite monks performed their customary obsequial rites in the courtyard adjoining the Tusiṯa Hall, where a number of altars had been erected for them. In front of these altars were a number of models of various kinds, boats, houses, torpedo-boats, figures of persons attired in various costumes, all beautifully made down to the smallest detail, but only of paper. Following the Cremation they were burnt near to the water's edge, in accordance with the old Chinese funeral custom, which is founded on the idea that such models have their spiritual counterparts, and that such will be of use to the departed spirit in the next world. As now performed in Siam, these foreign rites merely reveal the desire of the Chinese and Annamite communities to identify

[1] I have not seen the Siamese *paṅsakula* verse, but a Siamese to whom I showed the one used in Ceylon and quoted on p. 158, states that it is the same.

themselves with the general display of mourning for the loss of the monarch under whose protection they have dwelt, just as the Christian Churches also hold memorial services. But the custom is an ancient one in Siam, and I suggest that it was fostered to enhance the dignity of the monarchy in the eyes of the common people, even to persuade them that China and Annam were tributary States.

During the course of the Lying-in-State certain rites in connection with the urned remains were carried out. The base of the inner Urn is in the form of an iron grating, and from the outer Urn a copper tube passed down into the hollow catafalque where the depositions accumulated in a golden vase. Access to the interior of the catafalque was obtained by means of a small door on the western face, and each alternate day until the corpse was dry and no further liquids dripped from the tube, that is to say until about two months after death, an attendant entered and removed the vase. This was then borne in procession to Văt Mahădhătu where, ever since its foundation in the first reign, the sanies of kings and princes of high rank have been burned. They are first poured into a wide metal tray and covered with dry sugar cane and incense which absorbs them. The resulting compound is then burned and the ashes are kept to be mixed with those resulting from the cremation of the *paramaśaba*, to be disposed of as will later be described. After the sanies have ceased to drip from the Urn, flowers and odoriferous woods are placed within the catafalque.

During the Lying-in-State the sacred fire, to be used at the cremation, is kept burning on an altar in the Tusiṯa Hall in a lamp which is watched with great care. It was formerly the custom to preserve the fire from any building that had been struck by lightning. Thus :—

> "In the reign of P'ooti Yawt Fa (Rāma I), grandfather of his present Majesty (Rāma IV), the royal audience hall was destroyed by lightning. It is commonly believed that the fire taken from that conflagration, has been kept constantly burning in the palace, and is used on occasions like the above." [1]

Nowadays the sacred fire, like that which is used to light the Candle of Victory, is obtained from the sun by means of a burning-glass, and hence is ceremonially pure.

5. *The Funeral Pyre.*

Soon after the death of the late King, work began on the construction of the funeral pyre, called Braḥ Meru because it symbolizes Mount Meru, the home of Viṣṇu and Indra (Pl. XXIII). This great building was erected on the Royal Cremation Ground, a wide, grassy expanse near the

[1] *Bangkok Calendar*, 1864, p. 65.

PLATE XXIII.

[Photo : Narasingh Studio.

THE FUNERAL PYRE (BRAḤ MERU) OF KING RĀMA VI.

To face page 145.]

Grand Palace, which is also used for kite-flying and other sports when not required for Royal Cremations. The size and elaboration of the Braḥ Meru has been much reduced since the cremation of King Rāma IV; in fact, this is the feature which has suffered more than any other, as a result of the prevailing desire to economize. The expenditure in the case of the pyre used for the cremation of Rāma VI is said to have been only one-eighth of that lavished on the previous King's Meru.

The great expenditure on this structure is largely necessitated by reason of the fact that all the materials must be new, and can never be used again for a like purpose. Formerly, at least, the timber could only be given to the monks for the repair of their monasteries; but the fate of the materials used in certain recent princely cremations is better left unrecorded.

The Meru, which was illuminated by a multitude of electric lamps at night, stood in the centre of a square space of about an acre in extent, enclosed by a lattice *rājavăt* fence, which was decorated at intervals with tiered umbrellas. Against this fence, on the inner side, were built galleries and pavilions for the accommodation of monks, nobles, and officials, and with a most splendidly decorated pavilion for King Prajadhipok. Until the reign of King Rāma V the animal effigies which used to take part in the procession were also housed in these galleries. At each of the four corners were towers, formerly elevated high above the ground, but at King Rāma VI's cremation built at ground level. Each tower was for the accommodation of a party of four monks, frequently relieved by others, who chanted verses from the Buddhist scriptures on the Day of Cremation. Access to the interior of the enclosure was obtained by means of four gateways, one in the middle of each side. The Braḥ Meru erected in the centre was, in former reigns, an enormous structure, the skeleton consisting of four immense teak trunks, from 200 to 250 feet long, and each with a circumference of about 12 feet. These logs were obtained by royal order from four different provinces in the North, and were selected from virgin jungle. They were embedded in the ground 30 feet deep, their bases forming a square, and the trunks were made to lean slightly together to form a truncated pyramid. At the top they were joined by a roof upon which was erected a gilded *prāsāda* spire. The late King's Meru was erected in this manner, but the tip of the *prāsāda* spire was only about 150 feet above the ground. It was, however, very graceful, and the architects had shown great ingenuity in fashioning the upper part to represent the four faces of Brahmā, above which tapered the *maṅkuṭ*-like spire crowned by the late King's crest, which in turn was surmounted by a small tiered umbrella. Under the lofty roof of the great teak pyramid was built a floor at about 20 feet from the ground, which was reached by four terraced flights of steps, one of which was reserved for the King. The stairs and terraces were ornamented with tiered umbrellas and *devatā* figures holding large sunshades. On the floor of the Meru was erected the *braḥ peñcā*, or Pyre Proper, an octagonal pyramid diminishing by right-angled gradations, and terminating in a truncated top. The one used for the late King's Cremation was made of iron with gilt overlay. High above it hung a beautifully embroidered white umbrella of nine tiers, while the red and gold teak pillars were draped with heavy cloth of gold curtains, and each of the four sides of the open pyramid formed by these pillars was fitted with doors, on which conventional designs of birds and mythical figures were worked in silk. But one no longer saw the interesting painted scenes of heaven and hell, and the pictures illustrating life in the Siamese dependencies which used to ornament the walls of cremation buildings, nor the artificial lakes, hills, and houses that were in former reigns built around the Meru to give the semblance of Indra's paradise.[1]

In Old Siam a large part of the Cremation Ground, outside the square enclosure, was dotted with temporary buildings of many kinds, and their abolition, and that of the customs with which they were connected, has struck one of the greatest blows at the traditional Royal Cremation. Outside the enclosure and near the middle of each of the four walls was a platform on which was placed an artificial tree, the branches of which were heavily loaded with green and yellow limes. There was also a brilliantly decorated royal pavilion. Here the King stood on the Day of Cremation, and distributed wooden limes from a golden bowl to the nobles and high officials around him, while officials appointed for the purpose stood on the platforms and scattered the limes from the artificial trees amongst the eager people massed below. These trees represented the *Pārijāta* or *Kălpavṛkṣa* Tree of Indra's paradise or, according to the Buddhist interpretation, the four trees that will be found one in each of the four corners of the city in which the next Buddha is to be born, and which will bear not only money but everything else that man will need for his comfort under the coming Buddha's reign. Each wooden lime contained either a coin or a promissory note of a certain specified value, such as

[1] Although in most of the cremations of commoners that I have witnessed, the Meru consisted of a simple canopy erected on four posts over a pyre, on one occasion at Labapurī I saw a very interesting artificial mountain about 20 feet high from the side of which issued a figure of Indra mounted on his elephant. It was a definite attempt to represent the traditional Meru.

a boat, house, or garden, which when presented to the treasury were regularly paid. On the occasion of the late King's Cremation this distribution of limes was carried out on a very small scale only and on the day of the collection of the relics.

Other buildings were a large refreshment hall where all except the lowest classes could obtain food and drinks without charge; stands for the letting off of fireworks; and a great variety of theatrical entertainments and other side-shows. With the exception of the refreshment hall, all these were abolished in accordance with the wish of King Rāma V, who considered that such celebrations did not harmonize with the dignity which ought to characterize the royal obsequies. But this interference with tradition seems to me to be a mistake; such entertainments are highly appreciated by the people, and even commoners, unless very poor, do their best to provide at their cremations at least one theatrical performance, or nowadays a cinema. Such a reduction in the grandeur of the royal obsequies cannot fail to decrease the popularity of a Royal Cremation, and, what is more, decrease its impressiveness and sociological value.

6. *Transfer in Procession of the Urn from the Tusiṯa Mahā P̱rāsāda to the Braḥ Meru.*

On the morning of the Day of Cremation, and immediately after the last Buddhist service, the Urn was lifted down from the catafalque. During this process, and throughout the following rites, the mournful music of the Brahmans was played unceasingly. The outer Urn was removed, and the inner one was opened. The King removed the crown from the head of the *paramaśaba* and placed it on a small table. Then the corpse was removed from the Urn and placed on a bed covered with a white mat. Next all the gold ornaments and attire were taken off. Only the bones remained, and these, if they fell to pieces, were rearranged in the form of a human skeleton. The King, the Patriarch, and the nobles poured cocoa-nut water over the bones, which were then tied up in white cloth and replaced in the inner Urn.

In the case of the cremation of King Rāma VI, as soon as the above ceremonies had been completed, the inner Urn containing the remains was carried out of the Tusiṯa Hall and placed on a palanquin, the outer Urn being then replaced. Thus the *paramaśaba* was borne on the palanquin the short distance separating the Grand Palace from the neighbouring monastery, Văt Jetavana. It was an intimate personal procession, and has been well described as a family farewell to the Royal Remains which were leaving their home for the last time. Apart from a few ceremonial attendants and guards, only the

King and the royal princes down to the rank of *Braḥ Aṅga C̀au* followed the palanquin on foot, and the route was lined only by the servants of the palace, all attired in white.

When this procession reached the main road leading to the Cremation Ground, it met the Grand Funeral Procession already drawn up, and the Urn was transferred by means of the inclined plane to the Great Funeral Car (Pl. XXIV). Thenceforward the route was lined by almost the entire population of Bangkok, and large numbers of people who had come from outlying districts to pay their last respects to the late King.

The Grand Funeral Procession was composed of the following elements, and in the order below detailed :—

TERRITORIALS, BOY SCOUTS, AND TROOPS

Many units representative of all arms, with modern equipment, which need not be mentioned in detail.

THE ROYAL FUNERAL PARTY

Two three-tailed Flags
Four metal Drums
160 Red Drums of Victory
Twenty Silver Drums of Victory
Twenty Gold Drums of Victory
Two Headmen of the Pipe
Two Headmen of the War Drum
Twenty Blowers of the Foreign Bugle
Twenty-eight Blowers of the Siamese Bugle (horn-shaped)
Four Blowers of Conch Shells
Two Inspectors of the Bugle
Two seven-tiered Umbrellas, six five-tiered, and four Sunshades
Three Sword Bearers
One Bearer of the Priest's Fan of Honour

Royal Car with the Prince Patriarch reading the Scriptures

Four Sword Bearers
One Royal Umbrella
One Large Sunshade
One Royal Fan
Eight Representatives of Indra with lances
Eight Representatives of Brahmā with lances
Eight pairs of Civilian Guards (high officials of the Ministry of Justice)
Two seven-tiered Umbrellas, four five-tiered, and two Sunshades
Two Sword Bearers
Two seven-tiered Umbrellas, fourteen five-tiered, and twelve Sunshades
Six Sword Bearers

The Great Funeral Car bearing the Urn, and two officials dressed as *devatā*; drawn by a hundred Army Men and a hundred Navy Men, and with six Horses yoked to it.

One Royal Umbrella
One Large Sunshade
One Royal Fan

(Left side:) File of thirty-two Gentlemen-at-Arms. File of thirty-two Royal Pages.

(Right side:) File of thirty-two Gentlemen-at-Arms. File of thirty-two Royal Pages.

Plate XXIV.

[Photo: Narasingh Studio.

The Urn being transferred to the Great Funeral Car.

[To face page 148.

PLATE XXV.

[Photo: Narasingh Studio.

A ROYAL FUNERAL PROCESSION.

Sixteen Representatives of Indra and Brahmā, bearing silver and gold ornamental Trees (*bhum tòk mai ṅo'n dòṅ*)
Two seven-tiered Umbrellas, ten five-tiered, and eight Sunshades
Two Palace Officials with personal effects
Four Sword Bearers
Sixteen Pages with spears
Sixteen Pages with flowers
Four Chargers with eighteen men in attendance

KING PRAJADHIPOK'S PARTY

Eight Royal Lictors in two lines (bearing peacock feathers instead of rattans)
Monkey Standard | Garuḍa Standard
The King, walking
Royal Umbrella
Ten Aides-de-Camp
Princes of the Royal House down to *Hmòm Caus* of *bān dòṅ* (golden bowl) rank
Special Representatives of Foreign Sovereigns and States
Foreign Representatives and Ministers
Officials of Ministry of Foreign Affairs
Officials of Ministry of Royal Household
High Officials of other Ministries
Pupils of the Schools under the Royal Patronage
Two Battalions of the 1st Infantry Guards Regiment
Navy Band
Navy Men

The greater part of this long procession calls for no particular comments, since it is mostly composed of those bearers of ceremonial insignia of which enough has already been said in the chapter dealing with Coronation. The procession is on a very grand scale, due to the desire to pay the highest respect to the deceased monarch. But really the difference between the Coronation and the Cremation processions is rather one of degree and arrangement than of kind. It is to be noted that the Brahman blowers of the conch wear pointed hats from beneath which their long hair streams loose as a sign of mourning. This is the most important part that they now play in the Cremation ceremonies.

The features of greatest interest are the Cars of the Patriarch and of the Urn. These great vehicles, running on four wheels, are built up like a series of massive carved and gilded barges, but very short and broad, and seemingly superimposed in graduated sizes. At Aṅkor there were wheeled cars in the classical period, which Groslier thinks were drawn by men and used for funeral purposes.[1] If the modern Siamese Car was derived from that of Cambodia, it has greatly changed, and the boat-shaped build, the graceful *braḥ-dī-nàṅ* and tall spire, instead of the rectangular pavilion and *prāṅg*-like tower

[1] Gr., p. 101 and fig. 63, *b*.

of the ancient Khmer car, seem to betoken that Burmese, or rather Môn, influence, which has already been noticed in the case of the royal barges.

Unfortunately, several of the most remarkable features of the traditional Royal Cremation Procession must be spoken of as belonging to the past, since they have been omitted in recent times. These are as follows:—

(1) It was the custom, until the Cremation of the late King, for two young princes to ride on a Car between the Patriarch's Car and that bearing the Urn. A strip of silver cloth, 6 inches wide, was attached to the thighs of the Patriarch, whence it passed back to the princes in the second Car, and finally back to the Urn to which it was attached (Pl. XXV). One of the two young princes held the ribbon, and the other scattered roasted grains. This ribbon formed the mystic connection between the Book, the Royal Family, and the Urn, in the same way that a similar ribbon gave mystic connection between the Urn and the monks, during the Lying-in-State. When the Urn had been transferred to the Braḥ Meru, the silver ribbon was extended over the Urn, down the eastern and western sides of the *braḥ peñcā*, and thence on a Brussels carpet, protected by white muslin, nearly to the flight of steps on the east and west sides of the building. This ribbon was stretched between the Cars in the Cremation procession of King Rāma V, and even in that of the Queen Mother who died in 1922; if its omission at the late King's Cremation was due to the fact that he had no sons, perhaps we may hope for its restoration at some future time.

(2) The effigy of a rhinoceros took part in the procession, carrying a small pavilion on its back in which was the sacred fire (Fig. 1). It is interesting to note that a rhinoceros is figured in the reliefs of Aṅkor Văt,[1] though what its function was is not known. The sacred fire was apparently then carried on a palanquin, and such sacred fire processions are depicted on the reliefs at Bayon, Aṅkor, and Banteai Chhma.[2]

(3) After the rhinoceros there used to follow a host of more than sixty effigies of mythical animals, representing the denizens of the Himaphān or Himālayan fairyland. A complete list of them is given in the appendix to this chapter, and it will be seen that the names of some of them indicate Chinese origin, which is also borne out by their appearance. But many of them, especially the more human ones, are derived from India, and preserve the characteristics of Siamese styles of the Ayudhyā period. These effigies were drawn along

[1] A., iii, p. 237. [2] A., ii, p. 340, iii, pp. 168 and 261.

Fig. 1.—The "Rhinoceros", Bearer of the Sacred Fire.

[To face page 150.

in the procession on small wheels, and in small shrines on their backs they bore the King's offerings to religion. Their significance seems to be in connection with the Buddhist idea of every living creature from every plane of existence coming to worship at the feet of the Buddha; but they also have an earlier Hindu significance as we saw in connection with the Tonsure where they came to witness the initiation of Gaṇeśa. The rhinoceros and all the rest of the strange company were abolished by King Rāma V; but they still survive at Cremations in Cambodia.

To return to the proceedings at the Cremation of Rāma VI: When the great procession arrived at the Cremation Ground, the troops formed up in serried ranks facing each side of the Braḥ Meru enclosure, and the Great Funeral Car was halted at the northern entrance. Then the Urn was transferred to a gun-carriage (this is a modern substitute for a palanquin), and the King made the gesture of personally receiving the Urn thereon, the process being accompanied by the blowing of conches. Then followed the traditional circumambulation of the Urn around the Braḥ Meru within the enclosure. This is, of course, the Hindu *prasavya* circumambulation performed on inauspicious occasions with the left shoulder turned to the object in the centre. The process is known in Siamese as *uṯṯaravăṯra*.

The procession which thus three times circumambulated the Meru was necessarily a small one. First came the Prince Patriarch, carried on a palanquin, then the gun-carriage with the Urn, followed by the King and the princes walking. At the base of the Urn were wreathed the Siamese colours, at the front rested on a golden bowl the late King's Field Marshal's helmet, while behind was his Admiral's cocked hat. A rope of fresh flowers was placed round the foot of the Urn, and before it was carried the late King's personal flag draped with mauve ribbons of mourning. The gun-carriage was drawn by men of the Royal Palace Guards, accompanied by the usual insignia of rank, and shielded by a state umbrella, while during the circumambulation the ceremonial instruments were sounded.

The gun-carriage came to a halt at the eastern stairway leading up to the Meru, while the King proceeded to a throne facing the western entrance, so that he could supervise the placing of the Urn on the Pyre. All the other units of the procession now retired, leaving only the gun-carriage, surrounded by the scarlet-clad drummers and conch blowers who sounded their instruments ceaselessly while the inner Urn, the outer one having been removed, was hoisted up by means of the inclined plane on to the *braḥ peñcā*. The late King's insignia having been placed before the Urn, the gilt doors of the Meru were opened and the King ascended the steep staircase on the western side.

Lighting the candles before the Urn, the King knelt and did homage to the remains of his brother by raising the joined palms three times in the traditional manner. He then left at once for the Grand Palace by motor car. This was at about 11 a.m., and the final rites, which will be described in the next section, began at 4 p.m.

7. *The Final Rites.*

It was formerly the case for the Urn to remain in state on the Braḥ Meru for about fifteen days before the date of actual Cremation, which date was fixed by the *Braḥyā Horā*. Prior to these fifteen days, sacred relics were placed on the Pyre while the monks in the prayer towers, as well as large numbers in other parts of the enclosure, continued their chanting and the women their wailing until the Day of Cremation. But in the case of the late King, the remains were cremated the same day as the Urn was transferred to the Pyre.

The period from about 11 a.m. to 4 p.m. after the Urn had been placed in position, and before the final rites began, was left free for all such members of the public as were suitably dressed in mourning to enter the enclosure and pay homage with joined hands at the base of the Meru.

It was formerly the custom to remove the Urn from the Meru on the Day of Cremation to a neighbouring building, called the "pavilion of perfumes", where the long parcel of bones wrapped in the white shroud was removed from the Urn and laid on a white mat, to receive a last anointment with perfumed water by the King. In the case of the Cremation of King Rāma VI, since the remains had already been washed and anointed that day, they were not taken down from the Meru, but the inner Urn (the outer one having already been removed) was replaced by one of sandal-wood decorated with silver flowers. This operation took place while the public homage was in progress, as also did the preparation of the pyre. Fragrant wood was aid in order in cross layers on the platform, and a bellows was attached to the pile. Precious spices were laid amongst the wood, and green banana logs were laid round the pile to prevent the fire from spreading too far and endangering the structure of the Meru. Men armed with water ladles were also stationed in readiness.

When the King and Queen arrived in state palanquins in the afternoon, they took up their position in the royal pavilion facing the western side of the Meru. The Prince Patriarch preached a sermon, and fifty Lords Abbot chanted stanzas from the scriptures, the customary distribution of gifts to the officiating monks then taking place. The King and Queen then ascended the long stairway to apply the sacred fire. It was sunset and the masses of people stood in solemn silence. The King lit the sprays of sandal wood from the lamp containing the sacred fire and applied it to the pile which was kept alight by attendants, but not allowed to spread to the Urn at this time.[1] This was the supreme moment, and the first red flames were greeted by the roar of cannon, a fanfare of trumpets, and the playing of the National Anthem. The King and Queen knelt in final farewell before the pyre ; it was an impressive moment, and must have struck deeply into the hearts of the multitude, a moment which few who were present will ever forget.

Rising from their knees, the King and Queen stood and faced the Urn for a few moments before retiring to their thrones. Princes and princesses, the former by the northern and the latter by the southern staircase, then ascended and added their offerings of lighted candles and sandal-wood to the fire which was still kept within small compass, and not yet allowed to spread to the Urn. Thereafter the King and Queen returned to the Palace by state palanquins, but the stream of nobles and officials continued to pay homage at the Meru until it was quite dark, and long after that the awed populace continued to sit and gaze at the illuminated spire.

The rite of offering sandal-wood and candles at the Pyre which has been referred to in the last paragraph as a homage has really, according to Prince Damrong, a deeper significance which is understood by few Siamese. The underlying idea is that in placing these offerings on the Pyre the giver asks forgiveness for any wrong that he may have done the deceased during his lifetime. Originally a person whose conscience was quite clear had no need to perform this rite.

The Actual Cremation took place at 10 o'clock at night, behind the drawn curtains of the Meru, the fire not having been allowed to die out since the time it was applied by the King. The flaming pile was carefully watched throughout the night by the attendants, who stirred it with pokers and saw that none of the bones escaped the fire. In the morning only a thin wisp of smoke remained, and consecrated water was poured on the hot cinders, in analogy to the miraculous shower of rain that extinguished the pyre of the Buddha. Then more water was thrown on the ashes from the four jars which stood one at each corner of the *braḥ peñcā*, possibly symbolizing the earthly water that was brought by the faithful Mallas and thrown on the pyre of

[1] This is the procedure in the case of a king's cremation. In the case of the cremation of any other royal person, the King ignites the pile by means of a train of gunpowder without moving from his pavilion.

the Buddha after it had been extinguished by the celestial shower.[1]

The ashes were then given roughly the form of a human figure with the head turned towards the east. They were then stirred up and reformed with the head turned towards the west. Finally the process was repeated with the head turned towards the east. This is evidently symbolic of the rising, setting, and again rising of the sun—birth, death, and rebirth. A *satăpakaraṇa* rite was then performed by the monks in attendance, and the gifts of robes and food which the King had made to the monks during the Cremation ceremonies, were circumambulated three times around the Meru, *prasavaya*-wise (Pl. XXVI). While they thus circumambulated, the guards and insignia-bearers kept constantly crying "Hoo! hoo!". One might suppose that this was to keep off evil spirits, but Prince Damrong is of opinion that it is a relic of the far distant days when Buddhist cremations used to take place in deep jungle, and the cry served to prevent those who followed behind from losing their way.

Not until the above rites had been completed did the search for relics begin, in which the King and Queen, the princes and princesses, and the ladies of the palace took part. The little fragments of burnt bone relics (*ăṣṭhi*) were placed on a plate on a stand. In former reigns the King used to place some of them each in a gold locket, and hand them to the children of the deceased monarch, who kept them until their deaths, after which they were usually enshrined in a *stupa*. This division of the relics is quite in accordance with Buddhist tradition but was not carried out at the late King's cremation, since he had no children except his baby daughter. The remainder of the relics (all, in the case of King Rāma VI) were then perfumed and placed in a small golden urn, similar in appearance to the Great Urn, but only 50 centimetres high. They were then carried in state to the Grand Palace where they are kept, but are brought out on certain occasions to be honoured by the reigning King. The ashes (*ăṅgāra*) (Pl. XXVII), fragments of burnt wood, etc., together with the ashes previously produced at the burning of the sanies, of the first three kings of the dynasty are enshrined in Văt Braḥ Jetavana, those of Rāma IV are at Văt Pavaranivesa, those of King Rāma V at Văt Peñcamapabiṯra, while those of the late King Rāma VI are partly enshrined at Văt Pavaranivesa, and partly in the great *stupa* at Nagara Paṭhama. In the Ayudhyā period the ashes used to be tied up in white cotton cloth, then placed in a white bag embroidered with gold, and taken in a royal barge to be jettisoned in mid-river.

[1] *Mahā-Parinibbāna Sutta*, vi, 49, *SBE.*, xi, p. 130.

PLATE XXVI.

[Photo: Narasingh Studio.

BEARERS OF THE ROYAL GIFTS TO THE MONKS CIRCUMAMBULATING THE MERU.

To face page 154.]

Plate XXVII.

[Photo: Narasingh Studio.

The Ashes of the late Queen Mother borne in Procession.

CHAPTER XII

CREMATION (*continued*)

History and Function

1. *The History of the Siamese Royal Cremation.*

The Siamese Royal Cremation as it is, or rather as it was before it had been corrupted by the innovations and abolitions of the last fifty years, is undoubtedly a close copy of the Ayudhyā form. So far as the buildings of the Braḥ Meru are concerned, we know from the eighteenth century MS. already mentioned that the royal architects of Bangkok have closely followed the Ayudhyā model, and the *Annals of Ayudhyā* give the following interesting account of a royal cremation :—

> "His Majesty gave directions, that all necessary and suitable preparations be made for the cremation of the remains of H.M. the late King. The main building, which was to contain the urned remains, terminated in a spire and was 2 sen 11$\frac{3}{8}$ wahs high. Similar but smaller buildings at the four points of the compass, and interspersed around the square enclosure, which was set apart as the cremation lot, were decorated with gold, pinchbeck, silver, and other chats (umbrellas), and flags and other streamers and endless ornaments. The urned remains were placed in the gorgeous and beautiful car, and were escorted by a solemn procession of the magnates of the kingdom to the cremation buildings. The usual amusements, day and night ; religious ceremonies, plays, and theatrical performances were kept up for days, and the usual presents were made as at the cremation of all the kings of Siam. At the appointed day the torch was applied and the remains were reduced to ashes, and the usual ceremonies for preserving a few relics of the charred bones were observed." [1]

The seventeenth century European writers give but scanty details. La Loubère [2] mentions the use of mercury to drain the body, the large size of the pyres, the processions of mythical animal effigies, and the ignition of the pyre by the King, in the case of royal cremations, " without stirring out of his palace. He lets go a lighted torch along a rope, which is extended from one of the windows of the palace to the pile." Evidently the use of a train of gunpowder was not then understood. J. Struys [3] describes a funeral of a princess in more

[1] *Reign of King Narai* [i.e. Nārāyaṇa], translated by S. J. Smith, Bangkok, 1880.

[2] L. L., pp. 124 sq.

[3] Eng. ed., 1684, chap. viii.

detail than any other old writer: the Urn was borne to the Meru in procession on a car. A silk band passed from this to the car in which the princes rode. "Oranges" containing money were thrown to the people. The pyre was lighted by the King himself, accompanied by doleful music. The oldest account by a European writer is that of Mendez Pinto,[1] who refers to events of the year 1545, but unfortunately the cremation ceremonies he describes are quite un-Siamese and unworthy of credence.

The above evidence is sufficient to show that in every feature of importance the seventeenth century Royal Cremation was the same as it is to-day. We know that there were no violent cultural changes during the four centuries of the Ayudhyā period, and it was therefore about the fourteenth century that the Cremation took on its traditional Siamese form, as a result of the conversion of the Thai to Hīnayānism in the period when Sukhodaya was capital. Then Cambodia was also converted, but has retained to this day many Brahmanical features which have disappeared from Siam. This fact, coupled with the fact that the cult of the Deva-rāja was the principal royal religion up to the thirteenth century, even when Mahāyānism was practised, can leave little doubt that the Royal Cremation in ancient Cambodia was entirely Brahmanical.

We will first endeavour to pick out those features in the Siamese Royal Cremation that can definitely be traced to the Hīnayāna Buddhism introduced in the thirteenth century. Not all Buddhists practice cremation; the Burmese mostly bury their dead. But in preferring cremation, which is a method more in accordance with the Buddhist idea of the impermanence of matter, the Siamese are also adhering to the rules laid down by the Buddha himself. It was in response to the repeated request by Ānanda for information that the Buddha is said to have explained that His remains should be treated as was the custom with those of a Cakravartin, or Universal Emperor:—

> "They wrap the body of the king of kings, Ānanda, in a new cloth. When that is done they wrap it in carded cotton wool. When that is done they wrap it in a new cloth—and so on till they have wrapped the body in five hundred successive layers of both kinds. They then place the body in an oil vessel of iron, and cover that close up with another oil vessel of iron. Then they build a funeral pile of all kinds of perfumes, and burn the body of the king of kings. And then at the four cross roads they erect a *dāgaba* to the king of kings."[2]

Similar rites came to be accepted as the model for the cremation

[1] Eng. ed., 1663, chap. xlviii.

[2] *Mahā-Parinibbāna Sutta*, v. 26, *SBE.*, vol. xi, pp. 92 sq.

of Buddhist kings and distinguished monks in Ceylon. Thus King Uttiya—

"caused the dead body of the *thera* to be laid forthwith in a golden chest sprinkled with fragrant oil, and the well-closed chest to be laid upon a golden, adorned bier; and when he had caused it then to be lifted upon the bier, commanding solemn ceremonies, he caused it to be escorted by a great levy of troops; commanding due offerings (he caused it to be escorted) on the adorned street to the variously adorned capital and brought through the city in procession by the royal highway to the Mahāvihāra. When the monarch had caused the bier to be placed here for a week in the Pañhambamālaka—with triumphal arches, pennons and flowers, and with vases filled with perfumes the *vihāra* was adorned with a circle of three *yojanas* around, by the king's decree, but the whole island was adorned in like manner by the decree of the *devas*—and when the monarch had commanded divers offerings throughout the week he built up, turned towards the east in the Therānaṁbandhamālaka, a funeral pyre of sweet-smelling wood, leaving the (place of the later) Great *thūpa* on the right, and when he had brought the beautiful bier thither and caused it to be set upon the pyre he carried out the rites of the dead. And here did he build a *cetiya* when he had caused the relics to be gathered together. Taking the half of the relics the monarch caused *thūpas* to be built on the *Cetiya*-mountain and in all the *vihāras*. The place where the burial of this sage's body had taken place is called, to do him honour, Isibhūmaṅgaṇa." [1]

But Przyluski has shown [2] that in fact the cremation of the Buddha followed the simple customs usual for monks in those early times, and the idea of the Buddha having been cremated with the rites due to a Cakravartin is late. Almost all the rites described in the *Mahā-Parinibbāna Sutta* and other Buddhist texts refer to the Brahmanic ritual in use at the cremation of emperors. For example, the weeping of women, the multiplication of the wrappings of the corpse, the mention of an elaborate funeral procession (cf. that of Rāvaṇa, in *Rāmāyaṇa*, VI, iii), the use of perfumes and sandal-wood, a characteristic of royal cremations in the Epics, and the sprinkling of the pyre with milk or latex (cf. the use of cocoa-nut water in Siam), are all characteristic of the ritual in use at the cremations of Cakravartins. On the other hand, the usual washing of the corpse is omitted, because the Buddha was considered to be perfectly pure.

This tradition was preserved in Ceylon, and the Siamese kings of the Sukhodaya period no doubt imitated the ritual favoured by the Buddhist kings of Ceylon, but, since the early Siamese kings were imbued with the Khmer cult of the Deva-rāja, the Hindu-Buddhist

[1] *M.*, xx, 34–46.
[2] J. Przyluski, "Le Parinirvāṇa et les Funérailles du Buddha," Première Partie, Extrait du *Journal Asiatique*, 1918–20.

rites of Ceylon were grafted onto a very evident substratum of Khmer Brahmanism. Indeed, in the Siamese Royal Cremation to-day, we can distinguish only three important Buddhist features :—(1) the presence of large numbers of officiating monks, (2) their continuous chanting or preaching, (3) the *Satăpakaraṇa* rite.

As to the *Satăpakaraṇa* rite, the following note shows it to be still practised in Ceylon, and there can be no doubt that it was introduced into Siam from that source :

"The cloth which covers (the body) is removed and presented to the priest, who says :—

Aniccá vata saṅkhárá,
Uppádavayadhammino,
Uppajjitvá nirujjhanti
Tessam vúpasamo sukho.

Assuredly all that are born
Decay and pass away,
They are born and they cease to exist,
Their rest is happiness.

The priest departs, taking with him the cloth." [1]

Cremation was not an invention of Buddhism; it was known in Vedic India, although burial was certainly the earlier form. *Rig-Veda*, x, 18, which deals primarily with burial, also contains verses which were adapted for cremation and the collection of the relics. Up to modern times the remains of Brahmans and Kṣatriyas in India are cremated with rites which, though differing vastly in the main from those observed in Siam, show the following similarities: (1) the corpse is wrapped in a ceremonially pure cloth ; (2) gifts are made to the officiating priests ; (3) the corpse is washed ; (4) the body is apparelled in rich raiment and jewels ; (5) there is a funeral pyre ; (6) the near relatives approach and deprive the corpse of all the jewels with which it is adorned ; (7) the chief mourner walks round the funeral pyre three times ; (8) coins are distributed amongst those present ; (9) there are loud lamentations during the proceedings ; (10) the heir stirs the ashes with a stick, looking for any bones that may have escaped the flames ; (11) gathering up a portion of the ashes he throws them into the water, the remainder he collects into a heap, to which he gives the rough semblance of a human figure, supposed to represent the deceased ; (12) the anniversaries of the deaths of his mother and father must be observed with appropriate ceremonies, and liberal

[1] ***Journal of the Ceylon Branch of the Royal Asiatic Society*, vol. viii, No. 29, 1884, p. 233.**

gifts must be made to the priests.[1] Some of these features were no doubt borrowed by Buddhism from Hinduism at a very early period but others are purely Hindu and have reached Siam via Cambodia with a certain amount of influence from Śrīvijaya.

A study of such fragmentary records as we possess concerning the funeral customs of the ancient Khmers and their neighbours, the Cams and the inhabitants of the Malay Archipelago (before conversion to Islam), throws a little light on some of the Brahmanical features of the Siamese Ceremony. I shall therefore quote such notes as I have been able to collect concerning the funeral customs of these countries, and then see what deductions can be made from them.

(1) As regards the Ancient Khmers :—

The Chinese *History of the Leang* (A.D. 502–556) gives the funeral ceremonies of the people of Funan (the pre-Cambodian State), as follows :—

> "For mourning, the custom is to shave the beard and the hair. There are four methods of disposal of the dead : (*a*) throwing the dead body into a flowing stream, (*b*) burning it to ashes, (*c*) burying it in the ground, (*d*) exposing it to the birds." [2]

The seventh century Chinese chronicles give the following details :—

> "The children of both sexes pass seven days in lamentations, without food and without cutting their hair. The relations assemble with Buddhist priests and the priests of the Tao (Brahmans), and walk in procession with chants to the accompaniment of musical instruments. The corpse is burnt on a pyre of aromatic wood and the ashes are kept in an urn of silver or gold. Then the urn is thrown into the middle of a great river. Poor people use urns of baked clay painted in various colours. Sometimes the corpse is exposed on a hill-side to be devoured by beasts." [3]

(2) As regards the Cams :—

> "For people of high rank, the cremation had to be performed near to the mouth of the river, and in the case of the king the ashes were thrown into the sea. Ceremonies were performed in honour of the dead on the hundredth day and again in the third year." [4]

(3) As regards the inhabitants of the Malay Archipelago :—

Before the coming of Islam the peoples of the Malay Archipelago had two methods of disposing of their dead :—

> (*a*) By exposing them to vultures, etc., in very early times.
> (*b*) Cremation. Just as it was the custom in Cambodia to throw part of the corpse on gold plates to the dogs and vultures, so it is

[1] D., chaps. xxix and xxx. [2] C., p. 25. [3] C., pp. 62 sq.

[4] R. C. Majumdar, *Ancient Indian Colonies in the Far East*, vol. i, Champa, 1927, chap. ix.

still in Bali, the last stronghold of Hinduism in the Netherlands Indies. Before the coming of Islam, cremation was more general, especially in Java. The body was washed with a decoction of odorous plants, cinnamon, and salt, then wrapped in precious coloured vestments, and placed on a bed covered by a tent. Underneath were placed jars to receive the liquid depositions and the slave who collected these was set at liberty. After enough money for a pompous funeral had been collected the body was taken in ceremony to a bamboo pyramid called *wadah* [= Siamese Braḥ Meru ?] and was placed in a coffin and burnt. The ashes were carefully collected and thrown into the sea. Poor people, as with the Cams, buried their corpses until they could afford to burn them. Islam buries all bodies and the only remaining customs of Hinduism are the wrapping of bodies in costly cloths and sometimes the use of coffins.[1]

The above facts throw light on six points at least in the Siamese Royal Cremation, and I will proceed to deal with them in turn :—

(1) Exposure of the corpse to vultures: It used to be the custom in Siam at some time before cremation to cut off part of the flesh of the corpse immediately after death, and offer it to the temple dogs and vultures on gold or silver dishes. This was only done by the wish of the deceased; it long ago ceased to be the custom of royalty, and has now been prohibited by law in the case of commoners. It was given a Buddhist significance, and considered an act of great merit. In Cambodia it was practised in the case of a royal corpse as late as 1859, at the death of King Ang Duong.

Cheou Ta-kouan supposed that the chief method of disposal of the dead in Cambodia was to expose them to the dogs and vultures. Aymonier[2] states that this was always more common in Siam than in Cambodia and may have been in Cheou Ta-kouan's time a recent fashion brought in by the victories of the Siamese. I disagree with this, while admitting that the Siamese, in the eagerness of their recent conversion to Hīnayānism, might have been the first to revive and give a Buddhist significance to what I believe was a very ancient and widespread custom. The practice was evidently a very ancient one amongst the Khmers, since it is mentioned in the *History of the Leang*, and it was also common amongst the Malays, prior to the introduction of Islam. It survived in Siam until about thirty years ago in its primitive form as a means of disposing of the bodies of criminals and paupers, but even in these cases the bones were collected and either buried or burnt. I think that this, together with the method of throwing corpses into streams (mentioned in the *Leang*, and surviving

[1] Antoine Cabaton, "Ceremonial in use among the Malays at the death of their kings," *Revue du Monde Musulman*, March, 1908.

[2] A., iii, p. 631.

until quite recent times in Siam in the case of executed princes) are the two most primitive pre-Buddhist, pre-Hindu modes of disposal of the dead; they are probably very widespread amongst primitive peoples, and present a nice problem for the consideration of the exponents of the schools of common and independent origin.

(2) The Urn: The use of funeral urns is not confined to countries with an Indian civilization, but both Hindus and Buddhists have adopted them at least for the cremation of royalty. I suggest, however, that the magnificence of the Siamese Urn is largely a product of the Khmer cult of the Deva-rāja with a Burmese *prāsāda* spire added. The placing of jars under the corpse to collect the depositions, among the old Malays, is reminiscent of the process of draining the body in Siam and Cambodia, and if we had fuller information we should probably find many further resemblances in the preparation of the corpse for cremation. The Malays, prior to the coming of Islam, were much influenced by Śrīvijaya, if indeed they did not form part of that great empire, and if we had further evidence we should probably find that it was from that source that the Khmers derived many of their Brahmanical cremation rites.

(3) The survival amongst the modern Malays of burial in rich garments also suggests the derivation of the Siamese and Cambodian royal funeral ornaments and attire from Śrīvijaya.

(4) The throwing of the ashes into the sea or river is mentioned as the custom of the seventh century Khmers, of the Cams, and of the old Malays. It is in accordance with Hindu custom as still found in India, and is opposed to the Buddhist custom of burying the ashes and preserving the relics, and Siam in the Ayudhyā period compromised by casting the ashes into the river and keeping the bony relics.

(5) In Campā, ceremonies were performed on the hundredth day, and again in the third year. In India, rites are performed on the 30th, 45th, 60th, 75th, 90th, 120th, 175th, 190th, 210th, 240th, 270th, 300th, and the 330th day after death, and on the anniversaries of death.[1] These rites were the Hindu *śrāddhas*, and I suggest that the seventh,[2] fiftieth, and hundredth day rites and the annual homage to the relics in Siam and Cambodia are survivals of these.

(6) The Chinese historian of the *Leang* noticed that the early Khmers shaved their heads in mourning as they still do in Cambodia, and as they did until recently in Siam. It is a custom probably much older than Buddhism or Hinduism, and is almost world-wide. Its

[1] D., p. 496.

[2] But the seventh day rite has a special Buddhist significance in that, according to tradition, the Buddha was cremated on the seventh day after death.

origin presents as great a problem as does that of exposure of corpses to wild beasts.

To sum up :—

Despite the many gaps in detail, the evidence at our disposal is sufficient to show that the present Siamese Royal Cremation has not changed greatly since it took shape in the thirteenth to fourteenth centuries, when Sinhalese Buddhism was definitely established. The Sinhalese type of Royal Cremation was grafted on to the Khmer Cult of the Deva-rāja, inherited by the first Thai Kings. The Khmer Cult had been founded on Indian Brahmanism much elaborated by its passage through Śrīvijaya. Lastly we are able to recognize elements, such as placing a coin or gold piece in the mouth of the departed, shaving the head in mourning, and giving part of the flesh of the deceased to the beasts, which are survivals of very primitive prehistoric funeral customs.

It will now be possible for me to explain why I have included Cremation in the section of this book devoted to Ceremonies of Installation. In comparing the Brahmanical rites of the Coronation in Siam with those of the Royal Cremation, I have been struck with the resemblance between the two, and I suggest that the Cremation of the ancient Khmers was, in fact, a Spiritual Coronation. I am not going to maintain that all Funeral Ceremonies are to be looked on in this way, but it may be so, and religions like Buddhism would naturally obscure the idea and cause it to be forgotten. For the present I confine my theory to Cambodia and Siam where, especially in the former country, Divine Kingship—the cult of the Deva-rāja—reached its highest development. Most religions connect death with rebirth in another world, and to secure that rebirth in a happy state is the *raison d'être* of all funeral ceremonies (except those primitive ones designed to prevent the dead from worrying the living, which comes to practically the same thing). We have seen that according to Hocart [1] the theory of coronation is, or was, that the king (*a*) dies, (*b*) is reborn, (*c*) as a god; and if in Siam (*a*) and (*b*) are not definitely expressed, at least they are understood when the King takes on the divine attributes of the Hindu gods at his coronation. Moreover, when a king considers that his earthly power entitles him to rank as an emperor, he has himself consecrated again with the rites of Indra, king of the gods (*Indrābhiṣeka*). Surely, then, when a king really dies his apotheosis is most appropriately celebrated by an *abhiṣeka*, and this consecration would be accompanied by even greater pomp and circumstance than any during his lifetime, not only because it signifies the final step

[1] Loc. cit.

in supreme elevation, but because, whatever doubt there might possibly be in the mind of the king himself or of others as to deification during lifetime, the force of inspired tradition, of visions, and of the mystery of the unknown life beyond the grave, could leave no doubt in the minds of the people as to the possibility, indeed the certainty, of deification after death.

I do not deny the probability of an earlier ritual of cremation having existed before the cult of divine kings had reached its climax and the Royal Cremation of Siam and Cambodia may have been built up on such an earlier basis; but I do maintain that the theory explains the extreme complexity of the Siamese rites which have puzzled and shocked Christians by their apparent inappropriateness, and Buddhists as well, judging by the way in which the later Buddhist kings have sought to prune them.

For the sake of convenience I will once more quote Hocart's tabular analysis of the component parts of a typical Coronation.

(*a*) *The theory is that the King* (1) *dies*; (2) *is reborn*, (3) *as a god.*—(1) Of course actually happens, and (2) and (3) form the Brahmanic conception, though Buddhism substitutes Bodhisattva for god.

(*b*) *By way of preparation he fasts and practises other austerities.*—But, of course, the preparation is entirely spiritual, and those rites which have been described on p. 138 (2) are performed by the priests.

(*c*) (1) *Persons not admissible to the sacrifice, such as strangers, sinners, women, and children, are kept away, and are not allowed to know anything*; (2) *an armed guard prevents prying eyes.*—The same remarks as to the privacy of the more important ceremonies and the presence of guards apply to the Cremation as to the Coronation.

(*d*) *A kind of sabbath is observed*; *the people are silent and lie quiet as death.*—There is an extended period of mourning. This has disappeared from the Coronation, because the idea of death (previous to rebirth as a god) has been lost.

(*e*) *The King must fight a ritual combat* [(1) *by arms, or*] (2) *by ceremonies, and* (3) *come out victorious.*—The victory is, of course, entirely spiritual, even more so than was that of the Coronation. Most religions regard death as a victory over the flesh: Brahmanism attains it by sacrifice, and Buddhism by the conquest of desire. The Drums of Victory are present in the Cremation procession as well as at the Coronation.

(*f*) [(1) *The King is admonished to rule justly, and* (2) *promises to do so.*]—Nothing of this remains now, but there is no reason why there should not have been such an admonition, and promise, at one time. We have the analogy of the victims about to be buried alive at the city gates being admonished to guard them well. No doubt the deified kings of Aṅkor were believed to continue to take a strong personal interest in affairs of State, and were supplicated in times of danger. And I doubt not that the periodic homage to the relics of kings in Bangkok has some such origin.

(*g*) [*He receives communion in one or two kinds.*]—It has already been remarked, in connection with Coronation, that soma-drinking has disappeared from all Buddhist countries. So far as I know, there was no soma-drinking at death; but there is still a form of communion among the Hindus in India, where " the *purohita* pours a few drops of *pañcha-gavia* into the mouth of the dying man, by virtue of which his body becomes perfectly purified ".[1] If such a rite ever existed in Siam or Cambodia, it has now entirely disappeared.

(*h*) *The people indulge at one point in* [(1) *obscenities,*] *or* (2) *buffoonery.*—The theatrical entertainments, boxing, tumbling, etc., which were such a great feature of royal cremations until recent years, and which have appeared so *mal à propos* in the eyes of foreigners and recent Buddhist kings, are perfectly explicable on my theory that the Cremation is a Spiritual Coronation of the deified king.

(*i*) *The King is invested with special garments.*—We have seen that ancient monarchical garments are put on the corpse before it is placed in the urn.

(*j*) *He is baptized with water*—purificatory baths;

(*k*) *and anointed with oil*—not oil, but perfumes and cocoa-nut water in Siam. Purificatory bath and *abhiṣeka* are confused in Cremation as in Coronation.

(*l*) [*When a human victim is killed.*]—No relic of this could exist side by side with Buddhism in Siam, but Indian Hindu kings were accompanied in death by their wives and slaves.

(*m*) *And the people rejoice with noise and acclamation.*—The ceremonial music on conches, flageolets, and drums of victory, and the firing of guns, now regarded as signs of respect and ritual accompaniments.

(*n*) *A feast is given* in the Cremation, just as in the Coronation, roasted grains are scattered (but by the young princes) and not only monks, but all those who pay homage at the pyre are fed, and largesse is distributed, but now it takes the form of money contained in limes, while in the Coronation there was the scattering of gold and silver flowers.

(*o*) *The King is crowned*—when in the urn.

(*p*) *Puts on shoes;*

[1] D., p. 482.

(*q*) *And receives other regalia such as a sword, a sceptre, a ring, etc.*—the sword and sceptre have been displaced by Buddhism in favour of a candle and an offering of betel; but a gold chain is placed round the neck, a nine-tiered umbrella is hung over the Urn, and, when in procession, a page carries a fan.

(*r*) *And sits upon a throne.*—Catafalque or Braḥ Meru, the throne of Indra; the "invitation" to the corpse to be seated thereon is significant.

(*s*) [*He takes three ceremonial steps in imitation of the rising sun.*]

(*t*) *At the conclusion of the ceremonies he goes the round of his dominions and receives the homage of the vassals.*—The circumambulation around the Pyre symbolizes the god's journey round Mount Meru, especially if the deified king was a sun-god.

(*u*) *He receives a new name.*—The first three kings of the Bangkok dynasty had posthumous titles identifying them as Bodhisattvas, and we have seen that Khmer kings often received posthumous titles signifying that they had gone to the heavens of their favourite deities.

(*v*) [*The Queen is consecrated with the King.*]—An explanation of *satī* in India ?

(*w*) [*So are the vassals or officials either at the coronation ceremony or in the course of the King's tour.*]

(*x*) [*Those who take part in the rites are dressed up as gods, sometimes with masks.*]—But it is to be noted that the dead king wears a gold mask which represents the shining visage of a god.

(*y*) [*Which may be those of animals, thus identifying the wearer with some kind of beast.*]—But the presence of the mythical beasts in the procession is to be noted.

(*z*) *A King may be consecrated several times, going up each time one step in the scale of kingship.*—And, according to my hypothesis, Cremation is the final step.

2. *The Functional Value of the Royal Cremation.*

I have already indicated the functional value of certain parts of the Royal Cremation, but will conclude with a general summary. Cremation and Coronation are undoubtedly two of the most important, sociologically, of all the Royal Ceremonies of Siam. Perhaps they are not quite the most important since they occur comparatively rarely in the lifetime of most members of the public, whereas there are other annual ceremonies which from their more frequent occurrence perhaps do more to impress the people with the majesty of the kingship. Nevertheless, a Coronation or a King's Cremation once seen can scarcely be forgotten even by the most unimpressionable.

It is particularly important that a Royal Cremation should be celebrated with the greatest possible pomp, because death is the greatest danger that the idea of divine kingship has to combat. It strikes right at the roots of the whole conception, and instils doubt into the minds of a people who, until recently, had not dared even to contemplate the possibility of a king suffering from any mortal infliction; and now, with the spread of western education, modern scepticism, and the shadow of communism, the Royal Cremation plays an even bigger part than formerly in impressing on the people that the king is not dead, but has migrated to a higher plane, where he will work out his destiny as a Bodhisattva for the good of all beings. The mixture of Brahmanism and Buddhism is fortunate: the former lends itself more to the exaltation of the kingship, while the latter emphasises the royal protection of the people's religion and enables them to enter into the spirit of the ceremonies.

The Royal Cremation has another important sociological aspect: it shows, more strongly than does the Coronation, the new king's respect for his ancestors, for the dynasty, and for old traditions. It is also an example to the people in filial piety. Throughout history a new king, even a usurper, did well to honour the former occupant of the throne. A classical example of this is recorded in the *Mahāvaṁsa* [1]: The great Sinhalese king Duṭṭhagāmiṇi accorded full funeral honours to his fallen Tamil adversary Eḷāra, who, though a foreigner, had ruled Ceylon wisely and well for many years. On the other hand, the cold-blooded execution and deprivation of funeral honours of King Ṯāk by Rāma I, though considered necessary in those stern times, undoubtedly struck a blow at the people's respect for the kingship, which has only been repaired by the passage of years and the wisdom of later rulers.

As with the Coronation, it is the more public and stately parts of the Royal Cremation which have most sociological value in maintaining the respect of the masses for the kingship. They have no understanding of the significance of most of the rites, such as we have discussed in detail, but they have an innate love and respect for all forms of royal pageantry, and it is the magnificence of the state procession, the splendour of the Urn enthroned upon the catafalque, or the brilliantly illuminated Braḥ Meru, that impress them that their King is a great King; and the opportunity that is given them of paying homage by laying candles upon the pyre and thus storing up great merit, convince them that he is also a gracious one. But they miss the mythical monsters and the free theatrical entertainments, for they are a

[1] *M.*, xxv. 71–4.

light-hearted people, and these things mean much to them; and it is only to be hoped that what the Royal Cremation gains in dignity by these omissions may to some extent make up for the apparent diminution of the royal bounty.

APPENDIX TO CHAPTER XII

The following is a list of the mythical monsters, denizens of the Himaphān, whose effigies used to take part in Royal Cremation and Tonsure Ceremonies. Images of a few of these creatures are to be seen in the courtyard of the Chapel Royal. They are also depicted on the walls of Văt Braḥ Jetavana and other temples, while miniatures representing them are to be found in certain old manuscripts:—

Siamese Name.	*Description.*[1]	*Traditional Colour.*
Garudha	Garuḍa bird	vermilion
Garudha pèk dhaṅ	Garuḍa carrying flag	vermilion
Măcchāṇu	fish-tailed monkey	white
Kraḥpil păkṣā	monkey-bird	black
Vāyubhăkṭra	kind of bird	dark blue
Nak dăndimā	kind of bird	light yellow
Mayura gandharba	fairy-peacock	light yellow
Mayura verṭai	garuḍa-peacock	light indigo
Suparṇa-herā	crocodile-bird	light green
Gajpăksī	elephant-bird	white
Deb kinnara	man-bird	yellow
Ăbṣara sīha	woman-lion	yellow
Deb narasiṅha	man-lion	white and gold
Bānara maruga	monkey-deer	green
Siṅha bānara	monkey-lion	vermilion
Mărīṣa	demon-deer	white and yellow
Asura păkṣā	demon-bird	green, red wings and tail
Nak kāravik	kind of bird	light vermilion
Sŭ'a pīk	winged tiger	yellow
Deb păkṣī	fairy-bird	white, red wings and tail
(Name lost)	kind of man-lion	yellow and green
Kinnari	woman-bird	white or cream
Kraiṣara rājasīha	kind of lion	white
Gajasīha	elephant-lion	violet
Sindhaba năddhī	water horse	white, red tail and fins
Sindhaba kunjra	elephant-horse	green with black tail
Kraiṣara păkṣā	bird-lion	vermilion
Săṅplèn	kind of lion	light yellow
Hemarā ăśtara	swan-horse	piebald, white tail
Ăśtara vihak	bird-horse	yellow, vermilion, black
Tosīha	kind of lion	light yellow
Siṅga bŏ'ṅ	kind of lion	violet
Bayăga kraisīha	lion-tiger	yellow

[1] Where a description consists of two hyphened words, the first word usually refers to the appearance of the fore-part of the creature, while the second refers to the hind-part. This list is adapted from that recently published in Bangkok, together with a drawing of each species, by Nāy Kro'n Śilpabejra.

Siamese Name.	*Description.*	*Traditional Colour.*
Siṅha kinlen	kind of lion	dark blue and purple
Siṅha rāmăṅkara	dragon-lion	vermilion
Ṯo debăśtaṛa	lion-horse	green, red fins and tail
Mā́ draṅ krū'aṅ	caparisoned horse	"natural colour"
Jā́ṅ phū'ak	white elephant	light red (nat. col.)
Varī kuñjara	water elephant	purple, green fins and tail
Karinda p̱ăkṣā	elephant-bird	black, green wings and tail
Siṅṯo cīn	Chinese lion	yellow
Kihmī	kind of lion	yellow
Bayăgverṯai	tiger-garuḍa	yellow, green wings and tail
Rèṯjā́ṅ	rhinoceros	reddish purple
Kraiṣara năddhī	water lion	blue
Kilen p̱īk	winged lion	blue
Duraṅga kraisīha	lion-horse	vermilion
Ăśtara herā	horned lion-horse	violet
Bayăga kraisīha	tiger-lion	dark yellow
Sakuṇa kraiṣara	bird-lion	light yellow
Sakuṇa herā	crocodile-bird	light yellow
Haṅṣa	swan	dark yellow
Haṅṣa cīn	Chinese swan	vermilion
Kài ṯăṅkia	Tonquin cock	light yellow
Nāga p̱ăkṣiṇa	nāga-bird	vermilion
Nak deśa	kind of bird	vermilion
Nak hăśatin	elephant-bird	white, yellow wings and tail
Nak indrī	eagle	green wings, yellow tail
Kraiṣara gāvī	cow-lion	black and white
Duraṅga p̱ăkṣiṇa	horse-bird	"natural colour of horse"
Ṅāy sai	caparisoned lion	indigo
Măṅkra sakunī	dragon-bird	grey, yellow wings and tail
Kài sechvan	Szechuan cock	yellow
Sindhu p̱ăkṣī	water bird	dark blue
Kumbhī nimiṯra	fairy-crocodile	white, purple tail
Kài hakkiā́n	Hokkien cock	vermilion
Hemrāja	swan-lion	vermilion

CHAPTER XIII

THE WORSHIP OF DEAD KINGS

There was probably a time when a primitive form of ancestor worship was common to all the peoples of Indo-China and, together with animism, formed their only religion, as it does to-day for most Chinese. Later, this came to be overlaid by forms derived from India, and so we have to-day in Siam, so far as the common people are concerned, an inextricable mixture of Indian and Mongolian forms of ancestor worship. In the first place, it is customary for every one who can afford it to give a feast at New Year at which the spirits of the dead are supposed to attend. Lighted candles and flowers are placed before the urns and Buddhist monks come to take part in the feast and recite appropriate stanzas and receive *satăpakaraṇa* gifts. This reception of the ancestral spirits at New Year is, despite its Buddhist setting, identical with similar festivals of Chinese origin, which take place in Annam, Cochin-China, Tonquin, and Japan.[1] On the other hand, Gerini [2] has shown the resemblance between the three sets of oblations offered at the commencement of every domestic ceremony and the *Baliyajña*, *Devayajña*, and *Pitriyajña*, or offerings to all creatures, to the gods, and to the *Pitris* (spirits of the dead) which form so conspicuous a feature of the Hindu *Śrāddhas*.

Coming now to the immediate subject of this chapter, the worship of dead kings, we find that this is an extremely widespread custom, as Frazer has shown in the various volumes of the *Golden Bough*; in fact, it is the logical sequel to the belief in the divinity of kings, and as such will bring to a natural conclusion our studies of Ceremonies of Installation. So far as Siam is concerned, the proximate origin of the worship of dead kings is to be found in the cult of the Deva-rāja in Cambodia, which was also known in Java and South India. We have discussed in Chapter IV with almost sufficient detail the nature of this Deva-rāja Cult, and have seen that it combined deification with ancestor worship, the Royal God being either worshipped as a *Śiva-liṅga* or as a statue of Viṣṇu or Śiva, having the features of the deceased king. Special shrines were devoted to this cult, and of these the most famous is Aṅkor Văt. According to an ancient legend current among the modern Cambodians, Aṅkor Văt was the supernaturally built

[1] *GB.* vi, pp. 62 sqq. [2] Ge. (1), pp. 40, 41.

palace of a king who was miraculously reborn a second time on earth after a short stay in Indra's paradise. Cheou Ta-kouan, as would appear natural to a Chinese, supposed that it was the tomb of a dead monarch; and now Coedès [1] has shown that it was indeed the palace of a king, but of a dead one, under the name of Paramaviṣṇuloka, who was supposed to inhabit the central tower of the temple. This deified monarch to whom this Viṣṇu temple was dedicated was either Udayadityavarman II (1048–79) or Sūryavarman II (1112–1165).

The rulers of the first independent Thai kingdom at Sukhodaya retained, as we have seen, as much as they could of Khmer Hinduism the better to support their new-found majesty, at the same time revering and protecting the recently introduced Hīnayānistic Buddhism. The latter, at least in its popular form, was not incompatible with the worship of the dead king who, as a Bodhisattva, might be in a position to aid those still on earth; but this worship could no longer rank in degree or fervour with that which had been accorded to the Khmer Deva-rāja by Hinduism or even Mahāyānism. Nevertheless right down to the present day two methods of showing honour to the deceased kings of the dynasty remain, one of which is apparently Hindu, the other Buddhist.

In the former, the reigning king goes to pay his respects before the golden life-size statues of the deceased kings of the dynasty which are enshrined in niches in that fine cruciform building, surmounted by a tall Cambodian *praṅg*, situated within the precincts of the Grand Palace, and known as the Hò Braḥ Debpitara, or Pantheon (Pl. XXVIII). The King, on entering the shrine, lights candles and makes the usual obeisance with joined palms before the statues, and then retires; after which the nobles, officials, and members of the general public of both sexes crawl into the building on hands and knees, prostrate themselves before the statues, and pay homage with joined palms, and then they crawl out through another door. Surely this is very much what used to happen in the shrines dedicated to the Royal God in ancient Cambodia. The only difference between the statues of the Bangkok kings and the deified kings of the Khmers is that instead of being represented with the attributes of gods, they are true portrait statues; but this is an innovation of the Bangkok period, indeed the first three kings never allowed themselves to be portrayed, and their statues are based on the composite ideas of four old people who had seen all three kings and were ordered by King Rāma IV to instruct an artist.

The Buddhist method of paying respect to the dead kings takes the

[1] Coedès, *Les Bas Reliefs d'Angkor*, p. 59.

PLATE XXVIII.

[Photo : Bangkok Times Press, Ltd.

STATUES OF THE KINGS OF THE CAKRĪ DYNASTY IN THE PANTHEON.

[To face page 170.

PLATE XXIX.

[Photo: Bangkok Times Press, Ltd.

ROYAL RELICS PLACED IN STATE ON AN ALTAR IN THE AMARINDRĀ HALL.

form of placing the urned relics under a nine-tiered umbrella-of-state on an altar in the Amarindrā (Pl. XXIX) Hall or in the new Anănta Samāgama Hall, where the King and Queen light candles and incense-sticks, and pay the usual homage before the relics.[1] A chapter of monks recites stanzas, an abbot preaches a sermon, and the King lays down robes for the *Satăpakaraṇa* rite. Candles are also lit before the altar on which are the images of Buddha cast for the reigns which are being honoured. These images are cast merely as an act of merit, and as symbolizing the royal devotion to Buddhism. They do not represent the kings as incipient Buddhas, and are therefore not to be confounded with the statues in the Pantheon and the Brahmanic conception. Similarly, small images are cast for every year of each king's age, and are kept in the Căkrī Palace during his lifetime, and afterwards placed in the Chapel Royal.

At New Year, Coronation Anniversary, and on Căkrī Day, the latter kept on 6th April as a memorial to the accession of the Căkrī dynasty, the relics of all the deceased kings of the dynasty and their first queens are thus honoured, and reverence is also paid to the statues in the Pantheon as above described. On the anniversary of the death of King Rāma V and on that of King Rāma VI, the relics of these two kings only are honoured, each on the appropriate day, the relics of the Queen Mother, i.e. the first queen of King Rāma V, being also honoured with those of that king. But on these occasions there is no celebration in the Pantheon.

Although, on all the above occasions, the Chapel Royal is open for members of the general public to worship before the Emerald Buddha (after the King has left the building) and on Căkrī Day the public are also admitted into the Pantheon, yet the honouring of the actual relics is a semi-private affair, only the Royal Family, the nobles, and official world taking part in the homage. This was appropriate in the days when the people were kept at a distance from royalty, and when the only function that such ceremonies had was to increase the nobles' and officials' fear of, and respect for, the dynasty. But King Rāma V created in the hearts of his subjects an entirely new outlook with regard to the ruler, a deep personal affection for the sovereign who had done so much to relieve the hardships of his people, as apart from the ingrained traditional respect for the kingship. Hence, after his death, there arose a spontaneous desire for an annual opportunity for the people to pay public homage to his memory. This

[1] The classical Buddhist precedent of honouring relics is the occasion on which the Mallas paid homage for seven days before the relics of the Buddha (*Mahā-Parinibbāna Sutta*, vi, 50). It was, of course, founded on earlier Brahmanic usage.

was provided by the institution of a public holiday on the anniversary of his death, known as Cuḷālaṅkaraṇa Day (23rd October). On this day the great equestrian statue of King Rāma V, situated in the middle of the royal plaza, is surrounded with a *rājavăt* fence adorned with tiered umbrellas, and the base of the statue is massed with wreaths and artistic floral decorations, the tribute of schools, government departments, and commercial bodies. The King and Queen arrive by motor-car and, after inspecting the floral tributes, light candles and incense-sticks and offer flowers on the altar placed opposite the western entrance to the enclosure. Then they kneel and pay homage, while aeroplanes circle overhead. The National Anthem is played, and the King and Queen drive away. Throughout the day thousands of people take advantage of the opportunity to pay homage before the statue and, although music and refreshments are provided on both sides of the plaza, the occasion is celebrated with befitting dignity.

The fifth anniversary (1930) of the death of King Rāma VI was celebrated on an unusually grand scale, the ceremonies extending over three days, 25th, 26th, and 27th November. It has been the custom in recent years to commemorate the death of any notable person by the publication of a Siamese historical, literary, or religious work, selected from amongst the manuscripts preserved in the National Library. This is a very excellent custom which has done much to spread the knowledge and appreciation of the national literature. The enormous task of printing a new edition of the whole *Tripiṭaka* was undertaken by public subscription in order to commemorate the death of the late King, and this has recently been completed—1,500 sets, each of forty-five volumes. The completion of this great national work was celebrated together with the usual rites for the honouring of the relics of the late King. The special features were that on 26th November, part of the Scriptures were carried in procession from the Theological School at Văt Pavaranivesa to the Chapel Royal and there placed on the altar, together with the image of the Buddha (named Braḥ Buddhapatima Jayavadhana) for the sixth reign. The King lit candles before this image, before the Emerald Buddha, and before the *Tripiṭaka*. A sermon was preached, and a chapter of monks performed the consecration service. Afterwards the King proceeded to the Royal Pavilion erected on the lawn behind the Chapel Royal, where he witnessed lantern dances and other appropriate entertainments. Then he lit fireworks as a mark of worship, and took his departure. On the Royal Cremation Ground were a few theatres and other forms of entertainment for the public, but they were not on a very grand scale owing to the prevailing desire for economy. I noticed that the *Rāmāyaṇa* masked drama still holds first place among Siamese entertainments in the hearts of the populace. The Chapel Royal was also open for the public to pay their respects before the Buddha for the sixth reign, and the Emerald Buddha. Here again I mingled with the crowds that passed through the sacred fane and noticed their awed humility and deep respect when within the holy precincts. Next day the King visited the Chapel Royal once more, and presented food and other gifts to the monks who had officiated the day before. A *vian dian* rite performed by the Brahmans for the benefit of the sacred books—indeed a remarkable instance of the fusion of Buddhism and Hinduism in Siam—concluded the rites, after which the *Tripiṭaka* was taken back to the Theological School.

In the year 1932 will occur the 150th anniversary of the founding of the City of Bangkok, and very special celebrations are to take place as they did at the Bangkok Centenary, which will include the honouring of the relics of Rāma I the founder, of whom a bronze image, to be placed at the head of the new Mènāṁ bridge, is shortly to be cast in Italy.

One more method of paying homage to deceased kings in Siam remains to be mentioned: the setting of a photograph or lithograph of the particular king on a table, before which are made the usual offerings of lighted candles, flowers, and incense. This is now a very popular custom, both in government institutions and private houses, since every Siamese home possesses at least a cheap lithograph and can thus show its loyalty in this easy and practical manner. But it is of course quite a new custom, since the making of royal portraits only came into fashion after the middle of last century, after the belief that this was harmful to the person represented had been officially discountenanced. Indeed, the supposition that some part of the royal " soul " (if one may be permitted to use this loose term) might possibly inhabit the portrait,[1] would be an added stimulus to paying homage before it. It is also a modern means of expressing what remains of the worship of the living King, for whenever it is desired to honour him, especially on the occasion of a royal procession, portraits of the King set up on tables may be seen at almost every Siamese doorway along the route.

In determining the exact degree of " worship " that remains in the honouring of the relics, statues, and pictures of the deceased king at the present time, one must beware of generalization. One cannot, for example, compare the homage to the statues in the Pantheon with

[1] *GB.* iii, pp. 96 sqq.

the homage of the people before the equestrian statue of King Rāma V. In the former, respect for the abstract conception of the kingship is uppermost, and as such is a relic of the Khmer cult of the Royal God; whereas in the latter we have something entirely new, respect for the memory of a great sovereign and a good man, a loyal and spontaneous show of affection, which might, perhaps not inappropriately, be compared to the attitude of those gathered before the Cenotaph in Whitehall to honour the memory of those who fell in the Great War. I have been present both at the Pantheon on Căkrī Day and at the equestrian statue on Cuḷālaṅkaraṇa Day, and have endeavoured to analyse the attitude of the people. As I have said, one cannot generalize, and it seems that the attitude of mind on these occasions depends largely on the individual. The more ignorant portions of the masses seem to retain a good deal of that blind respect for the kingship as such, which probably characterized the Khmers in the days of the Deva-rāja cult—and popular Buddhism, with its desire to make merit and its prayers for material benefits offered before the altar of the Buddha, differs little from such popular worship amongst the Hindus. But it seems probable that, with the spread of education, the greater knowledge of the purer tenets of Buddhism and the substitution, gradual but inevitable, of respect for the Man in the place of respect for Divine Kingship, the attitude of mind in which respect is offered to the memory of dead kings, will tend to approximate more and more to that of other advanced nations, of whatever creed. In this coming change the present dynasty, who have long made themselves the true fathers of their people, have nothing to fear, and one cannot imagine the time when such days of remembrance will cease to have a sociological value.

PART IV

CEREMONIES CLOSELY CONNECTED WITH THE KINGSHIP

CHAPTER XIV

ROYAL AUDIENCES [1]

1. *State Audiences and the Reception of Embassies.*

With the establishment of modern diplomatic relations with foreign powers and the appointment of resident foreign representatives, State Audiences, such as were accorded to foreign embassies in the days when they were few and far between, have almost become a thing of the past. Intercourse with European powers and with America pursues its even course through the ordinary diplomatic channels, and when the King receives a diplomat or distinguished visitor he receives him in Private Audience in the Anănta Samăgama Throne Hall on the same quietly dignified lines as mark such occasions in Europe.

The State Audience takes place now only on great occasions such as following the Coronation, and on the Coronation Anniversary, and is simply the occasion for offering a congratulatory address to the King, who replies shortly in suitable terms. On the occasion of the Coronation of King Prajadhipok, I was fortunate in being present at the State Audience, and under unusual conditions. The setting was well fitted to inspire those present with a sense of the majesty of the occasion: Troops in brilliant uniforms lined the courtyards leading to the Amarindră Hall, where the audience took place. Officials in still more gorgeous uniforms, over which were draped gowns of silver or golden tissue, thronged the courtyards. Every department was represented, but perhaps the most numerous uniforms were the striking sky-blue and silver of the Mahhătlek and the black and gold of the officers of the Royal Household. The sun shone brilliantly, and the green, vermilion, and the yellow tiles of the temple roofs and the blazing gold of the great pagoda vied with the splendour of the uniforms in their combined effort to dazzle the human eye. The officials and nobles, the Diplomatic Corps, and a considerable number of European officials crowded into the Hall, which is of noble proportions, but with its decoration of light and dark green and silver appeared sombre in comparison with the splendour of the uniforms. The officials stood in groups and every now and then glanced towards

[1] The chief sources are the writings of the seventeenth century European ambassadors and missionaries, especially La Loubère and Gervaise. *Siamese Embassies to Europe*, by H.R.H. Prince Damrong, has also been found useful.

the heavy golden curtains which cut off a raised dais at one end of the Hall. It was there that at a given signal the King would appear.

I was anxious to see the proceedings from *behind* the curtain where were grouped around the golden throne chamberlains and pages of the Maḥhātlek, those officers whose duty it was to be in closest attendance upon the King, and I took up my position among them near the wall on the right of the throne. The King, wearing full state robes and the Great Crown of Victory, entered the curtained-off part of the Amarindrā Hall by means of a door leading from the Baiśāla Hall, and immediately ascended the throne, the chamberlains bowing their respects. As soon as the King had arranged his robes and signified his readiness, a fanfare resounded and three taps of two ivory blocks were the signal for the curtains to be suddenly drawn to reveal to the waiting officials the King on his throne of audience. The lighting was very cleverly arranged to present the King as the centre of a symmetrical picture of glittering gold. This golden audience throne called *Braḥ-dī-năṅ Budṯān Dòṅ* (Golden Hibiscus Throne) differs from the *Bhadrapiṭha* in being more highly ornamented and set on a tall tiered pyramid, carved with figures of *devatās* and *garuḍas*. It was flanked by tables bearing the regalia and by gold and silver trees, while above was reared the nine-tiered white umbrella. The King sat perfectly still, and seemed like an image in a niche. He listened intently to the address of homage and congratulation offered by Prince Barṇarăṅsī, who stood in front of the princes and nobles gathered in order of precedence below the dais. He moved only once, and that was to take from a chamberlain a scroll from which he read his reply. This completed, Prince Barṇarăṅsī intimated his acceptance of the royal commands, the officials bowed, the fanfare sounded, and the curtains immediately closed to blot from the eyes of those in the body of the hall this imposing picture. Once the curtains had fallen the King relaxed, and while he was relieved of his crown he smilingly joked with those around him. This part of the procedure was to me the most interesting, as it showed the quite pleasing and unassuming manner of a modern Siamese king when surrounded by none but his personal officers.

This magnificent State Audience was hailed at the time by some of the newspapers as a fine example of " veneration of the past ". If the journalists concerned had taken the trouble to discover what was the form of audiences in the past they might have observed that, except for the attire of the King, this occasion bore little resemblance to the State Audiences of old. To me it seemed that the modern lighting effects, the uniforms of the Maḥhātlek, and those of the nobles and officials, suggested rather a Court function of some Balkan capital. I noticed the presence of no antique uniforms such as give the impression of Old Siam to most of the State Ceremonies, but only that efflorescence of semi-European styles which was evolved in the last reign, but which has happily undergone considerable curtailment during the present one. This is especially fortunate in the case of the Kram Maḥhātlek, which department has been abolished, and the uniform of which, by no means unpleasing in itself, did much to mar the appearance of many a Court ceremony on account of its close proximity to the royal person. The structure and appearance of the type of throne used, the lack of all prostration, indeed the proceedings in general, made it difficult to connect the present spectacle with its prototype in Old Siam.

The State or Public Audience, being a non-religious ceremony, so far as anything connected with a divine monarch can be considered as non-religious, has changed more readily from time to time in accordance with the etiquette in use in those countries from which embassies were most frequently received. Thus, if the etiquette was originally entirely Hindu, which is suggested by its resemblance to that of Pegu and Ceylon, it was affected by Chinese influence at times when intercourse was more frequent with that country; while from the seventeenth century onwards Siam has been doing her best to withstand the repeated attempts of European countries to force their methods of diplomacy upon her. In the last century the missions of Crawfurd (1822) and Bowring (1856) are, especially the former, replete with the difficulties which they encountered as a result of mutual misunderstandings. Although Bowring succeeded in concluding a treaty, and establishing modern diplomatic relations, with the right of foreign representatives to follow their own customs when attending Court, it was not until the reign of King Rāma V that prostration was abolished for the Siamese themselves, and State Audiences assumed nearly their present form.

In the eighteenth century Siam was practically closed to Europeans, except the Dutch, there being otherwise only the abortive mission of Philip V of Spain in 1718. This seclusion was due to the sharp lesson which the Siamese had learnt at the end of the seventeenth century when a timely revolution only just saved Siam from becoming a French colony. The intercourse which nearly gave France possession of the country was marked by two embassies : (1) that of de Chaumont in 1685 of which we have full accounts in the writings of the ambassador himself, and those of the missionaries Tachard and Gervaise; (2) that of La Loubère in 1687–8. He, unlike any other early European ambassador, was able to forget his own difficulties sufficiently to give us a very valuable objective account of the Siamese etiquette. The French were also more sympathetic and willing to conform to the outward forms than were the ambassadors of other nations, and perhaps they had also greater knowledge, derived from their missionaries who had preceded them. Thus it is that although we have two early Dutch accounts of the forms of audiences,[1] and there was a Siamese embassy to Prince Maurice of Orange as early as 1607, it is from the French accounts that I take most of the following details as to the customs relative to State Audiences and the Reception of Embassies as they were at a time before they were corrupted by European influence.

The most striking point with regard to the Siamese idea of an embassy, and the one which most astonished the early European ambassadors, was that it was the custom in Siam and other Far Eastern countries to regard the foreign king's letter as the essential factor, to pay all respects to it, and to regard the ambassadors as mere messengers. But if this hurt the pride of the European ambassadors, it was as nothing to the insult which the Siamese monarchs felt, and rightly felt in my opinion, was inflicted upon them when they found that, in the case of the first British and the Spanish missions, the letter was not sent by the King, but by a governor-general. At first the Siamese were ready to believe that this functionary might be the King's brother, an *Uparāja* or Second King, but on learning that he was a mere official of State that had dared to address his Siamese Majesty, a person who would have been compelled to grovel in the dust before his king had he been a Siamese, their indignation was unbounded; for quite naturally they were unable to understand delegated authority. It was a similarly limited outlook that involved the British in so much trouble in Burma, where the King also felt himself degraded by the epistles he received directly from the Goompanee Min, or King Company, a term coined, somewhat ironically, I presume, to express that importunate body of merchants, the East India Company. There can be no doubt whatever that the French owed their success at the end of the seventeenth century largely to the fact that their letters were couched in glowing terms and emanated directly from their King. Later, the British appreciated the position and Sir John Bowring was charged with a letter directly from the Queen. Following our study of the conception of the kingship, the two ideas that the Royal Letter was alone worthy of respect and that only a king could address a king, will be readily understood.

[1] F. Caron and J. Schouten, 1662, and J. Struys, Eng. ed., 1684.

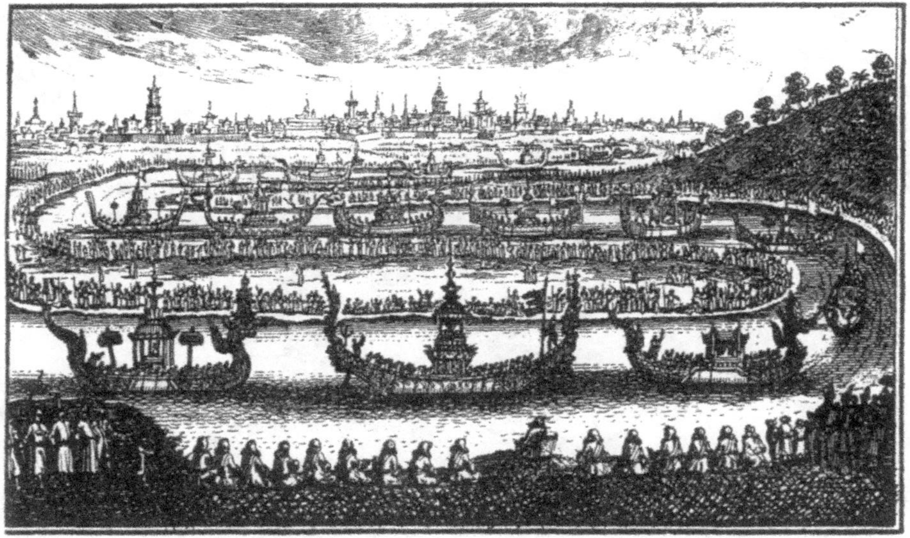

[*Reproduced from Tachard.*

FIG. 2.—ARRIVAL OF THE FRENCH EMBASSY AT AYUDHYĀ.

To face page 181.]

When a ship conveying a foreign embassy arrived at the mouth of the river, it was obligatory to unship all guns, and the ship proceeded independently to the capital. A procession of state barges was sent down to receive the letter and the ambassadors (Fig. 2). The Royal Letter was placed in a gold receptacle, and placed on the head of the Siamese bearer, as a sign of respect; then it was carried under a royal umbrella to a Throne Barge, and installed under the spire. The ambassadors followed in less splendid barges, and on arrival were accommodated with what degree of comfort the country could afford. The first audience was with the *Braḥ Glăṅ*, a sort of Minister of Commerce or Minister of Foreign Affairs, the two posts being regarded as the same in those days, since all foreigners appeared to be connected with trade. It was at these audiences that the ceremonial to be observed at the Royal Audience was decided, and several visits to the *Braḥ Glăṅ* were often necessary before an agreement could be reached, on account of the obstinacy displayed on both sides. The *Braḥ Glăṅ* refused to return the ambassador's visits because such was against etiquette until after the Royal Audience; nor were the ambassadors allowed to go about freely in the city, but were placed under a strict watch until after the Royal Audience. Then they were allowed complete freedom, and were supposed to be safe from all rudeness on the part of the populace, being considered to be under the King's protection; and they were also then allowed to engage in trading if they wished. Presents of food were frequently sent to them, and a sum of money was granted for their maintenance, it being the custom for the King to bear all the expenses of the mission while resident in the country. This was contrary to European custom, and an added insult in the eyes of the ambassadors was the fact that the amount of the payment, which would no doubt have been ample for the upkeep of Asiatic messengers, was to the Europeans a mere pittance. The British ambassadors refused to accept it, and this mutual misunderstanding was another obstacle in the way of the success of their missions.

According to Gervaise there was a marked difference in the mode of reception of the Letter, according to whether it was sent by a sovereign who was regarded as an equal or merely as a vassal. In the latter case the Letter was kept by the *Braḥ Glăṅ*, and a translation into Siamese was made; it was placed until the day of audience in a small house having a pyramidal shape, outside the city wall, and was presented to the King on the day of audience by a Siamese official. In the case of a king of equal rank the procedure was different: the ambassadors accompanied the Letter in full state to the palace, and were allowed to present it to the King themselves. This was the procedure followed in the case of de Chaumont and La Loubère, but Crawfurd was evidently treated as a vassal, for his letter was not even produced at the audience, and only the translation of it was read; nor were the interpreters belonging to the mission allowed to function. This mistake on the part of the Siamese of regarding the British in the light of vassals is understandable, since Crawfurd's letter came only from a governor-general, and hence the mission could not be considered to rank with that of a sovereign. The King would not consent to discuss a treaty with him, and he was told to confer with the *Braḥ Glăṅ*, who was regarded as the proper person to whom such a letter should have been addressed.

When at last the preliminaries had been settled, and the audience day had arrived, the ambassadors went in procession through the decorated streets, and were saluted by the guards, who were drawn up. The White Elephant and royal chargers were also on show for the occasion within the courtyards of the palace. When they reached the inner gate, the ambassadors were required to remove their shoes, also their swords or other weapons, no one being allowed to enter the King's presence armed. King Rāma IV was the first to waive this rule, when he allowed Sir John Bowring's officers to retain their swords. As a rule the members of the ambassadors' suite were not allowed to accompany them into the Audience Hall.

At the State Audiences at Ayudhyā the form of throne was peculiar and different from that used at Bangkok. It was, in fact, not in the Hall of Audience at all but in an adjoining room belonging to a higher storey, and from a window of which, situated about 10 feet above the ground, the King had a prospect of the Audience Hall (Fig. 3). The King's throne or seat could not actually be seen, and at the termination of the audience it was drawn away by unseen hands, and the shutters were closed. La Loubère remarks that this form of window throne was also in use in China, and I think it was probably derived therefrom, since embassies were exchanged between China and Cambodia from the third century A.D., and in the thirteenth century Rāma Gāṁhèṅ himself visited the Imperial Court. There were similar arrangements at Labapurī, which was a favourite residence of King Nārāyaṇa. The ruins still remain in tolerably good preservation. I have visited them personally, and found the Audience Hall very similar to that which existed at Ayudhyā, as figured by La Loubère. The modern arrangement of curtains and a comparatively low gilded throne is therefore an innovation of the Bangkok period. It was in use at the first Bangkok audience of which we have a record, i.e. in

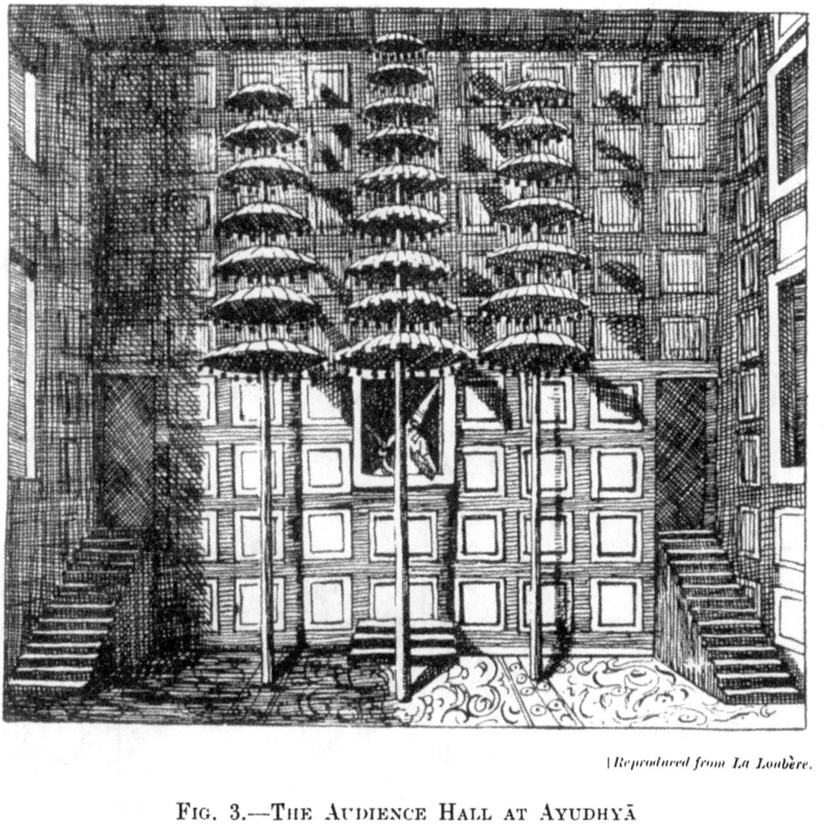

[Reproduced from La Loubère.

FIG. 3.—THE AUDIENCE HALL AT AYUDHYĀ

[To face page 182.

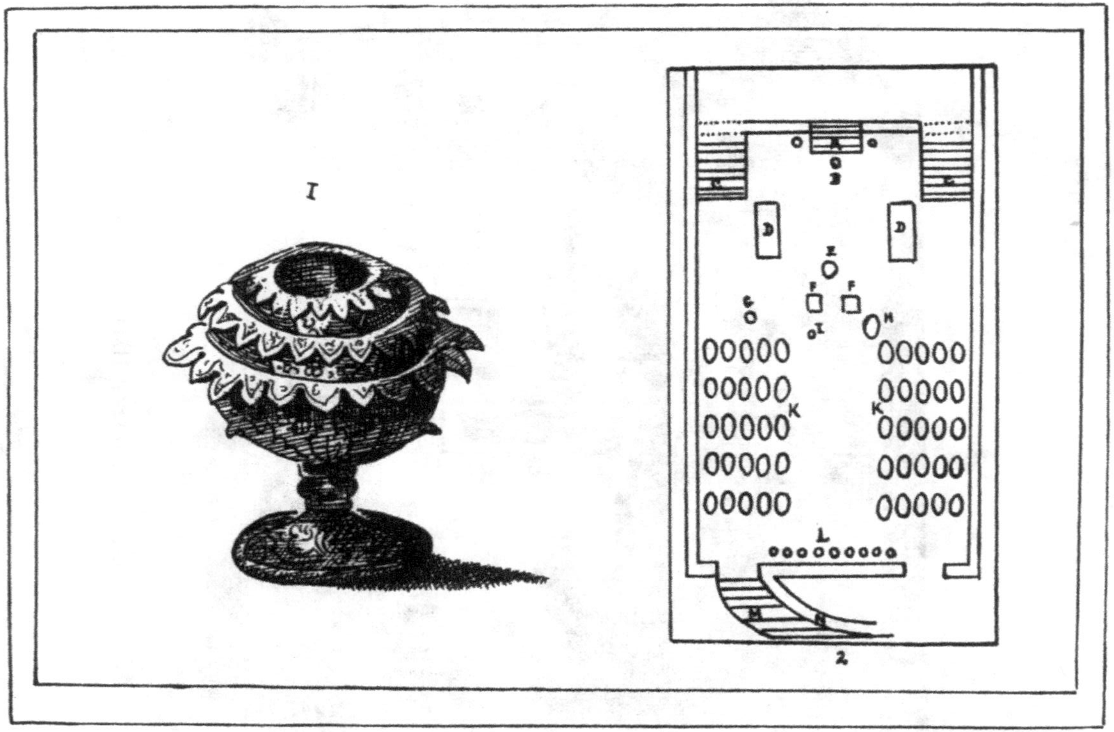

[Reproduced from *La Loubère*.

FIG. 4.—1, GOLD VESSEL FOR THE KING'S LETTER; 2, PLAN OF AUDIENCE HALL.

the reign of King Rāma II. On either side of the audience window was placed an umbrella of seven stages, and above it was reared one of nine tiers. The Siamese officers of State were arranged in the Audience Hall strictly in accordance with their order of precedence, the nearest about twenty paces from the window, and of course they were all prostrate throughout the proceedings. The ambassadors, and in the seventeenth century those French missionaries who were also allowed to be present to act as interpreters, were given whatever place the King thought suited to their rank, and they were allowed to sit or stand according to that relaxation of rule which the King had been prevailed upon to allow, but with special orders to keep their feet and the lower parts of their bodies hidden. When the King appeared, all paid homage by raising the joined palms three times and lowering the head until the forehead touched the ground, but the latter part was not insisted upon for Europeans. The same salute terminated the proceedings. The following interesting extract from La Loubère describes the arrangement of the Audience Hall during the State Audience at which his embassy was received[1]:—

"(*a*) Three Steps which are placed under the Window, where the King of Siam was, to raise me high enough to deliver him the King's Letter from hand to hand.

"(*b*) Three Parasols or Umbrellas.

"(*c*) Two pair of Stairs to go up into the place where the King of Siam was.

"(*d*) Two Tables covered with Tapestry, on which were laid the King's Present, which could be held there.

"(*e*) The Son of Mr. Ceberet standing, holding the King's Letter in a Gold Bason of Filigreen with a triple Story.

"(*f*) Two little square and low Stools, each covered with a little Carpet, for the King's Envoys to sit on. Monsieur de Chaumont had such another.

"(*g*) The Bishop of Metellopolis, Apostolick Vicar, sitting cross-legged.

"(*h*) Monsieur Constance prostrate at my right hand, and behind me to serve as my interpreter.

"(*i*) Father Tachart sitting cross-legged.

"(*k*) Fifty Mandarins prostrate.

"(*l*) The French Gentlemen sitting with their Legs across.

"(*m*) A little pair of Brick Stairs to go up to the Hall of Audience.

"(*n*) The Wall whereunto this pair of Stairs is fixed."

It will be noticed that one European, Monsieur Constance (*h*), was prostrate, like the Siamese officers. He was not a Frenchman, but the famous Greek adventurer, Constantine Phaulkon, who had

[1] See Fig. 4.

entered the Siamese Service some years before, and succeeded in rising to the position of the King's most trusted minister.

The gold vessel (Fig. 4) for the King's Letter, was of three stories. This was in accordance with the custom by which a triple-storied vessel was considered proper for the reception of the Letter of a king of equal rank to the Siamese king, one of only two stories being allotted to an inferior monarch.

The three steps below the window (*a*) were a modification introduced specially for La Loubère's embassy. It was the custom for the ambassador to hand up the letter to the King by means of a gold receptacle having a very long handle. De Chaumont, the previous ambassador, had for some reason difficult to understand thought this procedure derogatory to his dignity. He therefore held the vessel itself, not the end of its handle, and this obliged the King to stoop down, which he smilingly did, thereby showing a grace which seems to contrast favourably with the gauche manner of the ambassador. To guard against a repetition of this undignified scene the three steps had been erected.

The proceedings at a State Audience were short and formal. A prostrate secretary read a list of the foreign king's presents, the portable part of which were arranged on the tables before the window. The foreign king's letter was then presented in the manner above described, after which the prostrate *Braḥ Glăṅ*, his face nearly touching the ground, read the translation. Then,

> "The King [through interpreters] made three customary and formal questions. First: Were the king and royal family of the foreign country in good health? Second: Did the envoy have a good journey, and how long did it take? and Third: Was the rainfall satisfactory in the rainy season of his country, and were the people prosperous?" [1]

The King expected only short replies. He disliked anything in the nature of a harangue, and since the ambassadors were regarded only as royal messengers, not as plenipotentiaries, there was really no reason for a long discussion. An official gave the ambassadors a small present of betel from the King. This offering of betel to the ambassadors at various times, especially on arrival, long ago took the place of the old Hindu custom of offering scented water, golden bowls, and white cloth for ablution.[2] Other small presents such as umbrellas and Siamese cloth were sent to the ambassadors' residence, for they were expected to dress in Siamese fashion during their stay. Immediately after the presentation of betel, the audience terminated with the

[1] *Siamese Embassies to Europe*, p. 16.

[2] Gerini, *Impl. and Asiatic Quarterly Review*, x.

usual three obeisances, the King then withdrawing to the accompaniment of a fanfare of trumpets.

Cheou Ta-kouan, who describes a royal audience in Cambodia at the close of the thirteenth century, mentions that the King sat at a golden window; but I think this must then have been a recent innovation, for the *History of the Leang* (502–56) remarks that

> "when the king sits down he squats sideways, lifting the right knee, letting fall the left knee to the ground," [1]

and in the Aṅkor bas-reliefs the king is invariably shown seated in this position on a low throne of Indian style.

During the stay of the ambassadors they were shown the various sights of the city, especially the White Elephant, and the King usually granted them one or more private audiences. These differed from the State Audience mainly by reason of the fact that in them the King was not seated in the window, but in the audience chamber

> "in a wooden Tower joined to the Floor of the Hall, into which he entered behind, and immediately, by a Step higher than the Hall." [2]

Struys seems to describe a similar throne, although of gold, when he says:—

> "His supreme Throne is of massive Gold, made after the form of a pyramid, and so contrived that none can see him ascend." [3]

Possibly these thrones represent earlier forms of the tall *Braḥ-dī-nàṅ Budṯān Dòṅ* of the present day.

The ambassadors were also expected to pay their respects to the Second King, who received them in the same way as had the Supreme King, even asking the same formal questions. They had also to visit the high officials of the country, and on all occasions had to present gifts. A final State Audience of leave-taking took place after the conclusion of all business, and after this the ambassadors were prohibited from moving about the city, and were expected to leave immediately.

It was not the custom for the King to send a letter in return by the hands of the foreign ambassadors. He always sent an embassy of his own, if possible in his own royal ships. Such an embassy was sent to Louis XIV, and again to Queen Victoria, but in these cases it was impossible strictly to adhere to the custom of using a Siamese ship. A Siamese embassy consisted of three officers called respectively

[1] Pelliot, *BEFEO*. iii, 1903, p. 269.
[2] L. L., p. 109.
[3] *The Voyages of John Struys*, Eng. ed., 1684.

rājadūṭ, *upadūṭ*, and *trīdūṭ*, the first being the ambassador proper, but the fact that his title was never higher than *braḥ* indicates that he was not considered a very important personage.

Several other considerations throw further light on the Siamese conception of an embassy. The slowness and delays in completing all the preliminary arrangements, as well as the loftiness of the throne or audience window, the distant and reserved bearing of the King, and his condescension in making presents to the ambassadors, were all processes contrived to impress upon them the dignity and power of the King. Again, it was a maxim of Siamese kings to receive many embassies, but to send as few as possible. There was honour in receiving an embassy, but, on the other hand, there was always present the idea that the one who sent the first embassy was offering homage. The very great store that was set upon the reception of the presents, the King even sending secretaries on board the foreign ships to make an inventory before the gifts were actually presented, indicates the desire to regard them as tribute, if possible. This point of view was not unnatural since the main object of British and Dutch embassies to Siam and Burma was to ask for trade concessions, whereas the Siamese and Burmese desired only to be left alone. Another characteristic of the Siamese monarchs was their dislike of concluding a treaty. While prepared to make promises, they did not like to commit themselves to writing, an instinct of self-preservation, for they were not ignorant of the growth of British power in India, and they feared that they might sign away their sovereign rights.

It is hardly necessary to repeat that the difficulties experienced by European ambassadors were entirely due to a mutual misunderstanding. The Siamese system was well fitted to function in the way it was intended, i.e. for intercourse with the neighbouring vassal states, and with great China. There is a very interesting Sinhalese account of an embassy from King Kirti Śrī of Ceylon to the King of Siam in 1750.[1] Buddhism at that time had fallen to very low estate in Ceylon, and King Kirti Śrī sent to ask that a delegation of Siamese monks might be sent to improve matters. This was certainly a great honour for the King of Siam, and the Sinhalese king was regarded as being his equal. The result was that the ambassadors on returning from their mission, which was successful, expressed their great satisfaction at the kind treatment which they had received according to etiquette, which was exactly on the lines which have been described above.

[1] Translated in *Journal of the Royal Asiatic Society*, Ceylon Branch, vol. xviii, No. 54, 1903.

2. *Audiences to Officials and Petitioners.*

In the Laws of Manu, which have already been quoted in Chapter IV, it will be remembered that one of the chief duties of kings was to give audiences to ministers and officials and to hear those who might wish to present petitions ; and we have also mentioned that in the Coronation Audience the King promised to hear every official so far as opportunity might allow. Some of the audiences of Old Siam were in the nature of secret councils, which might be compared to the meetings of the modern Supreme Council of State, and Gervaise describes King Nārāyaṇa's audiences to his councillors as follows :—

> " After breakfast he goes into his Grand Council at eight o'clock and stays there until noon. There in the Council is Monsieur de Constance [Phaulkon the Greek adventurer], his first Minister, who tenders him an exact and faithful account of the chief affairs of the kingdom which need to be discussed. When he has finished, the King goes over all that he has said in the presence of the mandarins, his First Councillors of State, and asks their advice on these matters. They all prostrate themselves on the ground, leaning only on their elbows, unless they are excused keeping themselves in that posture while in the presence of His Majesty. Each Mandarin prefaces his remarks with a little compliment which he renders to the King approximately in these terms : ' Sire, since Your Royal and Divine word has seen fit to descend upon me who am but filth and dust, I place it respectfully on my head, and find in me the boldness to tell Your Majesty what I think of the matter that You have deigned to discuss with me who am but Your slave.' After they have all had their say, His Majesty then speaks giving his decision, unless he allows them to reply again. If, during the discussion of the matter in question, the King has noticed that some secret reason or private interest has prevented one of his councillors from saying sincerely and in good faith what he really thinks, then he suspends judgment until he knows that Minister's true feelings on the matter ; and, in order that the persons shall not feel injured by knowing that the Minister is being enquired about by His Majesty, the King sends secretly, and unknown to the other councillors, to question that minister on what he desires to know."

At eight o'clock in the evening the King again met his councillors :—

> " As he is accustomed to keep until the evening his decision on the matters of greatest consequence which have been conveyed to him in the morning, it is rare that anyone brings up new matter unless it is very urgent, so that the councillors have time to think over the morning's affairs during the day. This meeting of the councillors, however, does not end before midnight." [1]

[1] Gervaise, part iv, chap. 4, translation from the French (1684) by H. S. O'Neill, Bangkok, 1928, pp. 116, 117.

A seventh century Chinese account of a meeting of royal councillors in ancient Cambodia supplies us with the prototype of the above :—

> " There were five classes of high officials ; when they appear before the king they thrice touch the ground in front of the steps of the throne. The king orders them to mount up the steps, and then they kneel with their hands crossed over their shoulders. Then they sit in a circle round the king for discussing state affairs. When the meeting of the council is over, they kneel down again and take leave. At the gate of the throne-room there are a thousand guards in armour armed with lances." [1]

As to the presentation of petitions, Cheou Ta-kouan wrote of the procedure in thirteenth century Cambodia as follows :—

> " Each day the king holds audience twice for the affairs of state. The list is not restricted. Those of the officials or of the people who wish to see him sit on the ground and wait. After a while, one hears distant music in the palace, and, outside, conches are blown as a welcome to the king. An instant later one sees two palace girls draw back the curtain, and the king, sword in hand, appears at the golden window. Ministers and people joined their hands and lowered their foreheads to the ground. When the noise had ceased they could raise their heads. Following the pleasure of the king, they approached to sit down. In the place where the petitioner might sit, there was a lion's skin which was regarded as a royal emblem ; when the business was finished, the prince retired, the two palace girls let the curtain fall, and everyone rose from the ground." [2]

Gervaise gives rather a long account of this type of audience, which shows that after a lapse of four centuries the procedure was practically the same, though marked by a greater degree of servility on the part of the petitioner. As he gives interesting details which further illustrate the relations between the king and his subjects at that time, it will be worth while to quote his account *in extenso* :—

> " When he grants them an audience in his palace, it is always from the embrasure of one of his windows. Before the shutters are opened there are trumpets sounded to warn everybody that His Majesty is about to appear, and everybody bows his head towards the ground, and he who craves for an audience makes from a distance three deep bows to His Majesty. Then he steps forward three paces, to the spot that has been marked out for him. This position is always some distance from the window, more or less according to the superiority of the rank of the petitioner. When he arrives at this place he must make another three similar bows and remain there prostrated upon a mat or carpet, his hands clasped together and his head turned in such a way that he cannot look into the King's face. An interpreter by his side informs the great mandarin who is present, of the nature of the matter which the petitioner wishes to bring up, and the Minister or mandarin repeats this to the King, makes the three usual bows

[1] C., p. 61. [2] Pelliot, *BEFEO.*, loc. cit.

and prepares his Majesty to listen, by the prefatory compliment which he pays in these terms : ' Sire, Your slave craves permission to speak. He implores Your Majesty to suffer his unclean and defiled voice to reach the doors of your divine ears.' The King motions to him to speak, and after His Majesty has given the reply he thinks proper, the petitioner thanks him by making three more bows which end the audience. At this point a mandarin comes forward with a large silver dish filled with rich materials or some rarities of the country, of which a present is made on behalf of His Majesty to the one to whom it has pleased him to grant an audience. As soon as he has received them, the recipient puts them on his head to indicate the high esteem in which he holds such a gift, and he prostrates himself three times as he did on entering. The King then retires and the window is closed. If he has already received from His Majesty a coat or any other precious article, it is his duty to bring it with him to this audience, for it is by the display he makes of such gifts that he shows his gratitude and renders himself worthy of the continuation of these liberalities. It is most important that everyone shall be well prepared in what he shall say to His Majesty when he presents himself for an audience, and that he shall remember it carefully, for what is said there is written down in a record book which the King takes the trouble to look over from time to time, and often when one thinks least about it, he is pleased to question the same person on the same matters on which he has formerly spoken, so that His Majesty shall know if he is sincere and whether he may place confidence in him." [1]

Gervaise then goes on to remark that audiences were sometimes granted to petitioners at some place agreed upon outside the palace, for political reasons. But the ceremonial was only a slight modification of that in force at public audiences.

If any relic remains at the present day of these audiences to officials and petitioners, it is to be found, I think, in the Court Levees held on certain occasions, such as the King's birthday. I attended one of these in the magnificent new Anănṯa Samāgama Throne Hall, built at enormous expense in Italian style. The ceremonial was entirely European. The officials ranged themselves along the walls of the marble hall of vast proportions, illuminated by innumerable chandeliers, and decorated with splendid mural paintings representing scenes in Siamese history, the work of Italian artists. The arrival of the King, accompanied by the Queen, was heralded by the playing of the National Anthem by a military band. Their Majesties, preceded by a chamberlain carrying a wand of office, and accompanied by ministers of State, slowly walked round the hall, here and there pausing to exchange a few words with an official and inquiring as to the progress

[1] Gervaise, translation from the French (1684) by H. S. O'Neill, Bangkok, 1928, pp. 125–6.

of his work and his general well-being. Undoubtedly no one would have thought of presenting a petition at such a time; such a thing would be unheard of. But nevertheless it seems to me that the Court Levee, encased in western forms as it is, is the modern representative of the ancient petitioners' audience, giving as it does the opportunity for the King to exchange a few words with officials whom he probably never sees on any other occasions during the year.

There was still one other form of audience, perhaps the most interesting of all, which I have reserved for the last. In the famous stele of King Rāma Gāṁhèṅ of Sukhodaya we read:—

> "In the entrance to the gate (of the palace) a bell is hung up; if a subject of the realm has any trouble or any matter that distresses him within or torments his heart, and which he wishes to declare to his prince, there is no difficulty; he has only to ring the bell that is suspended there. Whenever King Rāma Gāṁhèṅ hears this appeal he questions (the plaintiff) concerning his case (and decides it) according to the right." [1]

This audience bell persisted until much later times in Siam, even if the call was not always answered and petitioners dared not to ring it; and it is mentioned in the classical Siamese work entitled *Sip-sòṅ Liam*. It was known in Burma,[2] and in Cambodia it lingered until the nineteenth century, under Norodom.[3] In fact, it was common to all the countries of the Orient—it is even mentioned in the *Thousand and One Nights*. But evidence that so far as Siam and Cambodia are concerned it was probably derived from India is to be found in the statement in the *Mahāvaṁsa*, that:—

> "At the head of his bed he had a bell hung up with a long rope so that those who desired a judgment at law might ring it." [4]

Whether it was derived from India or independently evolved by the early Thai nomads, it is undoubtedly an extremely ancient institution. It seems to take us back to remote patriarchal days when the king was indeed the father of his people and they were so few and their complaints so rare that he could deal with them all in person.

These various opportunities for officials and oppressed subjects to obtain access to the ear of their monarch must have been of considerable sociological importance in Old Siam. When high officers of State and judges were corrupt, and justice as at present understood was hardly known in Siam, it would obviously have a very salutary

[1] Coedès, *Les Inscriptions de Sukhodaya*, p. 45.

[2] An audience bell is mentioned in a Burmese and Talaing inscription (A.D. 1621) on such a bell, *Burma Research Society*, vol. xviii (1928), pt. i, pp. 21–34.

[3] Gr., p. 338.

[4] *M.* xxi, 15.

effect on the overbearing nature of the great nobles for them to know that any petty official might, if goaded too far, be led to try his luck with a petition before the King, who, however great a tyrant he himself might be, was the less likely to allow tyranny amongst his nobles; and, with the utter lack of proportion that characterized the government of Old Siam, the noble lord might himself be exposed with a cangue round his neck or be sent to cut grass for the royal elephants, only to be reinstated a few days later to his high position, but with, at least for a time, a very chastened outlook.

With the building up of a modern system of justice, with judges and ministers who have been educated up to a higher sense of public duty, still more perhaps through the publicity afforded by the open law-court and the newspaper, the necessity to maintain the right of petitioning the King has almost disappeared, though it is still resorted to in extreme cases.

The custom of prostration has frequently been mentioned above, since it was formerly a most important and inevitable characteristic of all intercourse between the subjects and the monarch of Siam. It was officially abolished by King Rāma V on the occasion of his Coronation, but it still lingers voluntarily, and especially in connection with the honouring of the relics and statues of past kings of the dynasty. The idea of never looking up at the King but always keeping the face parallel to the ground seems to be connected with that taboo mentioned in Chapter IV whereby the people were supposed not to be able to bear the radiance of the divine face. It has been suggested that the custom might be connected with a desire to avert the "evil eye", but I cannot find any evidence to show that the idea of the "evil eye" ever existed in Siam. Apart from the aversion of the face, the bodily prostration and the lifting of the joined palms is simply the servile method of offering homage to a deity or a king which seems natural to the Asiatic.

The following evidence indicates that the custom was not always in force: The seventh century Chinese chronicles, which have been quoted above, speak of the councillors as sitting, not grovelling; and Cheou Ta-kouan in the thirteenth century mentions the same phenomenon. Again, in the bas-reliefs at Aṅkor Văt, royal audiences are depicted in which the officials are seated in an attitude considered respectful in the East, but not prostrated in the modern way. The same fashion was evidently customary at Pagān, Burma, as is shown by the reliefs in the Ānanda Temple.[1] Relief No. 49 depicts King

[1] Reproduced in *Epigraphia Birmanica*, vol. ii, part 2.

Janaka on his canopied dais at audience with his ministers who *sit* with joined hands and feet concealed, while No. 33 shows a messenger kneeling before the Bodhisattva Temiya. Coming lastly to Sukhodaya, although there is no certain evidence on the subject, it is doubtful if such a great-hearted monarch as Rāma Gāṁhèṅ, the spirit of whose anxiety for the welfare of his subjects runs right through his famous inscription, could have brought himself to enforce prostration.

I conclude, therefore, that prostration was a comparatively late innovation in Indo-China, introduced by despotic monarchs not earlier than the fourteenth century. When the last traces of a patriarchal form of government had passed away, and fear was the chief support of despotic rulers, prostration had great sociological value. King Rāma V, who had endeared himself to the hearts of his people while yet a prince, was perhaps the first monarch since the rulers of Sukhodaya who was strong enough to break through the old tradition.

CHAPTER XV

THE OATH OF ALLEGIANCE

One of the most important State Ceremonies from the point of view of the upkeep of the established form of government in Siam is undoubtedly the Drinking of the Water of Allegiance (*bidhī śrīsăc-cpānkān*, or *thŭ'nāṁ*) which is still celebrated on the same impressive scale as it has been since the days of the Cambodian Empire.

The detailed regulations for the manner of taking the Oath by the various classes of officials are described at length by King Rāma V,[1] who rightly laid great stress on the proper carrying out of the ceremony. The rites take place with great splendour twice yearly, on the third day of the waxing of the fifth month (Chaitra), and on the thirteenth day of the waning of the tenth month (Bhādrapada). The Drinking of the Water takes place in the Chapel Royal in Bangkok, and also in one temple in each seat of provincial government. The water is previously hallowed in the usual way by the monks, who recite *mantras*, the sacred *siñcana* thread being stretched round the water-vessels, while the Court Brahmans also dip into the water the State Sword and other royal weapons, this being a rite of contagious magic, by the power of which any official meditating treason would be destroyed. It is said that persons have not infrequently in the past died of cholera after drinking the hallowed water, a result which no doubt did much to strengthen the general belief in the efficacy of the magic. On the day of the ceremony a Brahman reads out the Oath, and each official must drink the contents of a small cup, which he must drain to the last drop. Any appearance of difficulty in swallowing was, in the old days, considered as equivalent to an admission of disloyalty. The ladies of the palace, as well as members of the royal family, drink the Water of Allegiance, but, of course, with suitable privacy. Officials confined to their houses through illness are not excused from drinking the Water, but it is taken to their bedsides by royal pages or other officials. The following is a translation of the Oath of Allegiance made during the fourth reign, which I quote as I have not been able to obtain access to the original; but I understand that it is substantially accurate apart from a few obviously antiquated expressions which I leave unaltered :—

[1] *BRB.*, pp. 222 sqq.

" We, the slaves of the Lord Buddh, beg to offer to His Majesty, Prabaht Somdetch Pra Chula Chaum Klow [i.e. King Rāma IV] the King, this our personal oath, pledging our loyalty, in the immediate presence of the god Buddh, the sacred teachings and the sacred priests. We entreat the deity which protects the sectioned white Umbrella, and the guardian deities of all other places throughout the kingdom, to observe with their godlike eyes, and hear with their godlike ears, the pledges we make to Prabaht Somdetch Pra Chula Chaum Klow, the King, who has been crowned and placed upon the throne, and who, observing the ancient royal usages, treats graciously the priests, the ministers, and royal descendants, the official servants of His Majesty, military and civil, within and without, the provincial governors and their subalterns, the rulers of territories, states, and the entire population living within His Majesty's dominions. Hence it is proper that we gratefully perform our official duties, under His Majesty's feet faithfully, free from rebellious acts, physical, verbal, mental. If we, the slaves of our Lord Buddh, are not firmly fixed in true national gratitude, or if we meditate to His Majesty, Prabaht Somdetch, Pra Chula Chaum Klow, the King, with body, words or in disposition, or if we disclose our minds to the people or rulers of other regions that are hostile, and plot that others do evil to Prabaht Somdetch Pra Chula Chaum Klow, the King. If we see with our eyes, hear with our ears, or know that others are about to do evil to His Majesty, but delay with evil intent, with ingratitude, and lack of honesty, and with evil purposes toward Prabaht Somdetch Pra Chula Chaum Klow, the King, who is full of great mercy and incomparable graciousness: We pray the deities of lands and forests; the guardian deities; the atmospheric deities; the goddesses who care for the earth, especially the powerful deities who are located where is the great white Umbrella, emblem of royalty, may plague us with evil, destroy our lives, effect our destruction and death by breakage, by severance; cause our death by lightning and thunderbolts, by royal weapons, the powerful royal sword, by poison and the power of land and water animals; let there be some opportunity for the destruction of the perfidious ones; let swift destruction come; let us not escape all great disasters and consequences of all localities, which those who have the power can inflict for all offences. We beseech the power of the deities to plague with poisonous boils, rapidly fatal, and all manner of diseases the dishonourable, perverse, and treacherous, plague with untimely, wretched and appalling deaths, manifest to the eyes of the world; when we shall have departed this life from earth, cause us to be sent and all to be born in the great hell, where we shall burn with quenchless fire for tens and hundreds of thousands of ages and limitless transmigrations; and when we have expiated our penalty there, and are again born in any world, we pray we may fail to find the least happiness in worlds of pleasurable enjoyments; let us not meet the god Buddh, the sacred teachings, the sacred priests, who come to be gracious to animals, helping them escape misery, reach heaven and attain a cessation of births and deaths; should we meet them let them grant us no gracious assistance. If we remain firmly established in gratitude and honesty, and do not meditate the rebellion and evil that has been rehearsed, we beg the land, the forest and the atmospheric deities, and the four great guardians of the world, whose power extends to all the worlds of the gods, to the sacred foundations, forces and rulers of powerful nations, and the deities stationed in the great white Parasols of royalty, and the guardian deities that protect His Majesty by night and by day, and the deities that protect the palace, and the deities stationed to protect the twelve royal treasures, and all the deities, the armories, and ministers and great royal property; we entreat you all to assist, and protect us who perform all official duties faithfully; grant us prosperity and happiness in this and in other worlds; cause us to escape all the diseases and calamities that have been enumerated. We have received from His Majesty this water, pledging ourselves, therefore cause us to possess clear, unalloyed happiness, and to escape from all diseases and maladies; and grant us eminent prosperity, and brilliant, happy, fruitful lives, prolonged into very great age; and let us die in happiness resembling sleep, with an awakening in the abode of the gods, in the enjoyment of godlike possessions in heaven, for hundreds of thousands of ages and limitless species of beings. When we die and depart from heavenly and god-like worlds to be born again in human worlds, let us abound with goods, glorious and limitless possessions, and distinguished attendants in accord with our desires. We entreat the Lord Buddh, the sacred teachings, and the sacred priests, to grant the fulfillment of our desires in the way of heaven, and escape from the successions of life and death, and their attendant miseries, together with our fidelity and gratitude." [1]

It is known that the Ceremony of Drinking the Water of Allegiance in the Ayudhyā period was the same as that followed in Bangkok from the first reign onwards, King Rāma I having restored the ancient usage on his accession [2]; and it is mentioned by La Loubère in the seventeenth century.[3] There is no definite evidence for the practise of the ceremony at Sukhodaya,[4] but it was certainly in force in ancient Cambodia. On the pillars of a portico near the Phimeanakas at Aṅkor Thom are engraved eight inscriptions containing the names of numerous officials who swore allegiance to Sūryavarman I, each inscription being preceded by the Oath of Allegiance in Khmer, which has been translated as follows:—

"In 933 C.E. (A.D. 1011) the 9th of the waxing moon of Bhadra (August–September), Sunday. Here is the oath which we, belonging to the body of tamrvac (lictors) of the first, second, third, and fourth categories, swear all of us without exception, cutting our hands, and offering our lives and grateful and stainless devotion to H.M. Śrī Sūryavarmanadeva, who has been in complete enjoyment of

[1] *Siam*, M. L. Cort, pp. 123 sqq.

[2] *BRB.*, p. 231.

[3] L. L., p. 81.

[4] The passage in Rāma Gāṁhèṅ's inscription, supposed by Bradley (*JSS.*, vol. vi, pt. 2), to refer to this ceremony, has been shown by Coedès (*Les Inscriptions de Sukhodaya*, p. 47), to refer to an ordinary audience.

sovereignty since 924 C.E., in the presence of the sacred fire, the holy jewel, the Brahmans, and the ācāryas. We shall not honour any other king, we shall never be hostile (to our king), we shall not be the accomplices of any enemy, and we shall not seek to injure him (our king) in any way. We pledge ourselves to perform all actions which are the fruit of our grateful devotion towards His Majesty. If there be war, we pledge ourselves to fight faithfully in his cause without valuing our lives. We shall not fly from the battlefield. If we die a sudden death, not in war, or even if we commit suicide, may we obtain the reward due to the persons devoted to their lord. As our lives are dedicated to the service of His Majesty up to the day of our death, we shall faithfully do our duty to the king, whatever may be the time and circumstances of our death. If there be any affair, for which His Majesty orders us to go abroad, to learn everything about it, we shall seek to know it in detail. If all of us, who are here in person, do not keep to this oath of allegiance to His Majesty, may he reign long yet, we ask that he may inflict punishments of all sorts on us. If we hide ourselves, to escape carrying out the oath, may we be reborn in the thirty-two hells as long as there is the sun and moon. If we carry out loyally our promise, may His Majesty give orders for the upkeep of the pious foundations of our country, and for the maintenance of our families, as we are devoted followers of our lord H.M. Śrī Sūryavarmanadeva who has been in complete possession of the sacred royalty since 924 C.E., and may we obtain the reward due to faithful servants in this world and in the next."[1]

M. Coedès has remarked upon the similarity of this oath to the one still taken by officials at the Court at Phnompenh, there being, after a lapse of nearly a thousand years, little difference between the two other than the substitution of Buddhist terms for Brahmanical.

Though we have thus adequate material for tracing the history of the Siamese Oath back to Khmer times, we have no direct evidence as to the nature of the actual ceremony in ancient Cambodia. Nevertheless, there is reason to suppose that the ceremony was very much the same then as it is to-day, both in Bangkok and Phnompenh, because it seems very probable that it was derived from one of the forms of water ordeal practised in ancient India :—

"To whatsoever deity the accused happens to be devoted let (the judge) bathe the weapon of that deity in water, and give him to drink three handfuls of it. He to whom no calamity happens, within a week or a fortnight, (either to himself or) to his son, wife or property, is innocent beyond doubt."[2]

[1] Coedès, "Etudes Cambodgiennes," *BEFEO.*, t. xiii.

[2] Brihaspati, x, 23–4, in *SBE.*, vol. xxxiii, p. 318. In the Siamese version of the *Rāmāyaṇa* it is recorded that Pipek, brother of Rāvana, on going over to Rāma, was made to drink water, in which Rāma's weapons had been dipped, and to pray that it might destroy him should he break his oath. (Bastian, *Reisen in Siam*, pp. 518 sq.). But this may be a late interpolation.

In analysing the functional value of the Ceremony of Drinking the Water of Allegiance, several features of the Siamese Oath are of special importance. These are :—

(1) The substitution of Bhuddhist for Brahmanical terms (as compared with the early Khmer Oath).

(2) The introduction of a large number of animistic phrases, reference to guardian spirits, etc. (as compared with the early Khmer Oath).

(3) The greater detail in which the torments of the disloyal in future existences are described (as compared with the early Khmer Oath).

(4) The Oath is not entirely negative in either Siamese or early Khmer forms. It finishes up in a brighter vein, with reference to the rewards with which loyal officials may hope to be recompensed.

All these features have great bearing on the efficacy of the Oath, an efficacy which it retains at the present day. The very essence of the sociological value of such an oath and its accompanying water ordeal is that it is founded on fear, the emotion which is best developed in the subjects of barbaric kings. Now it would be going too far to say that the spirit of loyalty, as we understand it, never existed in Indo-China. It probably did. But that was before divine kingship reached such extreme elevation that it knew no limits to its power, and came to regard the people as mere chattels. Certain it is that any such spirit of loyalty, founded on the higher human emotions, passed away from Siam many centuries ago, and in the steady efforts of the educational and other government departments to reintroduce it, efforts which date from the memorable occasion on which King Rāma V first told his courtiers that they might stand in his presence, the people see an entirely new idea introduced from the West. In the ancient Khmer Oath we seem to have the oath of men who understood the meaning of the word patriotism, and whose loyalty was founded on higher motives than fear. It is still a long way removed from the Western idea of a man's word of honour being an all-sufficient oath, but the more restrained terms in which the damnation of the disloyal is described, and the absence of invocations of demons and spirits, the king himself being looked to for the punishment of traitors in this world, implies a people with some degree of self-respect. I do not mean to suggest that in the later centuries of the Khmer Empire the people were any less oppressed than were the Siamese of the Ayudhyā period; but their Oath seems to indicate that they retained some of the forms, if not the memories, of early patriarchal days. With the growth of tyranny in Siam in the Ayudhyā period, and the substitution of the milder religion of Buddha for Brahmanism, came the necessity to increase the efficacy of the Oath; and that was done by the elaboration of the details of the punishment and the introduction of the animistic phrases. Whoever was responsible for this introduction, if it was any one person, must have been a keen student of human nature. Kings were often too sunken in debauchery to wield in person the powers which their more vigorous forefathers had gained for them, Brahmanism was almost dead, Buddhism was perhaps as yet imperfectly understood by the masses, and though its hells make every conceivable provision for the discomfort of the damned, there were doubtless then as now, in Siam as in every other country, people who were ready enough to sell their souls to problematical devils in the next world, in return for the enjoyment of certain power and riches in this one. But there were still the *phī*: the elusive and dangerous spirits of the White Umbrella, of the Royal Weapons, and the guardian spirits of the city, who were jealous for the welfare of the king, not to mention the lesser sprites of house, garden, tree, and stream. They brought retribution swiftly, as any man could aver who had seen his neighbour smitten down with cholera in a single night. The belief in the power of *phī* is still very strong amongst nearly all classes of Siamese; how much more so must it have been amongst the ignorant and superstitious officials of Old Siam. It was this invocation of the spirits, then, that made the Oath of Allegiance such an effective support to Absolute Monarchy. Complementary to the fear aroused by this invocation, though far less important, was the last feature on our list. A slender hope is held out that the spirits would reward dutiful subjects for their loyalty. They seldom did, but a hope, however slender, of material rewards in this world, was probably a greater incentive to loyalty than anything that Buddhism could offer in the next.

The text of such an Oath as this does not reflect much credit upon the type of society that requires to use it, the more so as there is here no question of merely keeping up an old custom out of respect for ancient tradition. Drinking the Water of Allegiance is in Siam to-day definitely a powerful instrument for the support of the established form of government, and so long as a considerable percentage of superstitious, and half-educated, officials remain in the service, some of whom are not entirely disposed to turn a deaf ear to the alluring slogans of communism, so long will Siam be well advised to refrain from attempting to substitute a simpler and nobler form of Oath.

CHAPTER XVI

THE ROYAL BOUNTY

(a) Ṭulābhāra [1]

It has already been remarked that from the earliest historical times in India it has always been one of the foremost duties of kings to protect the established religion, and to confer lavish gifts upon the priesthood. In the days when the Brahmans were supreme it was, of course, to them that such gifts had to be made, and one of the most magnificent occasions on which this royal bounty was displayed was at the ceremony of *Ṭulābhāra*. At this ceremony, which was well known in India and is still practised in Travancore, the king, and sometimes the queen, were weighed in a balance (*ṭulā*) against gold or silver, which was given to the Brahmans.

Ṭulābhāra, despite the fact that the Brahmans had long ceased to be of much account in Siam, was performed at Ayudhyā in the ninth lunar month (Srāvaṇa), but fell into disuse in the middle of the eighteenth century. It was performed in the royal anointment pavilion (*braḥ-dī-nāṅ măngalābhiṣeka*), in the middle of which was placed a balance surrounded by curtains. The King went thither in a grand procession, riding on a palanquin, and accompanied by the Brahmans, nobles, and the first four ministers of State walking in pairs. The Queen, also seated on a palanquin, was accompanied by the wives of the astrologers (*horā*) and *grūs*, and the wives of the first four ministers, in pairs. They made nine *pradakṣina* circuits of the pavilion, and then the King entered the curtained enclosure. The Master of Ceremonies stood in front of the pavilion, the palace ladies sat outside the curtains, while the four *grūs* and the first four ministers of State sat inside the curtains. Of the latter, the *Braḥ Glăṅ* held the State Sword (*braḥ kharga*); the *Baladeba* held a guitar; the *Văṅ* held betel-flowers; and the *Yamarāja* held a standard of victory. One official blew a conch, another beat the big drum, another played the cymbals, and yet another beat the palace drum. The King mounted the right hand pan of the balance. In the left pan were placed the royal gifts, equivalent to the King's weight. Thus the King was weighed, and after him the Queen; and the royal alms were given to the Brahmans. Then the procession returned, and there was a

[1] Sources: *BRB.*, p. 535; *KM.*; *HV.* (not mentioned in *NN.*).

great feast, in the course of which it was said " the left is silver, the right is gold ", evidently with reference to the royal weighing, in which the royal gifts were silver, but the King was gold.

(b) Dòt Kaṭhina

1. *The Significance and Function of the Ceremony.*

We now proceed to study the Royal Bounty as displayed for the benefit of the Buddhist monks, which remains to the present day one of the most important and most flourishing of all Siamese State Ceremonies. *Dòt Kaṭhina*, which in its general sense means the laying down of robes for the monks, is a purely Buddhist observance, and is the only purely Buddhist festival which I deal with in this book. There are other important annual Buddhist feasts, such as (1) *Vaiśākha-pūjā*, in the sixth lunar month, which commemorates the Birth, Enlightenment, and Death of the Buddha ; (2) *Khau Barṣā*, in the eighth month, the beginning of the Buddhist retreat, and (3) *Māgha-pūjā*, held on full moon day of the third month, to commemorate the exposition of the Pratimokṣa made on that day by the Buddha to his 1,250 disciples of the four congregations ; while the full moon period of this month is also largely taken advantage of by the people for pilgrimages to the *Braḥ-pāda*, the sacred footprint of Buddha in the hills near Labapurī. But all these, although they are under royal protection, and the King is himself present at some of the religious services, listens to sermons and makes offerings to the priests, are not primarily royal ceremonies. They are popular ceremonies, and as such belong to a study of Siamese Buddhism. This may be the better realized when it is remarked that similar ceremonies continue to exist in Ceylon and Burma, where the kingship has passed away and the European government takes no active part in the proceedings.

On the other hand, although it is important to remember that the King of Siam protects *all* Buddhist activities, it is only in the Royal *Kaṭhina* that he takes a predominant part, a part eminently characteristic of the traditional Buddhist monarch. Indeed, the sociological value of the Royal *Kaṭhina* for the maintenance of social integrity and the continued prosperity of the Buddhist religion in Siam is exceeded by no other ceremony, for the following three reasons : (1) the King, by the lavishness of his gifts and his personal profession of faith at the altar, impresses upon the people in a truly regal way his belief in the national religion, and thus the love and respect which the people have for their monarch ; (2) the example of the King inspires the people with a desire to emulate his generosity, and by the *Kaṭhinas* of nobles and private persons which take place on a smaller scale all over the country, every monastery is provided for and the growth of the Buddhist religion is stimulated; (3) the Royal *Kaṭhina* processions by land and by water are almost the only occasions, other than the Coronation, on which the people can see their monarch pass by in the pomp and circumstance of Old Siam. While the State Processions on these occasions are not so magnificent as those which take place at the Coronation, yet I think they are of greater sociological value, for they take place, not once in a life-time, but every year, and the volume of the crowds that line the route can leave no doubt as to the great hold which royal pageantry still exercises over the minds of the people. Indeed, it is above all the frequency and regularity of these occasions which give them such great value.[1]

2. *Description of the modern Royal Kaṭhina.*

The period of the annual presentation of *Kaṭhina* robes is from the middle of the eleventh month (Āśvina or Āśvayuja) until the middle of the following month (Kārttika), i.e. October–November, the rains having then practically finished, and the Buddhist Retreat being at an end. There are four classes of *Kaṭhina*: (1) *Kaṭhina Hlvaṅ*, the King's *Kaṭhina*; (2) *Kaṭhina Cău*, the Prince's *Kaṭhina*; (3) *Kaṭhina Khun-nāṅ*, the nobleman's *Kaṭhina*; and (4) *Kaṭhina Brài*, the people's *Kaṭhina*. During the above-mentioned period, processions of one or another class of *Kaṭhina* are to be seen every day. When I lived near the river bank, some miles above Bangkok, I used to see the gaily decorated boats of the *Kaṭhina Brài*, with bands playing and everyone in the highest spirits and dressed in his best and brightest garments, passing up and down the river, and there were often two or three such processions in one day. I have also been present on two occasions at a nobleman's *Kaṭhina* (that of the former Lord Chamberlain), and on one occasion at a *Kaṭhina Cău* (that of Prince Dhāni Nivāt). I have also several times watched the King's *Kaṭhina* processions, on land and water, though it was not possible for me to be present in the Temple during the ceremony, as I was in the case of the other *Kaṭhinas*. But apart from the fact that the King's *Kaṭhina* is accompanied by greater dignity, and is not turned into a popular feast by the donor of the gifts for the benefit of his friends, there is little difference in

[1] It has been suggested to me that in Old Siam these processions had another important function. It was in similar processions of barges that warlike expeditions used to go down to attack places like Nagara Śrī Dharmarāja, and the annual *Kaṭhinas* gave the men valuable naval training.

the actual ceremonies within the temple, for Buddhism demands equal humility from all its devotees, whether king or coolie, and the King makes the same profession of faith when presenting the robes as does the humblest of his subjects.

The principal monasteries in the city and suburbs are designated *Văt Hlvaṅ*, that is, Royal Monasteries. These are under the special protection of the King, and expect to receive their *Kaṭhina* gifts from him. But there are so many of them that it would make too great a demand on the King's time to visit them all, and so nobles are appointed to represent him at the more distant ones. Some of the royal *Văts* are visited by the King by state carriage, or nowadays by motor-car. These *Kaṭhinas* take place with little or no show, and are of no great interest. I shall therefore confine myself to considering those great Royal *Kaṭhinas* which take place with the pomp of Old Siam. One of these takes the form of a procession by land, in the course of which the King visits the most important monasteries of the capital, Văt Braḥ Jetavana, Văt Pavaranivesa, and Văt Rājapabitra. As has been mentioned in Chapter VII, the Royal Coronation Progresses have adopted the features of *Kaṭhina*, the Progress by Land having lost its original significance as a *pradakṣina* circumambulation, and the Progress by Water having been added in analogy to the Water *Kaṭhina*. I shall therefore only note the main differences between the *Kaṭhina* Procession and the Coronation Progress.

The order of procession at the last Land *Kaṭhina* (*Kaṭhina Pak*) that I witnessed (14th October, 1930), was somewhat as follows (Pl. XXX) :—

Military Guards

Numerous units of modern troops, representative of all arms, and military bands

The Royal Party

A Nobleman	A Nobleman
Flag	Flag
A Nobleman	A Nobleman

Drum Major

Metal Drum	Metal Drum

Players of Ceremonial Instruments

Bearers of Royal Weapons

The King on a Palanquin; Sunshade, Umbrella, and Fan

Bearers of Royal Insignia

The King's offerings to Religion on a State Palanquin

State Chargers

H.R.H. the Prince of Nagara Svarga, mounted

(Left side:) File of Gentlemen-at-Arms with halberds
Processional Umbrellas. Red and Gold Drummers
Herald Trumpets
Supporters of H.M.

(Right side:) File of Gentlemen-at-Arms with halberds
Red and Gold Drummers. Processional Umbrellas
Herald Trumpets
Supporters of H.M.

PLATE XXX.

[Photo: Bangkok Times Press, Ltd.

THE KING ARRIVING AT A *VAT* ON THE OCCASION OF A LAND *KATHINA*.

[To face page 202.

Plate XXXI.

[Photo : Bangkok Times Press, Ltd.

Royal Barge taking part in a *Kaṭhina* Procession.

There is little that calls for special notice in this procession, since it is made up of elements which have already been considered in some detail in connection with Coronation, and which are characteristic of all royal processions. But the *Kaṭhina* is naturally on a smaller scale, although sufficiently impressive. The main difference which I noticed between this and similar processions in the last reign was the absence of the Maḥhātlek, abolished by the present King. In Old Siam such processions were swelled by the presence of numerous princes, each carried on a palanquin and surrounded by his own retinue bearing his insignia of rank. It is also to be noticed that the King wears plain white military uniform with plumed helmet, whereas in Old Siam he wore full monarchical dress and the *Kaṭhina* Crown, which is now seen only in Coronation Progresses. The innovation is not a happy one, and strikes one as most incongruous, affecting as it does the central feature of the Royal Party.

The last Water *Kaṭhina* (*Kaṭhina Nǎṁ*) which I witnessed took place on the next day, 15th October, 1930, when the King visited Văt Āruṇ, in accordance with old custom. Palace guards were drawn up at the landing-stage in front of the palace, and when the King arrived by motor-car the military band blared forth the National Anthem. The King was escorted down the jetty, beneath a royal umbrella, and embarked in a pavilion barge, accompanied by a number of noblemen. There was also a reserve pavilion barge for use on the return journey. It is interesting to note that on the occasion of *Kaṭhinas* the King does not himself ride in a *braḥ-dī-năṅ* barge, which supreme honour is reserved for the King's offerings to religion (Pl. XXXI); and in the *Kaṭhina* procession all the state barges are quite plain gilded structures without figure-heads, the great Haṅsa and Nāga barges being reserved for the Coronation. There were a number of drum barges and escort barges, but probably the whole number did not exceed thirty, whereas in the old days there were as many as 150 to 200, this number including those of numerous princes and nobles, whose rank was indicated by the varying degree of magnificence of the barges.

When the King reaches a *Văt* at which it has been arranged that he should present gifts, the palanquin, in the case of a Land *Kaṭhina*, is drawn up against a flight of steep brick steps, the King alighting and proceeding on foot to the temple between the files of a guard of honour, while the military band plays the National Anthem, in opposition to the blowing of the ceremonial conches. The path to the temple is carpeted with matting exclusively for the King to walk upon. In the case of a Water *Kaṭhina* the King alights similarly at the riverside landing of the temple. In Old Siam the handrail of the landing was wound with white cloth, as a sign that the landing might not be passed by any Siamese subject in a standing posture, or with covered head. Hence all boatmen rowing their boats standing, in gondola-like fashion, had to go down on their knees, just as they had to do before the palace, as a sign that the temple-landing was, for the time being, the King's landing.

3. *The Ceremony in the Temple.*[1]

On leaving the palanquin or barge, as the case may be, the King walks to the *uposatha*, or temple proper, and at the door takes one complete set of monk's robes from the hands of the official who is holding them, and then enters the temple. At the far end of the temple the great image of Buddha is seated on the decorated and illuminated altar, and the monks are seated in rows at the upper end. The King places the set of robes on a table specially prepared for the purpose, on which are five golden vases of flowers, five golden dishes of parched corn, five golden candlesticks with their candles, and five incense sticks. The number five represents the five Buddhas of the present world cycle, Gautama Buddha, the three Buddhas who preceded him, and the future Buddha, Maitreya.

The King then pays homage before the image three times with joined palms, each time repeating the Pāli salutation to the Buddha, "*Namo tassa bhagavato, arahato sammā sambuddhasa.*" The Abbot then lifts his fan and holds it before his eyes, so that he may not be distracted, and thrice repeats the same salutation. The King then proceeds formally to offer the robes to the priests, and the monks signify their acceptance, "*Sādhu, Sādhu!*" and the Abbot addresses the fraternity as follows:—

> "This *phā̌ kaṭhina* has been given to us by His most illustrious Majesty the King, who being endued with exceeding goodness and righteousness, has condescended to come hither himself, and present these garments to us, a company of Buddhist Priests, without designating any particular person by whom they shall be worn; but leaving it for us as a company, to decide who of us is most in need, and who of us has attained to the fifth degree of *Ānisaṅṣa* (fruitfulness in holy living), and who of us practise the eight rules of *Mātikā* (priestly etiquette)."

[1] There is a description of the Ceremony in the Temple at Royal *Kaṭhinas* in the *Bangkok Calendar* for 1863, but most of it is unreliable, being very elaborate, whereas the Royal *Kaṭhina* ceremony is, in fact, very simple. For the information in this section I am mainly indebted to my friend Braḥyā Prijānuṣāsanā.

The Abbot divides the robes in the King's presence, and the King makes a few other miscellaneous presents as well as special suits of robes for those monks who have distinguished themselves in the Pāli language. The monks then pronounce a short form of *paritta*, as follows:—

> "*Atireka vassasataṁ jivatu, dighāyuko hotu, arogo hotu, sukhito hotu; siddhi kiccaṁ, siddhi kammaṁ, siddhi labho, jayoniccaṁ (Paramindara) Mahārājavarassa bhavatu sabbadā. Khó thawāi phra: phón.*"

The last sentence is Siamese, and the whole has been translated as follows:—

> "May you live over one hundred years in the fullness of vigour, free from disease and happy; may all your wishes be fulfilled, all your works accomplished, all advantages accrue to you; may you always triumph and succeed, O Paramindra (the King's name), august Sovereign. May it be so forever! We beg to tender (to you) this blessing." [1]

The King then again pays homage before the image and leaves the temple. He spends about half-an-hour in each *Văt*.

4. *The Royal Kaṭhina in the Seventeenth Century.*

It is evident that the European travellers and missionaries who visited Siam during the seventeenth century were just as forcibly struck by the splendour of the *Kaṭhina* processions at Ayudhyā as is any modern observer. Tachard, Schouten, and Kaempfer all make mention of them, though the latter, who writes of Ktimbac (*Kaṭhina Pak*) and Ktinam (*Kaṭhina Nǎṁ*), confuses the latter with the ceremony of "Speeding of the Outflow".[2] But the best description of a seventeenth century *Kaṭhina* procession, as well as the earliest, is that of van Vliet, who was in charge of the Dutch East India Company's interests in Siam from 1629 to 1634, in the reign of King P̱rāsāda Dòṅ.[3] The account of the Water Procession is not specially interesting, except for the large number of barges (350 to 400) and of persons (20,000 to 25,000) which he states took part in it. This is probably no great exaggeration, for in those days Ayudhyā was very rich, and the king's outward show of magnificence was of the utmost social importance; and we must not forget that the queens and members of the harem accompanied the king in their barges.

[1] Ge (1), p. 115.

[2] Kaempfer, *History of Japan*, 1690–2, reprint of Scheuchzer's English translation, 1906, vol. i, p. 72.

[3] Van Vliet, *Description of the Kingdom of Siam*, Leyden, 1692, translated into English in *JSS.*, vol. vii, 1910, pt. i, pp. 23–6.

On the other hand, van Vliet's description of the *Kaṭhina Pak* is of great importance and interest because we know from the Siamese Annals that the Land *Kaṭhina* was not established in Ayudhyā until the reign of King P̱rāsāda Dòṅ, that is not prior to 1630, so that van Vliet must have witnessed some of the earliest of these land processions. To anyone who is acquainted with the topography of Ayudhyā, with its network of canals and absence of roads, it is easy to understand why the earlier *Kaṭhina* processions had always been by water. Indeed, the temples as well as the houses of the people were all situated along the banks of the waterways, and were most naturally approached by boat. The Thai were an amphibious people, and still are, in the neighbourhood of Ayudhyā and other riverine towns. In the early days of Bangkok the same conditions prevailed, and the sole means of communication by land was by means of narrow muddy lanes, ill-suited to a royal procession. But in the later period of Ayudhyā's history, just as in later times in Bangkok, better thoroughfares were made and temples were built which could be easily approached by land. Thus the *Kaṭhina Pak* came into being, and was probably modelled on the Coronation *pradakṣina* procession, which was a very ancient institution, and was always possible, even at Ayudhyā, on account of the flat open space which surrounded the city wall. On the other hand, we have seen that the Coronation Progress by Water is a late addition of the Bangkok period, in analogy to the *Kaṭhina Nāṁ*.

Van Vliet mentions that there was, in his time, only one Royal *Kaṭhina* by land, but many by water which took place at the end of October or in the beginning of November. His description of the land procession, which he says was not every year arranged in the same way, is of sufficient interest to be quoted *in extenso*, and is as follows :—

> " First come in stately order going from the palace to the principal temple called Nappetat [Nā Braḥ Dhātu] about 80 or 100 elephants, which are sumptuously decorated. On each of these elephants is seated, besides two armed men, a mandarin in his gilded little house having in front of him a golden basin containing cloth and presents for the priests. Then follow 50 to 60 elephants, on each of which are sitting 2 to 3 men, each of whom is armed with bows and arrows. After this come, also seated on elephants, the 5 to 6 greatest men of the kingdom, some of them wearing golden crowns but each with his golden or silver betel box or any other mark of honour given to him by the king. They are accompanied by their suites of 30 to 60 men afoot. Following those come 800 to 1,000 men armed with pikes, knives, arrows, bows and muskets and also carrying many banners, streamers and flags. Among these armed men are mixed about 70 or 80 Japanese who are gorgeously dressed and carry excellent arms.

The musicians who follow the soldiers play on pipes, trombones, horns and drums and the sound of all these instruments together is very melodious. The horses and elephants of the king are adorned copiously with gold and precious stones and are followed by many servants of the court carrying fruits and other things to offer. Many mandarins accompany these servants. Then follow on foot with folded hands and stooping bodies (like everyone who rides or walks in front of the king) many nobles, among them some who are crowned. Then comes the red elephant decorated very nicely with gold and precious stones. Behind this elephant follow two distinguished men, one of them carrying the royal sword and the other one the golden standard, to which a banner is attached. A gilded throne follows after them showing how former kings used to be carried on the shoulders of the people, and then follows His Majesty sitting on an elephant and wearing his royal garments and his golden crown of pyramidal shape. He is surrounded by many nobles and courtiers. Behind His Majesty comes a young prince, the legal child of the supreme king, who at present is eleven years old. The king's brother, being the nearest to the throne, follows then with great splendour, and seated on elephants in little closed houses come after this the king's mother, the Queen and His Majesty's children and the concubines. Finally many courtiers and great men on horseback, and 300 to 400 soldiers who close the procession. Altogether about six or seven thousand persons participate in this ceremony, but only his Majesty, his wives, his children, his brother, the four highest bishops and other priests enter the temple. Having stayed inside the temple for about two hours the king and the whole splendid train return to the palace in the same order as here described. The streets are very crowded with people from the palace to the temple, but everyone is lying with folded hands and the head bent to the earth. It is forbidden to anyone to look at the king's mother, his wives or children, and the people turn their faces when the royal family passes. Only strangers or foreign ambassadors are allowed to look at them."[1]

There are a few points in the above description which call for comment, as follows:—

(1) The presence of a red (white ?) elephant in the procession, and of war elephants, on one of which the king was mounted. Elephants were much prized in the Ayudhyā period because of their use in war, and hence took part in royal processions just as modern artillery does nowadays; and they were also considered as mounts most suited to the royal dignity, from very early times, and also were no doubt the most practical means of transport through the muddy lanes of Ayudhyā. But now that their military value has gone they have completely disappeared from the streets of Bangkok, except on certain special occasions. One, for example, sometimes appears in the procession of the Swinging Festival. But neither ordinary elephants,

[1] Van Vliet, loc. cit.

nor the white elephants, which are still maintained in Bangkok, ever take part in the *Kaṭhina*.

(2) Japanese settled in large numbers in Siam during the reign of King Ekādaśaratha (1605–10), and the Japanese bodyguard, of which van Vliet speaks, was instituted by that king. But shortly after van Vliet's time, in 1632, all Japanese were either massacred or expelled from Ayudhyā by King P̱rāsāda Dòṅ, who regarded their presence with apprehension.[1]

(3) In the Bangkok period, queens and palace ladies have ceased to accompany the royal *Kaṭhina*.

(4) Van Vliet's statement that the streets were crowded with people is certainly inaccurate, as we know from many other sources that right up to the time of Rāma IV the people were confined behind wicker fences during a royal progress. V̬an Vliet's remark on the conduct of the people during a *Kaṭhina Nǎṁ* is interesting, however. He says:—

> "Along the whole way which His Majesty passes, the houses, monasteries and temples are closed with mats, and nobody is allowed to stay in them in order that nobody may look at the king from a place higher than that of His Majesty."

Evidently the houses all along the river bank had to be completely evacuated, as a person even lying prostrate on the ground floor of a house near the river might very well be higher than the position of the king in his barge; and I observed at King's College, a two-storied building on the river bank, some miles above Bangkok, that the students were not allowed to remain on the upper floor when the King was passing in his motor launch.

5. *The Early History of the Kaṭhina.*

In the days of the Buddha, the tradition is that the ascetic monks refused all offers of new robes and dressed themselves only in such rags as they found in graveyards which they stitched together into the semblance of a robe; and they preferred a dirty yellow colour, for such was the colour of the dress of robbers and outcasts. In later times, even in Siam, there may have been ascetic monks who still followed this ancient practice, and then arose the custom of wrapping dead bodies in many unnecessary shrouds, for it was believed that by getting the monks to accept these robes, much merit would accrue to the dead person. This custom still survives, and in Royal Cremations it accounts for the *Satăpakaraṇa* Rite.

[1] Wood, *History of Siam*, 1926, pp. 159 and 176.

In later days, when monks had adopted more luxurious habits, they accepted perfectly new robes dyed yellow, but to maintain the semblance of the old asceticism the new robes had to be made from a number of pieces of cloth patched together, and so that too great care should not result in too well-made a garment, the monk's robe had, and still has, to be made in a single day and a night. The old meaning of the words *Dòt Kaṭhina* is "to lay down a pattern" in order to cut patchwork by it. The pattern is the *kaṭhina*, which in ancient times the monks of Buddha used in cutting their cloth in patches, to be sewed together to make their outer and inner robes. The cloth was cut with a knife, because it was considered sinful to tear it. But now the monks do not have to make their robes themselves, since the laymen save them the trouble, and although they do not use the *kaṭhina* as an aid to cutting the patches, but do it by eye, the work still retains the name, which, as we have seen, is also applied to the whole ceremony. The effect of this modification of old custom, which took place many hundred years ago, has resulted in the elevation of the monks from their former humble position, but it also has great value in providing one of the chief methods by which the laymen, and above all the King, can make merit and show their regard for religion in a practical way.

The inscription of King Rāma Gāṁhèṅ, A.D. 1293, gives the following important reference to Buddhism in general and *Kaṭhina* in particular:—

> "The inhabitants of Sukhodaya are given to alms, to the observance of the precepts and to charity. King Rāma Gāṁhèṅ, sovereign of Sukhodaya, as well as the princes and princesses, men and women, nobles and chiefs, all without exception, without distinction of rank or sex, practise with devotion the religion of Buddha and observe the precepts during the rainy season retreat. At the end of the rainy season there take place the *Kaṭhina* ceremonies which last a month. During these ceremonies they make offerings of heaps of money, heaps of areca, heaps of flowers, and of cushions and pillows. The offerings made each year amount to two millions. They conduct *Kaṭhina* ceremonies as far as the monastery of Araññikas, yonder, and when they return to the city, the procession stretches from the monastery of Araññikas to the border of the plain. There everyone prostrates himself while the lutes and guitars resound and hymns and chants are played. Whoever likes to play, plays; whoever likes to laugh, laughs; whoever likes to sing, sings." [1]

Thus, though we have few details, it appears that the *Kaṭhina* was an established institution in Rāma Gāṁhèṅ's time; but we know that it cannot have been so for long, since it was only in the thirteenth

[1] Coedès, *Les Inscriptions de Sukhodaya*, p. 45.

century that Hīnayānism was firmly established in the young State of Sukhodaya (although it had been established considerably earlier in the neighbouring State of Lāṁbūn), and the very mention of it in this inscription (it is, so far as I know, mentioned in no later ones) indicates that the King was very proud of a custom which he, in all probability, had himself introduced.

Further evidence in support of this is provided by King Rāma IV in an article called "Origin of *Văt* Visitations", published posthumously in the *Siam Repository*.[1] The author evidently bases his conclusions on some information derived from the Northern Annals to the effect that the *Kaṭhina* was introduced somewhat in its present form in the reign of Braḥ Rvaṅ, a name applied indiscriminately to most of the rulers of Sukhodaya, but more particularly to Rāma Gāṁhèṅ. He states that at that time the royal *Văts* were visited in the season of the full moons of October and November by the royal barges, containing baskets of cloths and baskets of food with branches placed in the centre of them, on which were suspended lanterns and strips of yellow cloth, the latter apparently in memory of less abundant times when the monks were obliged to search for rags on cremation grounds. The procession by water apparently took place at night, and the king was accompanied by nobles and palace ladies. He was received by the monks at each *Văt* and they let off fireworks in his honour, and the people gave themselves up to amusements.

But though, so far as Siam is concerned, the *Kaṭhina* originated in the thirteenth century when Hīnayānism had obtained Royal Patronage, nevertheless it is undoubtedly an extremely ancient ceremony in the older Buddhist countries. In Burma it has flourished since an early period as a state ceremony under the name *Kateindaw Pwe*.[2] Regulations for the *Kaṭhina* ceremony are laid down in the *Mahāvagga*, and in the Buddha's day, even if the *Kaṭhina* ceremony as we know it had not yet taken shape on account of the early asceticism of the monks which obliged them to seek cast-off rags, kings were very lavish in their gifts of food and pleasant monastic groves, and it cannot have been long before the discipline, at least of some sects, was sufficiently relaxed to enable them to accept robes. But though the *Kaṭhina* in its special form was a product of Buddhism, we cannot doubt that it was only an outgrowth of the age-old duty of Vedic kings to protect and bestow generous gifts on the Brahmans.

[1] April, 1868.

[2] *ERE*. iii, p. 35.

6. *The Royal Regatta.*

From the time of Sukhodaya it has always been the custom of Siamese kings to regale those who assisted and took part in the Royal *Kaṭhina* processions, and practically all members of the general public as well, with a feast to celebrate the termination of the royal merit-making. We have seen that mention is made of sports and amusements as following the *Kaṭhina* in the inscription of Rāma Gāṁhèṅ. In the Ayudhyā period, until 1767, this festival took the form of a regatta, in which the King's barge, the Queen's barge, and those of a number of officials took part in a race. From the result prognostics were drawn: if the King's barge lost, it betokened the prosperity of the realm; but if it won, it was a sign of impending calamities and famine.[1] This soothsaying was evidently a Brahmanical survival, since we find such rites connected with many Hindu ceremonies. As a state festival this was discontinued, but Prince Damrong considers that the popular annual beanfeast with boat races, which takes place annually on the eighth waning of the eleventh month in honour of the P̱āknāṁ Pagoda at the mouth of the river, is certainly the modern representative of the Royal Regatta, but it is entirely Buddhist and no prognostics are drawn. Graham[2] has incorrectly identified this P̱āknāṁ Water Festival as a survival of the Ceremony of the Speeding of the Outflow.

The Royal Regatta, or its modern equivalent at P̱āknāṁ, is of considerable social value, coming as it does immediately after the somewhat strenuous *Kaṭhina* season, and also affording relief and much needed amusement to the many young men who have just obtained freedom after their three months' sojourn in the priesthood.

It is natural in a hot climate, and with people who are more or less amphibious, that royal sports should be of an aquatic nature, especially in low-lying and swampy countries. That the Siamese Royal Regatta is in accordance with the traditional Indian idea of what should be the sport of kings, the following examples show:—

Thus in Pagān, an old capital of Burma :—

> "In the hot season the king (Narathihāpate, A.D. 1255–90) loved to sport at splashing water. He made a great shade from the palace to the river wharf and walled it in so that men might not see, and built a royal lodge for security thereby; and taking his queens, concubines, and all his women he was wont to go along a tunnel of cabins and sport in the water."[3]

[1] *KM.*, and *NN.*, p. 92.
[2] *Siam*, ii, p. 278.
[3] *Glass Palace Chronicle*, Tin and Luce, p. 168.

Again, in ancient Ceylon, we have :—

" The King Devānaṁpiyatissa, who had arranged a water-festival for the dwellers in the capital, set forth to enjoy the pleasures of the chase " [1];

and at a later period,

" When then the king had come into the capital as victor in battle and had raised the parasol (of sovereignty) he went to a festival at the Tissa-tank." [2]

Lastly, in Ancient India, there is the remark in *Ghāta Jātaka* (No. 454), that :—

" One day the king proposed that they should go and disport themselves in the water."

[1] *M.* xiv, 1. [2] *M.* xxxv, 38.

CHAPTER XVII

ROYAL ANNIVERSARIES

1. *The Anniversary of the Coronation.*

This festival, known as *Chăṯra Maṅgala* (literally the " blessing of the royal umbrella ") lasts for four days, which are, in this reign, 23rd to 26th February. It is a festival of comparatively modern origin, having been instituted by King Rāma IV, who wished Siam, in this respect, to follow the practice of other nations of the modern world.[1] The programme of ceremonies which he laid down has been followed ever since with such minor modifications as later kings have thought fit to introduce. The following were the rites as carried out on the last Anniversary of the Coronation of the late King Rāma VI, 9th to 12th November, 1925.

At 5 p.m. on the first day, in the Hall of Amarindrā, the annual memorial service in honour of the former kings of the dynasty was celebrated by a chapter of seventy-five monks in the King's presence. The miniature golden urns containing the relics of the five previous kings and their first queens were placed on an altar in the hall during the service. Before the service the King presented royal warrants conferring various ranks upon some fifty-two monks. Next day, also at 5 p.m., the King proceeded to the Tusiṯa Hall, where eighty high priests and abbots of the capital and the provinces celebrated a religious service, invoking prosperity for the kingdom. On the third day, at 10 a.m., the King again went to the Tusiṯa Mahā P̱rāsāda and, with the assistance of the members of the Royal Family and high officials, presented food to the monks who celebrated the service the previous evening. After this the Court Brahmans celebrated a benedictory service, the rites of which comprise a show of mumbling texts from their sacred books, performing a *vian dian* for the benefit of the nine-tiered White Umbrella (symbolical of the monarchy) to which they tie a strip of red cloth, and finally sprinkling the Umbrella and the Royal Weapons with lustral water.[2]

After 4 p.m. on the same day the King proceeded to the same Hall and, after lighting the candles at the altar, seated himself upon the throne, under the great Umbrella of State. The State trumpeters

[1] *BRB.*, pp. 56 sqq. [2] *BRB.*, p. 60.

blew a fanfare, accompanied by the drummers on the State metal drums. A royal scribe next read a decree promoting a *Cău Fǎ* Prince from *Kram Khun* to *Kram Hlvaṅ*, creating a *Cău Fǎ* Princess a *Kram Khun*, and promoting a *Braḥyā* to the rank of *Cǎu Braḥyā*. The King then handed the tablet of promotion to each recipient, poured lustral water on their heads and anointed them. Afterwards the King held a Chapter of the Order of Culā Còm Klǎu (an order confined to royalty), promoting certain members of the Order, and conferring the honour of knighthood and companionship on a number of new members. At the end of the Chapter the King retired to the Bimăn Ratya Hall, to hold a Chapter of the Ladies' Division of the same Order, and to make promotions and appointments. The King then proceeded to the Pantheon to light candles and incense, and to make obeisance before the statues of the former kings of the dynasty. Members of the Royal Family and officials also did reverence in the same way.

On this day, at noon, the Army and Navy fired a Royal Salute of 101 guns. At 10 p.m. on the 12th November there was a Court Levee, but the King was unable to attend in person by reason of the malady which shortly afterwards proved fatal.

The Anniversary of the Coronation of the present king (23rd to 26th February) is celebrated with almost the same detail as the above except that on the third day the King does not hold a Chapter of the Culā Còm Klǎu Order, nor are there any observances in the Pantheon. These features have in this reign been transferred to the King's Birthday Festival, and in their place the King now holds a State Audience in the Amarindrā Hall, similar to that which followed the Coronation, and which in the last reign was held yearly in connection with the King's Birthday.

The *Chătra Maṅgala* is of little historical interest, having originated in Siam so recently. On the other hand it is of the greatest sociological importance. Unlike so many Siamese royal ceremonies, the meaning of which has been entirely forgotten and the functional value consists only of inspiring respect for the hallowed past, the Coronation Anniversary definitely belongs to and is a product of New Siam. It was instituted after Siam had broken with the past, and was a manifestation of the desire of the learned King Rāma IV to bring his country into line with those more advanced countries of the West, and to inspire the people with the spirit of patriotism, something hitherto quite unknown to them. And yet the King was wise enough to found nearly all the component parts of the new ceremony on rites drawn from the stock of Siamese religion and culture—the material that lay ready to hand and was most easily understood by the people.

The rites may be analysed as follows:—

(1) Buddhist services of benediction: Naturally these predominate, King Rāma IV being such a staunch Buddhist, and the *Chătra Maṅgala* is one of those valuable occasions on which the King shows his interest in the people's religion by conferring degrees of learning on distinguished monks; and also shows his royal protection by presenting food to those who have officiated.

(2) The Brahmans, although they take but a small part, are not forgotten as they might have been by an equally staunch Buddhist, but less broad-minded, king. Their presence gives to the festival that stamp of compatibility with ancient tradition which it would otherwise lack by reason of its modern origin.

(3) The relics or statues of the former kings cannot be too frequently honoured during the course of the year as, especially in these days of communistic agitation, it is so important to preserve the people's respect for the ruling dynasty and the conception of the monarchy, quite apart from their love for the individual monarch.

(4) Semi-religious features such as the promotion of officials, and non-religious items of European origin, such as the Order of Culā Còm Klău, the Royal Salute, and the Court Levee, are all of value, applied in moderation, for the growth of self-respect, and the wholesome desire for advancement, the proper reward for services rendered to the Crown.

(5) Taken as a whole, and in the estimation of the millions who take no actual part in it, the *Chătra Maṅgala* must have the effect of calling to mind by its name alone the grand pageant of Coronation with which almost every Siamese is familiar, at least from the pictorial reproductions of it which are to be met with in almost every home throughout the country.

2. *The King's Birthday.*

This festival, like the Coronation Anniversary, is of comparatively modern origin in Siam, and the remarks which have been made as to the relative importance of the historical and sociological aspects of the latter also apply to the King's Birthday (*Kāra chalo'm braḥ janambarṣā*). It was founded by King Rāma IV[1] for similar reasons to those which prompted him to institute the *Chătra Maṅgala*. In Siam it had never been the custom for the birthday of anyone to be celebrated in any way, not even that of the Buddha; but King Rāma IV also instituted

[1] *BRB.*, pp. 663 sqq.

the festival of *Vaiśākha Pūjā*, which commemorates the Birth, Enlightenment, and Death of the Buddha. It is probable that the kings of ancient India celebrated their birthdays and, as King Rāma V remarks, that the ceremony of *Tulābhāra* was held on such occasions. The Siamese always remembered the day of the week of the lunar month on which they were born, and the name of the animal which presides over the particular year of the cycle of twelve animal years; this was important in connection with the horoscope with which every Siamese was provided, and which to a great extent controlled his conduct of life. This was the way in which the birthday of King Rāma IV was commemorated, and is still followed in Cambodia, where King Norodom instituted the Birthday Festival in imitation of the action of King Rāma IV.[1] But King Rāma V, in order to avoid confusion, fixed his Birthday Celebrations for 21st September, in accordance with the newly-introduced solar calendar. King Rāma VI's Birthday was on 1st January, and that of the present King is on 8th November. The duration of the festival has varied from five to three days, being at present of the latter extent. But when a king completes a cycle of twelve years, according to the old lunar reckoning, special celebrations are held in that year. This was the case in 1929, when King Prajadhipok attained the age of 36.

The ceremonies follow, with minor variations, the rules laid down by King Rāma IV. They are very similar to the ceremonies on the occasion of *Chătra Maṅgala*. On alternate days there is a service in the Amarindrā Hall by monks of the Mahā Nikaya Sect or the reformed Dharmayutika Sect, and a distinguished abbot preaches a sermon. The Candle of Victory is lighted at the beginning of the festival, and extinguished at the end. The special texts recited on this occasion are the Mahāsamayasutta and the Seven Parittas. On the following mornings the usual presentation of food to the officiating monks takes place. In the present reign the King chooses the occasion of his Birthday for the promotion of officials, the holding of a Chapter of the Culā Còm Klău Order, and the paying of homage before the statues in the Pantheon. The special feature of the Birthday Festival, as distinct from the *Chătra Maṅgala*, is that the King, on the day following his Birthday, takes a ceremonial bath, attended by the Brahmans, who accompany the proceedings with the usual ceremonial music, while the Army and Navy fire a salute of twenty-one guns. This ceremonial bath is not to be regarded as an *abhiṣeka*, but rather as a Hindu bath of purification.

In considering the sociological value of this festival, by far the

[1] L., p. 322.

most important feature is the illumination of the city which is carried out during the three nights of the celebrations. This was introduced in the reign of King Rāma V and the technique has now reached a very high standard. Not only the palace, and every government office, but the private house of every Siamese, so far as his means will allow, is brilliantly illuminated with designs which do great credit to the artistic sense of the people. Perhaps even more remarkable is the fact that every foreign firm, Chinese, European, and American, competes to offer the most striking evidence of their respect for the monarch under whose protection they flourish. The words *DRAṄ BRAḤ CARO'Ñ*, and their English equivalent LONG LIVE THE KING, flash in letters of fire from almost every building of any importance, and there could be no more obvious sign of the contented satisfaction of both Siamese and foreigners with the regime under which they live. The King and Queen greatly appreciate this spontaneous show of affection and never fail to drive round the city at night by motor-car, and to make a trip by launch to see the equally attractive illuminations of the riverside.

Part V

CEREMONIES RELATING TO AGRICULTURE

CHAPTER XVIII

CEREMONIES FOR THE CONTROL OF WIND AND RAIN

1. *Kite-flying.*

Despite the introduction of European sports, Kite-flying is still regarded by the Siamese as their national pastime, and as such has often been described by European writers. During the prevalence of the north-east monsoon, in every village and in every open space in the city, people, both young and old, are to be seen indulging in the amusement; and on the Royal Cremation Ground there is an annual Kite-flying Festival, which the King and members of the Royal Family attend, and prizes are presented to those who are successful in the competitions. The latter take the form of (1) contests between pairs of kites, the object of which is for one to bring down the other, and (2) competitions in which the owners of the most beautiful or original kites, all of which are invariably made of paper and bamboo, are suitably rewarded.

The above festival, and kite-flying in general, still retain great value as a suitable means of relaxation and gentle exercise in a hot climate, and as an occasion for popular social intercourse; but no Siamese now remembers that there was once not only a public festivity, but also an important Royal Ceremony in connection with kite-flying. At least, such is the opinion of Gerini,[1] who states that in the Ayudhyā period,

> "large paper kites were flown with the object of calling up the seasonal wind by the fluttering noise they made. The festival, which took place in the 1st month, Mārgaśīrṣa, was obviously connected with husbandry, as the wind prevailing at this season is the north-east monsoon, which when beginning to blow, sweeps the rain clouds away, so that fine weather sets in and the yearly flood quickly abates, the fields drying rapidly."

I have not been able to find any Siamese reference to kite-flying in the Ayudhyā period or earlier, except in the old legend *Suvarṇa-haṅṣa*, in which a lover is led to his lady by following the string of a runaway kite, and Gerini's conclusion seems to be based entirely on the passage in La Loubère,[2] which mentions that the kite

> "of the King of Siam is in the Air every Night for the two Winter-months, and some Mandarins are nominated to ease one another in holding the String."

[1] Ge. (2). [2] L. L., p. 49.

From this it appears that the Kite-flying was continued for many days in succession, until the desired result (the setting in of the north-east monsoon) had been obtained. It was thus a magical rather than a religious ceremony; but there seems to be no evidence as to whether it was derived from India or from China. I suspect from the latter, since we know that kite-flying has achieved a similar degree of elaboration in that country. In China also, kites were used to drive away the devil, and in Corea they were used as scapegoats.[1]

2. *Baruṇa Sātra* (*Rain or Varuṇa Festival*).[2]

This Ceremony has, from the days of Sukhodaya onwards, been performed in the ninth month (Srāvaṇa), a time when the commencement of the rains is urgently desired, and it has always been a ceremony of considerable importance in Siam, where the rice crop is absolutely dependent on the seasonal rains.

The ceremony was entirely Brahmanical until perhaps as late as the Bangkok period, when the usual Buddhist modifications appeared. There are now three degrees of the ceremony. The lowest is performed every year, just before the Ploughing Ceremony, when a chapter of monks prays for rain, and at which the King always attends if he can. In seasons when a lack of rain is becoming rather serious, the monks carry out in procession the special image as hereafter described, and recite stanzas. Only in years of great drought is the ceremony, both Buddhist and Brahmanical, performed in full; the last occasion being about thirty years ago. In ancient times, however, the Brahmanical rites were performed regularly every year with the intention of promoting the germination of seeds, but now they are, as already stated, reserved for times of great drought.

The Brahmanical rites were last performed almost exactly as they were in the time of Sukhodaya. Offerings of rice and other grains are first made to the Hindu deities which are then carried out from the Brahmanic temples in a procession resembling that of the Ploughing Festival. They are then placed in an enclosure without a roof, so that they are exposed to the full heat of the sun. The Brahmans, with dishevelled hair and wearing only a loin-cloth such as they use when bathing, take it in turns to read passages from their books before the gods, at the same time waving cloud-coloured flags. This they do twice a day for three days. Each evening they escort the images back to their temple, and formerly they used, in doing so, to make a *pradakṣina* circuit of the palace in order to honour the King.

[1] *GB.* ix, pp. 4 and 203.

[2] Sources: *BRB.*, pp. 540 sqq.; *NN.*, p. 87 (not mentioned in *KM.* or *HV.*).

Sir James Frazer [1] has given numerous examples of the widespread idea of controlling the rain by magic. Apart from the preliminary oblations to the gods, the Siamese ceremony exemplifies three widely known ways of producing rain by magic:—(1) the imitative magic of waving cloud-coloured flags; (2) the imitative magic of wearing bathing costumes, since "if you would make wet weather, you must be wet" [2]; (3) doing violence to the gods, i.e. exposing them to the sun with the intention of making them feel for themselves the unpleasant conditions, so that they may rectify them. This is, wherever it is practised, the last means adopted, after prayer and imitative magic have exhausted the patience of the oppressed.

The first two methods were not mentioned by Frazer as occurring in Siam since they were not mentioned by Bruguière from whom he quotes; but, on the other hand, Bruguière [3] states that if the Siamese "want dry weather, they unroof the temples and let the rain pour down on their idols". But I can find no Siamese authority for the practise of such a rite, which, if it occurred, must have been very rare.

Another method of producing rain which used sometimes to be employed was known as *Bāṁruṅ Ṅā*, which means "clashing of tusks". Two "must" elephants were tied to posts with strong ropes of sufficient length to allow their tusks to meet, but not long enough to allow them to inflict a wound. These animals being much excited by their "must" condition, would rush at each other in an attempt to fight and their tusks would clash, giving forth a loud sound. The animal which succeeded in forcing its tusks between those of its opponent and, with this leverage, in raising the other's head, was deemed to be the victor. The animals were then separated, and the mahouts indulged in a competitive dance and exchange of views regarding each other's skill and courage. This false combat was fought three times, followed by the dance and word war on the part of the mahouts. The movements, rhythm, and postures of the dance followed a set form.[4] It appears either that the clashing of tusks was a magical imitation of thunder, or that the mock fight was intended to inspire the rain gods with fear.

The Buddhist modifications now form the more important and popular, though less interesting, portion of the ceremony. The monks carry out in procession a certain image of the Buddha to the royal plaza, and they perform a religious service before it. The image is carried

[1] *GB.* i, chap. 5, esp. pp. 296–9. [2] *GB.* i, p. 272.
[3] *Annales de l'Association de la Propagation de la Foi*, v, 1831, p. 131.
[4] *BRB.*, pp. 564 sq. and F. H. Giles in *JSS.* xxiii, pt. 2, p. 67.

out into the open, no doubt in analogy to the procedure with regard to the Hindu gods, but the original magical idea has been lost, and the ceremony is rather a religious service of prayer. The particular attitude of the image carried in procession is the one known as *Braḥ-găndhāraḥrāṣṭara*, i.e. calling down rain, according to the following passage in the traditional life of the Buddha :—

> "When the Buddha stayed in Jetavana in the City of Savatthi, no rain fell and the rice withered all over the country. The water in the tanks, ponds and rivers was dried up and even the lotus pond from which the Buddha partook of water. Fishes suffered great distress, because the crows preyed upon them whilst the rest hid themselves in the mud. At that time the Buddha went with his alms bowl collecting food and when he saw this he felt pity. After having partaken of food the Buddha called Ananda asking him to bring him a bath cloth. Ananda said that the water was dried up since several days but the Buddha called for the bath cloth again, and when Ananda gave it to him, the Buddha covered his body with a part of it whilst he put the other part over his shoulder. He stood up near the pond, and is represented calling for rain with his right hand, and opening the left hand to catch the water, and then the rain was falling." [1]

As one might expect, the religious prayer offered to the Buddha on these occasions, being in accordance with the general procedure at other popular festivals connected with the national religion, is more appreciated by the masses of the people than the obscure and little understood rites of the Court Brahmans. Nevertheless, there is room for the latter, amongst a people given to superstition, and, taken together, the *Baruṇa Sāṭra* has still a strong hold over the people and great sociological value in enabling them to endure what must be a trying period of the year, considering that their very existence depends on the coming of the rains. The great power of this ceremony, as opposed to most magical ones, is that it can really never fail; it is, if necessary, kept up indefinitely—and rain must come sooner or later. Again, historical instances are recorded of rain having fallen immediately the ceremonies were undertaken, which is an example of the greater functional value of recorded history than of mere oral tradition, which sooner or later must forget or at least confuse such occurrences.

It is difficult to trace the path along which this Siamese ceremony has journeyed from India, by reason of the fact that perhaps no Brahmanic ceremony shows greater variations in detail in the various countries influenced by Indian civilization. In India itself there are

[1] Extract from translation of an essay of the Somtej Phra Paramanujit, the son of King Rāma I, quoted in *JSS.*, vol. x, 1913, pt. ii, p. 32.

many such variations which have been catalogued by Frazer,[1] and therefore it is not surprising that the rain-making ceremonies in the different countries of Indo-China show little resemblance to each other, and indeed they have probably been grafted on to local primitive cults.

In Burma there is a ceremony for the calling down of rain, called *Mōnāt Puzaw*, or worship of the Lord of the Clouds (presumably Varuṇa). It was of Indian origin, but apparently is now confined to prayer for rain by the Buddhist abbots,[2] and in Cambodia there is a rain-making ceremony called *Bauchea krabey*, in which a buffalo is sacrificed.[3] But neither of these forms throws any light on the evolution of the Siamese Brahmanic ceremony, which appears to be independently derived from India, and to be made up largely of late Tantric rites.

3. *The Speeding of the Outflow* (*lài ro'a* or *lài nẳṁ*).[4]

The Ceremony of the Speeding of the Outflow was formerly performed in the first lunar month (Mārgaśīrṣa). It was a magical ceremony designed to induce the dispersion of flood water, which at that time of year might be endangering the rice-crop. It was of great sociological importance, enabling the people to bear the strain of a period in which the entire fruits of the year's labour were in jeopardy, and the country was threatened with famine. It was not performed every year, but only after years of unusually heavy rainfall, when the floods assumed dangerous proportions, the last occasion being in the great flood year of A.D. 1831.

Probably it was discontinued because the King himself, and not the Brahmans, performed this ceremony, and it would not add to the dignity of the King if it continued to rain, as it sometimes did, after the ceremony; whereas the failure of a ceremony performed by the Brahmans would matter less. In fact, this was evidently felt as long ago as the seventeenth century by King Nārāyaṇa, since La Loubère says:—

> "The present King was the first that dispensed with this troublesome work, and it is several years since it seemed abolished; because, they say, that the last time he perform'd it, he had the disgrace of being surpriz'd with rain, although his Astrologers had promised him a fair day." [5]

The King, accompanied by the Royal Family, proceeded down the river in a grand procession of state barges. While officials beat gongs,

[1] Loc. cit.
[2] *ERE.* art. "Burma".
[3] L., pp. 574 sqq.
[4] Sources: *BRB.*, pp. 63 sqq., and *KM.*
[5] L. L., p. 43.

the King repeatedly waved the long-handled fan (*bŏjaḥnī*) in the direction of the sea, as an intimation to the flood-demon, i.e. the waters, to flow away rapidly. It was thus a rite of imitative magic, and is especially interesting as being, so far as I know, the only Siamese ceremony in which the King performs a rite, not as a god, but in the more primitive rôle of magician.

Most of the European writers, such as Diogo do Couto [1] in the sixteenth century, Le Comte de Forbin,[2] John Struys,[3] Tachard,[4] de Choisy,[5] and Kaempfer [6] in the seventeenth century, mention this ceremony. They all, however, make the mistake of confounding the royal fan with a sword with which, they say, the king cut the water. But this, as Gerini points out,[7] is absurd. They also, with greater accuracy, make mention of boat-races following the ceremony. These were a feature of the Ayudhyā period in this ceremony as in the Royal Regatta, and as they still are in the Cambodian ceremony. But Graham [8] was wrong in identifying the modern P̱āknāṁ Festival with the *lải ro'a*, since the former is without a doubt a relic of the Royal Regatta.

Disregarding the usual Buddhist modifications which were added on in the Bangkok period (the presence of Buddhist monks in the procession who invoke the Buddha, represented by the image known as *Braḥ Hām Samud*, i.e. in the attitude of calming the ocean) one might suppose that the ceremony was of Brahmanic origin, despite the fact that no Brahmans took part in it. This supposition is confirmed by the Cambodian ceremony [9] which survives up to the present day, and includes two rites not known in Siam: (1) a rite in which a Brahman, after invocation of the Hindu deities, cuts a leather thong stretched across the river between two boats by means of the sacred sword. The meaning of this rite has not been satisfactorily explained; (2) in which the king sprinkles himself with lustral water offered by the Brahmans. On the other hand, what would appear to be the essential rite of endeavouring to force the waters to disperse by waving the fan does not appear. Our knowledge of this ceremony is indeed fragmentary and unsatisfactory; it can only be said with reasonable certainty that the Siamese form is Brahmanic, and was derived from India, probably via Cambodia.

[1] *Decades*, quoted in Bowring, i, p. 101.
[2] *Memoirs*.
[3] *Voyages*, Eng. ed., 1684, p. 50.
[4] *Voyage de Siam des pères Jesuites*, Amsterdam, 1687, p. 221.
[5] *Journal*, Trevoux, 1712, p. 242
[6] i, p. 73, where he confuses this ceremony with *Kaṭhina nām̐*.
[7] Ge. (2).
[8] *Siam*, ii, pp. 278 sq.
[9] L., chap. xii.

Appendix to Chapter XVIII

My attention has recently been called by my friend, Monsieur René Nicolas, to a rain-making ceremony performed at Phnompenh in the reign of the present king Monivong of Cambodia. I thought it might be of interest to include it in this work, firstly, because it does not appear to have been published elsewhere, and secondly, because similar rites may have formerly been performed in Siam in connection with the *Baruṇa Sūtra*. The following is a copy of the programme for the celebration at Phnompenh, as I received it:—

Dimanche 18 *aout* 1929, *de* 18 *h* 15 *à* 20 *h* 15.

DANSES RITUELLES
exécutées
dans la salle du Trône du Palais Royal
à l'occasion de la
Ceremonie des Offrandes aux Anges (Buong-Suong) [1]
afin de solliciter la pluie pour la culture du paddy et la santé publique, suivies d'un thé offert par
Sa Majesté Prea Bat Samdach Prea Sisowathmonivong
Roi de Cambodge,
en l'honneur de
Madame et Monsieur Lavit
Résident Supérieur de Cambodge.

PROGRAMME

I. Présentation des mets, dans des plateaux d'or et d'argent, aux Anges des quatres points cardinaux par douze danseuses représentant quatre princes, quatre princesses et quatre ogres.

II. Ballet des offrandes aux Anges dites Buong-Suong exécuté par les danseuses à l'exception des quatre ogres qui sortent pour réapparaitre ensuite seuls sur la scène.

III. Danse d'ouverture exécutée par l'archange Vorchhun.

IV. Promenade à travers les airs de la déese des mers Mékhala qui détient un joyau merveilleux.

V. L'Ange-géant Réam-Eyso cherche à s'emparer en vain du joyau qui éblouit quand la déesse Mékhala le montre.

VI. Ballet des offrandes aux Anges dites "Chap-Robam" exécuté par l'ensemble de la troupe (Abondance de la saison pluvieuse, souhaits de bonne santé, de longévité et de bonheur).

[1] Siamese, *Braṅ Sraṅ* (guardian genii).

CHAPTER XIX

FESTIVALS OF FIRST FRUITS

1. *Dhānya-daha.*[1]

Until the end of the Ayudhyā period there was a State Ceremony of Harvest Thanksgiving, known as *Dhānya-daha*, or Burning of the Ears of Padi, which took place in the third month (Māgha). In the Sukhodaya period, according to Nāṅ Nabamaśa, the King was present at the burning of the padi, but Khun Hlvaṅ Hā Văt states that during the Ayudhyā period the ceremony was carried out as follows :—

An official dressed as a " temporary king " proceeded to the royal padi fields in a procession similar to that of the Ploughing Ceremony. A dais had been erected on the fields, and on this a tiered umbrella-of-state, made of various kinds of padi. The mock king seated himself on the dais and then set fire to the straw umbrella. His retinue was divided into two parties, one dressed in green and the other in red, representing respectively the followers of Indra and Brahmā.[2] These two parties of gods then ran to the burning umbrella and attempted to carry it off by force. Prognostics were drawn according to the party which was successful.

According to the *Baṅsāvaḥtāra* for the reign of King Paramakoṣa the rites consisted, perhaps in addition to the Burning of the Padi, of a ceremony of Carrying Home the Padi (*baraduk khẖu laṅ nai raḥdèḥ*). The King himself went out in state to the Crown padi fields, and loaded some of the grain on to a sled, which was drawn to the palace by members of the royal family by means of a rope of twisted padi straw. On arrival at the palace a tiered umbrella was fashioned from this rope, the juice was pressed from the grain and was mixed with cocoa-nut milk to form a gruel, which was presented to the abbots of the royal monasteries.

Taken as a whole, this ceremony is evidently a Sacrifice of First Fruits which, in the development of ritual, is a later stage than the primitive idea known as a Sacrament of First Fruits. Concerning such rites, Sir James Frazer[3] states that

[1] Sources : *BRB.*, pp. 118 sqq. ; *NN.*, p. 71 ; *HV.* ; the *KM.* simply says " *phau khẖu mài mī* ", i.e. " there is no burning of the padi ", the ceremony evidently having been in abeyance at the time the *KM.* was written.

[2] Gerini in Ge. (2) states that there were four parties, representing the gods of the quarters, but he cites no authority.

[3] *GB.* viii, p. 109.

"primitive peoples often partake of the new corn and the new fruits sacramentally, because they suppose them to be instinct with a divine spirit of life. At a later age, when the fruits of the earth are conceived as created rather than as animated by a divinity, the new fruits are no longer partaken of sacramentally as the body and blood of the god; but a portion of them is offered to the divine beings who are believed to have produced them. Originally, perhaps, offerings of first-fruits were supposed to be necessary for the subsistence of the divinities, who without them must have died of hunger; but in after times they seem to be looked upon rather in the light of a tribute or mark of homage rendered by man to the gods for the good gifts they have bestowed on him. Sometimes the first-fruits are presented to the king, perhaps in his character of a god; very often they are made over to the spirits of the human dead, who are sometimes thought to have it in their power to give or withhold the crops. Till the first-fruits have been offered to the deity, the dead, or the king, people are not at liberty to eat of the new crops."

The Burning of the Ears of Padi and the Conveying of it Home are two stages in an interesting series of superimposed rites, illustrating the evolution of the Sacrifice of First Fruits from a very early period. I will attempt to analyse this series as follows:—

(1) The Burning of the Ears of Padi was originally a sacrifice to Agni, and as such can be traced back to the Vedic offering of first fruits or *Āgrayaṇeshti*.[1]

(2) Later the king exercised his divine functions by himself receiving the fire offering (and we have seen that he was present at the ceremony during the Sukhodaya period).

(3) But, for reasons to be discussed in a later chapter, he afterwards appointed a substitute "temporary king" to take his place.

(4) A very interesting episode is the competition to obtain the spoil between the followers of Indra and Brahmā. The meaning of this is quite forgotten, and I have seen no attempted explanation of it. When reading the account of the Vedic *Āgrayaṇeshti* in the *Śatapatha Brāhmaṇa*, however, it at once occurred to me that I had found a possible explanation: The *Āgrayaṇeshti* oblations consisted of (i) a sacrificial cake on twelve potsherds for Indra and Agni; (ii) a mess of boiled grains for the Viśve Deva (All-gods), prepared with water or milk; and (iii) a cake on one potsherd for heaven and earth. That this oblation was due to them was explained by a myth which stated that the gods had performed a sacrifice in order to rid the world of the *asuras* who were poisoning the food of all men. But the gods could not agree as to the partition of the sacrifice:—

[1] *Śatapatha Brāhmaṇa*, ii, 4, 3, in *SBE*. xii, p. 369; and *Paraskara-Grihya Sutra*, iii, 2, in *SBE*. xxix, p. 338.

"Then they said, 'To which of us shall this belong?' They did not agree (each of them exclaiming), 'Mine it shall be!' Not having come to an agreement, they said, '*Let us run a race for this* (*sacrifice*) *: whichever of us beats* (*the others*), *his it shall be!*' '*So be it!*' *they said, and they ran a race.* Indra and Agni won, and hence that Indra-Agni cake on twelve potsherds; Indra and Agni having won a share in it. *And where Indra and Agni were standing when they had won, thither all the gods followed them.*" [1]

I suggest that the struggle for the spoils between the representatives of the gods in Siam is identical with the race between the Vedic gods. One must, of course, after such an immense lapse of time, allow for a certain amount of modification and confusion, due especially to the introduction of the mock king and the loss of the original meaning of the rite.

(5) The Conveying Home of the Padi, rather than being a distinct ceremony, seems to be a later stage in the series. It belongs to that late period when the reason for the "temporary king" has been forgotten, and the king wishes to resume his place as receiver of the first fruits. The erection of a royal umbrella of straw is in this case, as in the case of the "temporary king", a symbol of his being Lord of the Rice.

(6) The offering of rice-gruel to the monks is merely the addition of latter-day pious Buddhist kings. It cannot be considered as a sacrament of first fruits.

The Brahmanical Sacrifice of the First Fruits evidently spread from India to all the countries of Indo-China. In Burma it was known as the *Mahā-peinnē Pwedaw,* and the offerings from the king's hands were made to the Mahā-peinnē Nat at the Arakan Pagoda, Amarapura.[2] In Cambodia the ceremony, substantially the same as that of Siam, and from which the latter was probably derived, has been retained until modern times. It was mentioned by Cheou Ta-kouan in the thirteenth century in the words "after the rice harvest they burn rice in honour of Buddha", and, in its modern form, it has been fully described by Leclère.[3] It is called the *Thvoeu-bon Sdach Méakh*, the Sdach Méakh or King of the Month of Māgha, being of course the "temporary king" who officiates on this occasion. But the competition between the representatives of Indra and Brahmā is not mentioned, having evidently disappeared in the course of time. On the other hand, the Ceremony of Conveying home the Padi, which is also not mentioned, probably did not occur in Cambodia, and was a late Siamese modification.

[1] *Śatapatha Brāhmaṇa*, ii, 4, 3. 4, and 5.

[2] *ERE*. art. "Burma".

[3] L., pp. 292 sqq.

Dhānya-daha was naturally a ceremony in which the people took great interest, since it was necessary that it should be performed before they themselves could enjoy the fruits of their labours. It was, indeed, not only a royal ceremony, but was also a festival of the people, being celebrated on a limited scale in every town and village. And though the royal ceremony has long since ceased to exist, the harvest operations are still accompanied by oblations to the gods in rural districts. There is also much rejoicing, and a popular pastime at this season is known as *lĕn bleṅ*, or the singing of rhymes connected with harvest and love-making. I have myself witnessed this on one occasion, but a full description of it has been published by H.H. Prince Bidyaḷaṅkaraṇa.[1]

Since the popular harvest celebrations still retain such a hold over the people it seems probable that a revival of the ancient royal ceremony might be beneficial, as it would give official recognition to the present rural customs, and afford a stimulus to the people to work harder for the production of a satisfactory rice crop.

2. *Bidhī Sārada.*[2]

Until a few decades ago a festival known as *Bidhī Sārada*, which simply means the Feasting Ceremony, took place annually, from the last day of the tenth month (Bhādrapada) until the second day of Āśvina. It was revived by the present King in 1928, and again in 1930. As the ceremony took place, in accordance with ancient tradition, privately within the palace grounds, there was no chance of its awakening any interest amongst the general public, who have completely forgotten that there was once a popular form of the ceremony.

Sārada is a festival which completely lost its original significance during the course of the centuries, and one has to dig deeply in order to unearth that early meaning. Gerini[3] is, so far as I am aware, the only European author who mentions the ceremony, and he sums it up in few words as a half-year (autumnal) festival, originally Śaivic, now an occasion for merit-making; which is perfectly true as far as it goes, but it does not take us very far. King Rāma V, in his book, recognizes from the account of Nāṅ Nabamāśa that in early times the festival was entirely Brahmanic, consisting of the preparation of special food on which the Brahmans feasted and some of which was offered to the gods and manes. In later times the Brahmans took

[1] *JSS.* xx, pp. 101 sqq., "The Pastime of Rhyme Making and Singing in Rural Siam."

[2] Sources: *BRB.*, pp. 599 sqq.; *NN.*, pp. 89 sqq.

[3] Ge. (2).

little part, and the special food was presented to the monks as an act of royal merit-making, in accordance with Buddhist ideas; but the manes were not entirely forgotten, although not taken very seriously. King Rāma V, therefore, supposed that the original rites were Brahmanic, and corresponded to the Hindu *śrāddhas*.

In Cambodia there takes place a Buddhist festival of merit-making at the same time of year, though with rather more attention to the deceased ancestors than was evident in Siam. It is known as the *Thvoeu-bon-kant Boent*, which Leclère [1] translates as " Fête des morts ". It appears to me that both King Rāma V and Leclère have missed the point; and I take the somewhat bold step of attempting to show that this festival is not primarily a Feast of the Dead, but should be correctly classified as a Festival of First Fruits. In Siam, at least, it does not appear that there was any festival specially dedicated to deceased ancestors, and Gerini has remarked [2] that at the beginning of every domestic ceremony oblations, similar to those of the Hindu *śrāddhas*, are offered to the gods and *pitris*. In other words, the spirits of the dead are only remembered when something is required from them, i.e. their assistance in carrying out a ceremony, or (at New Year) their protection, or at least non-interference, during the coming year. I shall endeavour to show that *Sārada* was formerly a Festival of First Fruits.

As performed during the Ayudhyā and Bangkok periods, the ceremonies are as follows: For the three days during which the festival lasts, monks offer special prayers in the royal monasteries for the welfare of the kingdom, and *especially for seasonable rain during the time that it is required for the welfare of the growing rice.*[3] There is also a pavilion erected in the palace grounds where the Brahmans make offerings to the Hindu deities. On the first day, within the Grand Palace enclosure, the preparation of a special confection takes place, which rite forms the most striking feature of the festival. The process is known as *kvan khău dibya*, literally " mixing heavenly rice ", i.e. the food of the gods, which is significant. For this purpose eight of the usual ceremonial pavilions, with curtained roofs each supported on four posts, are erected in the palace grounds. Each pavilion is surrounded by a *rājavăt* fence decorated with paper umbrellas, and intended to ward off evil influences (Pl. XXXII). The ingredients used in making the confection, after having been prepared elsewhere, are brought to the pavilions and the sacred *siñcana* thread is passed round them. They are then poured into eight large pans about a metre in diameter,

[1] L., chap. x. [2] Ge. (1), pp. 40, 41. [3] *BRB.*, p. 629.

PLATE XXXII.

[Photo: Bangkok Times Press, Ltd.

"MIXING THE HEAVENLY RICE" IN THE *SĀRADA* CEREMONY.

[To face page 232.

PLATE XXXIII.

[Photo : Bangkok Times Press, Ltd.

"MIXING THE HEAVENLY RICE": A NEARER VIEW.

and a third of a metre in depth, one being placed on each dais. The ingredients are more than sixty in number, and include the various kinds of rice and other grain grown in the country, together with fruit juices, sugar, milk, butter, and water. As these ingredients have already been prepared, all that requires to be done during the actual ceremony is to stir them together. The result is something like mince-pie.

The stirring of the confection is the duty of thirty-two young ladies of royal degree, preferably of the rank of *Hmòm Cǎu*, but in the event of these not being available, they may be chosen from among those of the rank of *Hmòm Rāja Vaṅṣā* or *Hmòm Hlvaṅ*. They are attired in ancient Siamese style and also have the sacred thread passed round their heads. It is not always easy to find suitable young ladies, because it is essential that they should be very young, and that they should be virgins. The latter regulation probably had some earlier Hindu or pre-Hindu significance, but it is now explained on Buddhist lines, the virgins corresponding to the virgin Sujata, who offered the Buddha a dish of milk rice, in commemoration of which event the Siamese have a special image of the Buddha in the attitude of receiving the dish.[1] But the event in the life of Buddha took place in the sixth month (Vaiśākha).

At the four corners of the raised wooden frame into which the metal pan is fitted on the dais there is an image of a *devatā* (Pl. XXXIII). To these figures, previous to the commencement of the stirring, offerings of candles and flowers are made. It is not known for certain whom they are intended to represent, but the Siamese authorities suppose that they are the *grū* or spiritual professors who preside over the ceremony. Proximately, that is probably what they are, but I suggest that this is only the Hindu explanation borrowed by Buddhism. I think that they are the oldest feature in the ceremony, that they take us back to a time before Hinduism and Buddhism existed, and that they are in fact Spirits of the Corn.

A chapter of monks is invited to the ceremony, and when all is ready the King arrives and a proclamation is read to the assembly to the effect that, whereas the King has deemed it expedient to maintain (or revive) the ancient ceremony, it behoves all those taking part in it to pay attention to their allotted tasks in the spirit of kindness and charity. The proclamation ends with a pious wish that faith in the Buddha, the Law, and the Order may bring health and happiness to the King and prosperity to the country. The monks, holding one end of the sacred *siñcana* thread, recite passages from

[1] *JSS.*, vol. x, pt. 2, Fig. 5.

the sacred books, bless the King, and then retire. The King then sprinkles the virgins with consecrated water, after which they are conducted to their appointed stations, four to each of the eight pans.

As the stirring with long wooden ladles proceeds, the work becomes harder as the mixture thickens. The King then takes his departure, and the maidens hand their work over to strong men, and are later rewarded with some of the confection. On the evening of the day on which the *khău dibya* is made, some of it is partaken of by the King, and also by members of the Royal Family and high officials. But by far the most important part of the proceedings is the presentation every morning of the confection to the monks who have officiated at the special services in the royal temples, as well as the chapter who had recited scriptural passages at the stirring ceremony.

The offering of *khău dibya* to the *pitris* and to the *grūs* is, as already stated, no longer taken very seriously, but, at least until the modern revivals, it was always the custom to expose some of the food on tables, especially at cross-roads. The *grūs* are deceased spiritual professors, and the *pitris* are, of course, the ancestors. These offerings are the same as the Hindu *śrāddhas*, and the food thus offered is called *khău piṇḍa*. But the Siamese do not distinguish between the Hindu *ēkōddishṭa-śrāddha* offerings to the *pretas*, i.e. the spirits of those who have recently died and are wandering as ghosts, and the *sapiṇḍī-karaṇa* offerings due to those who have escaped from that stage and joined the company of the "fathers".[1] The Siamese *piṇḍa* offerings are made indiscriminately to all spirits of the dead. Their idea of the *preṭa* differs somewhat from that of the ancient Indians :—

> " It is a giant among *phī*, varying in height from ten to sixteen metres. It is the ghost of one who was an evil doer when alive. Its mouth is exceedingly small, even as the eye of a needle, so that it can never satisfy its hunger. The consequence is that its appearance is that of a skeleton. It cannot speak, but can make a noise like a whistle. There is one such *phī*, which is said to have been seen by many people, that appears in the Chinese graveyard on the Windmill Road [Bangkok]." [2]

But this loss of the original significance of the *preṭa* is not exclusively Siamese ; it is common to later times in India.

The ceremonies described above may be analysed as follows :—

(1) The *khău dibya* is made of every available product of the soil, together with milk and butter, the latter used in most Hindu oblations.

(2) The *devatā* figures which preside over the stirring are, I think,

---

[1] Barnett, *Antiquities of India*, p. 149.   [2] *JSS.*, vol. iv, part ii, p. 22.

to be regarded as descended from the Spirits of the Corn which at one time animated the confection with their vitality and were eaten sacramentally. In the course of the corresponding Cambodian ceremony, in some parts of the country the monks make images of the Buddha out of the rice presented to them mixed with a resinous substance. This seems very probably to be a relic of "eating the god".

(3) The virgins, as stated above, no doubt have an earlier significance than that attributed to them by Buddhism. There is a widespread connection between virginity and the fertility of cattle and plants, e.g. in the rites of the Roman Vestel Virgins who, like the Siamese maidens, were princesses.[1] Possibly the Siamese virgins taking part in this ceremony were originally goddesses of fertility. The rite of preparation by virgins does not occur in the Cambodian ceremony, according to Leclère,[2] where the royal ceremony consists only of the Brahmans offering oblations to the gods and *pitris*. Nor can I find anything to compare with it elsewhere. Possibly we have here the survival of an extremely ancient fertility rite on to which Hinduism, and later, Buddhism, have been grafted.

(4) Some of the confection is offered (i) to the King (god); (ii) to the Royal Family and officials (lesser gods); (iii) to the spirits of the dead; and (iv) to the monks. The latter, although of course so important in the modern aspect of the ceremony as a Buddhist merit-making festival, may be disregarded here, and the offering to nobles and officials is equally a late addition. What is of importance historically is the offering of the *khău dibya* to the King and to the *pitris*, which are exactly the classes of beings to which Frazer has shown that offerings of first fruits are made.

I think that the above evidence is sufficient for us to conclude that the *Bidhī Sārada* was once a Festival of First Fruits. Moreover, we can distinguish several strata in the development of the festival. We get a glimpse of what was perhaps an early rite of partaking of the Spirit of the Corn sacramentally, which possibly belongs to the early stock of pre-Hindu Indo-Chinese culture; and we see this developing into a Brahmanic sacrifice of the first fruits to the gods, the king, and the *pitris*. But now all this has been much obscured by Buddhist merit-making, and the Brahmans take only a minor part in the ceremony.

The earlier stages in this evolution are in accordance with what is found elsewhere; Frazer has shown that with a number of peoples

[1] *GB.* ii, pp. 228–9. [2] L., loc. cit.

"the sacrament of first-fruits is combined with a sacrifice or presentation of them to gods or spirits, and in course of time the sacrifice of first-fruits tends to throw the sacrament into the shade, if not to supersede it".[1]

This is exactly what has happened in Siam and Cambodia, with the addition of a still later stage in which either ancestor worship (Cambodia) or Buddhist merit-making (Siam) has caused the original significance to be forgotten.

It remains to find a satisfactory answer to the question: "Why has this seemingly important festival thus degenerated?", and I think that in tracing the ceremony back to India a satisfactory answer can be obtained.

Amongst the various Festivals of the First Fruits that are to be observed in modern times in different parts of India, the following has much in common with *Sārada*:—

> "In some parts of Northern India, the festival of the new crop is known as *Navan*, that is, 'new grain'. When the crop is ripe, the owner takes the omens, goes to the field, plucks five or six ears of barley in the spring crop and one of the millets in the autumn harvest. This is brought home, parched, and mixed with coarse sugar, butter, and curds. Some of it is thrown on the fire in the name of the village gods and deceased ancestors; the rest is eaten by the family."[2]

If this is the same as the *Mahā-navami*, described by Dubois[3] as a feast specially dedicated to ancestors, it took place at the new moon of October, i.e. approximately at the same time as does the Siamese *Sārada*.

Turning now to Vedic times I think we can find the common origin of these ceremonies in the *Sākamedha* offerings. Their performance required two days: firstly, offerings were made to the gods; then

> "in the afternoon takes place the Mahāpitriyagña, or (Great) sacrifice to the Manes (performed on a special altar and fireplace, south of the Dakshiṇāgni); which is succeeded by the Traiyambaka-homa, or offering to the Rudra Tryambaka, performed on a cross-way somewhere north of the sacrificial ground."[4]

The *Sākamedha* was a seasonal liturgy inaugurating the beginning of autumn; that and the fact that it included a special offering to the Manes make me think that it is the prototype of the Siamese *Sārada*. True, it was not specially regarded as an offering of first fruits. The latter was more definitely connected with the *Āgrayaṇeshti* which I have identified with the Siamese *Dhānya-daha*. But, as Dr. Barnett has pointed out,[5] there are various *Āgrayaṇa* feasts, in which

[1] *GB*. viii, p. 86. [2] *GB*. viii, p. 56. [3] *D*., p. 569.
[4] *Śatapatha Brāhmaṇa* in *SBE*. xii, p. 408, note 1. [5] *Antiquities of India*, p. 160.

the rites varied, namely, of rice in the autumn, barley in spring, millet in the autumn, or rainy season, and bamboo-seed in summer. It seems probable that the *Sākamedha* was an autumnal *Āgrayaṇa* festival.

This seems to suggest a reason why the original meaning of the *Sārada* was lost in Siam and Cambodia. In these countries there is but one harvest worthy of the name, and that is the rice harvest which was celebrated by the *Dhānya-daha*. Thus, while Indian colonists brought with them their autumnal festival of the first fruits, and perhaps sought to graft it on to some indigenous sacrament of the first fruits transposed from another time of year, in an effort to keep up the customs of their fatherland, the endeavour was doomed to failure, because this was not the rice harvest season in Siam.

CHAPTER XX

THE SWINGING FESTIVAL[1]

1. *The Reception of the Gods and the Swinging Proper.*

The important ceremony of *Ṭrīyămbavāy Ṭrīpavāy*, popularly known as *Lò Jiṅ J'ǎ* ("pulling the swing") is one of the most interesting as well as one of the most difficult to understand of all Siamese State Ceremonies. Not only is it of great historical interest, but it also retains considerable sociological value, but the latter is due mainly to the pageantry that accompanies it rather than to the ceremony itself. Almost all European writers of the Bangkok period have a good deal to say about this ceremony, which is not surprising, considering its spectacular nature, but little that is of any value for a serious inquiry. But it is remarkable that, so far as I know, none of the seventeenth century European writers mention this ceremony, which we know from Siamese sources was practised in the Ayudhyā period. In this section I shall deal with the Swinging Proper and the accompanying Reception of the Gods, while in the following section I shall make a thorough study of the little known rites performed by the Brahmans in their temples during the fifteen days of the gods' supposed stay on earth.

The Swinging Festival was formerly performed in the first lunar month, but was later changed to the second month. It was not only an important State Ceremony in Bangkok and in the former capitals, Ayudhyā and Sukhodaya, but was practised in the other chief cities of the realm in ancient times. At Nagara Śrī Dharmarāja the Swing still stands, but there is no longer a State Ceremony there.

According to the common Siamese belief, the purpose of the *Ṭrīyămbavāy Ṭrīpavāy* is as follows: Once a year the god Śiva comes down to visit this world and stays here for ten days. He used to arrive on the seventh day of the waxing moon in the first month and depart on the first day of the waning moon. But it was not difficult to postpone the date of his arrival until the second month; for, as King Rāma V remarks, the Brahmans, like the Pope, hold that they keep the keys of Heaven and, of course, Śiva could not come down till they had opened the door for him. Now, according to Siamese

[1] Sources: *BRB.*, pp. 77 sqq.; *NN.*, p. 70; *KM.*; *HV.*; and personal observation, to which I devoted considerable time, and for which I enjoyed special opportunities in the case of this ceremony.

Plate XXXIV.

[Photo: Narasingh Studio.

The Swinging in Progress.

[To face page 238.

notions, Śiva is a jovial god who likes to be amused; so the swinging and the acrobatic feats which accompany the procession are devised for his entertainment. On the contrary, Viṣṇu, who arrives on the day Śiva leaves, and stays only five days, is supposed by the Siamese to be of a quiet and retiring disposition. Accordingly, he is honoured only by the rites performed nightly by the Brahmans in the temple dedicated to him. It is strange that the Siamese conception of the characters of the two high gods is exactly the reverse of that held in India.

Śiva is received with great éclat. Divine beings like the Sun, the Moon, the Earth, and the Ganges assemble together and wait upon him. These lesser gods are represented by the carved panels which the Brahmans fix in front of the pavilions from which Śiva will watch the swinging.

For this ceremony the King appoints a nobleman to impersonate Śiva, and during the three days that the festival lasts this noble used to have almost unlimited powers and rights over certain of the State revenues. He was, in fact, a "temporary king" or "temporary god"—the two terms being almost synonymous in Siam—and this institution will be dealt with fully in Chapter XXII. It appears from the short account of Nāṅ Nabamāśa (who mentions the swinging, sprinkling of water, and circular dances) that during the Sukhodaya period the King was present at the ceremony, but during the Ayudhyā period the King remained in his palace on these occasions. The *KM*. makes much of a ceremonial bath which the King took on the occasion of the Swinging Festival, and this is also mentioned by Khun Hlvaṅ Hā Văt, but as there is no known instance of this having actually taken place, King Rāma V thinks that it probably refers to the time of King Nārāyaṇa, who is known to have favoured Brahmanism more than Buddhism, and probably wished to consider himself a Hindu on this occasion.

During the Ayudhyā period (as mentioned by Khun Hlvaṅ Hā Văt) and until the third reign of the present dynasty, it was only *Čău Braḥyā Baladeba* (Minister of Agriculture) who impersonated Śiva, but King Rāma IV, thinking that it was too much for this official to be expected to arrange for two great State Ceremonies every year, inaugurated the custom, which has been followed ever since, of appointing a different *braḥyā* of golden bowl rank to preside over the Swinging each year.

On the seventh day of the waning moon, in the morning, the procession of Śiva proceeds from the Buddhist temple of Văt Rāja-purāna, following the city wall, to the Swing. The god is supposed to have just arrived in this world. He wears a tall pointed hat representing a crown, a tunic, and long robe similar to that worn by the King on State occasions, and a *phā-nuṅ* of brocade. The mode of wearing the latter is called *pāv khun* ("slave of the king"), one side of the cloth being allowed to hang loose in front, i.e. only one side is tucked up behind and not both, as in the common practice. He is carried on a palanquin, accompanied by a royal umbrella, a sunshade, and several processional umbrellas, with a detachment of "drummers of victory", and pages bearing his insignia (Pl. XXXV).

The procession is made up differently each year. There are always a number of acrobats and persons dressed as sprites from celestial spheres, and sometimes Indra mounted on Airāvata; while nowadays it has become the fashion to add a long and incongruous array representing the department or industry with which the *braḥyā* is associated in ordinary life. In 1929 the procession was illustrative of the activities of the Ministry of War, with aeroplanes and the newly-purchased tanks; while in 1930, the *braḥyā* being a Chinese gentleman connected with commerce, there were model rice-mills on wheels, advertisements for certain makes of motor-car tyres, and walking bottles of whiskey—in fact, most Chinese firms took the opportunity to advertise their wares. The occasion was spoken of by the Siamese with pride as being a Siamese Lord Mayor's Show, and I noticed that, while there was little interest in the Swinging, which means absolutely nothing to the modern Siamese, vast crowds lined the route of the procession, which alone appears to be of any sociological value. But, however much one may regret these innovations, it must be said that to this "selling campaign" we owe the preservation of the Swinging Festival, which had almost reached the stage at which lack of interest and loss of significance are followed by abolition.[1]

The Swing is an enormous permanent erection some eighty feet high, which used to stand on a grassy plot in front of the Brahman temples, but now stands in the centre of a paved open space about a hundred yards from them. It consists of a pair of great red-painted teak pillars, like ship's masts, which slope slightly inwards, and are joined at the top by carved cross-pieces (Pl. XXXIV). On the occasion of the festival a plank is suspended from the lower cross-piece by means of ropes, and the central part of the plaza, around the Swing, is enclosed by a *rājavăt* fence. Before the procession arrives, the Brahmans carry out a swing-seat from their temple, and are supposed to hang it up; but, when the *braḥyā* arrives, the plank is taken back into

[1] I am informed on high authority that not long before this occasion the question of abolition was actually considered by the Supreme Council of State.

PLATE XXXV.

[Photo: Narasingh Studio.

THE PROCESSION OF "ŚÍVA" AT THE SWINGING CEREMONY.

To face page 240.]

Plate XXXVI.

[Photo: Narasingh Studio.

"Śiva" with his Insignia Bearers watching the Swinging.

the temple and another plank which has already been fastened to the swing-posts is let down, and it is supposed to be the same one as that which has been taken back into the temple. The reason for this is obscure, but it may be that it is to avert some evil omen.

On arrival, Śiva alights in the north-east corner of the plaza at a thatched hut or *śālā*, called the *mānab* or *māḷak*. He is then led to the furthest west of three pavilions (called *jamram*) of bamboo poles and white cloth which have been erected along the northern side of the plaza. In the middle of this pavilion there is a bamboo rail, covered with white cloth, for sitting on, and another one to lean against. The *braḥyā* sits on the rail. He crosses his left foot over his right knee and plants his right foot on the floor (Pl. XXXVI). Khun Hlvaṅ Hā Văt mentions this, and states that if the *braḥyā* were to allow both feet to touch the ground his property would be confiscated. The attitude may represent some *Yoga* discipline of ancient India. Four Brahmans stand on his right, two officials of the Ministry of War and two officials of the Ministry of the Interior of the rank of *hlvaṅ* stand on his left, while two conch blowers stand in front. As soon as he has arrived at the *jamram* he sends joss-sticks and candles to be offered in worship in the Buddhist temple (Văt Sudăśana) opposite; and sometimes he himself goes to worship at the temple, drums of victory being beaten while he enters and leaves. This feature is, of course, a comparatively late Buddhist addition.

When Śiva has taken up his position the swinging begins. There are three sets of swingers (*nārivăn*), with four men to each set. Their peculiar head-dress shows that they are supposed to be *nāgas*. For each set of swingers a reward is offered in a purse tied to the top of a slender bamboo pole erected some distance to the west of the Swing (Pl. XXXIV). In the first instance the purse contains twelve ticals, in the second ten, and in the third eight. When the swingers have climbed into the swing-seat they first do homage to Śiva, and then remain seated while the cradle gathers momentum as the result of a man pulling on a dependent rope. Then the man nearest to the purse gets on his feet, throws off his hat, and endeavours to snatch the purse with his teeth, while the man in the rear steers the cradle towards the pole. Several feints are made (evidently with the object of amusing the god—or the crowd) before the purse is seized. Success is greeted with applause, while any untoward accident is regarded as a bad omen. At the conclusion of each successful effort gongs are sounded and conches blown, and all the four swingers stand up and violently agitate the swing-seat by pulling the ropes, apparently in order to bring it to rest as rapidly as possible. They then once more pay homage to Śiva with joined palms and descend to the ground. After all three sets have performed their task, the swinging for the day is finished, and Śiva mounts his palanquin and is carried off in procession.

Next day there are only the Brahmanic rites in the temple, but on the day after that the swinging is again performed, but this time in the evening and with several additional features. The procession again sets out from Văt Rājapurāna and wends its way to the scene of the swinging, but on this occasion the *braḥyā* does not stop at the *mānab*, but goes straight to the western *jamram*, where he takes his seat and the swinging is carried out three times by the three sets of swingers as on the previous occasion, and they are rewarded with the same amounts of money. After the swinging is over, all the swingers bring a big brass basin, called *khăn sāgara*, full of water, and set it before the *jamram* in which Śiva is seated. They then perform a circular dance, called *senaṅ*, of three circuits around the basin, each *nāga* swinging a buffalo horn as he dances (Pl. XXXVII). Before the last circuit they run towards the basin and fill their horns with water, and after the completion of the last circuit they scatter the water from the horns over each other.[1] Śiva then rises and goes to the second *jamram*, and afterwards to the third. Each time the swingers follow him with their basin, dance the *senaṅ*, and throw water over each other. Then the *braḥyā* mounts his palanquin and is carried in procession back to Văt Rājapurāna.

It is the custom for the King to grant the *braḥyā* forty ticals for presiding over the ceremony, and the *braḥyā* himself presents to those who march in line with him (corresponding to aides-de-camp), four ticals each; the leaders of the procession one or two ticals each; those next to the leaders fifty satangs each; and all the others twenty-five satangs each. If the procession is big he must spend a large sum in feeding the men and giving them presents. Besides which, he must spend a little more in providing special costumes for his followers. All this, however, only applies to the "royal party" and the accompanying sprites and jugglers, not, of course, to the various elements which make up the enormous procession of this Siamese "Lord Mayor's Show".

It was King Rāma IV who first broke away from the old custom of remaining in his palace during the festival. He took great interest in the ceremonies and, following his usual custom, added Buddhist modifications to what was before a purely Hindu observance. In accordance with his idea that all State Ceremonies should conform

[1] The swingers do not use their hats as scoops, nor do they scatter the water over the crowd, as inaccurately stated by Graham in *Siam*, ii, p. 269.

PLATE XXXVII.

[Photo: Bangkok Times Press, Ltd.

THE CIRCULAR DANCE OF THE "*NĀGAS*".

[To face page 242.

PLATE XXXVIII.

[*Photo: Bangkok Times Press, Ltd.*

"ŚIVA" PAYING HOMAGE TO THE KING.

to Buddhism, cocoa-nuts, bananas, and sugar-cane were placed before the Emerald Buddha, and there was a service in which pop-corn was offered to the Buddha, in imitation of the offerings of the Brahmans in their temple. Buddhist texts were also recited for three days, and on the fifth of the waning moon food was offered to the monks who had officiated. These Buddhist observances thus became a preliminary to the Hindu festival.

The custom of the King being present as a spectator was also first introduced by King Rāma IV, and nowadays the King usually watches the ceremonies. This expression of the royal interest is much appreciated by the people, and especially acts as a stimulus to those who organize the procession. This comparatively recent innovation necessitated certain modifications in the programme. The King usually watches the swinging from the stone *śālā* on the wall of the Buddhist monastery, Văt Sudăśana, situated on the south of the plaza. The procession of Śiva is held up *en route* until it is ascertained that the King has arrived at the Văt. Then the mock "royal party" files before the *śālā*, the *braḥyā* walking, accompanied by his insignia bearers, he having alighted from his palanquin some distance away. Having arrived before the *śālā* he kneels on a mat and pays homage to the King in the usual way (Pl. XXXVIII). He then rises and proceeds to the *jamram*. It used to be the custom for the King to present to the *braḥyā*, at the time of the homage, 200 *kălpavṛkṣa* fruits, presumably containing coins to the value of forty ticals, the amount of the *braḥyā*'s reward for his services.

Leaving the question of the "temporary king" for later consideration, I shall here only attempt to trace the origin of the Swinging Ceremony itself. As with many other Siamese festivals it is, I think, quite clear that we have not to deal with one ceremony, but a whole series of ceremonies superimposed on one another. After much thought on this subject, I feel that, while it is not difficult to point to the origin of the Swinging, it is almost a superhuman task to endeavour to trace the misunderstandings and interpolations of succeeding ages. This is, of course, quite the opposite of the accepted view on the matter in Siam, where, the early significance of the swinging having been completely forgotten and obscured by later accretions, the latter are regarded as affording the true interpretation. I think that my article on the "Origin of the Swinging Festival"[1] was the first occasion on which the theory that the Swinging was originally a solar ceremony has been elaborated, although Gerini[2] had suggested as

[1] *Bangkok Times*, 27th Dec., 1930. [2] Ge. (2.)

much without, however, bringing forward any evidence from India in support of his supposition. Again, although Frazer, in my opinion, has failed to interpret the Siamese Swinging Ceremony correctly, he has nevertheless collected a great deal of valuable data on the various kinds of swinging practised in different parts of the world.[1] He has shown that swinging is performed with different objects in view by different peoples. If we disregard hook-swinging, which may or may not have been originally connected with the sun, there are two ceremonies of swinging known in India, and both of these are of solar origin :—

> " In the Rigveda the sun is called, by a natural metaphor, ' the golden swing in the sky,' and the expression helps us to understand a ceremony of Vedic India. A priest sat in a swing and touched with the span of his right hand at once the seat of the swing and the ground. In doing so he said : ' The great lord has united himself with the great lady, the god has united himself with the goddess.' Perhaps he meant to indicate in a graphic way that the sun had reached the lowest point of its course where it was nearest to the earth." [2]

That the Siamese *Lo Jiṅ Jā̆* was originally a sun ceremony is indicated by the following features : (1) It occurs about the time of the winter solstice ; (2) the swinging is performed from east to west, that is to say, in the direction of the course of the sun, and I have particularly ascertained that the swing-posts are oriented out of the plane of the transverse axis of the plaza in the centre of which they are situated so that the swinging should be performed exactly from east to west ; (3) the circular dances which follow the swinging probably symbolize the revolution of the sun and its rebirth on the occasion of its return to the northern hemisphere.

The ceremony was originally a rite of imitative magic, intended to coerce the god Sūrya into the fulfilment of his functions. It is not the up and down motion of the swing which is important, and which led Frazer erroneously to conclude that " the higher you swing the higher will grow the crops ". It was the to and fro motion of the swing which impressed the ancients, as symbolizing the path of the sun.

Turning now to the swinging as still performed in India :—

> " About the middle of March the Hindus observe a swinging festival in honour of the god Krishna, whose image is placed in the seat or cradle of a swing and then, just when the dawn is breaking, rocked

[1] *GB.* iv, pp. 277 sqq.

[2] *GB.* iv, p. 279. A confused form of the Vedic ceremony is also described in *Aitareya-Āraṇyaka*, i, 3 and 4.

gently to and fro several times. The same ceremony is repeated at noon and at sunset." [1]

This rite obviously symbolizes the three steps of Viṣṇu, as a manifestation of solar energy, through the seven regions of the universe, these steps being explained by the commentators as denoting the three places of the sun—its rising, culmination, and setting. In this connection, therefore, it is interesting to note that there are, before the altars of Viṣṇu and Śiva in the Bangkok Brahman temples, pairs of posts about four feet high, from which on certain occasions are suspended small swings on which the Brahmans rock to and fro the images of the gods. The original connection with the sun has been forgotten, and I understand that the Siamese Brahmans swing the effigy of whichever deity they desire to placate at the time.

I think that the above evidence leaves little room for doubt that the Siamese Swinging was originally a sun ceremony; and it is very interesting to find that some of the original features have survived from Vedic times in India.

The most noticeable and perhaps the earliest change that took place in the subsequent history of this ceremony was the substitution of Śiva for Sūrya. I think that this change can be explained without difficulty. Sūrya was a Vedic god who sank to comparatively low estate in Brahmanic times, and, with the growth of Śaivism, the original meaning of the ceremony was lost, and the Great God naturally came to usurp the place of the forgotten sun-god. The Swinging may have come to be regarded as symbolizing the functions of Śiva as Destroyer and Reproducer, and thus it would have retained its magical significance although now brought more closely into connection with agriculture as one of the many Hindu harvest festivals. As such the Siamese *Ṭrīyămbavāy* seems to have certain features in common with the Hindu *Holi* festival: The licence formerly allowed to the followers of Śiva remind one of the saturnalia connected with the Holi; and the fact that the whole ceremony is explained by the Siamese as having the object of amusing the god Śiva who "likes to see swinging" may have arisen from a misunderstanding of the Hindu saturnalia. Again, it has been suggested that the scattering of water by the impersonators of the *nāgas*, after the swinging, might correspond to the throwing of saffron water which is a feature of the *Holi*: but this also lends itself to another interpretation as being a distinct ceremony of rain-making, for the powers of the *nāgas* in this connection are well-known. Certainly the fact that the rôle of Śiva was formerly

[1] *GB.* iv, p. 279.

performed by the Minister of Agriculture points to a connection with a harvest festival.

B. A. Gupte [1] has shown that the *Holi* was originally a harvest festival of the wheat-producing tracts of western India connected with the spring equinox, and was later followed in rice-producing Bengal, where it was celebrated together with the *Dola-yatra* or swinging festival described above. This is interesting as indicating that the connection between swinging and harvest probably came into being before the arrival of the ceremony in Siam, i.e. it was probably never a purely solar ceremony in Siam. According to Dubois [2] the *Holi* (or *Pongul*) is in some parts of southern India celebrated during the winter solstice,

> "the period when the sun, having finished its course towards the southern hemisphere, turns to the north again and comes back to visit the people of India."

It seems, therefore, that this part of India retains a clearer recollection of the *Holi* having been connected with a solar ceremony than is the case elsewhere, and indicates that the Siamese ceremony has been influenced more particularly by the form of the festival known in southern India. It is also interesting to note that Dubois mentions that the festival was held in connection with the Brahmanical new year, *Mahā-Saṅkrānṭi*, and King Rāma V states that the Swinging Festival was made to coincide with the new year of the Brahmans.

It has already been mentioned that when the god Śiva arrives on earth in Bangkok he is accompanied by a number of other gods represented by painted panels and perhaps by the numerous sprites impersonated by those who precede the "royal party" in the procession. The Siamese explain their presence on the grounds that they have come to help in the entertainment of Śiva, but it appears to me that we have here an entirely distinct festival of the Reception of the Gods, which I have not been able to trace in India, although presumably it was derived from that source. In the second part of this chapter we shall have more to say concerning the way in which these gods are entertained during their stay in Bangkok.

One more point calls for notice here. According to my theory of the Swinging having originally been a rite of imitative magic intended to coerce Sūrya, and later Śiva, into the fulfilment of their functions, we should expect that the impersonator of the god would have been swung in the cradle of the swing. This we have seen was the case in

[1] *Hindu Holidays and Ceremonials*, Calcutta, 1916, p. 88.
[2] D., p. 572.

the Vedic ceremony where a Brahman swung himself ; and there is little difference between the Brahman swinging himself in Vedic times and his swinging the image of a god in modern India and Siam, for, in the words of Manu, " ignorant or learned the Brahman is a great deity." But the king is also " a great deity in human form ", and it therefore seems reasonable to suppose that, at times when the kingship was elevated at the expense of the Brahmans, the king at an early period, perhaps before the ceremony reached Siam, swung himself in imitation of the deity he was held to represent. Later, he was replaced by an appointed substitute. It would be interesting to know at what period it was that the Brahman, the king, or his substitute ceased to swing himself or be swung, and became a mere onlooker. It must have been at some time after the original significance of the swinging had been lost. And the change probably contributed in no small measure to the late idea of the ceremony being intended for the entertainment of the god.

In conclusion, I may say that my suggestion as to the influences which have played their parts in the evolution of this ceremony do not exhaust the possibilities. Gerini,[1] for example, puts forward what appears to me a far-fetched theory to the effect that *Ṭrīyămbavāy* symbolizes the Churning of the Ocean, the swing-posts representing Mount Meru and the ropes the serpent Śeṣa. This, at best, could be but a late interpretation. But I must repeat that in any attempt to trace the misunderstandings and interpolations of successive ages we are treading on exceedingly unsafe ground, beset with pitfalls. For the present I think we must rest content to have established, beyond all reasonable doubt, that the Siamese Swinging Festival retains features which take us back to Vedic times, and that it was in origin a purely solar ceremony.

2. *The Ritual of the Court Brahmans.*

In this section I shall deal in considerable detail with the rites which are performed in the Brahman Temple during the fifteen days of the gods' supposed sojourn on earth. I lay special stress on this section for two reasons: Firstly, because these rites are on very similar lines to those which the Brahmans perform in connection with the Coronation,[2] the New Year, and the Ploughing, but, whereas in these cases the ceremonies are performed within the Grand Palace or in special pavilions erected on the Crown Padi Fields where it is difficult to obtain facilities for studying them, in the case of the

[1] G. (2).

[2] With the addition of the fire offerings described on p. 72.

Swinging Festival the rites are performed publicly in the Brahman Temples where one may observe them with ease and comparative comfort. Secondly, there is, so far as I know, no account of these rites in any European language, and they are therefore unknown to European scholars. I met in Bangkok only one or two Europeans who had ever witnessed these ceremonies; in fact, very few even knew that there were such ceremonies. With the Siamese I found only utter indifference. The small temples were never uncomfortably crowded; and those who were present cared nothing for the rites, which were meaningless to them. Apart from a few superstitious old people desirous of obtaining some of the consecrated water, they were merely the poor dwellers in the vicinity who waited patiently each evening for the food, which, after having been offered to the gods, was distributed to those present. Broadly speaking, it was quite clear that had there been no food distribution there would have been no congregation. But this is not in itself a sign of decadence, for Hindu *pūjā* differs essentially from Buddhist and Christian worship in that the masses of the people can take little or no part in the services. The activities of the Court Brahmans do not, and never did, directly concern the common people. Their ceremonies are royal ceremonies, maintained by the King's desire.

I spent several evenings in the Brahman Temples during the Swinging Festival of 1930–1, and am indebted to the Department of Ceremonies (Kram Braḥ Rāja Bidhī) for permission to take flash-light photographs of the proceedings. The Head Brahman always received me well, and offered me tea and cigars; but neither he nor anyone else could suggest any explanation of the significance of the details of the complicated rites. But it is my hope that those scholars who have made a special study of similar Hindu *pūjā* in India may here find material to interest them.

On the sixth day of the waxing moon of the second month the Brahmans gather together, take a purificatory bath and "tie the vow" (*phūk braṭ*), that is to say, each ties a string round one of his arms. From that day until the period of their vows has expired they must live on a vegetarian diet and live apart from their wives. The *Braḥ Mahā Rāja Grū*, who presides over the rites, must observe the vows for fifteen days, and live within the Śiva temple. The others keep the vows for three days from the seventh of the waxing moon.

On the seventh day of the waxing moon, at dawn, the *Braḥ Mahā Rāja Grū* reads the hymn "Opening of the portals of Kailāsa", by way of invitation to the gods to come down. He then goes out to receive Śiva at the *mānab* as has already been described. At night

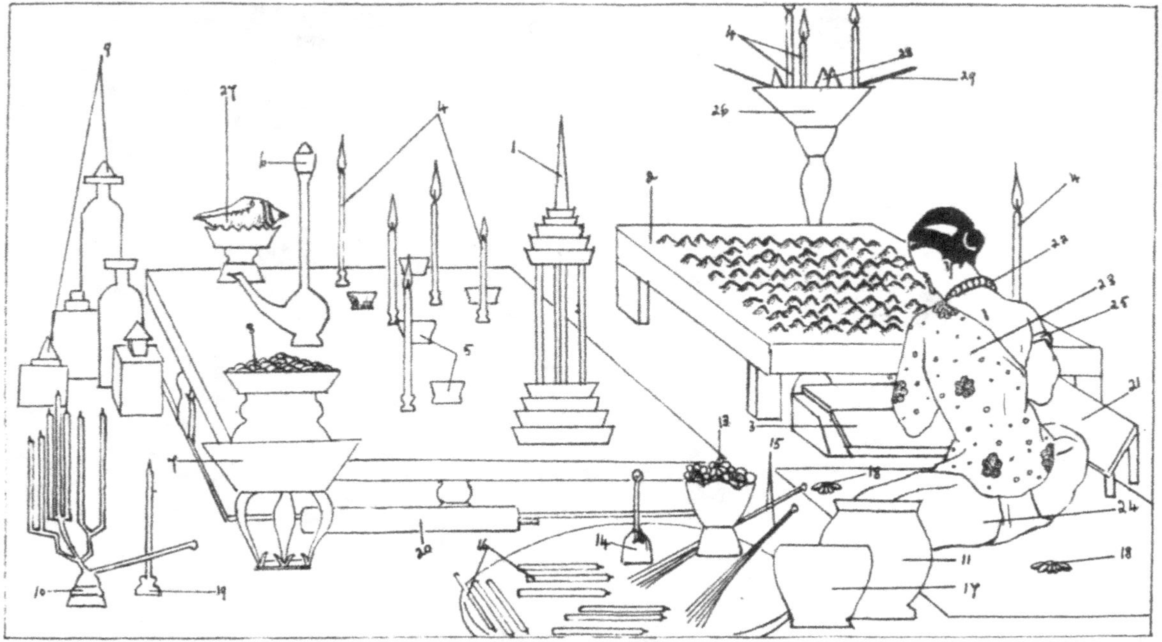

[*Diagrammatic sketch adapted from an original drawing by the Author. The figure of the Brahman is not drawn to scale (cf. Plate V).*

FIG. 5.—THE *BRAH MAHĀ RĀJA GRŪ* PERFORMING RITES IN THE ŚIVA TEMPLE ON THE FIRST DAY OF THE WANING OF THE SECOND MONTH, AT THE POINT IMMEDIATELY BEFORE THE SMALL IMAGES ARE BATHED AND PLACED ON THE *BHADRAPIṬHA* THRONE.

1. *Prāsāda* shrine, containing the small images, standing on the small altar; 2, "*Bhadrapiṭha* Throne" covered with little heaps of red, white, and green powder; 3, Sacred texts which the Brahman is reading; 4, 4, 4, Small lighted candles; 5, *Peñcagarbha* vessels containing sacred water; 6, Silver water-pot; 7, Red-gold dish for bathing images; 8, Red-gold bowl, filled with rose-petals, which will later be used for carrying the small images round the swan; 9, Scentbottles brought by the onlookers; 10, Candle-stick with seven candles; 11, Spittoon; 12, Brass tray for utensils; 13, Silver bowl with flowers; 14, Bell; 15, Brushes for sprinkling consecrated water; 16, Spare candles; 17, Glass jar containing consecrated water for use with brushes; 18, 18, Flowers placed by the Brahman around him at the cardinal points; 19, One of the candles marking off the area reserved for carrying out these rites; 20, Large candle later to be carried round the swan by the Brahman; 21, Stand for sacred texts when not in use; 22, Rosary for counting number of formulae, etc. (the Brahmanical cord is not shown); 23, Gauze upper garment embroidered with silver flowers; 24, Lower garment (*phā-nuṅ*); 25, Vow-cord; 26, Tall stand bearing offerings; 27, Conch embossed with gold, on small dish; 28, Offerings of food contained in plantain leaves; 29, Incense sticks.

To face page 248.]

the Brahmans gather in the Śiva temple, and the Head Priest performs the purificatory rites (*kraḥsūddhī aṯamasūddhī*) as follows: He takes his seat on a white mat with crossed legs and soles upturned; he puts on the Brahmanical cord (*sǎṅvāla brāhmaṇa*) and the finger-ring (*kau pil*) on the first finger of his right hand; he places flowers on the floor at the four cardinal points; he marks his forehead with the paste of sandal-wood and makes *unalom* signs on various parts of his body; he has a look of great concentration while he fingers the beads of his rosary, apparently enumerating the formulæ which he is reciting mentally; and lastly he takes up the branched candlestick (with seven lighted candles and a flower) in his right hand, and swings it to and fro before his face thirty-six times, at the same time ringing the bell with his left hand, while the other Brahmans blow the conch shells. After a short pause the same process is repeated twice more. Having thus been purified, the *Braḥ Mahā Rāja Grū* proceeds to consecrate four other Brahmans who crawl up to him and pay homage with joined palms, while he sprinkles their heads with consecrated water. They then crawl up to the altar and pay homage before it three times, their foreheads touching the ground. On a table before the altar pop-corn (*khaŭ-ṯòk*) has already been piled up, with a cocoa-nut on top of the heap. Into this cocoa-nut is stuck a candlestick with two lighted candles, while on a smaller table in front of the altar is a candlestick with four lighted candles and several dishes with flowers. On the large table, on either side of the heap of pop-corn, are bananas and other fruits, while under the table there is a pile of cocoa-nuts, and sugar-cane is stacked along the sides of the temple. The four Brahmans then stand in queue before the table and facing the altar, each one holding a plate of popcorn. They each recite a different *mantra* and these four *mantras* are called "Mahāveja-ṯu'k", "Korāyaḥ-ṯu'k", "Sāravaḥ-ṯu'k", and "Veja-ṯu'k" respectively. They then together recite a *mantra* called "Lòripāvāy". These recitations are punctuated by conch blowing by the other Brahmans, the conches being blown thirteen times in all, the thirteenth blast marking the conclusion of the first part of the ceremony. The *Braḥ Mahā Rāja Grū* then rises and advances to the table and faces the altar. He consecrates the offerings of fruit (known collectively as *ulup* or *utup*) by sprinkling it with consecrated water. He then, while standing before the altar, completes the consecration by swinging the candlestick and ringing the bell as before, while the conches are also sounded. He then reads a passage from one of the sacred books and offers flowers in a saucer at the altar. Having done this he retires and the candles on the tables are extinguished, and the cocoa-nut is removed from the top of the heap of pop-corn. In its place four jars of fruit are placed on the pop-corn. The four Brahmans who had previously officiated now go up in turn and each takes one of the jars of fruit and holds it up, at the same time reciting a short text. This process is known as *yak ulup* (" raising the *ulup* "), that is to say, offering the fruit to the gods. Finally the *ulup* is distributed among those assembled that they may eat it and thus secure good luck. This concludes the rites for the day in the Śiva temple; but the same proceedings are immediately repeated in the middle temple, that of Gaṇeśa.

On the eighth day of the waxing moon, at the break of dawn, the *Braḥ Mahā Rāja Grū* carries three wooden panels out of the Temple. Each is four cubits long and one cubit broad. One of them has the figures of the Sun (Braḥ Ādiṯ) and the Moon (Braḥ Candra) carved upon it, another has the figure of the Goddess of Earth (Nāṅ Braḥ Dharaṇī), and the third has the figure of Gaṅgā (Braḥ Gaṅgā). I have inspected these panels when they were in the Brahman Temple, where they are usually kept behind the altar of Śiva. They are carved in Ayudhyā style, painted and gilded, and probably date from the first reign of the present dynasty. Nāṅ Dharaṇī is the usual female figure represented as wringing out water from her long hair; Gaṅgā is a male figure; and the Sun and Moon are represented as discs beneath a gilded tiered umbrella, carved in low relief. These panels, which thus represent some of the lesser gods that have come to wait upon Śiva, are brought to pits which are situated in front of the three *jamrams* and are enclosed within *rājavăt* fences. The pits are paved with bricks and spread over with *darbha* grass (*hyā gā*), and each pit is supposed to be one cubit broad and four fingers deep. But since the enclosures are set up at the side of the hard macadamized road, I noticed that nowadays the Brahmans are content to make an artificial pit of clay raised on the surface of the road. One of the panels is placed in each of the pits, and made to lean against the enclosing fences. The figures of the Sun and Moon are placed in the eastern pit, that of Nāṅ Dharaṇī in the middle pit, and that of Gaṅgā in the western one. They are kept there for three days, and are taken back to the temple on the twelfth day of the waxing moon at dawn.[1]

It is commonly thought that the lowering of the panels into the pits causes the weather to be cold during the days that they remain in the pits. But no explanation is offered as to why it should be so. As King Rāma V remarks in his book: " We only hear the people

[1] The pits surrounded by *rājavăt* fences are referred to by Graham (*Siam*, ii, p. 268), as sentry boxes in which the Brahmans intone prayers!

shout that the boards have been placed in the pits, and so it is very cold. Probably they speak without knowing why it should be so, and simply because it is fashionable to make a remark like that. For it is naturally cold in the second month, and the people begin to murmur. Then some old man will observe that it will be colder still if the panels are lowered into the pits in the third month. He speaks as if it were a sober fact, without knowing that they are not placed in the pits in the third month, but during the *T̲rīyămbavāy*, long before the third month."

The rites already described as taking place in the Śiva and Gaṇeśa temples are repeated each evening until the first day of the waning moon, on which day a much fuller series of rites is performed, because it is on this day that Śiva leaves this world and Viṣṇu arrives. At dawn the Brahmans gather in the Viṣṇu temple, and the ***Braḥ Mahā Rāja Grū*** reads the hymn " Opening of the Portals of Kailāsa ", as an invitation to Viṣṇu to come down. In the evening they again gather together in the Viṣṇu temple, and conduct worship along the lines of the rites already described as taking place in the other two temples.

At night, as soon as the moon has risen, there is a procession, generally known as the " Procession of Nareśvara ", when Śiva leaves this world. The procession of Brahmans goes to the Grand Palace, where the King presents to them three small images, representing Śiva, Umā, and Gaṇeśa respectively. At the same time fireworks, representing the *Pārijāta* Tree of Indra's paradise, are let off outside the palace wall. It used to be the custom for the kings of the Ayudhyā period to follow the procession up to the temple, and this custom was also practised by King Rāma IV. The procession which I witnessed on 4th January, 1931, was made up approximately as follows :—

File of lictors bearing lotus-lamps.	Metal Drum *Braḥ Mahā Rāja Grū*	File of lictors bearing lotus-lamps.
File of red and gold drummers.	Brahmans blowing flageolets and conches	File of red and gold drummers.
File of umbrellas and sunshades.	Palanquin bearing the three small images and a large image of Śiva as Nātarāja	File of umbrellas and sunshades.
Brahmans bearing multiple candlesticks.	Palanquin bearing image of Gaṇeśa	Brahmans bearing multiple candlesticks.
Processional umbrellas and sunshades.		Processional umbrellas and sunshades.

When the procession has returned to the Śiva temple the ceremony proceeds after the following preparations have been made : At the eastern end of the temple (i.e. that furthest from the altar) there is placed a small low table called the *Bhadrapiṭha*, which is adorned with little heaps of coloured powder just as is the *Bhadrapiṭha* Throne used at the Coronation. On another low stand beside it are placed a conch shell, a silver water-pot (*klaśa*), and four cups of different metals, and one of crystal, called collectively *peñcagarbha*,[1] which are filled with consecrated water. On the stand are also placed five candlesticks with candles, and a small shrine with pointed *prāsāda* spire beneath which the three small images (each only about two inches high) are placed on arrival from the palace. A dish on a tall stand bearing small offerings of food rolled in plantain leaves, lighted candles, and incense sticks, is also placed near to the *Bhadrapiṭha*, and the bell, branched candlestick, and other paraphernalia are placed near at hand. Meanwhile, in the middle of the temple the small swing-posts have been decorated with banana leaves, a cradle has been suspended from the cross-beam, and on it has been fastened the gilded figure of a swan (*haṅṣa*) with its head facing eastwards (Pl. XXXIX). On the floor before the *haṅṣa* is placed a stone mortar (*śilāpat*) which is called the "mountain" (*păb boṯ*). On the stone mortar there is engraved a special *yantra* diagram, while a metal plate inscribed with another *yantra* is placed in the silver water-pot.[2]

The *Braḥ Mahā Rāja Grū* takes his seat on the white cloth before the *Bhadrapiṭha* and the ceremonies begin. He first performs the purificatory rites, and the ceremony of "raising the *ulup*" is again carried out as already described. But on this occasion the pop-corn is reserved for presentation to the King, and is not distributed among those present. The High Priest then recites two *mantras* called "Draṅ Sār" and "Ṯorabăt", pours the water out of the *peñcagarbha* into the silver water-pot, and offers incense, candles, and flowers to the gods. Then he dedicates the conch and water-pot by ringing the bell and waving the branched candlestick before them, while conches are blown. He reads the texts for bathing the swan, rises from his seat, and walks towards the swing. He places his foot upon the stone mortar, and pours sacred water from the water-pot on to the swan's head, and makes thumb-marks with paste on its neck, while conches are blown continuously. He lights a large candle that is fixed upon the swan's beak, and then he kneels, rings the bell, and waves the

[1] Gerini in Ge. (1), p. 174, supposes that *peñcagarbha* means "five receptacles"; but Mr. P. S. Śāstrī of the Royal Institute, Bangkok, is of opinion that Gerini was misled by the Siamese spelling of the word—which more probably refers to the Indian *pañcha-gavya*, i.e. the five products of the cow. The Siamese Brahmans have lost the use of *pañcha-gavya*, but retain the use of the five cups which appear to have been formerly connected with it.

[2] See Plate IV.

PLATE XXXIX.

[From a photograph by the Author.

CEREMONY IN THE ŚIVA TEMPLE.

[To face page 252.

candlestick before the swan, first with one candle lighted, then with all, conches being sounded. He then returns to his seat and reads a text inviting Śiva, Umā, and Gaṇeśa (Fig. 5). He takes a large bowl of red-gold and pours into it the contents of a number of scent bottles brought by the onlookers. He takes the three small images from under the *prāsāda* spire, lifting them by means of pieces of cotton fastened to them, and places them in the bowl, the scented water reaching up to the middle of each image. He then anoints the three images by pouring water on them from the conch and from the water-pot, while the conches are sounded. He makes a *mudrā* sign with his hands,[1] lifts the three images out of the bowl, places them on his head, and then carefully sets them upon the *Bhadrapiṭha*, after which he reads the texts called " Sar hlvaṅ ", " Mālai ", and " Sāṅvāl ". Then he takes the three images from the *Bhadrapiṭha*, places them in a smaller red-gold bowl filled with rose-petals, and, rising from his seat, walks towards the swan. Holding the bowl with the images in his left hand, and a large lighted candle in his right hand, he walks three times round the swan, pausing each time that he passes the mortar to put his foot upon it, which action is each time marked by the blowing of conches. The images are then taken from the bowl by two other Brahmans, who place them on the swan, and light a number of candles on the body of the swan and at the four corners of the swing-cradle. The *Braḥ Mahā Rāja Grū* then rings the bell and waves the candles before the swan while conches are sounded. From time to time after this the two Brahmans seated near by gently rock the swing. The High Priest, having now returned to his seat, proceeds to read the texts for offering worship to the swan and to the " mountain ". He reads the "praise of Kailāsa", just as he does when the King sits upon the *Bhadrapiṭha* Throne during the Coronation, and also reads the texts for " sending Umā ". He offers Bineśa Water (*nām̆ bineśa*), lights eight candles which are adorned with flowers and set up towards the eight cardinal points, and goes around them reciting " Tro Dvāra ". Two Brahmans then recite " Jă Klòm Haṅṣa " (lulling the swan ?) just as is done when the royal children are placed in the cradle for the first time, and conch shells are blown. Then the *Braḥ Mahā Rāja Grū* recites " Saṅ Sār " (sending news ?), " Saṅ Braḥ P̱en Ćau " (sending the gods), and " P̱it Dvāra Śivalai " (closing the gates of Kailāsa). Meanwhile the scented water in the large red-gold bowl, mixed, of course, with the consecrated water from the conch and water-pot with which the images had been

[1] Only one *mudrā* is known to the Siamese Court Brahmans, and this is the only occasion on which it is used.

anointed, is poured back into the scent bottles and returned to the owners, who receive the precious liquid with evident satisfaction. A Brahman also makes his way amongst the spectators, sprinkling the heads of all those present with a little of the sacred mixture. This brings the ceremony for the night to a close; the rites performed in the Śiva temple after the return of the procession being known collectively as *Jā Haṅsa*.

If I be permitted to hazard an explanation of the above complicated rites of *Jā Haṅsa*, I would suggest that they are expressive of two ideas, as follows: (1) Śiva, Umā, and Gaṇeśa, on their last night on earth, are undergoing a kind of consecration or *abhiṣeka* to fit them to carry out their duties for the benefit of mankind during the next twelve months. Hence the *Bhadrapiṭha* throne, the anointment, and the recitation of the same *mantras* that are used at the King's Coronation. There is nothing remarkable about this if we bear in mind the audacity of the Brahmans of Ancient India; the *Braḥ Mahā Rāja Grū* is simply acting the part of Brihaspati, the *purohita* of the gods (2) The rites connected with the *haṅsa* are a magical imitation of the homeward journey of the gods designed to help them on their way. Admittedly the swan is the traditional mount of Brahmā, but that is a minor modification after a lapse of so many centuries. Besides, Brahmā is forgotten and a swan is surely a swifter steed than Śiva's bull or Gaṇeśa's rat. The stone mortar is called the "mountain", presumably Mount Kailāsa, the home of the Śaivic deities. The images are placed upon the swan's back, and the swan faces the "mountain" and is rocked gently towards it, while the *mantras* "sending the gods" and "closing the door of Kailāsa" are recited. It seems that one could hardly wish for a clearer example of imitative magic. There are other rites which are unexplained, and may relate to other ideas; but my suggestions, which are only tentative, appear to afford a satisfactory explanation of the ceremony as a whole.

On the following morning (second of the waning), the *Braḥ Mahā Rāja Grū* and other Brahmans take the *ulup* which had been dedicated to the gods the night before and present it to the King. It consists of two plates of *khau mau* (half-ripe padi, husked and pounded flat), tender cocoa-nuts, plantain fruits, sugar-cane, and many kinds of cakes.

On the first and fifth days of the waning moon, shadow plays (*hnăṅ*) are shown in a shed opposite the Brahman Temple. This feature, together with the letting off of fireworks outside the palace, was introduced in the reign of King Rāma IV, presumably to increase the popularity of the ceremony with the people.

The ceremony of "raising the *ulup*" continues to be performed every evening in the temple of Viṣṇu only, until the fifth day of the waning moon, when a procession goes at night to the Grand Palace, and a small image of Viṣṇu is carried back to the temple. Then, in celebration of that god's return to his celestial abode, the rites are carried out in full as on the first of the waning, but this time, of course, in the Viṣṇu temple. This concludes the festival of *Ṯrīyămbavāy Ṯrīpavāy*, except for a Buddhist modification, introduced by King Rāma IV, in which a chapter of eleven monks is invited to recite Buddhist texts in the Brahman Temple, and is presented with food on the following morning. At the same time that the monks are being fed, the poor people bring their children to the annual public Tonsure Ceremony, performed by the Brahmans free of charge.

CHAPTER XXI

THE FIRST PLOUGHING[1]

The Ceremony of the First Ploughing, known as *Bidhī Carat Braḥ Năṅgăla*, or popularly as *Rèk Nā*, is entirely Brahmanical, and it takes place outside the city in the Crown padi field called *Duṅ Jam Poy* in the sixth month (Vaiśākha). The date fixed for the ceremony must be a *Śabha tithī*, a *Purṇa ṛkṣa*, or a *Sambhaḥ grauḥha* day, and not a *Phī phlia* day. In selecting the date for the Ceremony it is necessary only to be particular about the above factors; it does not matter if the date be inauspicious for any other reason. In the sixth month the *Phī phlia* days are the 1st, 5th, 7th, 8th, 9th, 10th, 11th, and 15th of the waxing moon, and the 1st, 5th, 6th, 7th, 8th, 10th, 13th, and 14th of the waning moon. The *Śabha tithī* days are merely those not included among the *Phī phlia* days. *Purṇa ṛkṣa* days are the 2nd, 4th, 5th, 6th, 8th, 11th, 14th, 17th, 22nd, 24th, and 27th days of the month. The *Sambhaḥ grauḥha* days are Mondays, Wednesdays, Thursdays, and Fridays.

On the afternoon of the same day that the Buddhist monks carry out the special image of the Buddha in procession in connection with the minor degree of the *Baruṇa Sāṭra*, the Brahmans also carry in procession the images of the Hindu gods to the Crown padi fields, where they place them on an altar in a ceremonial pavilion, and where they perform their rites along the usual lines, as fully described in the last chapter.

For the Ploughing Ceremony it is still the custom for the King to appoint a temporary substitute (Pl. XL), who in this case is always the Minister of Agriculture, the successor of the ancient *Baladeba*, or Head of the Department of Lands. Like the "temporary king" who presides over the Swinging (a post also filled by the *Baladeba* until King Rāma IV's time) this dignitary has, as will be shown in what follows, been shorn of his power, and no longer enjoys the perquisites which he used to during the three days of his annual reign.

On the morning of the day fixed for the Ploughing Ceremony the "temporary king" is carried on a palanquin in procession to the Crown padi field. This procession consists only of ceremonial drummers, processional umbrella-bearers, a bodyguard bearing ancient weapons, and pages carrying the insignia of the Minister, there being no pageant such as characterizes the procession to the Swing. On arrival at the

[1] Sources: *BRB.*, pp. 395 sqq.; *NN.*, pp. 78 sq.; *KM.*; *HV.*

PLATE XL.

[Photo: Narasingh Studio.

PROCESSION OF THE "TEMPORARY KING" AT THE PLOUGHING FESTIVAL.

[To face page 256.

PLATE XLI.

[Photo: Narasingh Studio.

THE FIRST PLOUGHING.

field, which is protected from the intrusion of evil spirits by *rājavăt* fences erected at each corner, the presiding official descends from his palanquin and goes to the pavilion of the Brahmans and lights incense sticks before the images of the deities. He then selects one of three *phā-nuṅ* offered to him by the Brahmans, and attires himself in one of them in the manner known as *pāv khuṇ*, already mentioned in connection with the Swinging. These three *phā-nuṅ* are of different lengths, and great importance attaches to his choice. Should he choose the longest the prognostication is that the rainfall will be abundant; should he choose the shortest there will be too little, while his choice of the one of medium length denotes that the rainfall will be average. He then takes the gilded handle of the plough, which has been wrapped in red cloth by the *Braḥ Mahā Rāja Grū*, and whips up the pair of magnificent oxen caparisoned in harness of red velvet and gold thread, while the Brahmans blow the conches. He then ploughs three concentric furrows, the Brahmans blowing the conches at the conclusion of each circuit. Four dowager ladies of the nobility, called *nāṅ devī*, then enter the field and hand to the Minister two silver and two gold rice baskets, containing seed-rice, hallowed by the *mantras* of the Brahmans and also of the Buddhist monks, which he scatters as he ploughs three more concentric furrows (Pl. XLI), while an official scatters holy water, an offering to the Goddess of Earth. Then the oxen are unyoked and seven vessels are placed before them containing respectively padi, Indian corn, beans, sesamum, rice-spirit, water, and grass, and whichever commodity the animals choose to partake of will be plentiful during the coming year. This ends the ceremony, and the "temporary king" then departs in state, but the vast concourse of people who have gathered to witness the proceedings, many of them having come from up-country, now burst on to the field and gather up the hallowed rice grains, which, mixed with their own seed-rice, are said to be very efficient fertilizers. Ploughing is also carried out simultaneously in two or three provincial centres by a local official deputed by the king.

It had never been the custom during the Bangkok period for the King himself to watch the proceedings at the Ploughing Ceremony until on 21st April, 1912, King Rāma VI witnessed the ceremony, and thus abolished what remained of a custom which had grown to remarkable proportions during the Ayudhyā period. The *KM.* says:—

"*Carat Braḥ Nāṅgāla* takes place in the month of Vaiśākha. *Cāu Braḥyā Cănda Kumāra* [a title of the temporary king] pays homage to the king in the hall of worship (*hò braḥ*). The king gives him the sword of State (*braḥ kharga*) and thus gives up his prerogatives (*draṅ braḥ karuṇālat braḥ parama deja*): he does not give orders nor call for the officers, nor leave the palace (*mi tai bo'k lūk khun mi tai satec òk*). As for the *Braḥyā Cănda Kumāra*, he has a mount for getting upon elephant-back, as if he were a king. He proceeds in state from the Buddhist temple, and for three days he entertains officials and nobles who take part in the procession." Khun Hlvaṅ Hā Văt makes mention of the ceremony as follows: "*Braḥ Inda Kumāra* [temporary king] represents the king and *Nāṅ Devī* impersonates the queen. They go to *Tuṅ Kèv* by boat, both wearing crowns. On land they proceed on silver palanquins; symbols of royalty are carried in their procession; the persons who follow them are called "*Maḥhătlek*"; and nobles armed with canes walk abreast the palanquin and make way. *Braḥ Inda Kumāra* yokes the bulls to the plough, and *Braḥyā Baladeba* leads them forward [from this it appears that the temporary king was not necessarily the Baladeba]. *Nāṅ Devī* carries the basket of padi and sows the seeds. After the plough has been driven round thrice the bulls are unyoked and allowed to eat the three kinds of rice, three kinds of pulse, and three kinds of grass. Predictions are made according to what the bulls eat."

It appears from the above that in the Ayudhyā period the wife of the "temporary king" was also accorded the honour of a "temporary queen", and played the part now filled by the dowager ladies. Khun Hlvaṅ Hā Văt makes no mention of the king giving up the sword of State, and it may be that this feature had already been dropped out in his time.

In the Ayudhyā period, and indeed during the early decades of the Bangkok period, it is said that the *Baladeba* was rewarded with the junks that came in during the Ploughing Ceremony just as he was with those that came in during the Swinging Ceremony, provided that he maintained his proper position with one leg raised during the swinging. He also collected the *Kāṁṭāk* taxes, as recorded by Khun Hlvaṅ Hā Văt, as follows: "During the three days of the rite, *Braḥ Inda Kumāra* has the right to take for himself all the boats, carts, and junks of the traders which come into the kingdom during that time. Again, the agents and servants of *Braḥ Inda Kumāra* are entitled to collect the taxes on markets and ferry boats everywhere. They are called *Danāy Kāṁṭāk*". The statement that *Braḥ Inda Kumāra* was entitled to take the carts and boats that arrived on the days of the ceremony seems to mean that he seized all the merchandise that came in. But King Rāma V states [1] that in truth it refers only

[1] Loc. cit.

to the tolls levied on boats and carts, which were assigned to him as his reward. He could not have had this income every year, for trade was then insignificant, and a junk or caravan of carts could not have always arrived during the days of the ceremony. The income that he derived regularly, every year, was the daily levy on markets and ferry boats which fell due on the days of the ploughing.

For the Sukhodaya period Lady Nabamāśa[1] supplies us with a very valuable account of the Ploughing Ceremony: "In the sixth month we have the ceremony of *Carat Braḥ Năṅgăla.* The Brahmans gather together, 'tie the vow,' and take the images of the gods to the hall of ceremony in the *Duṅ Laḥhān Hlvaṅ*, opposite the *Hān Khau* palace. The king dresses like an Indian (*yăṅ deśa*) and goes in procession on horse-back. The queen, the princes, and ladies of the harem who have been chosen by the king follow him in their carriages. *Ŏk Ñā Baladeba* dressed as a prince (*lūk hlvaṅ*) comes in procession, the Brahmans walking before him blowing conch shells and scattering pop-corn. When he has arrived at the shed in the middle of the *Laḥhān*, the king's bulls [i.e. the sacred bulls] are led out and yoked to the golden plough. The *Braḥ Mahā Rāja Grū* gives the plough and goad to *Ŏk Ñā Baladeba*, who pays homage to the king and ploughs first. Then Braḥ Śrī Mahosath, father of Nāṅ Nabamaśa, dressed in white in the manner of the Brahmans, ploughs with the silver plough, followed by Braḥ Văḍhaneh Śresṭhī dressed as a commoner (*yăṅ gahapatī*), who ploughs with the plough covered with red cloth. The king's astrologers sound the gong of victory and play upon musical instruments. The *Baladeba* and the others go around ploughing from left to right. The Brahmans lead the plough, blowing conch-shells, scattering pop-corn and flowers, and sounding the *păṇḍaḥvaḥ* drum. Khun Paripūrṇa Dhăññā, the superintendent of the king's farms, follows and sows seeds in the furrows. The event is celebrated with dancing and acrobatic feats all around the place. The bulls are unyoked and given five kinds of food to eat, from which the Brahman astrologers declare the omens. At the same time the queen asks her maid to set a dish of sweet porridge before the king, and the king's servants then distribute the porridge among the officials." In the above account the important point to note is that in the Sukhodaya period the king retained his power in full, was present during the ceremony, and merely deputed the *Baladeba* to plough for him, the other two officials representing respectively the Brahmans and the people.

Ploughing ceremonies are of world-wide distribution, but for our

[1] *N.N.*, p. 78.

purpose it is sufficient to note that in both the two main centres of civilization, i.e. India and China, from which the Siamese ceremony might have been derived, there were Ploughing Ceremonies in antiquity. At the Court of China a Ploughing Ceremony was instituted about 5,000 years ago, and until recent times the Emperor ploughed several furrows and scattered the seed. The corn grown on the holy field was collected and used by the Emperor in certain solemn sacrifices to the god Chan Ti and to his own ancestors. In the provinces of China the season of ploughing was similarly inaugurated by the provincial governors as representatives of the Emperor.[1] In Ancient India we have at least two classical examples of a Ploughing Ceremony. In the *Rāmāyaṇa* it is recorded that on such an occasion the child Sītā, who later married Rāma, was found by the officials in a furrow ploughed by Janaka, King of Mithilā. Again, there is the famous instance associated with the miracle of the child Buddha, when he caused the shadow of the jambu-tree to stand still (Pl. XLII):—

> "Now one day the king held the so-called Ploughing Festival. On that day they ornament the town like a palace of the gods. All the slaves and servants, in new garments and crowned with sweet-smelling garlands, assemble in the king's house. For the king's work a thousand ploughs are yoked. On this occasion one hundred and eight minus one were, with the oxen-reins and cross-bars, ornamented with silver. But the plough for the king to use was ornamented with red gold; and so also the horns and reins and goads of the oxen. The king leaving his house with a great retinue, took his son and went to the spot . . . the rāja clad in splendour and attended by his ministers, went away to plough. At such a time the king takes hold of a golden plough, the attendant ministers one hundred and eight minus one silver ploughs, and the peasants the rest of the ploughs. Holding them they plough this way and that way. The rāja goes from one side to the other, and comes from the other back again. On this occasion the king had great success."[2]

In weighing the evidence in favour of a Chinese or of an Indian origin of the Siamese Ploughing Ceremony it will be of value first to consider the ploughing ceremonies as performed in the neighbouring countries, Cambodia and Burma. The ceremony as still performed in Cambodia[3] is similar in all but insignificant details to the ceremony as performed at Ayudhyā, the *Okhna Pohulla-tep* (Minister of Agriculture) and his wife going in state to the Crown padi field where the former ploughs while the king remains within his palace, the ploughing

[1] *GB.* viii, p. 14 sq.

[2] T. W. Rhys Davids, The Nidāna-Kathā, or Commentarial Introduction to the *Buddhist Birth Stories*, p. 163.

[3] Leclère, *Revue Indochinoise*, 15 août 1904.

PLATE XLII.

[From a painting by a Siamese artist.

A SIAMESE REPRESENTATION OF THE MIRACLE OF THE JAMBU-TREE.

[To face page 260.

being followed by omens drawn from the selection of food made by the oxen. Probably at an earlier period the Khmer kings were themselves present at the ploughing, just as it was at Sukhodaya, and I think we need not hesitate to take the step of deducing that when the Thai obtained their freedom from the Khmer yoke they adopted the Ploughing Ceremony *in toto* from them.

Now a study of the Burmese first ploughing ceremony (or *Letwin Mingala*) as performed in the reign of Mindon Min, the last king of Burma but one, is by no means fruitless.[1] The most important difference between this and the Siamese and Cambodian festivals is that in Burma the chief part was performed by the king himself, who arrived in procession riding on the white elephant. Not only the king ploughed, with a gilded plough, but a long line of ordinary ploughs was ready drawn up for the ministers and high officials who also ploughed, and were obliged to continue long after the king had ceased. No scattering of seed and no omens from the oxen's choice of food are mentioned in Shway Yoe's account, and apparently the actual ploughing was the main, if not the only, part of the ceremony. Harvey [2] mentions a Ploughing Ceremony performed by King Bagyidaw (1819–37), and also an ancient one dating back to the early Pagān period :—

> "When Htuntaik, 569–82, a traditional chief of Pagān, was performing the rite, the oxen shied at his vestments flapping in the wind, and dragged the plough over him so that he died.[3]

The Burmese Ploughing Ceremony probably never influenced the Siamese or Cambodian form of the rite ; indeed, it is probably to the fact that there was so little cultural contact between Burma and Siam that we owe the preservation in Burma of a very ancient form of the ceremony which has much in common with the ploughing as performed in Ancient India. Thus we see surviving in a State of Indo-China down to modern times two features that were common to the ancient Indian Ploughing Festival : (1) the king himself guiding the plough, and (2) the use of a number of ploughs, and the participation of officials in the ploughing. We have seen that at Sukhodaya three ploughs were used, and that two of these were guided by the representatives of the Brahmans and of the people respectively, evidently a reduction from the grander scale on which the ceremony was carried out in Ancient India. And I think we cannot resist the conclusion that at an early period the Khmer King himself ploughed in person.[4]

[1] Shway Yoe, *The Burman*, chap. xxiv.

[2] *History of Burma*, pp. 295 and 362.

[3] *Hmannan* i, 218.

[4] Or we might have to go further back to Dvāravatī or Śrīvijaya.

The above evidence, and the fact that from Sukhodaya onwards the ceremony has always been attended and in part performed by the Brahmans, leaves little room for doubt that the ceremony as known in Siam during historical times was derived from India; and were it not that we know that there was also a Ploughing Ceremony in China, we should hardly be inclined to cast an eye in that direction. Yet I think we cannot entirely rule out Chinese influence. The only early writer on Siam who attempted to explain the custom was La Loubère, who evidently believed it to be of Chinese origin. He says :—

> "I suspect that this custom of causing the lands to be ploughed by the Prince, came from China to Tonquin, and Siam, with the Art of Husbandry." [1]

And the Jesuit fathers have placed it on record that the kings of Tonquin and Cochin-China in the seventeenth century took an active part in an annual ploughing ceremony held at their capitals. These countries have a purely Chinese civilization, and doubtless received the rite from their great neighbour. An important point of resemblance between the practice of Siam and China is the simultaneous ploughing of provincial governors at the same time that the state ceremony was performed in the capital. Thus it is very probable that the early Thai of Yunnan came in contact with some such Chinese provincial ceremony and carried with them the memory of it when they migrated southwards. We may therefore conclude that the early Thai were probably in possession of a Chinese form of the Ploughing Ceremony, but as they came in contact with the Khmers their early culture became almost entirely obscured by superimposed Brahmanism, so that the Siamese form of the Ploughing Ceremony, as known in historical times, retains perhaps no features which would enable us to state definitely that the Thai were in possession of an earlier Chinese form of the Ceremony.

There seems to be no doubt but that ploughing ceremonies, wherever performed, had primarily the object of ensuring a plentiful crop by means of magic. Frazer [2] compares the ploughing of the Rarian plain at Eleusis to the little sacred rice-fields on which the Kayans of central Borneo inaugurated the various operations of the agricultural year by performing them in miniature, and he concludes:

> "All such consecrated enclosures were probably in origin what we may call spiritual preserves, that is, patches of ground which men set apart for the exclusive use of the corn spirit to console him for the depredations they committed on all the rest of his domains."

[1] L. L., p. 20. [2] *GB.* viii, pp. 14 and 15.

That the Siamese rite has passed beyond this stage is evidenced by the fact that the people pick up all the grain and do not allow it to germinate on the Crown padi field as a reserve for the gods or spirits. Nevertheless, the offerings made to the Brahmanic deities in the ceremonial pavilion on the field point to some such idea having obtained at an earlier time. King Rāma V expresses his opinion as to the object of the ceremony in the following words:—

"The object of the king himself (or his substitute) ploughing first is to set an example to his people and induce them to be industrious in cultivating the land." I cannot agree with this; for although it no doubt expresses the functional value of the ploughing at the time King Rāma V wrote and gives *his* "object" in maintaining it, there was undoubtedly some earlier magical significance now forgotten and distinct from the functional value. This is indicated in both Siam and Cambodia, where it was formerly prohibited for the common people to commence to plough their land before the ceremony had been carried out, and by our whole theory of the *raison d'être* of "temporary kings", as explained in the next chapter. King Rāma V goes on to explain the subsidiary elements in the Ploughing Ceremony as follows: "The ritualistic elements [i.e. the omens drawn from the length of the *Baladeba*'s skirt, and from the oxen's choice of food, and also the fertilizing value of the hallowed grain] have been added to the simple act of ploughing because people are afraid of calamities like droughts, floods, and insect pests, and desire to secure an abundant harvest. They also need to know of the future beforehand, so that they can determine how to remedy what they fear and contrive what they desire." Here King Rāma V is on firmer ground. The Brahmanical soothsaying and the value attached to the hallowed grain as a fertilizer, the latter a good example of contagious magic, are definitely later accretions, added after the significance of the ploughing had been largely forgotten, to strengthen the efficacy of the ceremony. And it is to these later rites that is due the sociological value of the Ploughing Ceremony in Siam at the present day. The great crowd of people, a large proportion of whom are farmers seriously interested in the proceedings, anxiously study the length of the *Baladeba*'s *phă-nuṅ*, and the omens declared from the oxen's choice of food, and it may be said they are seldom disappointed with the auguries.[1] The actual ploughing has little or no meaning to them, but these

[1] Here is the latest example as recorded by the *Bangkok Times* for 22nd April, 1931: "The forecast states that the supply of rice, fish, meat, and fruits will be good, while at the beginning and towards the end of the season there will be abundant rainfall and during the middle it will be good. The supply of water will be sufficiently good."

omens usually are such as to have the effect of quieting their fears and of enabling them to go home and start their labours with a light heart and every confidence in the future. Again, it is said that inspection of the field after the crowd has dispersed with the coveted seed-rice has failed to reward the searcher with a single grain. This surely provides a useful index as to the continued sociological value of the ceremony. Should the Government ever have any intention of abolishing it, I suggest that a suitable time will have come when an official inspection of the Crown padi field, on the day following the First Ploughing, reveals an appreciable quantity of the sacred grain.

CHAPTER XXII

TEMPORARY KINGS

In this chapter an attempt will be made to define the functional value of the Siamese custom of appointing "Temporary Kings" on certain occasions. We have encountered this phenomenon in four of the State Ceremonies considered in this book, namely the Ploughing, Swinging, Tonsure, and *Dhānya-daha*. The table on page 267 sums up the known data which bear on this problem, and although there are gaps and no one ceremony gives us the complete story of the rise and fall of the Temporary King, nevertheless, by combining our evidence, we are able to trace the evolution of the institution. We can also distinguish five stages in this evolution which do not, however, bear an exact relationship to the four historical periods under which the evidence has been classified on the table.

These stages are as follows:—

Stage I: The King performed the chief rôle in the ceremony himself.

Stage II: The King appointed a substitute to perform his rôle in the ceremony, but was himself present as a spectator.

Stage III: The substitute became a "Temporary King", usurping the King's power, and enjoying royal privileges, while the King practically abdicated for the duration of the ceremony.

Stage IV: The "Temporary King" still performed the chief rôle, but was shorn of his power and privileges, and the King was again present as a spectator. This is a return to Stage II.

Stage V: The "Temporary King" is abolished, and the King resumes his rôle as the chief personage in the ceremony. This is a return to Stage I, but has as yet been reached only in the Tonsure and *Dhānya-daha* Ceremonies.

Frazer deals with the subject of Temporary Kings in *The Golden Bough*,[1] where he rightly concludes that,

> "The Cambodian and Siamese examples shew clearly that it is especially the divine or magical functions of the king which are transferred to his temporary substitute."

He considers these examples as comparable to the annual appointment of temporary kings in Samarcand, Upper Egypt, and Morocco,

[1] *GB.* iv, chapter 5.

and to the appointment in certain emergencies of a substitute for the Shah of Persia to protect him against some threatened evil. The underlying idea seems to be that the magical or divine functions of a king are a source of danger to him, and in countries where the welfare of the State depends so much on the welfare of the monarch, it would be natural to make use of every precaution to protect him against danger. The sociological value of the institution of the Temporary King was that it gave the king and the people the required confidence to enable them to carry out very important State Ceremonies in the belief that all danger of evil was thereby averted. This theory is supported by valuable evidence supplied by La Loubère to the effect that in the seventeenth century, when the power of Temporary Kings was at its height, there definitely was a tradition that the performance of divine or magical functions was attended with danger :—

> " For about an Age since, *and upon some superstitious Observation of a bad Omen, he labours no more* ; but leaves this ceremony to an imaginary King, which is purposely created every year. . . . *And by the same superstition has deterred the Kings themselves. It is looked upon as ominous and unlucky to the person.*" [1]

Two features characteristic of the third stage, that in which the conception of the Temporary King reaches its highest development, are of special interest. They are to some extent complementary. On the one hand, the Temporary King has special privileges and royal prerogatives, and is rewarded by certain levies and tolls ; on the other hand, should he not perform his duties properly, or, in the case of the Swinging Ceremony, fail to keep one leg raised from the ground when watching the swinging, he was deprived of his rank and otherwise treated with indignity. These are mild forms of features characteristic of the institution of Temporary Kings wherever found. An example of an extreme case is provided by the Roman Saturnalia, in which unusual licence was allowed to the slaves (cf. the licence of the followers of the Temporary King in Siam) and a soldier was appointed as mock king and was afterwards put to death. The rites were connected with the transference of public evil from the community as a whole to a chosen victim, and the licence and rewards were simply the payment considered due to the victim. In Siam we have the same idea of the transference of evil, though from the King more particularly than from the community as a whole, but it was never thought necessary to put the victim to death. Had Siam ever reached the logical conclusion arrived at in some other countries, it would have been in the Ayudhyā period, and we should have known of it. It is

[1] L. L., p. 20.

TEMPORARY KINGS

	CARAT BRAḤ NAṄGĀLA (Ploughing).	*ṮRĪYĀMBAVĀY ṮRĪPAVĀY* (Swinging).	*SOKĀNṮA* (Tonsure).	*DHĀNYA-DAHA* (Burning ears of padi and conveying padi home).
Pre-Sukhodaya Period in Indochina or in India	King ploughed in person in Ancient India. (This survived in Burma until extinction of Monarchy.)	Brahman swung himself in Vedic India. (When royal power was supreme, king may have performed this duty.)	No evidence.	Originally a Vedic offering to Agni (*āgrayaṇeshṭi*). At a later time the king may have impersonated Agni and set fire to the padi.
Sukhodaya Period	Substitute ploughed, but king was present and retained his powers.	Substitute impersonated Śiva, but king was present and retained his powers.	No evidence.	Substitute set fire to the padi, but king was present during the ceremony.
Ayudhya and Early Bangkok Periods	Substitute ploughed and enjoyed extreme privileges. King gave up his powers for three days and remained within his palace.	Substitute impersonated Śiva and enjoyed extreme privileges. King gave up his powers for three days and remained within his palace.	Substitute impersonated Śiva at the reception of the tonsurate prince on Kailāsa.	Substitute set fire to the padi, king not present. Also a later ceremony in which the king went in state and himself received the firstfruits.
Late Bangkok Period (Reign of Rāma IV, or later)	Substitute ploughs, but with reduced privileges. King retains powers and first came out to watch the ceremony in A.D. 1912.	Substitute impersonates Śiva, but with reduced privileges. King Rāma IV was first to break through old custom of remaining in palace, and was also first to watch swinging.	King Rāma IV inaugurated the custom of himself impersonating Śiva, at the Tonsure of his children, which innovation was followed by Rāma V.	Ceremony discontinued after fall of Ayudhyā.

To face page 266.

quite certain that she did not. Buddhism and the extreme respect for the King's person, or whatever represented it, were a sufficient guarantee against that. The fact that no very strongly defined evil ever befell the Temporary King in Siam, provided that he carried out his duties properly, enabled the selection for this office of a high official, i.e. someone in keeping with the dignity of a king (in Cambodia, a Brahman), who was ready to take the risk of possible danger in return for the power which he enjoyed during his short reign. This led, in course of time, to the office becoming an object of desire on the part of officials, and this, in my opinion, is the very factor which led to the decline in the status of Temporary Kings in Siam, represented by Stages IV and V in which, the *raison d'être* of the Temporary King having been forgotten, the King first appears as a spectator, and finally resumes his magical or divine functions in person.

Evidence in support of the statement that the object of creating Temporary Kings in Siam came to be forgotten is supplied by the following quotations: Sir John Bowring,[1] whose mention of the matter probably reflects the Siamese ignorance of the question prevailing in the days of King Rāma IV, says:—

> " The whole farce is probably intended to throw scorn upon popular influences and reconcile the subject to the authority of a *real* King."

Similarly, King Rāma V hazards a guess in his book to the effect that

> " The people of Ayudhyā wanted to make the ceremony efficacious by making the deputy seem to be the king himself come to plough."

While, in recent times, H.R.H. Prince Damrong puts forward the following explanation as to the origin of the Temporary King at the Swinging Festival:—

> " In a certain temple in Cambodia there is a stone inscription relating to a grant of the use of land to the temple by a Khmer King; it is stipulated that, should the King ever come to the country in which this temple is situated, the Brahmans must receive him with divine honours. We may have here the origin of the rites performed by the Brahmans for the reception of the Phya who presides over our swinging festival and who represents the sovereign of the country. During the course of the swinging ceremonies, this official is still received by the Brahmans into the city as though he were a god upon one day, and is similarly escorted out of it again by them upon another."[2]

This is ingenious, but quite unconvincing, because it offers no explanation of the Temporary King in other Siamese ceremonies, and fails to take note of the fact that we are dealing with an institution

[1] *Siam*, i, 159. [2] *JSS.*, vol. xiii, part 2, 1919, p. 19.

of world-wide distribution. Finally, in the last Swinging Festival (December, 1930) when a Chinese *braḥyā* was chosen to preside, no one who saw the spirit of elation evinced by the celestials of Bangkok from merchant down to coolie, and the zeal with which the elaborate procession was prepared, could have been in the least doubt as to the extent of the honour believed to have been conferred upon the Chinese community.

The institution of the Temporary King in Siam has thus undoubtedly lost its earlier functional value of enabling the people to carry out important rites without fear of evil consequences, yet, so long as it lingers in its modified form in the Swinging and Ploughing Ceremonies, it retains a certain value as a support to ancient tradition and popular respect for the country's past, and nothing that serves that end and is otherwise harmless should be lightly abolished. For the popular view would, and does, regard Stage V as a modern innovation, and not as a return to Stage I, but the annual appearances of the Temporary King recall time-honoured tradition and the glory of Ayudhyā. Not that there is any probability of Stage V ever being reached in the Ploughing or Swinging Ceremonies; Western influence, and the new belief that a monarch is more usefully occupied in guiding the prosaic affairs of a modern government than in exercising his divine and magical functions, are much more likely to bring total abolition in their train.

As to the origin of the institution of Temporary Kings in Siam, the fact that the idea was in process of development during the Sukhodaya period suggests that it was proximately derived from Cambodia, and the Khmers may have received the idea from India, where the following example of a somewhat similar institution is cited by Frazer [1] :—

> "In Bilaspur it seems to be the custom, after the death of a Rajah, for a Brahman to eat rice out of the dead Rajah's hand, and then to occupy the throne for a year. At the end of the year the Brahman receives presents and is dismissed from the territory, being forbidden apparently to return. . . . The custom of banishing the Brahman who represents the king may be a substitute for putting him to death."

[1] *GB.* iv, p. 154.

PART VI

MISCELLANEOUS STATE CEREMONIES

CHAPTER XXIII

THE WHITE ELEPHANT

I suppose no one feature connected with the countries of Indo-China has contributed more lavishly to the fund of material on which European writers from the seventeenth century onwards have drawn in their search for the sensational than has the White Elephant. This is perhaps not surprising, considering the unusual nature of the cult connected with this animal, but I shall here endeavour to confine myself to a discussion of its historical and sociological importance. I was privileged to witness some of the ceremonies in connection with the reception of the White Elephant for the present reign, and I shall therefore base my account on what I saw on that occasion, while, as regards the past, I shall make extracts from comparatively little-known sources.

After all that has been written on the subject, it is almost a platitude to state that the White Elephant is not white, but that it is merely an albino which, if perfect, should have pink and yellow eyes, a light reddish-brown skin, white at the edge of the ears and at the top of the trunk, white toe-nails, and red hair. The term "white elephant" is a figment of the European imagination, for the Siamese never regarded it as such, their term *Jăṅ Pho'ak* meaning simply, albino elephant.

For the moment it will be sufficient to state that by the common people the capture of a *Jăṅ Pho'ak* at the beginning of every reign is looked upon as an auspicious event, and the possession of one or more of these animals as royal appanages is regarded as an outward sign, hallowed by ancient custom, of the greatness of the monarchy. The underlying significance, now rapidly becoming forgotten by the lower classes, will be discussed later. But it may be said at once that there never was any actual worship of the White Elephant as commonly supposed, and there is very little regard for its sanctity, or other respect for it than that which its great size and strength naturally inspire. Even as an auspicious omen at the beginning of a reign it is doubtful if any Siamese would express himself so enthusiastically on the subject as did the late King Rāma VI in the following passage, in the speech which he made early in his reign:—

"During the first year of our reign several portents of the highest traditional import have made themselves manifest, and the augury

T

they convey convinces us that prosperity, and not calamity, shall continue to be the lot of our Thai Race. The discovery of the Monkey Standard, the Garuḍa Standard, and the Bow and Arrow of Rāma's strength are sure manifestations that warriors have not yet ceased to exist in the Land of the Thai, and inspire us all with confidence that the defence of our national independence will not be altogether futile. The appearance of the White Elephant at the same period is likewise a portent that the Kingdom of Siam will not fall to a low estate, unable to stand on an equal footing with the nations. All these portents have created a deep impression upon us, and we doubt not upon the minds of every one of you also."

The White Elephant for the present reign (Pl. XLIII) was born in captivity in 1926, its mother being one of the elephants of the Borneo Company's herd, employed in the extraction of teak, so its appearance was not of a very romantic nature. It was presented to the King by the Company, and the mother was lent until such time as its distinguished offspring should be weaned. The two elephants were brought down from the North in a specially constructed railway carriage, supplied with electric fan and shower-bath, and made several stops of two or three days' duration *en route*, in order to give the animals a chance to rest, and to give the people of some of the provincial towns an opportunity to pay homage and enjoy the festivities arranged by the provincial governors to commemorate the auspicious occasion. At each stopping place the elephants were led to a specially erected *śālā*, where a chapter of monks intoned appropriate stanzas, and at night the populace were regaled with theatrical performances. At the last stopping-place, P̲āṅ Paḥ In, a few hours' journey by rail from Bangkok, and the seat of the King's summer palace, the animals arrived on 12th November, 1927, and the King, in accordance with ancient custom, made the journey up-river by launch to meet them. After inspecting them the King returned to Bangkok by water.

On the 15th the train bearing the elephants arrived at the royal station at Bangkok. As they were detrained a chapter of monks chanted stanzas, and the animals then took their place in the elaborate procession which had been organized for the occasion. The route which the procession took from the railway station was lined with masses of people all eager to get a view of the unusual sight; but it was certainly only curiosity that inspired them, and not religious awe. The procession entered the Tusit̲a Park where the elephant stable is situated.[1] I have called it a stable, but it is more properly

[1] There are other elephant stables in the Grand Palace, but they are now only used at times when the White Elephant's presence is required there on a state occasion, such as the Coronation.

PLATE XLIII.

[Photo: Narasingh Studio.

THE WHITE ELEPHANT OF THE PRESENT REIGN.

[To face page 274.

PLATE XLIV.

[Photo: Narasingh Studio.

THE WHITE ELEPHANT OF THE SIXTH REIGN.

designated a *braḥ-dī-năṅ* or palace, and it is certainly built in the traditional style of Siamese temple or palace architecture. The procession was a pageant rather than a state procession in the usual sense. On its way to the stable it filed past pavilions accommodating the King and Queen, the Royal Family, and officials. Except for the bearers of ceremonial weapons and standards, and those in charge of the young elephant, its mother, and the White Elephant of the sixth reign (Pl. XLIV), the procession was made up entirely of girls mostly drawn from the ranks of the official classes. There were companies of girls dressed in the costumes of various foreign countries, others dressed to represent flowers, while others were mounted and armed with breastplates and lances to represent the amazons of ancient days. There were companies of dancers, and the masked actors of the ***Rāmāyaṇa*** also passed in review. The elephants having reached their station, the various troupes of actors and acrobats, whose stages were erected in different parts of the park, began to perform, ostensibly for the benefit of the White Elephant, but perhaps it would be more truthful to say for the amusement of the general public, who were allowed free access to this royal park on the evenings of the three days during which the celebrations lasted. Meanwhile, in the elephant "palace", as soon as the animals had entered it, a chapter of Buddhist monks intoned formulæ, while the Brahmans also performed their rites in a special pavilion.

Next morning (16th), the White Elephant was bathed, and the King arrived to take part in the anointing ceremony. Having lit the candles of worship before an image of the Buddha, the King awaited the auspicious moment of nine hours, twenty-six minutes and twenty-four seconds. The young elephant, who was extremely playful and appeared to have no respect for the ceremonies, was securely tied to upright posts on the inside of the enclosed platform, and the King mounted a dais on the outside of the rail. At the auspicious moment the Head Brahman struck the gong of victory, while other Brahmans blew conches, the monks began to recite stanzas of victory, and the King anointed the White Elephant (Pl. XLV). He also fed it with red sugar-cane on which had been inscribed the name by which the animal was to be known in future, viz. Braḥ Savetra Gajedejna Dilok; together with a string of titles somewhat similar to those taken by the King at the time of his coronation, i.e. honorific epithets of a kind appropriate either to a King or to a noble White Elephant [1]:—

[1] Carl Bock, who visited Siam in 1881, gives the full style and title of the White Elephant then recently captured, which I quote as follows, together with Prince Prisdang's translation :—

The elder members of the Royal Family also took part in the anointment followed by the Brahmans. The officials of the Elephant Department then dressed the White Elephant in full state, with the insignia of the rank of *Braḥyā Jǎṅ*; and a golden cord was placed round its neck to signify that the *khvǎñ* (spirit) of a *Braḥyā Jǎṅ* was being retained. Miniature trees were placed at the four corners of the platform on which the elephants stood. Food was presented to the monks who had officiated, and the King conferred promotion and reward upon those who had been connected with the White Elephant and attended it hitherto. It is obvious that the above ceremonies must be considered in the light of a form of *abhiṣeka*, the King anointing the White Elephant and conferring upon it a style and title. Possibly the feeding of the animal with red sugar-cane is a relic of the sacrament which accompanies coronation ceremonies in many countries, but of which we have been unable to find any trace in the Siamese *Rājābhiṣeka*. The mention of the retention of the *khvǎñ* is remarkable, and suggests that the form of *abhiṣeka*, which the ceremonies represent, is rather an initiation than a coronation.

A digression must here be made to consider the accoutrements of the White Elephant. Some idea of their evolution can be gained by a comparison with the ancient Khmer bas-reliefs. The harness of the Siamese White Elephant shows much fewer parts than that of the elephant depicted on the reliefs of Bakong, which was a common draught elephant; it is also simpler than that of the Siamese war-elephant, because it was not usually ridden except by the necessary mahouts, and therefore did not require a howdah. As La Loubère remarks[1]:—

> "The King of Siam never mounts the White Elephant, and the reason which they give is, that the White Elephant is as great a Lord as himself, because he has a King's soul like him."

Nevertheless, it appears that the King did ride the White Elephant in former times in Siam, as is indicated by a passage in the stele of

"Phra Sawet Sakonla Warophat ako udom chat visute thi mongkon sri sama sakon loma naka net adisaya sawet viset san komon la phan prom kra khoon paramintara narane soon siamma tirat pha hana nat mahan tadet kotchera ratana phiset chaloem phop kiet kachon chop charoen sak phra chak phon parun vibun sawat akka nakin ratana phra soet loet fa."

"An elephant of beautiful colour, hair, nails, and eyes are white. Perfection in form, with all the signs of regularity of the high family. The colour of the skin is that of lotus. A descendant of the angel of the Brahmans. Acquired as property by the power and glory of the king for his service. Is of the highest family of elephants of all in existence. A source of power of attraction of rain. It is as rare as the purest crystal of the highest value in the world" (*Temples and Elephants*, p. 26).

[1] L. L., p. 43.

PLATE XLV.

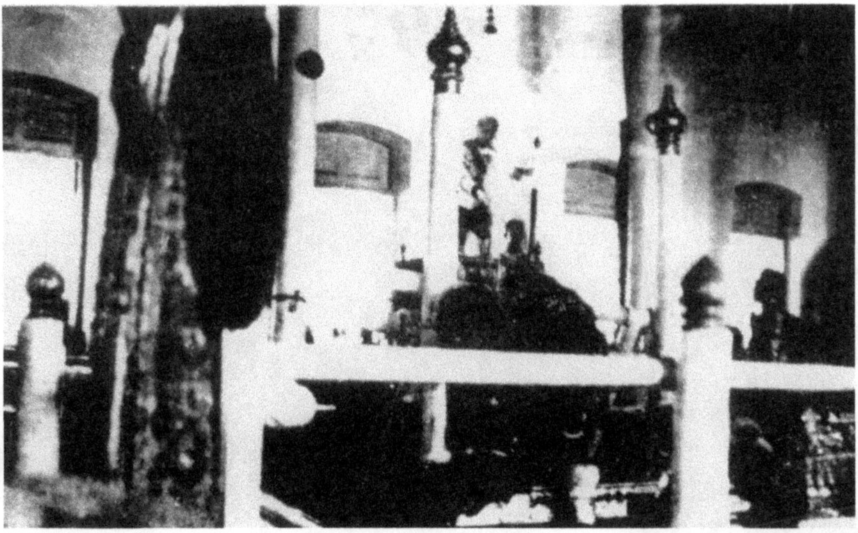

[Photo: Narasingh Studio.

THE KING ANOINTING THE WHITE ELEPHANT OF THE PRESENT REIGN.

To face page 276.]

Rāma Gāṁhèṅ, which is incidentally the first known mention of the White Elephant in Siam. The passage is as follows:—

> "On the days of the new and full moon the King orders the White Elephant named Rucāśrī to be caparisoned with the saddle ornamented with gold and ivory on the right and left; the King mounts it and goes to pay his devotions to the venerable chief of the Araññikas and then returns." [1]

Similarly, in early times in Burma, the King is referred to as

> "the exalted, who rides upon a White Elephant" [2];

and Batuta, who wrote in A.D. 1350, says the King of Ceylon was in the habit of riding on a White Elephant on state occasions.

Some of the Khmer reliefs show elephants wearing crowns, and Groslier [3] illustrates an example which might well represent a White Elephant with its magnificent *mokhut* and saddle cloth. The modern Siamese White Elephant does not wear a crown, but only a highly ornamented head-cloth, sometimes in three overlapping pieces which might represent the tiers of the *mokhut*. It also wears a saddle-cloth ornamented with the royal arms. Groslier [4] also shows examples of elephant "bells", but the modern White Elephant does not carry bells, though it does carry, as also do the other royal elephants, suspended from its head, a pair of yak's hair tufts, to keep off the evil spirits, which spring from bell-shaped holders, and appear to be similar to the bells figured by Groslier. On the other hand, the yak's tufts are not figured in the reliefs, and may therefore be a Siamese addition.

It will be understood that the attention shown to the young White Elephant on its arrival was of short duration, and that it soon faded from the public eye. It is well known that the White Elephants were forgotten and neglected during the closing decades of last century, but, if the noble animal does not enjoy very much royal favour nowadays, a growing knowledge of the conditions necessary for the welfare of animals, coupled with the fact that the White Elephants are much in demand as a tourist sight, has led to a general improvement in their condition, which at present might be described as the happy medium between the total neglect which was their lot during preceding decades and the pampered state which they enjoyed, and which often brought about their death from indigestion, in the days of Old Siam. The reception of the young White Elephant and its mother in 1927

[1] Coedès, *Inscriptions de Sukhodaya*, p. 47; Bradley's translation of this passage in *JSS*. vi, is inaccurate.

[2] *Epigraphia Birmanica*, vol. i, part 2, Môn inscription, iii, face D.

[3] Gr., Fig. 68. [4] Gr., Fig. 67.

was, of course, only a revival brought about by a King with antiquarian interests and a strong believer in the undoubted fact that to keep up old customs is a valuable means of inspiring the people with a respect for the past, and a spirit of loyalty to the Crown. When I visited the young animal on the occasion of the celebrations I noticed that, although carefully prepared food was arranged on gold plates in the vicinity, the White Elephant was, in fact, fed in quite an ordinary manner, the precious vessels being kept well out of the way of the playful youngster. I was, in common with other members of the public, permitted to offer it sugar-cane, which was considered an act of merit.

To see the White Elephant as it was in the days of its glory one must go back to the reign of King Rāma IV. It was this pious king who, even in his official letter of welcome to Sir John Bowring, the British Ambassador, could not refrain from adding the following postscript :—

> " I have just returned from old city Ayudia of Siam fifteen days ago with the beautiful She Elephant which your Excellency will witness here on your Excellency's arrival."

The following information is extracted from the writings of Mrs. Leonowens [1] :—

> In those days, when the governor of a province was notified of the appearance of a white elephant within his domain, he immediately commanded prayers and offerings to be made in all the temples, while he sent out a formidable expedition of hunters and slaves to take the precious beast and bring it in in triumph. As soon as he was informed of its capture, a special messenger was despatched to inform the king of its sex, probable age, size, complexion, deportment, looks and ways ; and in the presence of his Majesty this bearer of glorious tidings underwent the painfully pleasant operation of having his mouth, ears, and nostrils stuffed with gold. Especially was the lucky individual, perhaps some half-wild woodsman, who was first to spy the illustrious monster, munificently rewarded. A wide path was cut for the animal's passage through to the jungle, and on arriving at the river-bank he was installed in a floating palace of wood, surmounted by a gorgeous roof, and hung with crimson curtains. The roof was thatched with flowers, the floor overlaid with gilt matting, while an obsequious crowd bathed him, perfumed him, fed him, sung and played to him. At a point some seventy miles from the capital, he was met by the king and his court, all the chief personages of the kingdom, and a multitude of Buddhist monks and Brahman priests, accompanied by troops of players and musicians who conducted him with all honour to his stable-palace. A great number of cords and ropes of all qualities and lengths were attached to the raft, those in the centre being of fine silk. These were for the king and his noble retinue, who with their own hands made them fast to their gilded barges, the rest being secured to the great fleet of lesser boats. Thus the White Elephant was escorted to the

[1] *The English Governess at the Siamese Court*, pp. 141 sqq. Also P. i, 152 sqq.

capital in triumph, there to be anointed by the king and fêted with theatrical entertainments for nine days, while his tusks were ringed with gold and he was robed in purple. Whenever he went out for his bath his head was shielded by a royal umbrella, while pages waved golden fans before him. He was fed with the finest of royal food from plates of gold and silver, and, should he fall ill, he was attended by the king's own physician, while priests daily repaired to his palace to pray for his safe deliverance, and to sprinkle him with consecrated water.

To the above account I may add that it was formerly the custom to provide young White Elephants with a large number of human wet-nurses. I have in my possession a photograph, taken about a dozen years ago, of a Siamese woman suckling a young elephant, probably a white one.

It is perhaps not generally known that lullabies were composed to induce the White Elephant to sleep, and that a eulogy was recited immediately such an animal was captured in order to persuade him to resign himself to his new mode of existence. The following is a translation of the latter:—

"With holy reverence we now come to worship the angels who preside over the destiny of all elephants. Most powerful angels, we entreat you to assemble now in order that you may prevent all evil to His Majesty the King of Siam, and also to this magnificent elephant which has recently been brought. We appeal to you all, whom we now worship, and beg that you will use your power in restraining the heart of this animal from all anger and unhappiness. We also beg that you will incline this elephant to listen to the words of instruction and comfort that we now deliver. Most royal elephant! We beg that you will not think too much of your father and mother, your relatives, and friends. We beg that you will not regret leaving your native mountain and forests, because there are evil spirits there that are very dangerous, and wild beasts are there that howl, making a fearful noise, and there too that bird *hassadin* which hovers round and often picks up elephants and eats them; and there are also bands of cruel hunters who kill elephants for their ivory. We trust you will not return to the forest, for you would be in constant danger. And that is not all, in the forest you have no servants, and it is very unpleasant to sleep with dust and filth adhering to your body, and where flies and mosquitoes are very troublesome. Brave and noble elephant! Why should you wish to wander free? The forest is full of thorns, bushes and marshes. Why should you wish to cross the valley and mountains? There you must drink muddy water, and there the stones will cut your feet. O Father Elephant! We entreat you to banish every wish to stay in the forest. Look at this delightful place, this heavenly city! It abounds in wealth and everything your eyes could wish to see or your heart desire to possess. It is of your own merit that you have come to behold this beautiful city, to enjoy its wealth, and to be the favourite guest of His most exalted Majesty the King." [1]

[1] *Siam*, M. L. Court, New York, 1886, pp. 210 sq.

This curious practice has the sanction of antiquity, as Mr. F. H. Giles has pointed out,[1] for Megasthenes, the Greek ambassador at the court of the Hindu emperor Chandragupta, about 300 B.C., whose capital was at Pātaliputra (modern Patna), records that Indians sang songs to the accompaniment of music to soothe and coax wild elephants recently captured.

The following extracts from the *Annals of Ayudhyā*, relating to events in the seventeenth century, will serve as a further illustration of the esteem in which the White Elephant was held by the Siamese of Old Siam :—

"In the Siamese Civil era 1020 [A.D. 1658] year of the Cock, H.M. took a boat excursion to Nakon Sawan. While at this place H.E. Phya Chakri informed H.M. that Khun Srikhaun Charin of the province Sri-sawat had reported that while he was out gathering information in the forests of Hui sai, Nai Ahnsui had captured a she white elephant, over sixty inches high. Her ears, tail, and her general appearance were beautiful. The capture was made on Tuesday, in the second lunation, second of the waning. H.M. gave orders that H.E. the governor of Tanahwasee (Tenasserim), and all skilled in the management of elephants go and bring to him the white elephant, H.M. then returning to Ayuthia, the capital. The white elephant was brought to the capital in the second lunation, fifth of the waxing, and a magnificent boat procession received her and brought her to a stall near the palace. H.M. conferred upon his great and distinguished acquisition the following name : Phra-intra-aiyarah-warnawisutti-racha-kirini. The astrologers and wise sages, and princes, ministers and nobles were required to make demonstrations of gladness for three days. After which beautiful ornaments and utensils were made for the decoration and use of the white elephant, and Phra Sri-sittikarn was appointed to care for the animal. Nai Ahnsui, the son of Khun Sri-khaun Charin who captured the elephant, received from H.M. the title Khun kachen-taun-aiyarah-wisutt-rach-kirini, and presents of a silver box with a golden rim, and 96 dollars, a cotton and silk waist cloth and a silk coat, and to this man's wife H.M. presented a silver bowl with lotus petal rim, weighing dollars 24, and its accompaniments and dollars 18, and a calico waist cloth. H.M. promoted Khun Sri-khaun-charin, the father of Nai Ahnsui with the title Luang Sawats Kachentara, and presented to him a silver box inlaid with the figure of an elephant's ear, and gold ornaments for his box and 96 dollars, a cotton and silk waist cloth, and a silk jacket. As Nai Ahn Sui, when he captured the elephant, thought her eyes were defective, and was about to let the precious prize go, H.M. gave only such presents. To the elephant driver, and the elephant keeper, H.M. made the presents usually given when a white elephant has been obtained. To the bearer of the letter of information reporting the capture of the animal, and to the man who delivered her each received from H.M. a present. The value of the presents made on this occasion amounted to dollars 846. The political servants who are required to pay their annual quota of block

[1] *JSS.* xxiii, pt. 2, 1929, p. 65.

tin, and who assisted in leading to the capture, and the Government servants who have in charge the white elephant and who assisted in the present instance each received some token of royal favour for their service."

Again :—

" In the Siamese civil era 1022, year of the Rat, second of the decade [i.e. A.D. 1660], the provincial officials of Nakon Sawan sent a dispatch to the Samuha nahyok department, that one of the officers of the elephant keepers, had captured a white elephant about 80 inches high. The animal was a very pretty one and it was captured in the forests of the province, Nakon Sawan. H.E. Chao Phya Kosa Chakri (Minister of the North), presented this glorious intelligence to H.M. the King of Siam. This was a source of immense gratification to the King of Siam, who promptly gave orders to the ministers and their subaltern officers, who have in charge the royal elephants, to go up and receive this eminent beast, and bring it to Ayuthia, and that all necessary preparations be made for an ornamental and grand procession by land and by water as was customary for such auspicious acquisitions. The lordly animal was to be placed in a shed outside of the Royal palace, and appointed a grand festival, at which Buddhist priests and Brahmins were to officiate, to be enlivened with music, theatricals and other amusements to interest the public for some days, after which the highly-prized acquisition was to be conducted to its shed within the palace walls. H.M. honoured it with the dignified and imposing title, Chao Phya Broma Chentara Chatratant and provided for the royal beast gold decorations, ornamented with the nine distinguished gems, and designated leading men of the elephant department, and masters of tens to be in attendance upon the lordly white elephant. The fortunate man who captured the animal was elevated to the rank of Khun Mun. According to ancient custom he had honours, clothing and money showered upon him as usual. Those who were associated with him and assisted in the capture were each rewarded, and received certificates exempting them from every description of taxes, and they were dismissed to return to their homes, and engage in their usual vocations.

" The Khun Mun who was appointed to superintend, have in charge and care for this lordly elephant, diligently taught it till it understood human language, and could do a number of deeds. All who were under sentence of severe penalties for grave offences and were in prison, and for whom none could have interceded, prepared vows and promised votive offerings to this white elephant, and then presented to the elephant their written petition. The elephant took these petitions up in his proboscis, raised it in adoration to the King, and presented them to him, and thus entreated for the petitioners' pardon. Whenever H.M. made his appearance at the lordly elephant's shed, on such occasions H.M. reached forth his hand, received from the elephant the petition, read it, acquainted himself with the contents and out of regard to the lordly beast, granted to the beast the request of the petitioner. All thus pardoned, upon their release brought to the royal beast, the votive offerings they had bound themselves to give. After the acquisition of this animal, many criminals, sent petitions in this way and through the beast obtained their pardon. H.M. the King became very meritorious being the possessor of a male and female white elephant, as special royal seats, and H.M.'s wonderful power was known in all parts of the world, among the great and small nations and H.M.'s enemies greatly respected and feared him." [1]

Not only in Siam, but also in the other countries of Indo-China, was the White Elephant an object of desire. Especially was this the case in Burma, as we know from the accounts of Ralph Fitch, who travelled throughout Burma in 1582, and of Father Sangermano, who was in Burma some two hundred years later. It is not surprising, therefore, to find that the desire for the possession of the sacred animal was on more than one occasion the cause of war. Thus it was that in the middle of the sixteenth century, King Cakravarti of Ayudhyā, who was the proud possessor of no less than seven white elephants, and had been persuaded to take the title of "Lord of the White Elephant", aroused the jealousy of King Bayin-Naung of Burma, who sent to demand two of the animals. His request was refused, whereupon he immediately declared war on Siam, and was not satisfied until four white elephants, instead of the two he had originally demanded, had been handed over.[2]

We have seen with what esteem the White Elephant was regarded during life, that it was received with all honours befitting a king, that it was anointed and named after the manner of a royal *abhiṣeka*, that in health it was served in its own palace by royal pages, and in sickness it was attended by the king's physician. It is not therefore surprising to find that after death it was honoured by a royal cremation.

In recent times the occasion of the death of a White Elephant has, as one would expect, not occasioned very much notice or alarm:—

"On the occasion of the last death a few Brahmins, the white monkey, and some physicians, only, attended the death-bed. After the elephant was dead, an excavation was made in the ground near its head, and incense burned. The carcase was then covered with white cloth, dragged on board a barge, and taken outside the city. It was not cremated, but was left to decay, the bones and tusks being afterwards collected and preserved. For three days Brahmins remained praying in the stable."

Mrs. Leonowens, however, gives a graphic picture of the consternation which the death of a White Elephant caused in the reign of King Rāma IV. In 1862 a magnificent White Elephant had been captured

[1] Reign of King Nārāyaṇa, translated from the *Annals of Ayudhyā*, by S. J. Smith, Bangkok, 1880.

[2] Wood, *History of Siam*, pp. 117 sq.

[3] "The Decadent White Elephant," in *Imperial and Asiatic Review*, vol. xi.

and a splendid pavilion had been erected in front of the Grand Palace to receive it. The whole nation was filled with joy, until there came the awful tidings that it had died.

> "No man dared tell the King. But the Kralahome—that man of prompt expedients and unfailing presence of mind—commanded that the preparations should cease instantly, and that the buildings should vanish with the builders. In the evening his Majesty came forth, as usual, to exult in the glorious work. What was his astonishment to find no vestige of the splendid structure that had been so nearly completed the night before. He turned, bewildered, to his courtiers, to demand an explanation, when suddenly the terrible truth flashed into his mind. With a cry of pain, he sank down upon a stone, and gave vent to an hysterical passion of tears; but was presently consoled by one of his children, who, carefully prompted in his part, knelt before him and said: 'Weep not, O my father! The stranger lord may have left us but for a time.'"

Only the brains and the heart were cremated, the carcase, shrouded in fine white linen, being floated on a barge down the river. Shortly afterwards the king showed Mrs. Leonowens its tusks and a part of its skin preserved, at the same time reading the following curious description of the deceased monster:—

> "His eyes were light blue, surrounded by a salmon colour; his hair fine, soft, and white; his complexion pinkish white; his tusks like long pearls; his ears like silver shields; his trunk like a comet's tail; his legs like the feet of the skies; his tread like the sound of thunder; his looks full of meditation; his expression full of tenderness; his voice the voice of a mighty warrior; and his bearing that of an illustrious monarch." [1]

Van Vliet has left us a short account of the death and obsequies of a White Elephant during the reign of King P̱rāsāda Dòṅ of Ayudhyā. He states that

> "In the commencement of the reign of the present king, a young white elephant was caught which suddenly died in 1633. His Majesty was so upset by this, that all the slaves, who had guarded and assisted the animal were executed. Besides this, the king paid reverence to the dead animal, ordered it to be buried near one of the famous temples, and a small house of a pyramidal shape was built over the grave. But after it had been buried a short time, it was dug up and was burned with a splendour, even greater than that which has been displayed for the most famous mandarins. All remains which had not been consumed by the fire, were collected in a box, buried at the temple, and a beautiful pyramid was erected over it." [2]

Finally, it is interesting to note that the White Elephant is not without the crowning dignity of a special "pantheon" corresponding

[1] *The English Governess at the Siamese Court*, pp. 144 sq.
[2] *JSS.*, vol. vii, pt. i, 1910, p. 100.

to that of the kings. In the Chapel Royal of the Emerald Buddha are to be seen twenty-one statuettes of elephants, each with its name carved on the pedestal. These represent the White Elephants which have added to the splendour, prestige, and prosperity of the Royal House of Căkrī of Siam.

In endeavouring to trace the history of the White Elephant Cult in Indo-China we naturally look to India, at once the home of the elephant and of the culture which has been adopted by most of the peoples of Indo-China. If we had gone to Africa, also the home of the elephant, we should also have found the White Elephant regarded as a sacred animal in Abyssinia. But it is unnecessary to seek for any connection between Indo-China and Abyssinia for, as Sir James Frazer has shown in the various volumes of *The Golden Bough*, albino animals are held to be sacred in many parts of the world. This fact probably supplies us with the origin of the White Elephant Cult in pre-historic times. White animals were esteemed because they were rare, and especially would this be so in the case of the White Elephant which is not only extremely rare, but belongs to a species which, even in its ordinary form, was always venerated on account of its strength, size, and value in war. In the earliest times the White Elephant came to be regarded as having a magical significance. In the *Vessantara Jātaka* the White Elephant was regarded as a rain maker, and we have seen that this is one of the epithets used in connection with the Siamese White Elephant. Van Vliet [1] has the story of a White Elephant that turned black, and afterwards red, much to the consternation of the officials in charge; while it is clear from several remarks in the *Baṅṣā-vaḥtāra* of Hlvaṅ Prasoeṭh, that the royal elephants were closely watched for omens. For instance,

> "the chief elephant Phraya Chaddanta uttered a noise like that produced by the sounding of a conch-shell,"

following which an accident befell the king. On another occasion

> "the chief elephant Svasti Mongol and the chief elephant Keo Chakraratna were fighting with each other, and the left tusk of the elephant Svasti Mongol got loose. On this the soothsayers forbade the preparations for a war."

Again,

> "In Phitsnulok on Wednesday the 8th of the 10th waxing moon (A.D. 1547), marvellous events happened, inasmuch as the Menam Sai in Phitsnulok rose over the banks of the river for three soks. Furthermore the apparition of a female form resembling an elephant was seen; it had the appearance of a trunk of an elephant; the

[1] Loc. cit.

ears were large and it was seen sitting at the temple Prasād in Phitsnulok." [1]

I have mentioned these examples, and many more could be collected, because they seem to indicate that the early pre-religious significance of the White Elephant has survived in Siam until comparatively modern times, and we may indeed have here the relics of an early indigenous White Elephant Cult followed by the peoples of Indo-China long before the grafting on of imported Indian interpretations. In support of this is the fact that the elephant hunters of the Gorāja table-land in Eastern Siam have retained until the present day an elaborate system of spirit-worship, and early beliefs in connection with elephants, with which Mr. F. H. Giles has dealt at length in *The Journal of the Siam Society*.[2]

The great religious systems of India each gave their special interpretations to the already existing cult of elephants. In Hinduism the first of all elephants is the magnificent Airāvata, the derivation of whose name is referred to the word Iravat, signifying "produced from the ocean" in accordance with the mythical churning of the ocean.[3] It is frequently referred to in Hindu mythology and in the *Rāmāyaṇa*. It is the mount of Indra, and in India possesses one and sometimes three heads, representing the three great gods, Brahmā, Viṣṇu, and Śiva, but in Siam is more frequently represented as having thirty-three heads in consonance with the heaven of the thirty-three gods (*tavatu'ṅsa*).

In Buddhism the White Elephant was cast for the rôle filled by the dove in Christianity :—

> "Then the future Buddha, who had become a superb white elephant, and was wandering on the Golden Hill, not far from there, descended thence, and ascending the Silver Hill, approached her from the North. Holding in his silvery trunk a white lotus flower, and uttering a far-reaching cry, he entered the golden mansion, and thrice doing obeisance to his mother's couch, he gently struck her right side, and seemed to enter her womb." [4]

But it is mainly to the part taken by the White Elephant in several of the *Jātakas* that the animal owes its fame and sacredness in the eyes of all pious Buddhists. Perhaps the best known of these ancient stories is the *Vessantara Jātaka*, in which Prince Vessantara gives away the magical rain-producing elephant, the most valued possession of

[1] *JSS.*, vol. vi, 1908, "Events in Ayudhyā from Chulasakaraj, 686–966."
[2] Vol. xxiii, pt. 2, 1929.
[3] Dowson's *Hindu Classical Dictionary*, p. 9.
[4] Rhys Davids, *Buddhist Birth Stories*, p. 150.

his country. In several *Jātakas* the Bodhisattva himself is born as a White Elephant, most notably in the *Chaddantha Jātaka* where he is a noble six-tusked elephant. The *Mati-posaka Jātaka* is most interesting to us because it shows how the bounty lavished on White Elephants by pious Buddhist kings in Siam was founded on the example set by ancient Indian kings:—

> "I, my lord, have seen a splendid elephant, white all over, and excellent, fit for the king's riding! . . . And the king caused the city to be decorated. The trainer led the Bodhisattva into a stable all adorned and decked with a screen of many colours, and sent word to the king. And the king took all manner of fine food and caused it to be given to the Bodhisattva."[1]

This passage might almost refer to the reception of a White Elephant in the heyday of the cult in Siam. One more *Jātaka* may be mentioned—the *Dumedha*—which tells of a king who was jealous of the beauty and honour of his White Elephant.

A Greek source affords us independent evidence of the esteem in which White Elephants were held about 300 B.C., and here again the events described might almost have occurred in Siam in the days when Ayudhyā was capital of the realm:—

> "Megasthenes gives a story of a white elephant which was caught and kept by its owner; there arising between the two a great friendship and love. The king, hearing of this white elephant, commanded that it be made over to him, but the owner refused and fled to the jungle with his animal. The king sent men in pursuit, and a great fight, in which the elephant fought on the side of his master, took place. The king's men were put to flight, and the elephant nursed his master, who had been wounded, bringing him to convalescence. It is not recorded that the king obtained possession of this animal, but the story goes to prove that over 2,000 years ago the white elephant was the object of desire on the part of a monarch, and the same is amply proved by the *Jātaka* stories in which the white elephant plays an important part."[1]

We thus see that three different points of view have become fused together to produce the historical White Elephant Cult of Indo-China in general, and Siam in particular. These are:—

(1) The animistic or magical, still surviving in the taboos and propitiatory rites of the Gorāja elephant hunters and only awaiting some such ill-omened event as the sudden death of the young White Elephant of the present reign, to be revived amongst the superstitious lower classes of the capital.

(2) The Hindu, represented by the many-headed elephant of Indra, to be seen in the masked performances of the *Rāmāyaṇa*, sometimes

[1] *Jātaka* No. 455, edn. of Cowell. [2] F. H. Giles, loc. cit.

also in the procession of the Swinging Festival, and on the one tical silver pieces, but now perhaps altogether without religious or magical significance.

(3) The Buddhist, according to which the animal is still half seriously regarded by some as being animated by the soul, if not of a Bodhisattva, at least of some being in an advanced stage of the journey towards Nirvāṇa, though there is not, nor has there ever been, any idea of worship, in the proper sense of the word. Indeed, this Buddhist idea has now almost degenerated into a supposition that the White Elephant is a sign of the King's merit.

To these may be added the severely practical official point of view, in accordance with which it is realized that the White Elephant has always been an important adjunct of Siamese royalty and may yet for many years continue to help to inspire the common people with a wholesome respect for the monarchy.

A few words remain to be said about the white monkey and the white crow, which are the companions of the White Elephant in captivity. Apart from the fact that these animals are prized on account of their rarity, there is also a mythological interpretation. The white monkey represents Hanumān, the monkey hero of the *Rāmāyaṇa*, or, according to the Buddhist interpretation, the monkey who offered honey to the Buddha; while I suppose that the white crow may represent the sacred bird Garuḍa.

CHAPTER XXIV

FEASTS OF LAMPS

1. *The Hoisting of Lamps on Poles (Còṅ P̱ariaṅ).*[1]

The term *Còṅ P̱ariaṅ* means, literally, the hoisting of fat (*p̱ariaṅ* = fat). According to ancient usage, lanterns were raised on posts, as will shortly be described, on the first day of the bright fortnight and lowered on the second day of the dark fortnight of the additional month, if the year had one ; if it had not, they were raised on the fourteenth day of the bright fortnight of the twelfth month, and lowered on the first day of the bright fortnight of the first month. According to the astrologers the lanterns were to be raised on the day on which the sun entered Scorpio and the moon was in Taurus. An alternative method was to raise the lanterns when the Pleiades were visible throughout the night.

On the appointed day, in the morning, the King sprinkled the "posts of the lamps of victory" (*sau gom jăya*) with lustral water, and anointed them with fragrant unguents. Then the posts were raised. There were three of these wooden posts, and they had nine-tiered umbrellas of white cloth erected over them. There were also three lamp-posts called *sau gom jăya p̱raḥdiap*, and these had seven-tiered umbrellas above them. They were all painted white, and hung with little bells. The lanterns were bamboo frames covered with white cloth. Around them were one hundred "attendant" posts of bamboo. These had three-tiered umbrellas and lanterns of bamboo framework covered with paper. The ceremony took place within the precincts of the royal palace, where the posts were erected, and where the Brahmans in a special pavilion erected for the purpose prepared the candles each morning. These were smeared with cow's fat in accordance with a very ancient Brahmanical custom, and presented to the King together with a conch full of lustral water for sprinkling the posts. Twenty-four candles were burnt in the "lanterns of victory" each night, each candle lasting about three hours. King Rāma IV used always to come out and light the candles in the lanterns himself. King Rāma V sometimes did so, and sometimes did not. In the latter case the Brahmans sent the candles and sacred fire into

[1] Sources : *BRB.*, pp. 9 sqq. ; *NN.*, pp. 63 sqq. ; just mentioned in *KM.* ; also mentioned by Gervaise (edn. of 1688, p. 159), and by *L.L.*, p. 48.

the palace where the King lit them, and his sons brought them out and set them up. If the King was away from the capital, the ceremony was performed in the palace in which he was staying. It was also performed in the palace of the *Uparāja*, and, in the royal palace, outside the quarters of the princes and princesses. The *Côṅ Pariaṅ* fell into disuse in the latter part of the reign of King Rāma V, but since then it has on one occasion been revived, in the last year of King Rāma VI's reign.[1]

In Siam it was always realized that *Côṅ Pariaṅ* had originally been a Brahmanic ceremony, the worship of the three gods Śiva, Viṣṇu, and Brahmā, represented evidently by the three posts crowned with nine-tiered umbrellas, while the three posts crowned with seven-tiered umbrellas possibly represented their *śaktis*, and the " attendant posts " their heavenly courtiers. But later it came to be popularly regarded as having a Buddhist significance: the worship of the relics of the Buddha, the " Crest-Jewel " in the " Heaven of the Thirty-three Gods ", and the footprints of the Buddha found on the ridge of sand of the Narmadā and worshipped by the Snake people (Nāgas). King Rāma IV fostered this interpretation by introducing, in his customary way, the recital of Buddhist texts in the evening and the feeding of monks in the morning before the lantern posts were set up. In this connection it is interesting to note that a corresponding royal ceremony was celebrated by the Buddhist kings of Ceylon.[2]

For the original of the Brahmanic festival we must, of course, turn to India. It can, without a doubt, be identified with the Hindu *Diwali* or *Dipawali*, which is still celebrated in India by all householders at the same season as the *Côṅ Pariaṅ*. Dubois [3] says:—

> " At the end of November or the beginning of December the Deepavali (feast of lamps) is celebrated. It occupies several days. Every evening while it lasts the Hindus place lighted lamps at the doors of their houses or hang paper lanterns on long poles in the street. This feast appears to be specially dedicated to fire. But as it is held at a time when most of the cereal crops are ready for harvesting, the cultivators in many places are then in the habit of going together in procession to their fields, and there offering up to their crops prayers and sacrifices of rams or goats, in order, as it were, to give thanks to their crops for having ripened and become fit for the food of man."

Gerini [4] apparently considers that the ceremony in Siam was also connected with agriculture, being performed in order

[1] As recorded in the *Bangkok Times* for 2nd Nov., 1925.
[2] Knox, pp. 160, 161.
[3] D., p. 571.
[4] Ge. (2).

"to retain the water from draining off the padi fields, for the ears of rice would not attain maturity if the yearly inundation were to abate so early".

This is presumably a conjecture, since I find no evidence for it in the Siamese literature on the subject. On the contrary, it seems always to have been regarded in Siam as a form of worship of the three gods (later given a Buddhist significance) just as in India, as Gerini [1] himself admits,

"it is essentially a festival in honour of Vishnu and his consort, for it is known that on the 11th day of the new moon of Kārttika the god awakes from his four months' sleep, and that his victory over king Bālī (Vamana avatara) took place at this season."

Nevertheless, it must be admitted that Brahmanic worship was seldom, if ever, performed without a definite object, and the connection of *Dipawali* with agriculture in India is significant. In Siam the *pūjā* was kept up long after its object was forgotten.

2. *The Kaḫṯikeyā Festival.*[2]

This Brahmanical ceremony was abolished in the early years of the present century. Formerly it was performed in the first Siamese month, but King Rāma IV ordered it to be performed in the twelfth. In making this change to the twelfth month (Kārttika), when the moon is in conjunction with Pleiades, King Rāma IV was guided by the name of the ceremony. No doubt it was originally performed in the twelfth month, but had been transferred to the first month at the time when the Swinging Festival was transferred to the second month. There seems to have been a connection between the Kaḫṯikeyā Festival and the Swinging Ceremony (when the latter was performed in the first month), and it was also connected with the *Còṅ Pariaṅ*, being performed about the middle of the same month, sometimes a little earlier and sometimes a little later. The nature of the relationship between these ceremonies will be discussed later.

The features of this ceremony were as follows: Three platforms, each four cubits high, were erected in front of the temples of Śiva, Gaṇeśa, and Viṣṇu. By the four sides of each platform, facing the four cardinal points, were raised four mounds of sand and cowdung called "mountains", each a cubit high, and shaped according to one of the *yantra* diagrams in the Brahmanical books.[3] The Brahmans also brought three new pots which were covered with plaited ropes, and were called "jewel-vessels" (*pāṯra kèv*). A zinc tube containing nine cotton wicks, and bags of padi, pulses, and sesamum, were placed in

[1] Loc. cit. [2] *BRB.*, pp. 17 sqq. [3] See Plate III.

the pots. Then they brought twelve sticks, each four cubits long, called "divine clubs" (*mai debdăṇḍa*). The ends of these sticks were wound with strips of cloth, so that they could be soaked with oil and lighted. At nightfall the *Braḥ Mahā Rāja Grū* consecrated the sticks and pots and lit the wicks in the latter. He also sprinkled the sticks with lustral water and anointed them. Having placed the pots on posts near the platforms, he lit the ends of the sticks and threw them at the "mountains" one after another, until he had thrown all the twelve. Omens were drawn from the way in which the sticks fell, east representing the King, south the priesthood, west the ministers and officials, and north the people.

The *Braḥ Mahā Rāja Grū* then made oblations of parched rice to the "jewel-vessels" in which fire was kept burning in front of the temples for three nights. On the third day the vessels were taken inside the temples, and the fire put out with lustral water, which concluded the ceremony.

It is quite clear that the making of predictions by the casting of sticks at the hillocks is no part of the original rite, but is one of the late soothsaying modifications which the Brahmans added on to most State Ceremonies with the object of showing their own importance and flattering the King. But it was this soothsaying which was nearly always discontinued, as a result of the growth of education, long before the main part of the ceremony ceased to be performed. The Kaḥṯikeyā Festival is no exception and the soothsaying connected with this ceremony was abolished many years ago, and what was the nature of the predictions is now forgotten. But, as King Rāma V naïvely remarks,

> "perhaps the predictions were uniformly good every year till at last the King could remember them and ordered them to be cut out."

As to the significance of the main ceremony, it seems that the Siamese have no clear ideas. King Rāma IV, who was uncertain as to the purpose of the Brahmanical rites, was at a loss to know where Buddhist modifications might be added on; so he did nothing beyond restoring the observance to its original month. King Rāma V suggested, in view of its coming shortly before the Swinging Festival, that the lamps were lit outside the temples to welcome the gods who were about to come down to earth; but this quite obviously has the appearance of a very late attempt to explain the forgotten original meaning. The resemblance between this ceremony and the *Còṅ Pariaṅ* is striking, and they both occur about the same time. Gerini [1]

[1] Ge. (2).

has noticed this resemblance, and identifies the Kaḥṯikeyā ceremony as the Śaivite counterpart of the Vaiṣṇavite ceremony of *Còṅ P̱ariaṅ*. It was, he considers, a fire festival in agreement with Kaḥṯikeyā's legendary birth from fire, corresponding to the celebrations held in Southern India on full-moon day of this month, when rice-meal buns are made, with a cavity in the centre filled in with *ghi* and provided with a wick which is lit; at the same time bonfires are kindled on the mountain tops in honour of Kaḥṯikeyā. Both these ceremonies of lamps are, of course, in their present form, of comparatively late origin, having presumably been derived from some early Vedic worship of Agni, which was in course of time forgotten, but came to be interpreted in accordance with the mythology of the later Brahmanic gods. This was in turn forgotten in Siam, and in both the *Còṅ P̱ariaṅ* and the Kaḥṯikeyā Ceremony the respective Vaiṣṇavite and Śaivite dedications of the two ceremonies were lost, and the gods were worshipped indiscriminately.

3. *Lòy Braḥ P̱raḥdīp or Lòy Kraḥdòṅ*, i.e. *the floating of lamps at night.*[1]

This ceremony is performed twice a year, for the three nights of the fourteenth and fifteenth waxing and first waning of the eleventh month (Āśvina), and again one month later in the twelfth month (Kārttika). On both these occasions little rafts, made of plantain stems and decorated with flags, paper umbrellas, incense sticks, and lighted candles, with offerings of food and flowers, are set adrift on the river by people living near its banks. Formerly, at least, the King himself went down to the royal landing and set a raft adrift while all the palace ladies did likewise. These rafts of the royalty and nobility were on a more elaborate scale than those of the common people, and all exercised their greatest ingenuity in producing the most beautiful and original forms, model barges, floating houses, etc. When I lived close to the river bank I often watched the making and launching of these rafts by the people who dwelt near by, and it was always a very pretty sight to see the river at night covered with thousands of bobbing lights, on their way out to be swallowed up by the sea.

Neither the Buddhist monks nor Brahman priests play any official part in this ceremony; so it is not easy to trace its origin. For the observance of the eleventh month, the people have invented a Buddhist significance, the launching of the illuminated rafts being regarded

[1] Sources: *BRB.*, pp. 25 sqq.; *NN.*, pp. 63 sqq.: part of *NN.*'s account was translated and published by King Rāma IV in the *Siam Repository*, April, 1869.

as an act of worship of the footprint of the Buddha on the sandy bank of the Narmadā. Round fish-pies, some of large size, are made and partaken of, and the ceremony is celebrated contemporaneously with the festival of the ending of the Buddhist retreat. It may thus be looked upon sociologically as a means of popular merit-making and amusement at this happy season of the year. But there also lingers the animistic belief in the propitiation of the spirit or spirits of the river.

There is evidence for supposing that the earlier significance of both these occasions of lamp-floating was Brahmanic. Gerini [1] has suggested that the observance in the eleventh month is the traditional continuation of the Hindu *Dyuta* or *Kojagara* festival, held at full moon in honour of Indra and Lakshmī, when lamps were also lighted; while the observance in the twelfth month is undoubtedly connected with the Kaḥṯikeyā Festival. In support of these probabilities we have the evidence of Nāṅ Nabamāśa. She states that there was in her time no ceremony of *Lòy Kraḥdòṅ*, but she, being the daughter of a Brahman, wished to honour the genii of the river in Brahmanical fashion. She accordingly made a *Kraḥdòṅ* of great beauty and elaboration, such as she alone had the skill to make. The King, happening to see it, was much struck by its beauty, and was filled with the desire to light and launch it. But, as he was an ardent supporter of Buddhism, and knowing that it was made by Lady Nabamāśa with the intention of honouring the Brahmanical deities, he had scruples about doing so. However, he overcame his scruples by declaring:—

> "The property such as pyramids and spires dedicated to Buddha on the banks of this river, or his sacred relics, bones, hair, etc., wherever they may be in the subterranean regions concealed from the eye, under the river, or in places which Buddha has pressed with his feet, when moving in his might, or in his natural state, if these prints are in this river, or in the ocean which receives the stream of this river, all these articles that are suitable offerings to Buddha I reverently dedicate to him with this elegantly decorated *Kraḥdòṅ* offering. Whatever merit becomes complete by these offerings to Buddha, that merit I cheerfully make over to the genii of the river who are venerated by Cău Còm Nabamāśa as the owner of the *Kraḥdòṅ*."

The King set adrift the *Kraḥdòṅ*, and his example was followed by all the courtiers and nobles, and the King ordered that the custom should become an annual observance. It was observed regularly during the Ayudhyā period, and is mentioned by La Loubère.[2] In the early

[1] Ge. (2). [2] L. L., p. 48.

reigns of the Bangkok dynasty it was observed with great splendour, but King Rāma IV reduced the expenditure on it.

We cannot lay much stress on the fidelity of the details in Lady Nabamaśa's story; but we can take it as evidence of a definite tradition that the *Lòy Kraḥdòṅ* was first introduced into Siam as a Brahmanical ceremony later to be modified in accordance with the growth of Buddhism. But, though the *Lòy Kraḥdòṅ* seems to have been connected with festivals dedicated to the later Brahmanic gods in India, it probably grew out of older oblations made to the sacred rivers, especially the Ganges, and continued down to the present day. And very probably the Brahmanic form of the observance was merely grafted on to an indigenous Thai animistic worship of the spirit of the river, with which their lives were so intimately bound up. And even now, despite the teachings of Buddhism, the Spirit of the Mènāṁ or "Mother of Waters" is by no means forgotten.

CHAPTER XXV

MINOR BRAHMANICAL CEREMONIES

1. *The Worship of the Sacred Bull* (*Chavian Braḥ Go Kin*).[1]

This ancient ceremony was once performed in the second month (Pauṣa), but it was discontinued several centuries ago. From the account of the ceremony in the *KM.* we learn that the Sacred White Bull (representing Nandi, the mount of Śiva), was led out from the royal stables, its horns and hoofs adorned with gold ornaments decorated with the nine gems, and with golden medallions and tassels hanging from its ears. A silk cord was passed through its nostrils, and it was tied to a richly ornamented post on a dais two cubits high. Gold and silver and silken cloths were heaped under the belly of the sacred animal, and it was made to stand facing the north. A sacred fire was lit in front of it, and *p̱a̱i-śrī* trays of food were also placed before it. It was fed and watered by the King's children from vessels of gold. The four chief Brahmans stood at the four corners of the dais sacrificing to the sacred fire all through the night. Early in the morning the King arrived in procession with ministers bearing the various insignia of State, and the *Baladeba* carrying a tray of parched rice. The King carried a golden lotus, and the Queen a silver one. The procession circumambulated the Sacred Bull nine times auspicious-wise, and after that there was a banquet. The ceremony took place within the royal palace enclosure Gerini [2] considers that this festival may have originated from the Hindu one of letting loose the sacred bull (Vrsotsarga), which was, however, performed on full moon day of Kārttika, or even in Āśvina.[3] The ceremony was probably connected with agriculture or the multiplication of cattle, but, at this distance of time, and without further evidence, it is impossible to judge its sociological value.

2. *Viṣṇu's Sleep.*

The Siamese accounts of ceremonies for the eighth month (Āṣāḍha) are almost entirely devoted to the great Buddhist festival of *Khău Barṣā.* There are, however, indications that at an early period in

[1] Known only from a description in *KM.*, quoted in *BRB.*, pp. 68–9 ; not mentioned in *HV.*, the ceremony evidently having been abolished before that was written.

[2] Ge. (2).

[3] *Paraskara Grhyasutra*, iii, 9, in *SBE.* xxix, p. 353.

Siamese history there were Brahmanical celebrations in this month which have now been almost completely forgotten. It appears that the Āṣāḍha, or Midsummer, Festival (seventh to fourteenth of the waxing) was once known in Siam, and that after this the Brahmans began their retreat and fasts. A couple of sentences in *NN.*[1] indicate that there was also a royal Brahmanical ceremony in this month. It is stated that in the centre of a pond in the royal temple grounds a dais was erected on which the King lay down, and was sprinkled by the Brahmans. Gerini[2] identifies this with the day on which Viṣṇu is supposed to commence his four months' sleep on the Milk Sea, and which is still celebrated in India by a festival on the eleventh waxing. According to this the pond represents the sea, and the dais the serpent Śeṣa, Viṣṇu's mythical couch. It is an interesting example of the Siamese king's identification with Viṣṇu, and of his imitating the god's actions, for the good of the realm.

3. *Śiva's Night* (*Śivārāṭrī*).[3]

This festival was celebrated from very early times in Siam, but was discontinued after the fall of Ayudhyā. It was, however, revived by King Rāma IV, but has again fallen into disuse. It occurred on the full-moon day of the third month (Māgha), and was of course a strictly Śaivite festival.

In the evening the High Priest of Śiva (*Braḥ Mahā Rāja Grū*) carried out the usual preliminary rites common to all Brahmanic ceremonies. He then set up four poles from which was suspended, by means of strings, an earthen pot full of water, but with a hole in the bottom. Under the pot was placed a stone *liṅga*, symbolic of Śiva, which stood on a base having the form of a *yoni*, symbolic of Umā (Śiva's *śakti* or cosmic energy).[4] The *yoni* was provided with a spout from which the water which dripped from the pot over the *liṅga* and ran down into the *yoni*, was collected in vessels. This went on all through the night, and just before dawn the Brahmans cooked some rice mixed with honey, sugar, milk, and butter, which was distributed and partaken of by all those present. At daybreak they all went down to the canals and bathed, and then they returned and anointed their heads with some of the water which had been collected from the *liṅga*. It was a rite of purification, and the Brahmans

[1] *NN.* p. 83. [2] Ge. (2). [3] *BRB.*, pp. 123 sqq.

[4] This apparatus is still to be seen by the curious amongst the dust-covered lumber behind the altar in the Śiva temple. The present Head Brahman recently informed me that his father had performed the ceremony in days gone by.

believed that the consecrated water washed away all impurities and sins.

The ceremony was in early times derived from India, where it is still practised, but on the fourteenth waning of the same month:

> "At the time of the new-moon in the month of February the Liṅgayats, or followers of Śiva, celebrate with great pomp their feast *Śiva-ratri* (Night of Śiva). This lasts three days, and during the course of it the Liṅgayats wash and purify their *liṅgam*, cover it with a new cloth, and offer it sacrifices of a special character. They also visit their *jangamas* or *gurus*, and present them with gifts." [1]

In Siam the festival can hardly be regarded as a royal ceremony; it was rather a ceremony performed by the Brahmans for their own benefit. But it was probably fostered by the Siamese kings as the means by which the Brahmans purified themselves before performing more important ceremonies connected with the welfare of the King and the State.

4. *Snāna, or Gajendrāsva-snānam.*[2]

This ceremony, which signifies "the sprinkling of the lordly elephants and horses", was carried out twice yearly, in the fifth month (Chaitra), and again in the eleventh month (Āśvina). It was not abolished until the reign of King Rāma V, but had for some time only been performed on a reduced scale, the elephants and horses filing in procession past stands from which they were sprinkled with lustral water. The ceremony was originally a lustration of arms, a general purification of the army, like the Hindu *Nīrājanā*. While the sprinkling of the elephants was in progress, the Vṛddhi-pasa Brahmans (i.e. those in charge of auspicious rites in connection with elephants) uncoiled, in the royal elephant warehouses, the ropes and nooses stored therein for elephant catching, and performed a hook and noose dance in honour of Viṣṇu, simulating the capture of elephants. This took place on the third day of the waning. Next morning the ropes and nooses were coiled up again and stored away.

In ancient times *Snāna* was a general review of the army, with the object of seeing that all its equipment was kept in proper order and efficiency. Ceremonies of this sort are mentioned in the *Annals of Ayudhyā* as being performed prior to the launching of campaigns, and must have been of considerable sociological value in keeping up the spirits of the soldiers, and inspiring them with confidence in their none too trustworthy weapons.

[1] D., p. 568.

[2] *BRB.*, pp. 271 sqq. *NN.*, pp. 73 sqq.; *KM.*; Ge. (2).

5. *Top-spinning (Bidhī Geṇḍaḥ or Dǐn Khǎn).*[1]

This Brahmanical ceremony was discontinued several centuries ago; in fact it may have ceased to be performed even before Ayudhyā was founded, since there is no mention of it in the *KM.*, and it is known only from fragmentary descriptions of it in the old Brahmanical treatises and in *NN.*

Top-spinning was performed in the seventh lunar month (Jyaiṣṭha), and attracted large crowds of people who were eager to learn the fortunes of the realm as foretold by the Brahmans on this occasion. Three tops "as large as pumpkins" and made of the nine metals which correspond to the nine planets, symbolized the three gods of the Hindu triad, and were carried out in procession from the temple of Śiva. They were spun on a board by means of a silken string of five colours, ten cubits long. Omens were drawn from the length of the spin and the kind of noise emitted from the tops. If they spun long and loudly the Brahmans announced that the glory of the King would shine forth over foreign lands, the prosperity and riches of the people would increase, and the boundaries of the kingdom would be extended. If the contrary occurred, the Brahmans interpreted the omen as indicating danger to the realm during the coming year.

A ceremony, characterized by such extravagant prognostications as the above, could only flourish among a conquering and unsophisticated people, and was thus well suited to the early Thai. But with the stern experiences of military reverses, and the spread of the elevating teachings of the Buddha, such soothsaying ceremonies were the first to fall into disuse, and are now only found in connection with the Ploughing Festival, where, however, the Brahmans confine themselves within the more modest limitations of predicting the extent of the rice crop.

6. *New Year.*[2]

There are really three Siamese New Year Festivals, which used to take up most of the fifth month (Chaitra) but which have now been officially combined to be celebrated on the first of April. This date is really the civil (modern solar) New Year's Day, introduced in 1889, to fall invariably on 1st April; but the lunar and astrological (old solar) new years, essentially religious, and connected with the old calendar adopted from India on the basis of the Saka era reckoning, are still used by the Brahmans in the arrangement of their ceremonial

[1] *BRB.*, pp. 452 sqq.; *NN.*, p. 82.
[2] *BRB.*, pp. 133 sqq., and Ge. (2).

calendar, and also celebrated by the masses to whom the new civil New Year means nothing.

Truṣ, or lunar New Year, is celebrated during three days: the fifteenth waning of Phālguna (fourth month); the first waxing of Chaitra (fifth month) or New Year's Day, and the day following. The ceremonies carried out at this period are (1) a general expulsion of evil [1]; (2) the King pays homage to his ancestors and the people hold a popular festival of ancestor worship [2]; (3) the drinking of the water of allegiance takes place on this occasion as at half-year [3]; the ceremony of *Snāna* used to take place, as it also did at half-year [4]; the Brahmans performed a *homam* sacrifice as in connection with the Coronation.[5]

It will thus be seen that New Year is a time when a number of mportant ceremonies take place, all of which have been or will be dealt with elsewhere in this book. But there remains one Brahmanical rite, the actual rite of changing from the Old to the New Year, which may most appropriately be dealt with in this chapter. This rite, which is known as *Sămbăcchara-chinda*, is performed by the *horā* at the same time that the Brahmans are offering their *homam* sacrifice. The rite consists in changing the name of the animal denoting the place of the year (*Sămbăcchara*) in the duodenary cycle, after which the year is designated, but not the " figure " or serial number of the year in the era, the altering of which is to be effected later on *Meṣa-saṅkrānṯi*, i.e. at the completion of the astrological (solar) year.

The *Saṅkrānṯi*, or astrological (solar) New Year falls on either the 12th or the 13th April, the date of the assumed entrance of the sun into Aries, according to the traditional local (Hindu-imported) reckoning. The day is termed *Mahā-saṅkrānṯi* day (substantially the same as *Meṣa-saṅkrānṯi*), and with it commences a three days' festival, the year's serial number in the era being changed on the third day, which is actually regarded as New Year's Day (solar). This is one of the seventeen occasions in the year on which, according to the *KM.*, the King must take a ceremonial bath of purification,[6] and he afterwards sprinkles the sacred images. For the people this season is one of much rejoicing and merit-making by washing the images in the temples, building hillocks of sand for covering the monastery courtyards, sprinkling the monks as an act of respect, and making offerings of candles and incense before the images.

[1] See Chap. XXVII. [2] Chap. XIII. [3] Chap. XV. [4] p. 297. [5] p. 72.

[6] Siamese texts refer to these ceremonial baths as *mūrdhābhiṣeka*, literally " anointment of the head ", but it has been shown in Chapter VI that the Siamese confuse the negative rite of lustration with the positive one of unction.

CHAPTER XXVI

THE PROPITIATION OF SPIRITS

The lower one goes in the social scale in Siam, as perhaps in every country, the more one finds that superstitions and the belief in the existence of spirits who require propitiation come to the fore at the expense of the established religion. So it is that in Siam, despite the teachings of Buddhism, which especially denounce such beliefs, the spirits of the dead and other innumerable varieties of *phī*, all more or less objectionable, make considerable demands on the time of the Siamese, at least of the uneducated classes, in order to keep them at bay. The Government, as a body, if not individually, is supposed to be above such things, especially since it is the official upholder of the Buddhist religion, and hence we find that the State affords this vast host of *phī* little recognition, other than ruthlessly to drive them out of the city every New Year. There are, however, or were until well on in the Bangkok period, certain powerful *phī* whom even the King and the Government could not afford to ignore. It seems probable that these genii, together with all the common varieties of *phī*, have survived from a period long anterior to the introduction of Buddhism and Hinduism into the country, and may have been part of the "original" stock of the early Thai and other races of Indo-China. But since these beliefs are so widely spread amongst primitive peoples, it is very difficult to say definitely in any particular case whether it is indeed indigenous, or has been introduced, say, from India, in a more or less Hinduized form; the fact that a primitive belief has been dressed in Hindu garb is, however, no proof that it has been imported from India, for we know that wherever Hinduism went the Brahmans did their best to canonize whatever of the native beliefs they were not powerful enough to suppress. Thus, though it is probable that the Brahmans formerly took part in the ceremonies connected with spirit-worship, such rites are not to be confounded with such purely Brahmanical rites as the sacrificing to the gods and demi-gods of the Hindu pantheon, which is a preliminary to most Hindu State Ceremonies.

The details which I have been able to collect with regard to State Spirit Worship are unfortunately rather scant, for two reasons: (1) because such ceremonies have almost completely died out, and no living person has any memory of them, and (2) because owing to the very nature of such primitive rites, there were probably never any written records of them; and early Bangkok kings were not sufficiently interested in them to record what was remembered of them by survivors from the destruction of Ayudhyā. The following comprises such information as I have been able to collect on the subject:—

1. *Animism.*

I define animism as that primitive belief of the savage, according to which every tree, river, and mountain, in short every natural feature, especially such as have some special peculiarity such as a very large tree or tall mountain, has its guardian spirit, dryad, or goblin. This still forms one of the largest classes of *phī*, which demands the respect and propitiation of the Siamese peasants, more particularly in the northern part of the country. Probably it is several centuries since these ceased to receive the serious attention of Siamese royalty, and the only definite record that I can find of it is in no less distinguished a document than the famous inscription of King Rāma Gāṁhèṅ, as follows:—

> "In yonder mountain is a demon-spirit, Braññā Khabuṅ, that is greater than every other spirit in this realm. If any prince ruling this realm of Sukhodaya reverence him well with proper offerings, this realm stands firm, this realm prospers. If the spirit be not reverenced well, if the offerings be not right, the spirit in the mountain does not protect, does not regard; this realm perishes." [1]

From this we see that the animism of the early Thai still enjoyed the royal protection, despite the fact that the Kings of Sukhodaya had adopted much of Khmer Brahmanism and were fervent Buddhists as well. But it appears that there was only one spirit who was thought worthy of the royal patronage, and it was a mountain spirit. Probably this class of spirit always enjoyed a pre-eminent position, and may have been the earliest type of guardian spirit of a city. It is probable that Văt Phukhao Dòṅ (Temple of the Golden Mount) at Ayudhyā was originally a shrine dedicated to the spirit of a mountain, who was also the guardian of the city. It was the *deva* of the Missaka-mountain that appeared to King Devānaṁpiyatissa of Ceylon in the form of an elk-stag, and led him to Mahinda, the apostle of Buddhism.[2]

Another example of animism in connection with Siamese Kings is the belief in the existence of a guardian genie resident in the royal nine-tiered umbrella. This idea, as has already been mentioned in an

[1] *JSS.*, vol. vi, pt. ii, p. 29; and Coedès, *Inscriptions de Sukhodaya*, p. 46.
[2] *M.* xiv, 3.

earlier chapter, was also present in Burma: in one of the *Jātaka* reliefs in the Ānanda temple at Pagān, the Bodhisattva Temiya is depicted on his couch, over which is a single-tiered white umbrella, from which the goddess is seen issuing in order to give Temiya advice not to become king.[1] Similarly in Ceylon, as King Duṭṭhagāmaṇi "thus reflected the *Devatā* of the parasol observed his thought".[2] Evidently, therefore, the idea of the Spirit of the Umbrella in Siam has been derived from India. But if the Umbrella were originally derived from the tree, I suggest that the genie was originally a tree-spirit.

2. *Guardian Spirits of Cities.*

On the verandah of every Siamese house, or in a shady corner of the garden, is set up a small wooden "doll's house" on a pole, called *Śāl Braḥ Bhūmi*, or "Shrine of the Sacred Grove", corresponding to the Burmese *Nat Sin.* This is the shrine of the *Cău Dī* (Spirit of the Place) and before it the people of the house offer incense sticks, flowers, and rice, especially when any domestic crisis, such as the birth of a child, is pending. Similar *Śāl Braḥ Bhūmi* are to be seen in every street, every field, even in the sacred precincts of the monasteries. They are the most tangible evidence of the survival of pure animism in Siam to-day; and the guardian spirits of the city, which still receive official sanction, are but a development of the same primitive point of view.

Every city in Siam that ever attained any degree of independence boasted its guardian genie, and, for example, when I visited Sukhodaya, the ruins of its shrine were pointed out to me. A similar shrine exists in Bangkok at the present day, called *Śāl Cău Hlăk Mo'aṅ*, and until the year A.D. 1919 there used to be another called *Śāl Cău Hò Klòṅ*. I have personally visited the former, but details concerning the latter I take from Bastian[3] and Graham.[4] The *Śāl Cău Hlăk Mo'aṅ*, or "Shrine of the Pillar of the Lord of the Country", is a small brick building crowned by a Cambodian *prāṅg.* In the small and dark interior there stands a carved and gilded pillar of wood, draped in red cloth. This pillar is the home of the Guardian Spirit of the City, and around it are grouped phallic emblems, images of lesser *phī*, and paper votive offerings in piles. A recent visit to the *Śāl Cău Hlăk Mo'aṅ* (18th December, 1930), supplied the following additional information: The person who was sacrificed to make the *Cău Hlăk Mo'aṅ* is buried underneath the post. On one side, leaning against the wall, I noticed

[1] *Epigraphia Birmanica*, vol. ii, pt. 2, No. 6.
[2] *M.* xxviii, 6.
[3] *Reisen in Siam*, p. 96 sq.
[4] *Siam*, ii, pp. 284, 285.

another post, also draped in red cloth. I was told that it is the post of the *Ċau Hlăk Mo'aṅ* of Dhanapurī which was removed to this site from the short-lived capital on the other side of the river. People who are not in good health still come to pay homage before the *Ċau Hlăk Mo'aṅ*, and I was told that it is still much respected. Printed slips were in readiness to be sold to those who come to ask their fortunes. It is also still the custom for a person desirous of obtaining a boon—such as a rise in salary—to make a mental promise beforehand to the effect that, should he obtain that which he desires, he will make an offering to the *Ċau Hlăk Mo'aṅ*. This offering varies from some flowers or food placed in the shrine to a theatrical entertainment, and the promise is always kept.

Śāl Ċau Hò Klòṅ used to stand near Văt Braḥ Jetavana, and was so called on account of its proximity to the foundations of the former *Hò Klòṅ* or " Hall of Drums ", which in the early reigns of the present dynasty was a tower on the top of which drums were beaten to warn the populace in the case of fire or other danger, but which has long since disappeared. This shrine was especially dedicated to a guardian spirit called Ċau Ceṯ in the person of a small image dressed in the traditional costume of a *devatā*. Brahmanic influence in this shrine was evident in the presence of Braḥ Kāḷa, the god of death, mounted on an owl, and also probably by two images of godlets known as Braḥ Draṅ Mo'aṅ and Braḥ So'a Mo'aṅ. But Ċau Ceṯ was a true *phī*, since he was manufactured by the sacrifice of a suitable individual, as also, presumably, was the spirit of the *Ċau Hlăk Mo'aṅ*. When the *Śāl Ċau Hò Klòṅ* was pulled down in 1919, owing to its delapidated condition, Ċau Ceṯ and his attendant spirits were removed to the *Śāl Ċau Hlăk Mo'aṅ*, where both they and the Guardian Spirit proper continue to receive offerings. But, in the present work, it is the extent of the official recognition which the *Ċau Hlăk Mo'aṅ* receives that is of special interest. This manifests itself, or did until recently, in two ways: (1) It used to be the custom, at least until A.D 1910, to issue periodical invitation cards by royal command, requesting the honour of the presence of Ċau Ceṯ at forthcoming religious ceremonies. Such cards were until that year stuck on the door of the shrine. (2) In the oath of allegiance taken twice yearly by all officials, the *Ċau Hlăk Mo'aṅ* is still invoked, and his vengeance called down on any traitor.

Thus it seems that the Guardian Spirit of the City is by no means forgotten, that he still retains a sociological value, and in case of national danger no doubt he would come in for a considerably greater share of attention, as he did in times past.

3. *Guardian Spirits in Great Guns.*

It appears that one of the guardian spirits of Ayudhyā had taken up its abode in a big gun, and the following account is interesting as showing what great faith was put in the guardian spirit by the king and people in time of national danger, this referring to the period immediately before the fall of Ayudhyā in A.D. 1767. But since it comes from a Burmese source, it must be received with caution.

> "Finding that every attempt against the enemy had always resulted in failure, the King of Siam ordered that the great gun called Dwāra-wadī, which had been regarded from ancient times as the guardian of the city, should, after the customary propitiatory offerings had been made to the presiding spirit, be brought out from the building where it had been carefully kept, mounted on the northern wall of the city, and fired against the enemy. He also ordered that all the inhabitants of the city, both men and women, young and old, should, with suitable offerings, propitiate the guardian spirits of the city, the country and the weapons. In compliance with this royal command, the great gun was brought out with due ceremony and, with the help of mechanical appliances, raised and mounted on the northern wall of the city and directed against Nemyo Thihapate's camp. It was then loaded with an ample charge of powder and all kinds of shot, such as bar-shot, chain-shot, shrapnel, elongated bullets, etc., and fired with a fuse. The fuse burned alright, and so did the priming powder, but the charge in the gun failed to ignite. Although repeatedly tried, the gun failed to discharge its load of shot. So the charge was taken out to discover the cause, and to the amazement of the officers and men, it was found that the powder had dissolved and the water trickled down the mouth of the gun. The Siamese officers were alleged [by the Burmese] to have exclaimed that when even the great guardian gun of the city, a thing inanimate, had gone over to the side of the King of Ava, they who were animate beings, could not but submit." [1]

This is probably not an isolated incident of a city's guardian spirit residing in a big gun; indeed, the association of ideas seems obvious. It reminds me of the well-known cannon that lies close to the road near Batavia, Java, half-buried in the ground. There is a tradition that it will one day be joined by its mate which lies in another part of the island, and on that day the rule of Europeans in Java will cease. When I saw it a few years ago it was surrounded with heaps of flowers and paper offerings, and, like the *Cau Hlăk Mo'aṅ* at Bangkok, was said to be particularly revered by barren women.

4. *Foundation Sacrifices.*

Closely allied to the Spirits of the *Śāl Cau Hlăk Mo'aṅ* are the *phī*, whose duty it is to guard the gates of the city, although now they are

[1] *JSS.*, vol. xi, pt. iii, p. 47. Intercourse between Burma and Siam, as recorded in Hmannan Yazawindawgyi.

forgotten and receive no attention, for the gates have disappeared, and every Siamese knows that the walls, or what remains of them, are no protection to the city. But they are of special interest because we have fairly detailed accounts of their installation, whereas there seem to be no accounts of the manufacture of Cău Cet̠ and the *Cau Hlăk Mo'aṅ.*

Bruguière gives the following account of the ceremony as performed in the early days of Bangkok:—

> "Whenever a new gate is to be built in the city wall, or an old one repaired, three innocent human victims have to be immolated. The King secretly sends an officer to the gate about to be repaired; this man has the appearance of wishing to call somebody, and from time to time repeats the name to be given to the gate; which excites the attention of passers-by, and they turn their head to see what it is. The first three who do so are seized by men stationed for the purpose, and their death is irrevocably fixed; no service, no promise, no sacrifice can deliver them. Within the gate is a ditch, and at a certain height above it is a great beam; this beam is hung by two ropes, and suspended horizontally almost in the same way as in a wine-press. On the appointed day for the sacrifice, a splendid banquet is prepared for the three victims, after which they are led in ceremony to the ditch, and the king and court come to salute them. The king charges them in particular to guard well the gate confided to them, and to give notice of the approach of enemies, or rebels to take the city. Instantly the ropes are cut, and these victims of superstition are crushed by the load that falls on their heads; the people think that they are transformed into the genii called *phī.*" [1]

Frazer [2] remarks that the building of human shadows into foundations in various parts of Europe is a latter-day modification of the foundation sacrifice, and, on the other hand, he cites an even more brutal form of the sacrifice than that described by Bruguière as occurring in Bima, a district of the East Indian Island of Sumbawa. There,

> "when a new flag-pole is set up at the sultan's palace a woman is crushed to death under it; but she must be pregnant. The notion may be that the ghost of such a woman would be more than usually fierce and vigilant." [3]

From the account of van Vliet, who was in Siam from 1629 to 1634, it seems that a similar custom was in vogue in Siam during the Ayudhyā period. He wrote as follows:—

> "The kings counted their subjects so little that if palaces, towers or resting places had to be built for them, under each post which was

[1] *Annales de L'Association de la Propagation de la Foi*, v (1831), pp. 164 sq.
[2] *GB.* iii, pp. 89 sqq.
[3] Ibid., p. 91.

put into the ground a pregnant woman was thrown and the more near this woman was to her time the better. For this reason there was often great misery in Judia [Ayudhyā] during the time that palaces or towers had to be built or repaired. For as all houses in Siam are built at a certain height above the ground and stand on wooden posts many women have endured this suffering. Although this description seems to be fabulous, these executions have really taken place. The people, who are very superstitious, believe that these women after dying turn into terrible monsters or devils, who defend not only the post below which they are thrown, but the whole house against misfortune. The King usually ordered a few slaves to catch without regard all the women who were in a pregnant state. But out of the houses no women were taken unless in the streets nobody could be found. These women were brought to the queen, who treated them as if they were of high birth [cf. " temporary kings "]. After they had been there for a few days, they were thrown into the pit with the stomach turned upwards. After this the post was put on the stomach, and driven right through it."

He then goes on to say that in 1634 the king renewed seventeen gates, for which sixty-eight women were required, but five of them gave birth on reaching the palace. This was considered to be a miracle, so the king decided to liberate all the women except four.[1]

Though the belief in guardian spirits which led to these human sacrifices was extremely widespread, and was probably an outgrowth of primitive animism, it seems probable that the Siamese form was influenced by India, where such customs were once prevalent. Thus in the *Takkariya Jātaka* (No. 481):—

> " The chaplain said to the king of Benares at the erection of a new city gate, 'My lord, a great gate is possessed and guarded by great spirits. A Brahman tawny brown and toothless, of pure blood on both sides, must be killed ; his flesh and blood must be offered in worship, and his body laid beneath and the gate raised upon it. This will bring luck to you and your city.' "[2]

A note on this *Jātaka* by Cowell states that the sacrifice was meant to propitiate the spirits disturbed by the digging. But I see no evidence for this supposition, at least in the Siamese rite. It seems quite clear that the victims were themselves more or less deified ; they were feasted before execution and propitiated afterwards ; they were not offered as sacrifices to any other spirits. The custom also flourished in Burma. " Tepathin, guardian spirit of the city-gate of Pagān " is mentioned in the *Glass Palace Chronicle*,[3] and the Sarabha Gateway is guarded by two figures in niches, one on each side, and, as

[1] *JSS.* vii, i, pp. 18–20.
[2] *Jātakas*, Cowell's edition, iv, p. 155.
[3] Trans. of Tin and Luce, p. 16.

I noticed when I visited Pagān in 1929, they are still reverenced by the people of the neighbourhood.

> " Their origin is obscure, but they are said to represent the Popa Maungdaw and Hnamadaw, brother and sister *Nats* of Popa Hill " [1];

but I suggest that they represent the spirits of gate-guardians manufactured in the usual way. At the founding of Mandalay the proper sacrifices were supposed to have been carried out, but evidently Thibaw, who thought nothing of wholesale murder, had his doubts as to whether the kind-hearted King Mindon had performed the work thoroughly. He therefore meditated the immolation of several hundred victims and was only restrained by fear of the effect it might have on the British. But it is quite clear that he was not thinking of propitiating the spirits of the soil, but was desirous of strengthening the city's spiritual defences. There was in Burma a special annual ceremony called *Paya Pwe*, or Feast of the Shrines, in which royal offerings were sent to the shrines of the *nats*, and to the city gate guardians.[2]

It is indeed amazing that such barbarous customs could have existed in Siam as late as the beginning of the nineteenth century, and in Burma until the extinction of the monarchy—two countries in which the religion of the Buddha was pre-eminent and where to kill an insect was accounted a sin. Yet such is the force of tradition, that it needed the adverse expression of foreign opinion to bring about the abandonment of these rites. They formed no part of Siam's true religion, but held her, as it were, in a vice; and their abolition is one of those changes for the better which Siam owes to contact with the West.

[1] Taw Sein Ko, *Archæological Notes on Pagān*, p. 16.
[2] *ERE*. art. " Burma ".

CHAPTER XXVII

THE EXPULSION OF EVIL

In *The Golden Bough* [1] Sir James Frazer has noted several features characteristic of the Expulsion of Evil, wherever ceremonies to that end are practised; and we shall see that these features are not wanting in Siam. In the first place, there are two methods of Expulsion—the *immediate* and the *mediate*—which are identical in intention, that intention being the total clearance of all the ills that have been infesting a people. In both cases the evils are considered as invisible and intangible, but in the former case they are directly expelled, while in the latter a material vehicle is used—a boat, a litter, or a human scapegoat.

In the second place, a general clearance is resorted to periodically, the interval between the celebrations is commonly a year, and the time of year when the ceremony takes place usually coincides with some well-marked change of season—in Siam the beginning of the rainy season, when cholera frequently begins its ravages and the expulsion of the demons gives the people some degree of confidence in the future In Siam, as in many other countries, the annual expulsion marks the New Year.

Thirdly, this period is frequently marked by unusual licence. In Siam this takes the mild form of a certain amount of popular amusement and joviality, and a feast of ancestors.

The last two of Frazer's generalizations apply more particularly to the General Expulsion of Evil which takes place at the Siamese New Year, but the present chapter will be a suitable place in which to discuss also certain more specialized forms of the Expulsion of Evil or Exorcism, most of which are now almost or quite extinct in Siam and about which very little information is obtainable.

1. *The General Expulsion of Evil at New Year.* [2]

This is an example of the *immediate* Expulsion of Evil, and the rites are really extremely primitive, although overlaid with Buddhist modifications. The ceremony of freeing the palace and city from evil spirits takes place at *Ṯruṣ* (lunar new-year). Chapters of Buddhist monks draw the sacred *siñcana* thread round the various buildings of the Royal Residence, round the palace walls and, formerly, round the city wall. Seated within the palace enclosure and, formerly, in

[1] *GB.* ix, chapter v.

[2] *BRB.*, pp. 133 sqq.; *NN.*, p. 71 sq.; Ge. (2).

the centre of the city, at the eight gates and in the forts on the city walls, they recite an uncanonical compilation known as *Āṯānāṯiya Suṯra*, believed to be of great efficacy in the expulsion of demons. Guns are also fired at various points within the palace and city, with the object of frightening away all evil spirits. This firing is called *yiṅ pū'n āṯānā*, i.e. firing to drive away evil. In earlier times the function of the guns was performed by gongs.

There are also popular celebrations at this season. The people carry protective rings of unspun cotton thread on their heads, and threads of the same material around their shoulders, so as to be freed of evil influences on New Year's Day. The monks are also invited to the people's houses, where they free the premises from evil by means of their recitations, and are afterwards entertained with food. There is much rejoicing and popular amusement at this season, as is usual in most parts of the world on occasions when people believe themselves freed from evil influences. As long as such beliefs remain in Siam, the ceremony will retain its functional value as affording periodical relief from the mental stress and worry of everyday life.

2. *The Public Scapegoat.*

Though I have not been able to obtain corroborative evidence from any Siamese source, it would appear from the following passage that the idea of the *mediate* Expulsion of Evil by its transference to a human Scapegoat was practised in Siam in the seventeenth century, presumably in connection with New Year.

> "There is one day in the year, in which they practise a ceremony, somewhat resembling that of the Scape-goat, which was customary among the Jews. They single out a woman broken down by debauchery and carry her on a litter through all the streets to the sound of drums and hautboys. The mob insult her and pelt her with dirt; after having sufficiently exposed her through the whole city, they throw her on a dung hill, and sometimes on a hedge of thorns, without the ramparts, forbidding her to enter them again. This inhuman and superstitious ceremony is founded on the belief that this woman thus draws upon her all the malign influences of the air and of evil spirits." [1]

We have already seen that the idea of the Scapegoat was known in Siam in a specialized form with regard to the institution known as "temporary kings". The Public Scapegoat would not, therefore, seem entirely incompatible with Siamese custom.

3. *The Expulsion of Disease.*

In May, 1820, an epidemic of cholera broke out, which was one of the worst recorded in the history of Siam:

[1] Translation of Turpin's *History of Siam*, chapter 3, in Pinkerton's *Travels*, vol. ix, p. 579.

"Corpses which there was no time to burn were heaped up in the monastery 'like stacks of timber' or else left to float about in the river and the canals. The people fled in a panic from the capital; the monks deserted the monasteries, and the whole machinery of government was at a standstill. The king even released the royal guard from their duties in the palace. There were great ceremonies of propitiation; the Emerald Buddha and the precious relics kept in the monasteries were taken out in procession through the streets, and on the canals of the city, attended by high dignitaries of the Church who scattered consecrated sand and water. The king and the members of the royal family maintained a rigorous fast. The slaughter of animals was completely forbidden, and the king caused all supplies of fish, bipeds, and quadrupeds, offered for sale, to be bought up in order that they might be liberated. All criminals, except the Burmese prisoners of war, were released from prison. The scourge abated at last after taking 30,000 victims within a few months." [1]

This appears to be an example of magical methods having given way to religious ones. The prayer and carrying round of the sacred images probably replaced an earlier observance in which the cholera demon was driven from the city, perhaps encased in some material vehicle.

The above occasion is mentioned by King Rāma V in *BRB.*,[2] where he states that the three images carried about, each in a separate procession, were the Emerald Buddha, the Lord of Victory (Braḥ Jăya), and Braḥ Hằm Samud (Buddha in the attitude of calming the ocean). He also states that the people were divided in their opinion as to whether the scourge was caused by the machinations of evil spirits or whether it was brought about by the Buddha's anger. He wishes that the people would realize that diseases are caused by specific germs, and states that the ceremony may be considered as abolished. His desires have been vigorously followed up by the propaganda of the Department of Public Health, to some extent with success, though not to the exclusion of private magical observances, which are still more to the taste of the superstitious masses than is any amount of vaccine.

4. *A Ceremony of Palace Exorcism.*

I translate the following curious passage from the *KM.*: "If any persons quarrel and stab each other so that blood is shed within the precincts of the royal palace; or if a female slave should have a miscarriage in the palace, propitiatory offerings must be made to the gods. Ceremonial pavilions must be erected at each of the four gates and *pa̱i-śrīs* with offerings placed under the gates. The sacred thread

[1] R. Lingat, "History of Văt Mahādhātu" in *JSS.*, vol. xxiv, pt. 1, 1930, p. 14.

[2] *BRB.*, pp. 158 sqq.

must be passed round the palace. A chapter of monks must be invited to recite stanzas for three days. The Brahmans must come and offer sacrifices to the guardian genii (*baḥlīkarm bvaṅ svaṅ*) in accordance with custom. Let there be dancing (*raḥpāṁ*), *biṇbādya* bands with gong and drum, and orchestral music (*turiyatanṭrī*), and lanterns lighted at the four gates. When the ceremony is finished the fœtus must be carried out of the city and cast away. Thus is the evil omen averted and the city saved from calamity."

The casting away of the fœtus is, of course, an example of the *mediate* Expulsion of Evil, the fœtus being regarded as the vehicle of the evil.

5. *A Royal Exorcism.*

No doubt there were, formerly, in Siam as in Cambodia, specially prescribed Brahmanical and Buddhist rites for the exorcism of any evil spirit, especially one of disease, which was believed to have taken possession of the King or any member of the royal family. I cannot find any Siamese record of such rites, however, but think it may be of interest to quote Mrs. Leonowens' account, for she was probably the only European who has ever had the opportunity of witnessing such a ceremony. However, her story must be taken with the utmost reserve and full allowance for missionary bias and untrained powers of observation. The events which she relates refer to the occasion on which an unfortunate slave-girl, named "May-Peâh", who had liberated her mistress from the harem, was put on trial for the offence. In order that she should not be persuaded to betray her accomplices she had heroically cut out her tongue, and so was unable to speak.[1] She was about to be put to the torture when an old and respected *yogi* who was present announced that in his opinion she was not to blame, since she was possessed by an evil spirit, and should be exorcized.

> "'Let her be exorcized' said the Chief Judge of the Supreme Court, whose secretary was making minutes of all that took place during the trial. On which the queerest-looking woman of the party, an old and toothless dame, drew out a key from her girdle and opened some wooden boxes from which she took a small boat—a sort of coracle—a long grey veil of singular texture, an earthen stove, whereon to kindle a charcoal fire, and some charcoal; out of the second box she produced some herbs, pieces of flint, cast skins of snakes, feathers, the hair of various animals, with dead men's bones, short brooms, and a host of other queer things. With the charcoal the old woman proceeded to light a fire in her earthen stove; when it was red-hot she

[1] In support of Mrs. Leonowen's story, or at least, as evidence that such things *are* done in Bangkok, we have the following incident recorded in the *Bangkok Times* for 27th April, 1931: "A Chinese woman took a pair of scissors and clipped off her own tongue with them at a Chinese boarding-house on Friday evening."

opened several jars of water, and, muttering some strange incantations, threw into them portions of her herbs, repeating over each a mystic spell, and waving a curious wand which looked like a human bone, and might have been once the arm of a stalwart man. This done, she seated the prisoner in the midst of the motley group, covered her over with the veil of grey stuff, and handing the short hand-brooms to a number of her set, she, to my intense horror, began to pour the burning charcoal over the veiled form of the prisoner, which the other women, dancing around, and repeating with the wildest gestures the name of Brahma, as rapidly swept off. This was done without even singeing the veil or burning a hair of May-Peâh's head. After this they emptied the jars of water upon her, still repeating the name of Brahma. She was then made to change her clothes for an entirely new dress, of the Brahminical fashion. Her dressing and undressing were effected with great skill, without disclosing her person in the least. And once more the yogi laid his hands upon her shoulders, and whispered again in her ears, first the right, and then the left. But May-Peâh returned the same intimation, shaking her head and pointing to her sealed lips. Then the old wizard, Khoon-P'hikhat—literally, the lord who drives out the devil—prostrated himself before her, and prayed with a wild energy of manner; and, rising suddenly, he peremptorily demanded, looking full in the prisoner's face, 'Where did you drop the bunch of keys?' The glaring daylight illuminated with a pale lustre the fine face of the Laotian slave, as for the third time she moved her head, in solemn intimation that she could not or would not speak. To see her thus, no one would believe but that, if she willed, she could speak at once. 'Open her mouth and pour some of the magic water into it,' suggested one of the 'wise women'. But they who opened her mouth fell back with horror, and cried, 'Brahma, Brahma! an evil fiend has torn out her tongue.' And immediately the unhappy woman passed from being an object of fear and dread to one of tender commiseration, of pity, and even of adoration. So sudden was the transition from fear and hate to love and pity, that many of the strong men and women wept outright at the thought of the dreadful mutilation that the fiend had subjected her to. Now came the last and most important question, 'Was the exorcism effectual?' To prove which a small taper was lighted and put into the witches' boat; and the whole company betook themselves to the border of the stream to see it launched. The boat swept gallantly down the waters, and the feeble lamp burned brightly, without even a flicker—for it was a calm day—till it was brought to a stand by some stones that were strewn across the stream. Then the yogi raised a shout of wild delight, and all the company re-echoed it with intense satisfaction and pleasure. And, in accordance with the king's instructions, being acquitted of any complicity with the devil in the abduction of the princess, the prisoners received each a sum of money, and were set at liberty." [1]

The significance of the boat is obviously that it is a vehicle for the expulsion of the evil, one of the most obvious vehicles for such a purpose that would occur to a riverine people accustomed to cast all their refuse into the water.

[1] Leonowens, *Romance of Siamese Harem Life*, pp. 197 sqq.

GENERAL CONCLUSIONS

CHAPTER XXVIII

GENERAL CONCLUSIONS

Since the various Siamese State Ceremonies have as far as possible each been made the subject of a separate and self-contained study, it will only be necessary here to draw together certain threads which run throughout the book, and to give a summary of the chief conclusions at which it has been possible to arrive.

We have seen that the evolution of the State Ceremonies bears out, in the main, what is known of the history of Siamese Culture as a whole as based upon the results obtained from the study of the inscriptions and chronicles of Siam and the neighbouring countries, of which a summary was given in Chapter II. Here and there we can detect what appear to be survivals of the primitive stock of culture possessed by the early Thai nomads, e.g. the placing of a gold ring in the mouth of the dead king; the *khvăñ* spirit of the tonsurate, perhaps a very early conception of the soul; the propitiation of spirits, especially the guardian spirits of mountains; and the cult of white animals, particularly the white elephant; while many of the Agricultural Ceremonies were probably grafted on to primitive animistic and magical rites practised by the early Thai. But it is perhaps impossible to say with absolute certainty whether any apparently primitive feature is in fact purely Thai, or whether it was one of the more primitive beliefs introduced in later times from China or India.

The first foreign influence brought to bear on the early Thai culture was Chinese, though it can now hardly be said to survive in connection with any Ceremony, with the possible exception of the First Ploughing. Early Chinese influence was undoubtedly swamped by influences from India many centuries ago, and in later times China has left her mark only on the etiquette connected with the Reception of Embassies.

Indian influences reached Siam to some extent directly, but they came mainly by way of the earlier Indianized kingdoms of Dvāravatī, Śrīvijaya, and Cambodia. Little is at present known as to the nature and extent of the influences of the first two kingdoms, but there can be no doubt that the Brahmanism which forms the basis of most of the Siamese Royal Ceremonies was derived from Cambodia, where similar Brahmanic ceremonies are performed to this day. Though Peguan Buddhism had reached the neighbouring Lao State of Lāṁbūn and become the established religion there at least a century before the Thai threw off the yoke at Sukhodaya, it is doubtful if Hīnayānism became definitely established at Sukhodaya before the thirteenth century, when missions were received from Ceylon. From that period dates the introduction of the great Buddhist festivals like the *Kaṭhina*, but royal ceremonial remained predominantly Hindu, since the Thai rulers sought to imitate the splendour of their former Khmer suzerains. Even as late as the second half of the seventeenth century there was a Siamese King of Ayudhyā (Nārāyaṇa, 1656–84), who is known to have favoured Brahmanism. On the whole, however, the trend of development was in favour of Buddhism, which culminated in the reign of King Rāma IV (1851–68), with the addition of Buddhist modifications to nearly every State Ceremony. I have characterized these Buddhist modifications as late, because most of them seem to have appeared in Siam only in fairly recent times, and this was because the Siamese for centuries modelled most of their royal ceremonial on that of the ancient Khmers. But many of the ideas contained in these later Buddhist modifications are extremely ancient and were probably introduced in imitation of the forms in use amongst the early Buddhist kings of Ceylon.

In studying the Siamese State Ceremonies we have frequently been brought in contact with important phenomena of wide application and great general interest. In the first place, we have made a close study of the Siamese conception of the Divine Kingship, have noted the taboos with which it is hedged around, and have seen how functionally important is the institution in the social life of the Siamese people. We have often seen the King performing his divine or priestly functions, and in one ceremony at least (the Speeding of the Outflow) we have seen him acting in his more primitive rôle as magician. Lastly, we have considered the King as protector of the people's religion, on the occasion on which he confers the *Kaṭhina* gifts on the Buddhist priesthood.

A generalization of considerable importance is the theory that the Ceremonies of Coronation, Investiture of the Queen, Tonsure, and Cremation are all derived from some earlier Installation Ceremony. This theory is particularly interesting with regard to the Cremation, since it appears to throw light on the significance of many apparently incongruous rites.

The theory of "Temporary Kings" has been considerably elaborated in this work. It has been shown by comparative methods that a series of stages can be traced in which the King first performed his magical and divine functions in person, afterwards retiring in favour of an appointed substitute when the belief had arisen that such duties were dangerous to the monarch. Finally, when this belief has been forgotten, a stage is reached at which the King resumes his early functions.

A characteristic of Siamese State Ceremonies, which is brought out most clearly in the section dealing with the Ceremonies Relating to Agriculture, is the fact that one rarely has to deal with a single ceremony performed with a single object in view, but rather with a series of superimposed rites, the objects of which have often been forgotten or confused. This is more particularly to be found in the older ceremonies, and in none more than in the Swinging Festival, the elucidation of which presented one of the most complicated but also one of the most interesting problems in the whole work. I also believe that it is a matter of some importance to have been able to place on record from personal observation an account of the complex and little understood ritual of the Court Brahmans in connection with the Swinging Festival, and the accompanying Reception of the Gods. This ritual may be abolished at any moment, following which the opportunity for studying it at first hand will have gone for ever.

With reference to the ultimate derivation of most of the Siamese State Ceremonies from India it is satisfactory to note that it has been possible to trace the more important features in nearly every ceremony back to their Indian prototypes. In most cases this result seems to have been achieved with reasonable certainty, so that I feel confident that the light of further knowledge is more likely to strengthen than to destroy most of the theories that have been built up in the course of this work. In most of the ceremonies, however, fuller knowledge is very much to be desired, and there are many gaps which require to be bridged. Only in the Coronation are we possessed of anything like the amount of evidence which we should like to have in the case of every ceremony, and which, in the Coronation, enables us to trace back many ideas step by step to very ancient times.

Turning now to the sociological aspect of the work, I think that it has been made quite clear that most of the Siamese State Ceremonies still retain very considerable importance in connection with the maintenance of the social integrity of the State. The chief function now performed by State Ceremonial is the preservation of the popular respect for ancient tradition, particularly with reference to the Absolute Monarchy. The Siamese are as yet quite unsuited to any other form of government, and, were the abolition of the kingship to come about in the near future, the whole social fabric of Siam would undoubtedly collapse like a house of cards. As has been frequently pointed out in the course of this book, it is the brighter side of Court Ceremonial, the pageantry of the royal *Kaṭhina* processions, and the splendour of the

Coronation, which most impress the minds of the masses, and any attempt to curtail the traditional glamour surrounding the Divine Kingship is bound to react unfavourably on the established form of government. But though this is the chief, it is not the only type of functional value that the State Ceremonies retain. A large section of this work has been devoted to the numerous Agricultural Ceremonies of the Siamese, and it is natural that a people whose welfare depends so largely on the abundance of the rice crop should have paid so much attention to the elaboration of ceremonies of this type. Some of these ceremonies, especially the First Ploughing, may almost be said to retain their former functional value in full, in enabling thousands of superstitious farmers to set about their agricultural operations with confidence that their efforts will be rewarded. Again, it may be said that belief in the power of spirits remains unabated with a large section of the population who still turn to them, and to the half-forgotten Hindu gods for help in worldly matters which they cannot expect from Buddhism. More particularly is the *Ca̓u Hlăk Mo'aṅ*, or Guardian Spirit of the City, not forgotten, and I doubt not but that the exclusion of his name from the Oath of Allegiance might have an adverse effect on the loyalty of some of the less worthy of the King's servants.

Finally, I should like to call attention to what seems to me to be a bright omen for the future prosperity of Siam. While many of the old ceremonies have been abolished or curtailed, it is only fair to mention that there has, in recent years, been a tendency for those in power to continue to cater for the Siamese populace's unflagging desire for pageantry and ceremonial display. Thus many new observances have crept in to fill the places of those which have lost their significance. The process was begun by King Rāma IV when he instituted the King's Birthday and Coronation Anniversary celebrations. Now we have the Trooping of the Colour, and Degree Day at the University, on both of which occasions a chapter of monks is in attendance to chant stanzas of victory; while, when the King anoints a new gunboat, it is something more than the European custom of breaking a bottle of champagne. Naturally these rites are mainly Buddhist, but, however much we may regret from a historical point of view the passing of Brahmanism, it cannot but be admitted that this bringing into line of the national religion with the modern State Ceremonies of a progressive people is sociologically sound, and augurs well for Siam's future. With the growth of education the change to a democratic form of government is certain to come sooner or later, and the beneficent influence of Buddhism manifested in every Ceremony of State will probably do much to mollify the dangers of the period of transition.

INDEX

Abhiṣeka (anointment) of kings, 70, 74, 76, 79, 121 ; of queens, 116–18 ; of tonsurate, 130, 131 ; of images, 253–4 ; of white elephant, 276.
Ablution, 184 (and see Bath, ceremonial).
Absolutism of the monarchy, 24.
Address, modes of, 40.
Agni Purāṇa, cited, 107.
Āgrayaṇa feasts, 236.
Āgrayaṇeshti, 229, 236.
Agriculture, Minister of (see *Baladeba*).
Aitareya-Āraṇyaka, cited, 244 fn.
Aitareya Brāhmaṇa, cited, 80, 81, 83, 95, 121.
Amazons, 47, 109.
Ambassadors (see Embassies, reception of).
Ancestors, homage to, 30, 90, 169–74.
Animals, mythical, of the Himaphān, 128, 150, 167–8.
Animism, 301.
Aṅkor bas-reliefs, 59, 93, 96, 100, 109, 110, 111, 113, 115, 149, 150, 185, 191, 277.
Anniversaries, royal, 213–17.
Anointment (see *Abhiṣeka*).
Antagada Dasao, cited, 75, 77 fn., 80.
Anthem, National, 6.
Apsaras, as figure head, 114.
Army, purification of, 297.
Āṣāḍha festival, 296.
Ashes, disposal of, after cremation, 154–61.
Aśoka, missions of, 12.
Astrologer (see *Horā*).
Asuras, 122.
Atharva Veda, rejected by Siamese, 55.
Audience, general, at coronation, 88–9 ; to palace ladies, 89 ; special, 90 ; State, 177–86 ; to officials and petitioners, 187–92.
Ayudhyā, foundation of, 14.

Bakus, 60, 61.
Baladeba (Minister of Agriculture), 22, 199, 239, 256–9, 263, 295.
Bālī, 113, 122.
Barges, royal, 33, 111–15, 203.
Bath, ceremonial, of kings, 74, 216, 239, 299 ; confused with anointment, 76 ; of queen, 118 ; of tonsurate, 128, 130 ; of royal corpse, 139 ; of Brahmans, 248.
Bell, audience, 190 ; in Brahmanic ritual, 249–53.
Betel Nut Set (regalia), 83, 101.
Birthday, King's, 215–17.
Blood of royal persons tabooed, 37–8.
Boat, as vehicle for expulsion of evil, 312.
Bodhisattva, king regarded as, 31, 166.
Bodyguard, Royal (*Ṭāmrvac*), 110.
Brahmā, 129, 148, 149, 228, 229.
Brahmans, Cambodian, 58–60.
Brahmans, Indian, 57–8 ; duties of, 61.
Brahmans, Siamese, dress of, 54 ; sects of, 54 ; temples of, 54 ; distribution of, 57 ; books of, 55, 63 ; initiation of, 57 ; origin of, 61 ; hair loosened as sign of mourning, 149 ; ritual of, at Swinging Festival, 247–53.
Braḥ-pāda, 200.

Brihaspati, cited, 196.
Buddha, " Emerald," 71, 89, 310.
Buddha, image of, " calling down rain," 223–4 ; image of, " calming the ocean," 226, 310.
Buddha, life of, Siamese version cited, 49, 87, 97, 224 ; Burmese version cited, 117 ; Sinhalese version cited (see *Nidāna-kathā* and *Mahā-Parinibbāna Sutta*).
Buddhist Religion, King's acceptance of the Headship of, 89.
Buddhist ritual, 54 fn.
Buddhist sects in Siam, 91, 216.
Buddhist services of benediction, 73, 77, 84, 87, 213, 216.
Bull, sacred, worship of, 295.
Burma, Siamese intercourse with, 15, 19–20.

Cakravartin, king regarded as, 31 ; cremation of, 156.
Căkrī Day, 171.
Căkrī Dynasty, 15, 17.
Cambodia, influence of, 13–15.
Candle of Victory, 73, 216.
Candles, in Brahmanic ritual, 249–53.
Cars, funeral, 149–50.
Ceylon, religious intercourse with, 14, 15, 19, 186.
Chank (see Conch).
Chargers, royal, 88, 109.
Chăṯra Maṅgala, 213–15.
Cheou Ta-kouan, 56, 101, 109, 113, 160, 170, 185, 188, 191.
Chignon, Brahmanic, 54, 59, 96.
Children, royal, not allowed to remain in palace, 40.
China, intercourse with, 15, 18, 182.
Chinese rites at Royal Cremation, 143.
Circumambulation, *pradakṣina*, 102 fn., 107, 131, 199, 202, 222 ; *prasavya*, 151, 154.
Cities, guardian spirits of (see Spirits).
Cocoa-nut water, used for bathing royal remains, 147, 157.
Cocoa-nuts, thrown to drowning royalty, 33.
Command, first, of crowned king, 86.
Conch, 72 and fn.
Concubines (see Harem).
Còn P̱arian, 288–90.
Consecration ceremonies compared, 123–5.
Cord, Brahmanic, 249.
Corn, spirits of the, 233, 235.
Coronation, Ceremony of Actual, 82–7 ; Anniversary of, 213–15.
Corpse, royal, bathing and adorning the, 139–40 ; preparation of, for burning, 147.
Cremation, history of, 155–62 ; function of, 165–7.
Crow, white, 287.
Crowns, royal, 83, 95–8, 129, 140 ; of white elephant, 277.
Cuḷālaṅkaraṇa Day, 172.

Damaru, 77 fn.
Dance, *dèṅvisai*, 121 ; at Cambodian rain-making ceremony, 227 ; circular, at Swinging Festival, 242, 244 ; for exorcism, 311.
Darbha grass, 78, 83, 250.
Days, auspicious, for First Ploughing, 256.
Deification of kings (see Kingship, divine).
Deva-rāja (Royal God) Cult, 29, 59, 86, 169, 170.
Dhānya-daha, 228–31.
Dharmarāja I, King, 14, 16, 60, 85, 98.
Dhanapurī, 15, 17.
Diffusion, theory of, 4.
Dipawali (see *Diwali*).
Directions, eight, worship of the, 72.
Disease, expulsion of, 309–10.
Diwali, 289.

Dogs, corpses offered to, 159, 160.
Draṅ Dharma, King, 16, 57.
Dress, of Brahmans, 54 ; of kings, 77 ; of queens, 117 ; of tonsurate, 129 ; of royal corpse, 139 ; of Buddhist monks, 208–9.
Dvāravatī, 13, 18.
Dyuta festival, 293.

Earth, Goddess of, 87, 109, 250, 257.
East, quarter faced by king at coronation, 79.
Elephants as rain-makers, 223, 284.
Elephants, sprinkling of (see *Snāna*).
Elephant, White, a royal *ratna*, 88 ; whisk of tail of, 83, 100, 119 ; at *Kaṭhina*, 207 ; reception of, 274–5, 278 ; anointment of, 275 ; naming of, 275, 276 ; accoutrements of, 276–7 : in reign of Rāma IV, 278–9 ; eulogy recited to, 279 ; in seventeenth century, 280–2 ; cremation of, 282–3 ; omens drawn from, 273, 284 ; a cause of war, 282 ; significance and history of the cult of, 284–7.
Embassies, reception of, 177–86.
Eunuchs, 50.
Evil, expulsion of, 308–12.
Execution of royal persons, 37–8.
Exorcism, palace, 310–11 ; royal, 311–12.

Fan, 83, 100, 110, 226.
Fiftieth day rites, 143.
Figwood (*udumbara*), 78, 81, 102.
Fire, sacred, for cremation, 144, 150, 153.
Fire sacrifices (see *Homa*).
Fireworks, 147, 172, 210, 251, 254.
Flowers, gold and silver, scattered, 87.
Flowers, in ritual, 249.
Food, taboos relating to, 37 ; offered at lying-in-state, 142.
Footprint, sacred (see *Braḥ-pāda*).
Fruit offerings in Brahmanic ritual, 249, 254.
Fruits, First, festivals of, 228–37.
Functional method of social anthropology, 3, 5, 7.
Functions, magical, priestly or divine, of kings (see King).

Gandharvas, 110.
Gaṇeśa, temple of, 54, 55 ; ritual in temple of, 250 ; image of, borne in procession, 77, 251 ; tonsure of, 127.
Gaṅgā, at Swinging Festival, 250.
Garuḍa, 88, 110, 113, 287.
Gems, the Triple, 78 ; Girdle of the Nine, 83, 101 ; Ring of the Nine, 130.
Ghosts (see *phī*, and *pretas*).
Girdle, Brahman, 83, 86, 101 ; of the Nine Gems, 83, 101.
Glăṅ, Braḥ (Minister of Commerce and Foreign Affairs), 22, 181–4, 199.
Glory, Buddhist (see *Sirotama*).
God, eating the, 235.
Gods, doing violence to the, 223 ; reception of the, 238–47.
Grains, roasted, scattered, 77, 129, 150.
Ground, king not supposed to touch, 36.
Grū, Braḥ Mahā Rāja (High Priest of Śiva), 72, 74, 77, 83, 248–55, 257, 296.
Grūs (pandits), 199 ; (deceased spiritual professors), 233–4.
Guns, fired at coronation, 77 ; fired at cremation, 141, 153 ; fired to expel evil, 309 ; guardian spirits in (see Spirits).

Hair, tabooed, 32–34 ; modes of dressing, 54, 59, 96, 97, 149.
Hair-cutting of kings, 34.
Haṅsa, as figure-head, 114 ; in ritual, 252–4.

Hanumān, 110, 113, 287.
Harem, constitution of, 46–9; function of, 49–52.
Harihara, images of, 54–5.
Hat, royal, 89, 98.
Head tabooed, 32–4.
Hīnayānism, introduction of, 13.
Hīnayānistic conception of kingship, 31.
Historical method, 3.
Holi festival, 245–6.
Homa, 72.
Horā, 44, 62, 102, 129, 199, 299.
Horoscope, royal, inscription of, 102.
Housewarming, 118–20.
Hundredth day rites, 143, 161.

Illumination of Bangkok, 217.
Independent origins, theory of, 4.
India, cultural influence of, 18–19.
Indra, 122, 123, 129, 134, 146, 148, 149, 228, 229, 230.
Indrābhiṣeka, 80, 121–3.
Initiation of Brahmans, 57: of princes (see Tonsure).
Inscriptions, 7.
Insignia, of officials, 22; of tonsurate, 131, 144; of temporary king, 240, 256.
Installation, ceremonies of, compared, 123–5, 133–5, 163–5.
Investigation, methods of, 3.

Japanese in Siam, 208.
Jātakas, cited, 76, 93, 94, 95, 99, 100, 101, 103, 107, 116, 284, 285, 286, 302, 306.

Kaḥṯikeyā Festival, 290–2.
Kailāsa, Mount, 31, 61, 71, 122, 127–8; "opening the portals of," 56, 63, 83, 86, 248, 251; "closing the portals of," 63, 253.
Kălpavṛkṣa (*Pārijāta*) tree, 123, 146, 243, 251.
Kaniṣka, King, mission of, 13.
Kaṭhina, 200–12; significance and function of, 200; description of modern, 201–4; ceremony in the temple at, 204; in the seventeenth century, 205–8; early history of, 208–10; followed by regatta, 211.
Kauṭilīya-artha-śāstra, cited, 44.
Khău Barṣā, 200.
Khvăñ (see Spirit, *khvăñ*).
King, daily life of, 42–6; dress of, 77, 139, 203; exercise of divine and priestly functions by, 79, 91, 118, 130–2, 174, 229, 266; exercise of magical functions by, 226, 266; ceremony before death of, 138; dead, worship of, 169–74.
King, Second (see *Uparāja, Mahā*).
King, Temporary, 132, 228–30, 239, 256, 265–9; pays homage to king, 243; rewards of, 242, 258.
Kings of Siam, list of, 16–17.
Kingship, Divine, 29–32, 86 (and see Deva-rāja).
Kite-flying, 221.
Kojagara festival (see *Dyuta*).

Lamps, feasts of, 288–94; hoisted on poles, 288–90; floated at night, 292–4.
Language, Court, 39.
Lao, 13.
Lavā, 12.
Leaves, in ritual, 72, 74 fn., 130.
Letter, Royal, reception of, 181, 184.
Levees, Court, 189, 214.
Libations, 87, 109, 257.
Libation Vessel (regalia), 83, 101.
Light-waving rite (see *Vian dian*).
Limes, containing coins, 146.
Liṅga, 29, 110, 169, 296.
Literature, Siamese, 7–9; European, 9–10.
Lokapāla, 78, 82.

Lòy Kraḥdòṅ, 292–4.
Lying-in-State, 141–4.

Māgha-pūjā, 200.
Magic, contagious, 193, 263; imitative, 223, 226, 244.
Magical rites, at Assumption of Royal Residence, 119.
Mahābhārata, cited, 44.
Mahā-navami, feast, 236.
Mahā-Parinibbāna Sutta, cited, 107 fn., 154, 156, 157, 171 fn.
Mahāvagga, cited, 210.
Mahāvaṁsa, cited, 32, 92, 93, 94, 95, 97, 98, 100, 103, 157, 166, 190, 212, 301, 302.
Mahāyānism, introduction of, 13.
Maḥhātlek (Lord Chamberlain's Department), 22, 177, 203, 258.
Maitreya Buddha, 32, 204.
Manasara, cited, 107.
Mantras, Brahmanic, 55–7, 83, 84, 249, 251–4; Buddhist, 73, 193.
Manu, cited, 30, 35, 37, 45–6, 58, 61, 116, 187, 247.
Marriage, royal, 48, 116.
Mask, gold, on face of corpse, 139.
Matriarchy, 68–9.
Mercury, use of, at cremation, 140, 155.
Meru, Mount, 31, 71, 122–3, 144–7.
Ministers of State, 22.
Miscarriage, expulsion of evil after, 310.
Monkey, white, 287.
Môn-Khmers, 12.
Moon, at Swinging Festival, 250.
Mortar, stone, in ritual, 252–4.
Mountains, spirits of (see Spirits).
Mourning, regulations for, 142, 161.
Mudrā, 253.
Mūrdhābhiṣeka, 299 fn.

Nāga, figure of, at *Indrābhiṣeka*, 122–3.
Nagara Paṭhama, 13, 154.
Nagara Śrī Dharmarāja, 14, 57.
Nāgas, as figure-heads, 114; impersonated in Swinging Festival, 241–2, 245.
Name, personal, of king tabooed, 38–9.
Nanchao, 13, 18.
Nandi, 54, 295.
Nārada, cited, 30, 58.
Nārāyaṇa, King, 16, 225, 239; daily life of, 43–4; audiences of, 182, 187.
Nareśvara, King, 16, 106.
Nareśvara, procession of, at Swinging Festival, 251.
New Year, 298–9.
Nidāna-kathā (in *Buddhist Birth Stories*), cited 81, 93, 119, 260, 285.
Nīrājanā, 297.

Oath, king's, to Brahmans, 79–80, 86; of allegiance, 193–8.
Observation, personal, 10.
Ocean, churning of the, 123.
Octagonal Throne, ceremony on, 77–82.
Officials, ranks of, 22; promotion of, 214–16.
Oil, not used for anointment in Siam, 76, 79.
Omens, importance of, in Siam, 62; drawn from boat-races, 211; drawn from oxen's choice of food, 257, 259, 263; drawn from length of *Baladeba*'s skirt, 257; drawn from appearance of elephants, 273, 284; drawn from casting of sticks, 291; drawn from top-spinning, 298.
Omkāra, 86.
Ordeal by water, 196.
Origins, independent, theory of, 4.
Outflow, speeding of the, 225–6.

Padi, burning of, 228–31; carrying home the, 228–30.

Pai-śrī offerings, 73, 131, 295, 310.
Palace, Grand, 71.
Palanquin, royal, 110.
Pāli dialogue (at Coronation), 78–9, 83–6.
Pañcha-gavya, 252 fn.
Pandits, Court, 44, 77, 78.
Paṅsakula verse, 143, 158.
Pantheon, homage to statues in, 170, 215.
Parākrama Bāhu, King, influence of, 14, 97.
Pāraskara Grihya-sūtra, cited, 229 fn., 295 fn.
Pārijāta tree (see *Kălpavṛkṣa*).
Paritta suttas, 73, 129, 205, 216.
Patriarch, Prince, 75, 88, 91, 138, 152.
People, divisions of the, 22.
Phā-nuṅ, 54, 77, 117, 122, 240, 257.
Phaulkon, Constantine, 183, 187.
Phī, 137, 198, 300–3, 305.
Phimeanakas, 71, 195.
Piṇḍas, 234.
Pitris, 169, 232, 234, 235.
Ploughing, First, 256–64.
Portraits, royal, honoured, 173.
Pradakṣina (see Circumambulation).
Prāpṭābhiṣeka, 70.
Prāsāda Doṅ, King, 16, 205, 206.
Prāsāda spire, 114–15, 145, 252–3.
Pretas, 234.
Procession, Coronation, by land, 108; Coronation, by water, 111–12; Tonsure, 129; Cremation, 148–9; *Kathina*, 202–8; at Swinging Festival, 240, 251; at First Ploughing, 256; at reception of White Elephant, 275.
Prognostics (see Omens).
Progresses, State, 106–15.
Prostration, 24, 59, 142, 191–2, 208.
Purohita, 58, 60, 61, 62, 79, 80, 85, 87, 103, 254.
Pusyābhiṣeka, 121.
Pyre, funeral, 144–7.

Quarters, guardians of (see *Lokapāla*).
Queen, 68, 116–18.

Rain, control of, 222–7.
Rajābhiṣeka, 70.
Rājasīha, as throne covering, 83.
Rājasūya, 70, 74, 75, 77, 79, 81, 87, 93, 99, 103.
Rājavăt fence, 122 fn., 145, 172, 232, 240, 250.
Rāma I–VI, kings of Căkrī Dynasty, 17.
Rāma IV, King, daily life of, 42–3; harem of, 46–7.
Rāma Gāṁhèṅ, King, 14, 16, 182, 190, 192, 195 fn., 209, 211, 277, 301.
Rāmādhipatī I, King, 14, 16.
Rāmādhipatī II, King, 122.
Rāmāyaṇa, cited, 87, 96 fn., 99, 101, 113, 121, 123, 157, 173, 196 fn., 260, 285, 287.
Ranks, social, 21–2.
Ratnas, royal, 88, 93, 116.
Rāvaṇa, 96.
Receptacle (regalia), 83, 101.
Reforms, of King Rāma V, 23; of King Rāma VI, 23.
Regalia, list of, 83; significance of, 86; possible derivation from magicians' implements, 92, 99; the five chief, 92.
Regatta, royal, 211–12.
Relics, royal, collection of, 154; homage to, 171, 215.
Religion, the popular, 24.
Residence, Royal, Assumption of, 118–20.
Rhinoceros, bearer of the Sacred Fire, 150, 168.
Rhyme-making, 231.
Rice, mixing the heavenly, 232–5; consecrated, sown at First Ploughing, 257 (and see Padi).
Rig-Veda, cited, 107 fn., 158, 244.
Ring, of nine gems, 130; placed in

mouth of royal corpse, 140; of Head Brahman, 249.
Rings (regalia), 83, 101; use of, at king's hair-cutting, 34.
Rites, magical (see Magical rites); purificatory, 72, 249.
Rivers, the five principal, 74; spirits of (see Spirits).

Sacrament of First Fruits, 228.
Sacrifice, of First Fruits, 228; human, at foundation of buildings, 304–7.
Sākamedha, 236, 237.
Śakti, 55, 289, 296.
Śăkti nā, 22, 53.
Saṃskāras (initiation rites), 126.
Sandal-wood, 152, 153.
Săṅgharāja (see Patriarch, Prince).
Saṅkrānti, 299.
Sanies, burning of, 144.
Sanskrit texts, 55.
Sārada Ceremony, 231–7.
Śāstras, references to, in Siamese texts, 55.
Satăpakaraṇa rite, 142, 143, 154, 158, 169, 171.
Śatapatha Brāhmaṇa, cited, 30, 36, 74, 75, 77, 79, 81, 83, 86, 87, 95, 99, 102 fn., 103, 106, 107 fn., 229, 230, 236.
Scapegoat, public, 309.
Sceptre (regalia), 83, 100.
Sebhā, recited at king's hair-cutting, 34.
Second King (see *Uparāja, Mahā*).
Śeṣa, 296.
Seventh day rites, 143.
Shadow plays, 254.
Śiladitya, King, missions of, 13.
Siñcana (sacred thread), 73, 102, 110, 131, 193, 232, 233, 308, 310.
Sirotama (Buddhist glory), 97.
Sister-marriage, 68, 117.
Śiva, introduction of worship of, 13, 19; temple of, 54; images of, 54, 123, 251; High Priest of (see *Grū, Braḥ Mahā Rāja*); impersonated at Tonsure, 130–2; impersonated at Swinging Festival, 239; watches the Swinging, 241; ritual in temple of, 247–54.
Śiva's Night, 296–7.
Slippers (regalia), 83, 99.
Snāna, 297.
Sokănṭa (see Tonsure).
Soothsaying (see Omens).
Soul, 173 (and see Spirit, *khvăñ*).
Spirit, *khvăñ*, 33, 34, 131, 276, 315.
Spirits, of umbrella, 73, 194, 198, 213; guardian, of cities, 73, 194, 198, 302–3; of the corn, 233, 235; of rivers, 294; propitiation of, 300–7; of mountains, 301; guardian, of great guns, 304; guardian, of foundations, 304–7.
Śrāddhas, 161, 169, 232, 233, 234.
Śrīvijaya, 13, 18.
Standards, royal, 110.
Stick (regalia), 83, 100.
Style and title, handed to the king, 83; inscription of, 102; of kings of Cākrī Dynasty, 104–5.
Succession, 67.
Sugrīva, 96, 113, 122.
Sujata, 233.
Sukhodaya, independence of, 14.
Sun, king's equivalence to, 35–6, 78; at Swinging Festival, 250.
Sunshade, 110.
Suvarṇabhumi, 12.
Swan (see *Haṅsa*).
Swing, the great, 240; the small, in Śiva temple, 252.
Swinging Festival, 238–55; solar origin of, 243–5; processions at, 240–2, 251.
Sword, of Victory (regalia), 83, 98, 193, 199; Personal (regalia), 83, 101.

Taboos, 32–42.
Ṭāk, King, 15, 17, 18, 32, 166.
Tamil hymn, 55, 56.
Thai, 13.
Thread, sacred (see *Siñcana*, and Cord, Brahmanic).
Throne, Octagonal, 78, 81 ; *Bhadrapitha*, 83, 129, 252–4 ; Golden Hibiscus, 88, 178, 185 ; Window, 182–5.
Title (see Style).
Tonsurate, reception of, on Mount Kailāsa, 130.
Tonsure, 126–36 ; function of, 135–6.
Top-spinning, 298.
Tradition, value of, 5, 6.
Ṭraibhūmi, 127.
Transliteration, system of, 11.
Tripiṭaka, honoured, 172–3.
Ṭruṣ, 299.
Ṭulābhāra (royal weighing), 199, 216.

Udumbara (figwood), 78, 81, 102.
Udumbara, King, 8, 16.
Umā, images of, 54.
Umbrella, single-tiered, 110 ; processional, 110 ; straw, 228–30.
Umbrella, White, 78, 83, 93–5, 141 ; spirit of, 73, 194, 198, 213.
Unalom scroll, 131, 249.
Uparāja Mahā, 22, 52–3, 180, 185, 289 ; function of, 53.
Urn, Water (regalia), 83, 101.
Urns, funeral, 139, 154, 161.

Vaiśākha-pūjā, 200, 216.
Vājapeya, 71, 81.
Vedas, reference to, in Siamese texts, 55, 60.
Vehicles, traditional, of kings, 109.
Vian dian rite, 102, 131, 173, 213.
Victory, king's, at coronation, 78, 80–1.
Virgins, in *Sārada* Ceremony, 233, 235.
Vishṇu, Institutes of, cited, 50, 58.
Viṣṇu, temple of, 54 ; images of, 55, 122, 123 ; High Priest of, 72 fn., 77 ; ritual in temple of, 255.
Viṣṇu's Sleep, 295–6.
Viṣṇu worship, introduction of, 13, 19.
Viṣvakarmā, 123.
Vow, tying the, 148, 259.
Vultures, corpses offered to, 159–60.

Wailing of women at cremation, 139, 142.
Water, consecrated, 74, 249, 253, 254 ; of allegiance, 193.
Weapons, royal, 106, 193, 198, 213.
Weighing, royal (see *Ṭulābhāra*).
Wind, control of, 221.
Women, pregnant, sacrifices of, 305–6.

Yak's hair tufts, 112, 277.
Yak's tail whisk (regalia), 83, 100.
Yantra diagrams, 56, 72, 252, 290.
Yoni, 296.

SUPPLEMENTARY NOTES ON SIAMESE STATE CEREMONIES

BY

H. G. QUARITCH WALES

Author of *Siamese State Ceremonies*, 1931

LONDON
BERNARD QUARITCH, LTD.
5–8 LOWER JOHN STREET, GOLDEN SQUARE
1971

THE RIVER-BATHING CEREMONY AS LAST PERFORMED IN 1887.

PREFACE

The subject of my 1931 book is one which George Coedès in his review of it considered " d'importance primordiale pour la connaissance du pays ". Hence it is undoubtedly worthy of the continuing attention of scholars. That I had not done full justice to an absorbing subject I was aware when in my preface I called it a pioneer work, and on the penultimate page spoke of the many gaps that required to be bridged. Now " forty years on " there could be no question of my attempting a revised edition. For one thing that could well have meant the loss of everything deriving from that contact with the " atmosphere " of the Court to which I then felt very close. That is surely something worth preserving now that we begin to realize that the era ending in 1932 still belonged to that Old Siam which then appeared to have closed some half century earlier.

With few exceptions the kind of penetrating studies that I hoped to see as paving the way for a definitive work of the future have not yet materialized. Phya Anuman Rajadhon's excellent series of articles in *JSS*, designed to salvage the memories of disappearing customs, have brought valuable elucidations whenever they have sufficiently approached our inquiry ; and Kenneth Wells' book mentioned below has admirably filled the lacuna on Siamese Buddhism. But it is because my book is still regarded by many as a standard work that it has seemed worth while, indeed a matter of duty, to repair at least some of its shortcomings.

These Notes have been made possible partly by the fact that I never lost interest in the Ceremonies, occasionally looking again at those texts which form our main sources and noting particulars which I might well have included. But I must add that this has not involved any thorough-going re-study of such texts. Again I would take the opportunity of stressing that any future use of the voluminous writings of King Rāma V will always involve judicious selection, bearing in mind that the royal author was addressing a contemporary Siamese audience. Further, and perhaps most fruitfully, these Notes have benefited from constructive criticisms made by two of my reviewers: firstly the painstaking analysis by G. Coedès which appeared in *BEFEO*, Vol. XXXII, 1932, pp. 331–338 (abbreviated Coedès, rev.) ; and secondly, from the Indian side, an unsigned review that appeared in the *Journal of Indian History*, Vol. XI, pt. 3, 1932 (abbreviated *JIH*, rev). But where I have not referred to a point raised in either of these reviews it does not mean that I have not given it my consideration. Finally there have been my own corrections of some errors that escaped the notice of even the most meticulous reviewers and correspondents; as well as references to matters that have occurred to me as a result of wider reading or are consequent on the general progress of related researches. The only ceremony of which I here give a full account is the River-bathing ceremony which was not included in the book. The omission of this spectacular ceremony was however soon made good by an article I devoted to it in a journal, of which a corrected version is here given, accompanied now by an illustration of the last occasion on which it was performed.

In addition to stimulating further research by specialists in Siamese culture it is to be hoped that these Notes will increase the interest and usefulness of the book to readers who have in the past found that it has some bearing on their own particular fields.

H. G. Q. W.

CONTENTS

Notes on the following chapters of
Siamese State Ceremonies : *Page*

I Scope and Sources 7
II An Outline of the History of Siamese Culture . 7
III Social Organization of the Siamese 8
IV The Kingship 8
V The Court Brahmans 10
VI Coronation 11
VII Coronation 11
VIII Coronation 11
IX Higher Grades in Royal Consecration (*Puṣyābhiṣeka* and *Indrābhiṣeka*) 14
X Tonsure—and other Initiations 16
The River-bathing Ceremony 16
XI Cremation 21
XII Cremation 21
XIII The Worship of Dead Kings 22
XIV Royal Audiences 23
XV The Oath of Allegiance 23
XVI The Royal Bounty 27
XVII Royal Anniversaries 27
XVIII Ceremonies for the Control of Wind and Rain . 28
XX The Swinging Festival 28
XXI The First Ploughing 29
XXII Temporary Kings 29
XXIII The White Elephant 30
XXIV Feasts of Lamps 30
XXV Minor Brahmanical Ceremonies (*Snāna*) . . 30
XXVI The Propitiation of Spirits 31
XXVII The Expulsion of Evil 33
XXVIII General Conclusions 33

CHAPTER I

SCOPE AND SOURCES

p. 3, l. 24. The desired research into Siamese Buddhism has now been adequately undertaken by Kenneth E. Wells, *Thai Buddhism, its rites and activities*, Bangkok, 1939.

p. 7, l. 28. Exceptions to the disappointing character of Khmer inscriptions are referred to in the Notes for page 121 and Chapter IX below.

p. 8. The 1916 edition of the *Evidence of Khun Hlvaṅ Hā Vǎt* is an incomplete edition of the translation made in the fourth reign from the Môn version (part of which was translated into English in *JSS* xxviii and xxix, 1935 and 1936). This incomplete printed edition from the Môn version lacked the section on ceremonies which was utilized by King Rāma V, who had access to the manuscript. A later discovered Burmese version, translated into Siamese in 1911, was printed by the National Library in complete form in 1925, under a title meaning *Evidence of the People of Ayudhyā*, it now being realized that several Ayudhyan prisoners of war had contributed the information. It was not available to King Rāma V, but is referred to in these Notes when (very rarely) there is any reason to do so.[1]

CHAPTER II

AN OUTLINE OF THE HISTORY OF SIAMESE CULTURE

pp. 12, 13. There is no evidence to connect Nagara Paṭhama with Suvarṇabhumi and Aśoka's mission. The Buddhist remains there do not appear to date from earlier than the sixth century A.D. and are not Mahāyānist. However at Ůdòṅ (U T'ong), not far away, Buddhist remains of Amarāvatī style possibly of the third or fourth century A.D., have been found. The region then seems to have formed part of the Fu-nan empire, the independent Môn kingdom of Dvāravatī not coming into existence until the sixth century. It remained independent until early eleventh century and its art style was late Gupta not Sarnath. Though Hīnayāna Buddhism was predominant in Dvāravatī, there is evidence of some Hinduism, but no reason to believe that Mahāyānism, though known, ever took root.[2] After the conquest of Dvāravatī by

[1] The bibliographical reference in my *Ancient South-east Asian Warfare*, page 125, note 1, is inaccurate.

[2] Cf. H. G. Quaritch Wales, *Dvāravatī*, London, 1969.

the Khmers, early in the eleventh century, many Khmer temples were erected, but they were not, as stated in the text, all Brahmanic : Phimai and Labapurī were Buddhist. It is not now thought that the Thai established the Yunnan kingdom of Nanchao.

p. 14, l. 1. It is doubtful whether the Thai ever had any contact with Mahāyānism in Yunnan ; they were probably purely animistic as they moved into the Indochinese river valleys.

p. 14, l. 9. *For* 1276 *read* about 1275.

p. 14, l. 14. *For* 1317 *read* about 1317.

p. 18. As Coedès pointed out in his review, besides borrowings from Chinese culture, the possibility of common origins has to be kept in mind.

p. 19, l. 4. Indian Mahāyānist influence : the route followed cannot be so definitely defined as stated by me. There is no evidence for its introduction into South-east Asia before the sixth century ; and no reason to believe it ever influenced the Thai.

p. 19, l. 16. Indian Śaiva Brahmanism : *for* between the eighth and twelfth centuries A.D., *read* fifth to seventh centuries.

p. 19, l. 28. Sinhalese Hīnayānistic influence : Peguan influences did not in fact reach Northern Siam about the twelfth century. The Buddhism of Lāṁbūn in Northern Siam was not Peguan, but reached that region in the eighth century, having been brought by Môn colonists from Labapurī, one of the centres of the Dvāravatī kingdom.

p. 20, l. 7. To what extent the Siamese were indebted to the earlier Indianized civilization of the Môns (of Dvāravatī) is a matter on which it is not yet possible to speak with any certainty.

CHAPTER III

SOCIAL ORGANIZATION OF THE SIAMESE

The subject of this chapter is treated more fully in my book *Ancient Siamese Government and Administration*, London, 1934, repr. New York, 1965.

CHAPTER IV

THE KINGSHIP

pp. 29 sq. What is said here of the Royal God, or Deva-rāja cult, of the Khmers would have to be modified considerably in view of the progress of research. It differs in important respects from the *liṅga* cults of Central Java and Champa, and cannot be traced to a South Indian origin. At least, as Coedès has put it, " if it comes from purely Indian ideas it has been extended in Cambodia in a way that its origins cannot completely explain ".[1] The manner in which this extension is due to local factors has been studied by me in *The Making of Greater India*. One result of this extension which concerns the Siamese is that through Khmer influence the divinity of the king was more extreme than in Indian theory. It is probably to this, rather than to any Buddhist conception, that the Siamese owe their ideas on divine kingship. But while the Khmer royal religion had a chthonic bias, it would seem that the Siamese more readily comprehended and accepted those Indian ideas which stressed the uranic or solar aspect of divinity.

p. 31, l. 2. Besides the calling down of Viṣṇu and Śiva to animate the new king at the Coronation, there is another indication of the survival of the cult of the Royal God. The statues of Buddha cast for each reign (see Chapter XIII) were considered by Coedès (rev.) to be more than a mere act of merit. As he says, " Les Siamois n'en savent pas plus ou n'en veulent pas dire plus ". This comment, in my opinion, would apply equally to the attitude of those modern Siamese who would deny that the divinity of the king, etc., was ever taken seriously.

pp. 33 sq. The *khvăñ* spirit is referred to in this book mainly in connection with the Tonsure (Chapter X). A detailed study of the beliefs and rites connected with this spirit has been published by Phya Anuman: "The Kwan and its ceremonies", *JSS*, Vol. L, pt. 2, 1962, pp. 119–161. The corresponding Cambodian beliefs in *pralin* (vital spirits) have been studied by Mme E. Porée Maspero, " La Cérémonie de l'appel des Esprits vitaux chez les Cambodgiens ", *BEFEO*, XLV, pt. 1, pp. 146–183.

p. 36. The King was not supposed to touch the ground. Coedès (rev.) suggested that, if the king represented the sun, the taboo was inspired by fear that the feet of the sun god would burn the ground, causing calamities.

p. 37. It was taboo to spill royal blood. Rather than being due to respect for the royal blood, Coedès (rev.) again stresses the magical import of the taboo, suggesting that it was based on fear that the king's blood would burn the earth. In a very interesting note on " The Manner of executing Princes of the Blood Royal ", F. H. Giles[2] quotes and interprets a difficult reference in *KM* to the mode of execution of princes in the Ayudhyā period, and the ceremonial dance that preceded

[1] G. Coedès, " Note sur l'Apothéose au Cambodge ", *Bull. Comm. Archéolog. de l'Indochine*, 1911, p. 48.

[2] " Analysis of van Vliet's Account of Siam ", *JSS*, xxx, pt. 2, p. 203.

it; he also gives some details as to the method followed under the Bangkok dynasty, on information supplied by a high personage. His conclusion that " it was deemed improper that the blood of a Prince should stain Mother Earth " seems not far removed from Coedès' suggestion.

p. 39. The personal name of the King was taboo. The first three kings of the Căkrī dynasty did have personal names, phonetically transliterated as Duong, Chím and T'āp respectively (Coedès, rev.). The *posthumous* names of the first two kings were given by the third king, after the names of Buddha images he had dedicated to them (*BRB*, pp. 234–236), and nothing to do with Bodhisattvas. The posthumous name of the third king, meaning " the lord seated on the head (of his subjects) " was given by Rāma IV.

p. 40, l. 5. For *sevay* read *svey*. For this and other corrections in transliteration I am indebted to Coedès, rev.

CHAPTER V

THE COURT BRAHMANS

p. 55, l. 1. The images labelled as Harihara after they had been transferred to the National Museum are so labelled only hypothetically, owing to their mixed attributes. Coedès (rev.) states that all these images, even if in Khmer or Indian style, are of Siamese make and not earlier than the fourteenth century.

p. 56, l. 5. Another *mantra* " Pūjā muraị " (mentioned on p. 63 under Vol. D) was recognized as Tamil by *JIH* reviewer. Recently other Tamil chants have been recognized in the National Library collection, and a preliminary study of them and of the scripts used has been made by J. R. Marr,[1] to which the reader is referred for details. The scripts used are evidence of contact with both South India and Cambodia.

p. 61, l. 6 from bottom. The origin from Mount Kailāsa claimed by the Cambodian Brahmans may have a rational explanation in their possible derivation from a South Indian spiritual line who call themselves Kailāsa-paraṃparā (Sanskrit) or Kayilāparamparai (Tamil), suggests J. Filliozat.[2] This is paralleled to a certain extent in the

[1] J. R. Marr, " Some Manuscripts in the Grantha Script in Bangkok ", *Bull. School of Oriental & African Studies*, XXXII, pt. 2, 1969.

[2] J. Filliozat, " Kailāsaparamparā ", *Prince Dhani's Felicitation Volumes*, II, pp. 241–248.

interpretation given by A. B. Griswold[1] of the story of eight Indian monks who told King Kyanzittha of Burma about their former residence on Mount Gandhamādana, which might not be an imaginary place in the Himalayan fairyland, but an abode in Orissa that copied it.

p. 62, l. 6. In the Ayudhyā period the *purohita* was certainly a Brahman, a head of those Brahmans concerned with the administration of justice.[2]

p. 62, l. 8. According to the *KM*, if their prognostications proved false, the astrologers were liable to severe punishment, as indeed they were for other faults.

p. 62, l. 10 from bottom. That the astrologers took the steamship schedules into consideration is doubted by Coedès (rev.), and he cites an instance in 1930 when, following a fatal accident to a lady-in-waiting on a journey to Indochina, the king publicly blamed himself for having ignored the astrologer's dates.

p. 63, l. 7 from bottom. *For* " Guśatī sănveyak lòṁ jăṅ " *read* " Tuṣṭi saṅvey klòm jăṅ ".

CHAPTERS VI, VII, AND VIII

CORONATION

p. 67, l. 3. *For* law of A.D. 1360 *read* *KM* of 1458.

p. 67, n. 3. For *Kaṭhmāy* read *Catmāy.*

p. 71, l. 6 from bottom. *For* the temple containing the beautiful jewel of the monastery of the divine teacher *read* the temple of the Master (Buddha) [made of] the sacred jewel. (Coedès, rev.).

p. 72, last line. *After* New Year Festivals *add* also *Laṅ Sraṅ* (*BRB*, p. 163).

p. 73, notes 2 and 3. On *paritta suttas*, *sāy siñcana* and Candle of Victory K. Wells, op. cit., may also be consulted.

p. 74. Plate VII, showing the King in the Ablution Pavilion, may be compared with the famous painting in Cave 1, Ajanta, showing the ceremonial bath of a prince.

p. 77, l. 8. The statement that the Siamese national lower garment (*phă-nuṅ*) was not derived from Cambodia is questioned by Coedès (rev.), and no doubt rightly. He points out that on the Aṅkor Văt

[1] A. B. Griswold, *Burma, Korea, Tibet*, London, 1964, p. 31. The story is from the *Glass Palace Chronicle*.

[2] Cf. H. G. Quaritch Wales, *Ancient Siamese Government and Administration*, p. 99 and Chapter VIII.

reliefs the Khmers wear the *sampot*, identical with the Siamese *phā-nuṅ*, while the Siamese on those reliefs wear a skirt or wide trousers. The classical Khmer feminine lower garment was, however, a skirt or sarong (cf. p. 118).

p. 81, l. 14. In the Vedic *Rājasūya* there was actually a symbolic foray or sham fight ; but, comments the *JIH* review, " it must be remembered that the *Rājasūya* is a ceremony of the coronation of one who has already established his overlordship by a series of conquests, or by acknowledgement of his overlordship, so that the representation of a fight is quite in place. The idea is absent in the Mahābhiṣeka of Indra."

p. 82, end of section 6. If no longer recognized, there is surely an underlying magical significance in this ceremony on the Octagonal Throne, designed to bring the king's realm as a microcosm into harmony with the universe.

p. 83, l. 3. The Whisk of the Yak's Tail : for *jāmri* read *cāmarī*.

p. 90, l. 3. For *upathămabhak* read *upatthambhak*.

p. 95, l. 6. If we can explain the multi-tiered umbrellas of Siam on the theory of accumulation of honour, this can only mean that recognition of an underlying cosmological symbolism, with the tiers representing heavens and the shaft the axis of the universe, has been lost. Neither in the Ceremony on the Octagonal Throne, nor in the Coronation Progress, does there seem to have survived any vivid consciousness of cosmo-magical symbolism, though this was a feature of many Southeast Asian civilizations. Cf. R. Heine Geldern " Conception of State and Kingship in Southeast Asia ", *Far Eastern Quarterly*, November 1942.

p. 96, l. 21. *For* Syam Kut *read* Syāṃ Kuk.

p. 97, l. 13. The relief in a certain temple at Sukhodaya refers to one of the Jataka reliefs of Văt Śrī Cum (L. Fournereau, *Le Siam Ancien*, Vol. II, pl. XI).

p. 97, l. 14 from bottom. *For* the Indo-Javanese art of Śrīvijaya *read* Central Javanese art.

p. 98. The Sword of Victory. Coedès (rev.) denies the existence of a Jayavarman II tradition concerning the *Braḥ Kharga* and says that later Cambodian kings adopted the sword from Siam. Originally the *phgak* had been the Khmer royal weapon, the sword merely an emblem with which feudatories, including the Thai, were invested. The latter had thus given it leading status when they became independent, and it was in this role that the Cambodians later accepted it. The *phgak* has been incorporated in the Siamese regalia (p. 83) as the " hostage sword " or " weapon of the prisoners of war ".

p. 100. As to the Sceptre *JIH* review points out that we have the *danda*, or rod of punishment, in Sanskrit literature, and in Tamil literature the sceptre itself is referred to under a term meaning " rod of righteousness ".

p. 102, l. 24. For *janam* read *janma*.

p. 104, l. 6. *For* in a thirteenth century inscription at Aṅkor Văt, and believed to refer to the founder of that temple *read* a post-thirteenth century inscription and referring to a post-thirteenth century king (Coedès, rev.).

p. 104, l. 7 from bottom. *For* dharmikrājā *read* dharmikarājā.

p. 104, n. 1. *For* A.ii, p. 258 *read* A.iii, p. 238.

p. 105, l. 9. *For* agulaya *read* atulya.

p. 105, l. 17. *For* sakla *read* sakala.

p. 105, l. 20. *For* kruṇā *read* karuṇā.

p. 106, l. 12. The Long Handled Sword was evidently a Japanese sword. Such were in use in Malaya (G. B. Gardner, *Keris and other Malay weapons*, Pl. 50.4), and in Cambodia (Gro. Fig. 55 L).

p. 107, l. 18. " Solar *origin* " is too strong a term.

p. 109, l. 6. The coronation procession of King Sisowath cannot be invoked as evidence of the origin of the Siamese royal procession, since by this time Siamese influence in Cambodia was strong (Coedès, rev.).

p. 109, l. 17. The chariot is a typically Khmer form of royal vehicle, but for ceremonial purposes only, as a result of Indian Epic influences. It was not used in warfare.[1]

p. 109, l. 27. The Cambodian king changed his head-dress each time he changed his vehicle, probably symbolizing his representation in turn of each of the kings of the cardinal points. This would be as part of the symbolism which regards the city as a microcosm corresponding to the macrocosm of the universe or city of the gods.[2]

p. 111, l. 18. For *Rājakicavinicachāy* read *Rājakicavinicchāy*.

p. 113, l. 15 from bottom. Cheou Ta-Kouan was probably speaking of junks, not of royal barges. Later he describes the royal barges quite correctly (Coedès, rev.).

p. 115, l. 4. I should not now speak of the Burmese *prāsāda* (*phyathat*) being " evolved in Burma ", but rather of its being derived from a lost temple type of Bengal.[3]

p. 115, l. 17. The Chinese junk is depicted on the reliefs of the Bayon, not of Aṅkor Văt. The paddles of the barges on the reliefs were not thrust through holes in the sides ; they were used as oars and

[1] H. G. Quaritch Wales, *Ancient South-east Asian Warfare*, p. 84.
[2] G. Coedès, *Pour mieux comprendre Angkor*, 1947, p. 98.
[3] H. G. Quaritch Wales, *The Making of Greater India*, 2nd edn, p. 49.

thrust through gaps below screens. This applies to the war barges only, and was the only means of giving the rowers some protection.[1]

p. 117. The Siamese lower garment: see my correction in the Note to page 77 above.

CHAPTER IX

HIGHER GRADES IN ROYAL CONSECRATION

p. 121. *Puṣyābhiṣeka.* This is mentioned in stanza xix of the inscription of Prāsāt Hè Phkā.[2] The Khmer king Rajendravarman obtained the throne in the month of Puṣya and had received the *Puṣyābhiṣeka* consecration.

pp. 121–123. *Indrābhiṣeka.* In *BEFEO,* XXXII, p. 74, n. 4, Coedès observed that the correct date of the performance of this ceremony in the reign of Rāmādhipatī II is A.D. 1496, probably on the occasion of the king's twenty-fifth birthday. With regard to my translation of the difficult passage in *KM* which describes this ceremony, Coedès (rev.) made a number of corrections and improvements which are incorporated in the following:

"For the royal ceremony of *Indrābhiṣeka* a Meru, of a height of 1 *sen̆* 5 *vā*,[3] is built in the middle of an open space. There Indra sits on the Meru, surrounded by Isindhara and Yugundhara mountains, one *sen̆* high; and there stands Karavika Mountain 15 *vā* high and Mount Kailāsa 10 *vā* high. On the inside are golden umbrellas, in the middle are red-gold umbrellas, and those of silver are outside. Outside these again is a *rājavăt* fence with umbrellas of five colours. Within the umbrellas stand figures of *devatā*, and outside them is a *rājavăt* fence. Paper umbrellas and figures of giants (*yăkṣa, gandharba, rākṣaṣa*) stand at the foot of the Meru; and there are figures of various kinds of lions (*gajasīha, rājasīha, sin̄to, kilen*) goat-antelopes, elephants, cows, buffaloes, tigers, bears, and *devatā* all over Kailāsa. On the summit of Meru sits a figure of Śiva and graceful Umā. Figures of Indra and *asuras* are in the middle of the Meru; Viṣṇu sleeps on the water at the foot of the Meru, and a seven-headed *nāga* encircles the Meru. Outside the open space stand *asuras*, and outside the walls are dancing halls. Lictors are dressed as 100 *asuras*, and pages represent 100 *devatā*. There are Bālī, Sugrīva, Mahājambhū, and a train of 103 monkeys.

[1] Cf. P. Paris, "Lex Bateaux des bas reliefs Khmers", *BEFEO*, XLI, pt. 2, p. 354, where he also discusses the more remote ancestry of the craft.

[2] G. Coedès, *Inscriptions du Cambodge*, Vol. IV, p. 87.

[3] 1 *vā* = 1 fathom, 1 *sen̆* = 20 fathoms.

They pull the ancient *nāga*; the *asuras* pull the head, the *devatā* pull the tail, and the monkeys are at the end of the tail. One side of the Meru is gold, one side is red-gold, one side crystal, one side silver, the Yugundhara mountain is gold, the Isindhara is red-gold, Karavika and Kailāsa are silver. On the surrounding space outside are elephants, horses, and the four divisions of the army. Officials of 10,000 marks of dignity wear diadems,[1] and put on coats and silk *phā̆-nuṅ* of honour. Those of 5,000 grade wear golden hats and put on coats and splendid silk *phā̆-nuṅ*. Those of 3,000 wear hats of foreign silk and coats and silk *phā̆-nuṅ*. Those of 2,400 to 1,200 marks of dignity carry silver and gold flowers according to rank, with flowers and pop-corn to pay homage. Brahmans of various sects sit within the enclosure. On the first day there is a penance [a preparatory retreat]; on the second and third days they start the building; on the fourth the construction is finished; on the fifth day they pull the ancient *nāga*. On the sixth day they make three pools of angelic water, a three-headed elephant, a white horse, a king of oxen, the king of Garuḍas and Nang Tārā [meaning Śrī, since it is the products of the churning which are being referred to] before the king's seat. They take arms, elephant weapons, and ropes for catching elephants, and steep them in water. A hundred men dressed in brocade and led by Śiva, Viṣṇu, Indra, and Viṣvakarmā, and carrying their emblems, come to salute the king. On the seventh day the Brahmans render homage and on the eighth day the princes pay homage, on the ninth day they offer the elephants and horses and the four divisions of the army; on the tenth day they offer the twelve treasuries; on the eleventh day they offer the taxes; on the twelfth day they offer the city; on the thirteenth day they offer the consecrated water; on the fourteenth day they make offerings to the *devatā*; on the fifteenth day the king makes presents to the princes; on the sixteenth day to the officials; on the seventeenth day the king rewards the Brahmans; on the eighteenth day there are offerings of *kalpavṛkṣa* fruits;[2] on the nineteenth, twentieth and twenty-first days gold and silver flowers are scattered. For a month theatricals are performed. They build a standing effigy of a giant 1 *sĕn* high. The pages represent monkeys and go out through openings in its ears, nose, eyes, and mouth, and the king drives a royal car scattering alms about the city. This is the end of *Indrābhiṣeka*."[3]

[1] These are of a certain kind described by Coedès in *JSS*, xvi, p. 38.

[2] See page 146.

[3] The above translation now appears to me to be entirely satisfactory. However, in comparing it with the partial translation given by Prince Dhani in connection

Coedès points out in *BEFEO*, XXXII, p. 74 that *Indrābhiṣeka* is mentioned in a Bayon inscription where it explains the king's going into a quiet retreat before the rite, and also the next bas-relief scene where athletes and jugglers are performing, as was also the case in connection with the Siamese ceremony.

In my last paragraph in the text on this ceremony I was at a loss to appreciate the connection between the churning and the idea of an *Indrābhiṣeka*. This evoked an enlightening response from *JIH* review: " The connection is intimate. *Indrābhiṣeka* is a ceremony symbolizing the re-installation of Indra in his position after having lost his wealth and position as the result of the slaying of Vṛitra, and the recovery of it was after a long period of penance by the churning of the ocean of milk."

CHAPTER X

TONSURE—AND OTHER INITIATIONS

Apart from correcting *Sikkhā* for *Sikjā* in the fifth line of p. 126, and mentioning that the *Traibhūmi* of A.D. 1776 referred to on p. 127 is King Ṯāk's recension, the first version going back to the reign of King Lu'dai of Sukhodaya, I say no more on the Tonsure Ceremony. The other initiation rites (*samskāras*) mentioned on p. 126 would not qualify for consideration in a work on state ceremonies, and have moreover been dealt with by me elsewhere.[1] Exception should, however, be made for the River-bathing Ceremony, and it was in view of this omission that I published an article on it not long after my book made its appearance.[2] A few errors and omissions in this were shortly afterwards noted by R. Lingat,[3] which are taken into account in this revised description.

THE RIVER-BATHING CEREMONY

Naḥhānaḥ ṯittha maṅgalam (Pāli, *tittha* landing-place, *nahānam* = bathing, *maṅgala* auspicious) is the classic term applied to the River-bathing Ceremony in Siam, but the popular form of the ceremony

with his interpretation of the supposed representation of the ceremony on a lacquer screen in the Grand Palace (*Artibus Asiae*, XXIV, 3/4, 1961, pp. 276, 281) one notices a few discrepancies.

[1] H. G. Quaritch Wales, " Siamese Theory and Ritual connected with Pregnancy, Birth, and Infancy ", *Journ. Roy. Anthrop. Inst.*, Vol. LXIII, 1933, pp. 441–451.

[2] H. G. Quaritch Wales, " Naḥhānaḥ Ṯittha Maṅgala, the River bathing Ceremony in Siam ", *Bull. School of Oriental Studies*, Vol. VI, pt. 4, 1932, pp. 957–962.

[3] R. Lingat in *JSS*, Vol. xxvii, pp. 127 sq.

was formerly known as *bidhī maṅgala laṅ dā sòn vāy nām* "auspicious rite of taking the child out to bathe at a river (or sea) landing and teaching him to swim". The name of the popular form of the ceremony is interesting as showing that in former times the ceremony retained its early function of marking a definite stage in the development of the child, an occasion on which it was taught to swim, and after which it would be regarded as more independent and capable of taking care of itself. This stage of initiation was immediately antecedent to that marked by the tonsure, after which the initiate was regarded as having definitely bidden farewell to childhood days. The importance of the river-bathing ceremony in the social life of a people like the Siamese, whose welfare largely depended on their being amphibious at an early age, is evident. But like most of the other *saṃskāras*, probably as a result of the influence of Buddhism, the popular ceremony lost its hold on the people and died out about 180 years ago, after which the ceremony as performed for *Cau Fā* princes and princesses, in practice only the heir apparent, alone remained in favour. This royal ceremony was performed in the ninth, eleventh, or thirteenth year of age, and is called simply *bidhī laṅ sraṅ* "the bathing ceremony". It will be seen from the account which follows, that the observance has lost its early function and degenerated into a rather meaningless ceremonial bath and *abhiṣeka*, in analogy to many other royal ceremonies.

I am not aware of the existence of any record of the manner in which the popular form of the ceremony was performed, but there is material for a fairly detailed description of the river-bathing ceremony of *Cau Fās*. The following account refers to the first occasion on which the *laṅ sraṅ* was revived at Bangkok, after the destruction in A.D. 1767 of the old capital, Ayudhyā, and it became the model for future royal ceremonies of the kind.[1]

In the year A.D. 1813 the eldest son of King Rāma II by a royal mother attained the age of nine years, and his father reflected that, whereas in the first reign tonsures had been performed in the style of those of Ayudhyā, the river-bathing ceremony of *Cau Fās* had not yet been carried out. The older people who had seen this ceremony at Ayudhyā had nearly all died, and the knowledge of the way in which it should be carried out would soon be lost. Accordingly, at the coming of the fourth month (Phālguna), Prince Cau Fā Kram Hlvaṅ Bidakṣa

[1] My authority is Prince Damrong's *History of the Second Reign*, pp. 144–149, the author basing his account on the contemporary Bangkok annals by Cau Braḥyā Dibākravaṅṣa, together with the official regulations for carrying out the ceremony.

Mantrī and Cau̍ Braḥyā Śrīdharmādhirāja were appointed superintendents of the river-bathing ceremony of the young prince.

The preparations for the *laṅ sraṅ* resembled those for the *sokănta* (tonsure of *Cau̍ Fās̍*) except that instead of a Kailāsa mountain being built within the Grand Palace enclosure, a four-sided spire-roofed shrine (*maṇḍapa*) was erected on a pontoon, similar to those used for Siamese floating houses. The pontoon was moored at the royal landing, and the *maṇḍapa*, which stood on the central part of the pontoon, was built of figwood (*udumbara*) covered with white cloth, and had carved doors at each of the four sides. Beneath the *maṇḍapa* the pontoon was cut away to make a bathing-pool, with a floor beneath the water-level made of a trellis of strong bamboo laths, protected on the outside by the meshes of a net, while the inside of the floor and walls of the bathing pool were covered with cloth. Thus a safe artificial bathing place was constructed, into which the river water was admitted but from which noxious aquatic animals were excluded. Running round the edge of the bathing pool, at the water-level, was a foot-board on which people could stand, and to which access was obtained from the floor of the pontoon by means of three ladders, a silver one on the north, a gilded one on the south, and a so-called " crystal " one on the eastern side, which was nearest to the landing-place. On the western edge of the pool, within the *maṇḍapa*, was placed a seat of two stages for the *mūrdhābhiṣeka*, while three artificial prawns, of gold, red-gold, and silver respectively, three fish of similar materials, a pair of gilded coco-nuts, and a pair of silvered ones, were also placed at hand. Possibly the artificial prawns and fish were meant to represent the wonderful aquatic fauna of the Anotatta lake in the Himālayan fairyland, while it may be presumed, on the analogy of the bundle of coco-nuts carried on royal barges in lieu of life-belts, that the gilded and silvered coco-nuts used in this ceremony were intended to be used as floats by the young prince.

The *maṇḍapa* was surrounded by three concentric rows of *rājavăt* fences, decorated with gold, red-gold, and silver umbrellas respectively. At the four corners of the *maṇḍapa* the Brahmans placed tables to support the chank-shell water, and the consecrated water called *nām̍ krat* " sharp or powerful water ", for sacrificing for victory. During the ceremony, soldiers armed with lances, the handles of which were draped in gold, stood within the middle fence, ten men to each of the three exposed sides. Between the middle and outer fences stood soldiers armed with iron swords, fifteen to each of the three sides. Outside the outer fence there were soldiers armed with swords, sixteen to each of the three sides, while in the water near the raft there were soldiers similarly armed, to the number of sixteen on each of the three sides. On the north side of the pontoon, outside the fences, stood soldiers armed with flint-locks. Pavilion-barges were moored alongside the landing, while monkey barges, garuḍa barges, guard boats, and war barges with figure-heads representing various animals, the paddlers wearing red hats and coats, cast anchor in a circle to the number of thirty-nine boats. There were boats manned by crocodile hunters, and boats casting nets in order to catch any malignant beasts which might enter the protected circle, and endanger the safety of the young prince during the ceremony. Inside the Grand Palace enclosure, a pavilion was erected for the Brahmanic rites and a hallowed circle (*brahdèṅ maṇḍala*) was prepared in the Tusiṯa Mahā P̱rāsāda (throne hall) for the recitation of auspicious stanzas by the Buddhist monks. Protective threads (*sāy siñcana*) of unspun cotton were passed round each of the places at which rites were to be performed in order to preserve them from evil influences, as in the Tonsure ceremony.

On Friday, the fourth day of the waxing of the fourth month, the young prince was attired in white in the Baiśāla Dakṣina section of the Royal Residence, whence, in the afternoon, he proceeded in state accompanied by a procession similar to that of the Tonsure, by a circuitous route partly outside the palace wall, to the Tusiṯa Mahā P̱rāsāda. There the king, who had gone by a more direct route, was waiting to assist him from his palanquin. The palace ladies led him by the hand and invited him to have his feet washed by the pages in a silver basin. When this had been done he entered the throne hall, sat down within the hallowed circle, and listened to the recitation of *paritta suttas*. Afterwards the king entered and lit candles of worship, repeated the *śīla* precepts, and remained to listen to the *paritta* recitations until they were finished. The palace ladies then led the prince to the mounting stairs, and the king assisted him to mount his palanquin, after which he returned with the procession to the Royal Residence. Similarly, on the following two evenings, the prince went in state to listen to the Buddhist recitations, but this is to be regarded merely as the preparation which is the prelude to most important royal ceremonies.

On Monday, the seventh of the waxing, in the morning, fifteen monks went to recite auspicious stanzas at the bathing place. When the prince arrived in state, the king assisted him from his palanquin, and the palace ladies led him to the landing where he removed his shoes and ornaments. As the auspicious time drew near, the king led the prince by the hand from the landing to the " raft of scented water ". Then Prince Bidakṣa Manṯrī took the young prince by the hand and, following the king, they went to the *maṇḍapa*. The king sat upon a chair within the *rājavăt* fences, and the prince sat on a cushion near the chair. The *Braḥ Mahā Rāja Grū* (High Priest of Śiva) floated the gold, red-gold, and silver prawns and fish, and the two pairs of gilded and silvered coco-nuts in the bathing pool. The *horā* (astrologer) made an oblation to the water at the auspicious time of 7.18 a.m. Officials beat the Gong of Victory, sounded the conches and other musical instruments, and fired signal guns in the bows of the barges, all at the same time. The king carried the young prince to the " crystal ladder " and Prince Cau Fā Kram Khun Iśarānurăkṣa (the Uparāja) received him in his arms and carried him down to the bathing pool. He let him seize the coco-nuts and bathe in the river water in the pool. Then he brought him up and placed him on the anointment seat, where the young prince was sprinkled by the king with water from a dextrorse chank. The *Săṅgharāja* sprinkled him with water which had been consecrated by means of the recitation of Buddhist *mantras*, the senior members of the royal family sprinkled him with water from sacred lotus gourds, and lastly, the Brahmans offered chank-water and *nāṁ krat*. When this bathing in scented waters was finished and the young prince had changed his wet robes and was dressed in royal ceremonial dress, he was accompanied by Prince Bidakṣa Mantrī to the landing. There the procession was already drawn up, its members having now donned red garments. The king having assisted the prince to mount the palanquin, the procession returned in state to the Royal Residence via the circuitous route outside the walls, but the king proceeded to the Tusita Mahā Prāsāda and made offerings to the monks who had officiated. Later, the prince, having removed his ceremonial attire and dressed himself as usual, went by the short inner route to the Tusita Mahā Prāsāda and made offerings to the monks, afterwards returning by the same way.

Meanwhile in the Căkrabartibimān section of the Royal Residence officials had set up three *pai-śrīs* of gold, silver, and crystal respectively bearing offerings of food; and in front of these they had placed the young prince's throne. In the afternoon, the young *Cau Fā*, dressed in the attire of a prince of the highest rank, went in state procession to the Căkrabartibimān, where the king received him and escorted him to the golden throne prepared for him. He was now about to relinquish the personal name that had been given him at the naming ceremony a month after birth. At the auspicious time of 2.36 p.m. the ceremonial instruments were sounded, and a golden plate (*subarṇapaṭa*) was presented to the prince, on which were inscribed his new style and title, as follows: Cau̓ Fā̓ Maṅkuṭ Sammuṯidevāvaṅṣa Baṅṣa Iśrakṣāṯriya Khăṯiya Rājakumāra. Then the taper-waving rite (*vian dian*) was performed by the Brahmans, for the benefit of the prince. The final rite of the *laṅ sraṅ*, as of the Tonsure, was the *sambhoj*, or feast, in which the young prince partook of a small quantity of coconut milk mixed with food from the *pai̱-śrīs*, as nourishment for his *khvăñ* spirit. This rite was repeated twice again, on the eighth and ninth days of the waxing, being thus performed thrice in all.

It should be remarked that it was more usual and proper in Siam to change the names and title of persons of the royal family after they had undergone the tonsure, for not only does that ceremony symbolize a more complete break with childhood, but there is also the classical Indian precedent of the god Khandhakumāra, whose name was changed to Mahā Vighneṣa after tonsure.

Owing to the lack of *Cau̓ F̱ā̓* princes the *laṅ sraṅ* was not again performed until January 1887, in honour of the future King Rāma VI. Extant photographs as well as a skilfully made model in the National Museum enable us to appreciate that the ceremony was celebrated with a splendour which even more than the Tonsure may be held to vie with that of the Coronation itself.

CHAPTERS XI AND XII

CREMATION

p. 137, note 1. With regard to source (2) for *Kaṭhmāy* read *Catmāy*. The title was misunderstood by me since the work is actually a description of two eighteenth-century cremations, only the second one, that of Princess Yodhādeb, at the beginning of the last Ayudhyan reign, being complete and detailed. However it tells us nothing that is not already known from the Bangkok royal cremations, but serves to confirm the close adherence of the latter, at least the earlier ones, to the Ayudhyā model. Possibly it was the minute description of the Meru, and especially of the arrangement of the decorations and fixing of the curtains [1] together with the accompanying plans of the buildings, that led to my error, in the course of a too cursory examination. Surprisingly, no one has called attention to this.

p. 140, l. 7. Gold was also placed in the mouth in Burma and Annam. For its magical powers see J. Przyluski "L'or, son origine et

[1] This was commented on by Prince Dhani in *JSS*, liv, pt. 2, 1966, in connection with a recent re-edition of the Ayudhyā record.

ses pouvoirs magiques ", *BEFEO*, XIV. In China it represented the *yang* principle (De Groot, *The Religious Systems of China*, I, p. 269). In the *Śatapatha Brāhmaṇa* (*SBE*, XLIV, p. 203), gold is held to bestow immortality.

p. 141, last line. The comparison of the catafalque with Baksei Chamkrong should not be too closely pressed; for the Siamese it is essentially a Meru, just as is the pyre, and the great Urn resembles *prāsāda* spire (also a Meru). See *BEFEO*, XL, pt. 2, p. 319 footnote.

p. 143, l. 13. *For* fifteenth *read* last.

p. 144. *The Funeral Pyre.* For a recent study of this structure with architectural plans, see Phya Anuman Rajadhon "The Golden Meru", *JSS*, xlv, pt. 2, 1957, pp. 65–71. The author's suggestion (p. 66) that the Urn is a phallic symbol can scarcely be accepted.

p. 150, l. 30. Coedès (rev.) points out that the rhinoceros figured in an Aṅkor Văt relief was there as the mount of Agni in the legend of Bāṇa (*Mem. EFEO*, II, pl. 402). Consequently the rhinoceros as bearer of Fire was indeed known at Aṅkor Văt, though the relief is a late one.

p. 159, l. 4. *Delete*: with a certain amount of influence from Śrīvijaya.

p. 161, l. 17. *Delete*: if we had further evidence we should probably find that it was from that source [Śrīvijaya] that the Khmers derived many of their Brahmanical cremation rites.

p. 162, l. 9. There is no evidence that the Cult of the Deva-rāja was inherited by the first Thai kings.

p. 162, l. 10. *Delete*: the Khmer cult had been founded on Indian Brahmanism much elaborated by its passage through Śrīvijaya.

p. 163, l. 17. *The theory is that the King . . . is reborn.* The squatting position in the Urn (and in Cambodia the two pieces of cloth probably symbolizing amnion and chorion) may be intended to represent the position of the foetus, thus symbolizing rebirth. (Cf. *BEFEO*, XL, pt. 2, p. 318, and Leclère, *La Cremation et les rites funeraires*, p. 27.)

CHAPTER XIII

THE WORSHIP OF DEAD KINGS

p. 169, l. 9 from bottom. For the cult of the Deva-rāja see Notes to pages 29–30.

p. 171. *Add at end of first paragraph*: Coedès (rev.) considered that these statues in fact represent more than simple acts of merit, whatever the Siamese know or care to admit. Without being a true portrait statue, an image made to commemorate a reign must have a certain relation to the royal person. Coedès thus thought that it probably derives from the Khmer apotheosis : " C'est la vieille tradition khmère des statues de *Kamrateṅ jagat* transposée dans le bouddhisme siamois ".

Besides the Buddha images cast for the kings of the Bangkok dynasty, Rāma IV also had images cast to commemorate the 34 kings of Ayudhyā and Dhanapurī (*BRB*, pp. 238 sqq.). But only those of the reigning dynasty were provided with umbrellas.

CHAPTER XIV

ROYAL AUDIENCES

p. 190. The idea of the audience bell persisted in the nineteenth century, though the bell was replaced in Rāma IV's reign by a drum, now in the National Museum. Coedès (rev.) thought that a Chinese origin of the custom was possible.

CHAPTER XV

THE OATH OF ALLEGIANCE

The Drinking of the Water of Allegiance (*Bidhī śrīsaccapānakāla* or *thū' nām*), of such vital importance to absolute monarchy, was no longer performed after 1932, its place having been taken by Constitution Day.[1] Here I propose to extract from *BRB* a few more details of the old ceremony.

Within the *siñcana* thread, or hallowed area in the Chapel Royal, the statues of the Buddha representing the kings of the Cākrī dynasty, were placed on a throne, with below them the Brahmanic books, statues of Śiva, Umā, Viṣṇu and Brahmā, three arrows and the Diamond Spear. On one side was placed the Sword of Victory, and on the other the royal title tablet. Other royal weapons, candles and utensils were also arranged before the Buddhas. Twelve silver bowls, with two basins between them were placed on a bench, all within the area enclosed by the sacred thread.

In earlier reigns few monks took part in the ceremony, but Rāma IV increased the number to thirty-seven, equal in number to the statues

[1] For this see K. Wells, op. cit., p. 203.

that had been cast to represent the kings of Ayudhyā, Dhanapurī, and Bangkok up to that time. (This was naturally one of the occasions on which the royal relics and statues were honoured.) The evening before the ceremony a scribe read a *prakāśa* [1] praising the dynasty, exhorting officials to fidelity and finally appealing to the *devatā* in the manner usual to *prakāśa*.[2] Then the monks recited *parittas*, and the Brahmans passages from their books, in preparation for the next day. *Biṇbādya* music (drums and gongs), but not *mahorī* (strings) was played.

In the morning, after the monks had been fed, the water for the Oath was prepared. A Brahman read certain verses giving the water power to destroy the disloyal. The language of this proclamation is Siamese but so archaic as to be scarcely intelligible. Rāma V believed it to date from the beginning of the Ayudhyā period and to have been introduced from India. There is nothing Buddhist about it; first Viṣṇu, then Śiva, and finally Brahmā are invoked and the creation is described. Then the king is praised, the false are cursed, the loyal promised reward.[3]

An innovation was made by Rāma IV to take place at this juncture, and it is especially interesting because so different from his usual Buddhist modifications. A document is known which tells us how this innovation came about. In 1853 the king was presented with some ornamental canes and after due consideration he decided to have three arrows made from them for this ceremony, because Bangkok is the city of Rāma or Viṣṇu. Details are given of their manufacture. At an auspicious time a rites hall was set up in the arsenal. Iron was brought and struck to form the arrow-heads, while *biṇbādya* music was played. Before images of the Hindu deities the shafts were affixed with appropriate ritual, a piece of gold engraved with a mystic symbol being placed in each socket, and auspicious names were given to each arrow.[4] Feathers were attached with gold wire. At the waxing of the tenth moon, the arrows were taken to a sacred lake at Labapurī, where a rites hall was set up and monks chanted. At the auspicious moment the arrows were dipped in the lake while *biṇbādya* music was played and the Gong of Victory sounded. Cannon were fired four times and small arms continually. After a *vian dian* rite had been performed the three arrows were taken in procession to a *văt* and Brahmanic *yantras* were inserted

[1] See below, Notes to Chapter XXVI.

[2] Full Siamese text in H.R.H. Prince Damrong's *Prakāśa Kāra Rājabidhī*, Vol. I, pp. 1–20.

[3] ibid., Vol. I, pp. 21–28.

[4] Cf. H. G. Quaritch Wales, *Ancient South-east Asian Warfare*, pp. 149 sq., for another example of magic sword-making in Siam.

in each shaft. The arrows were then taken in procession back to Bangkok in time for the Oath-taking ceremony of the tenth month.

Here we may note the sound psychology of Rāma IV in recognizing that there was little scope for his usual Buddhist additions. More immediate effects in the way of putting teeth into the Oath might be achieved by representing Viṣṇu as a powerful local deity. In making these arrows the king enlisted the full power of this local Viṣṇu's wrath against any who should threaten the security of Rāma's capital (Bangkok). At the same time, so far as Buddhism was concerned, the identifying of the officiating Buddhist monks with the number of the previous Siamese kings, may be seen as a shrewd move to associate his predecessors with the sanctions. It should be added, however, that Rāma IV introduced the practice of the king also taking the Oath, this implying a certain reciprocity.

To return to the ceremony of Drinking the Water at the point where we left it. An image of Viṣṇu, armed with a bow, was placed in the middle of a basin filled with the consecrated water. The *Braḥ Mahā Rāja Grū* dipped each of the three arrows in the water, then made obeisance with joined palms. A secretary then read the Oath. The translation I reproduced from Miss Cort's book, though not very literal (e.g. as to the mention of specific guardian deities) gives an adequate idea of it. At line 2 p. 194 I inadvertently inserted Rāma IV, instead of Rāma V. The original of this translation is available in *Prakāśa*, Vol. I, pp. 28–36.

The Brahman acting as chief of the Vaiṣṇavas then received the royal weapons from an official. With a white cloth around his hand, and drawing the weapons from their scabbards, he dipped each in the water in each silver pot and basin. Some of the weapons used, notably the Sword of Victory and the Diamond Spear, also the Gun, were made in the first reign, others were made subsequently. After the dipping the monks recited *gathas*, and *biṇbādya* music was played without cease. Then the Brahmans added to the water in each vessel a little of the water into which the three arrows had previously been dipped, also some scented water which they had consecrated; so the water when actually drunk had a composite potency.

The princes drank the water inside the Chapel Royal, the officials in front of it, a somewhat shortened version of the Oath being read outside. The positions to be taken up by the various grades of nobles and officials inside and outside the Chapel, the regulations for taking the Oath by the chiefs of the Môns (resident in Siam), by the wives of officials, by the members of the royal family in the palace, and the attire considered suitable, are all described in much detail in *BRB*.

As taken in the provincial towns, the Oath was similar though comparatively short.[1] Officials of the dependent provinces had to come up to the chief town of the province on which they depended. The ceremony took place at an important *văt*, and the governor's sword of office was used.

King Rāma V states that there were five kinds of occasion for taking the Oath, as follows: (1) On the king's accession; (2) twice yearly, that at the fifth month being more important than that at the tenth; (3) for defeated enemies; (4) formerly some of the soldiers had to take the Oath every month, but in the fifth reign this was changed so that it was taken only on enlistment; (5) Army officers had to take the Oath on appointment to a new rank.

The hostage Lao and Khmer princes in Rāma III's reign had to come and take the Oath at the Chapel Royal, like ordinary officials, but the Malay rulers took an Oath according to Islam in the council chamber. In these earlier Bangkok reigns Europeans in the government service had to take the Oath administered by a Christian priest, in the Palace department. For both the Europeans and Malays in the government service the wording of the Oath was altered according to their respective religion. This is confirmed by La Loubère for the Ayudhyā period. He states that the king required all in his service to take an Oath of Allegiance, whatever their nation or religion.

There were some differences in the Ayudhyā period Oath-taking not previously mentioned by me, as follows: the *KM* states that death was the punishment of officials who did not come to the ceremony, or falsely gave illness as excuse for staying away. Equally on pain of death it was forbidden to wear gold or red-gold rings at the ceremony, to eat before it, or to fail to pour the last drops of the water from the cup onto one's head—evidently in token of humility. The same rules are laid down in the Cambodian *KM*, and were apparently practised until recent times.[2] In a passage not previously referred to by me Leclère makes remarks about the servility of the Cambodian oath similar to those I made about the Siamese. But whereas I compared the Siamese Oath adversely to that of the ancient Khmers he contrasted the Cambodian Oath to that of the proud and independent Malay who dipped his own weapon into the water previously consecrated by a royal weapon, letting some drops fall on his tongue.

Though it is obvious that the use of royal weapons to fortify the consecrated water implied contagious magic, the Oath itself being essentially an appeal to the *devatā* is certainly no less religious than

[1] The text is published in *Prakāśa* . . . Vol. I, pp. 26–28.

[2] L., pp. 645 sqq.

magical, both in regard to the cursing of offenders and the blessing of the loyal.[1]

CHAPTER XVI

THE ROYAL BOUNTY

p. 201, note 1. For further description of these warlike processions see the account of the royal progresses to vist the Buddha's Footprint in *JSS*, Vol. xxviii, 1935, pp. 8 sqq., and the account of King Nārāyaṇa's expedition against the Lao given in the (partial) translation of *HV* in *JSS*, Vol. xxix, pt. 2, 1936, pp. 124 sqq.

p. 211, note 1. *For* 92 *read* 93. The Regatta is also mentioned in *HV*.

p. 212. As royal bounty should also be included the *pia hvăt* monetary gifts distributed to officials in November. I have dealt with this in my *Ancient Siamese Government and Administration*, pp. 42, 226, 236.

CHAPTER XVII

ROYAL ANNIVERSARIES

p. 214, l. 7. Coedès (rev.) points out that high officials of commoner origin, and even European officials, were admitted to the Order of Culā Còm Klău.

p. 215, l. 6 from bottom. For *janam* read *janma*.

p. 216, l. 1. The festival of *Vaiśākha Pūjā* was not instituted by Rāma IV, but was first performed in Bangkok in 1817, and may be of earlier origin (*BRB*, p. 427).

p. 216, l. 2. Indian kings celebrating their birthday is mentioned in the *Agni Purāṇa*.[2] As mentioned above, in connection with *Indrābhiṣeka*, it appears that in the Ayudhyā period the twenty-fifth birthday was especially celebrated.

p. 216, l. 3 from bottom. I omitted to mention the Releasing of Bad Luck (*BRB*, pp. 689-692) which was performed at this time. Up to 1878 it was a Brahmanical rite but since then the Brahmanic texts have been replaced by Buddhist *suttas*. The manner in which these are recited to " release bad luck " on the King's birthday is explained by Wells, op. cit., pp. 200 sqq.

[1] Cf. E. Crawley, *Studies of Savages and Sex*, London, 1929, pp. 271 sq.
[2] Beni Prasad, *The State in Ancient India*, 1928, p. 331.

CHAPTER XVIII

CEREMONIES FOR THE CONTROL OF WIND AND RAIN

p. 221, l. 8 from bottom. Kite-flying in the Ayudhyā period is mentioned in *Evidence of the People of Ayudhyā*, p. 250, where its purpose is said to have been " for calling up the wind ".

p. 224, l. 5. The meaning of the term applied to the attitude of the Buddha referred to here is " image of the Gandhāra kingdom " and is illustrated in *JSS*, Vol. x, 1913, p. 32 (Coedès, rev.). For fuller information on the Buddhist features of *Baruṇa Sāṯra*, see Wells, op. cit., pp. 190–195.

p. 225. Coedès (rev.) referred to the existence of another rain-making rite, in which a female cat played the chief part, and was known as the " procession of madam cat ", but on the details of which he had no information. As a purely popular rite it is barely mentioned in *BRB*, p. 564, and is indeed outside the scope of the present work. However, we now have a detailed description of it, and of other popular rain-making rites, from the pen of Phya Anuman Rajadhon.[1]

p. 226, l. 11. Coedès (rev.) thought that the early European writers in referring to the water being cut with a sword might have actually observed another ceremony, which would have been similar to a Cambodian rite in which a sword is used. Presumably he had in mind the Cambodian rite mentioned lower down on the same page.

CHAPTER XX

THE SWINGING FESTIVAL

p. 238, l. 2. *Ṯrīyămbavāy Ṯrīpavāy*. *JIH* review connects these words with the " well-known (Tamil) poems Tiruvempāvai of Māṇikkavāsákar and Tiruppāvai, the Vaiṣṇava hymn of Āṇḍāḷ, both of them of similar import, sung usually early in the morning in the respective shrines of Śiva and Viṣṇu, in Mārgaśirṣa, the first month of the year of Viṣṇu ".

p. 241, l. 5 from bottom. It is said that in earlier times those swingers who failed to snatch the purse were liable to be roughly handled. There is support for this in *Evidence of the People of Ayudhyā*, p. 251, where it is stated that such unsuccessful swingers (referred to as Brahmans) were buried up to the waist, and their swing-seat was buried too.

p. 242, ll. 15 and 21. For *senaṅ* read *sneṅ*.

[1] " Fertility rites in Thailand ", *JSS*, Vol. xlviii, pt. 2, Nov. 1960, pp. 37–42.

p. 246, l. 18. With reference to my suggestion that the Siamese ceremony has been influenced more particularly by the form of the festival known in southern India, it is of interest to note what Soma Sundara Desikar, Pandit, Tamil Lexicon, Madras University, wrote to me in a letter dated February 8th, 1939. After referring similarly to the Tamil poems mentioned above, he adds that Swinging " is a common festival in all the Śaiva shrines of South India and probably dates from the 5th century A.D. It has found its way strangely enough into Vaiṣṇavism which adopted it sometime after the 9th or 10th century A.D. The festival proper is in honour of Śiva and finishes off on the first or second day of the waxing moon in December–January, generally taking place about Christmas time . . . It therefore becomes necessary to seek for light in these matters in the Tamil country."

p. 249, l. 7 from bottom. *Ulup*. The writer of the above letter further remarked that " the word ' *ulup* ' is *uluppai* in Tamil and means presents of fruits, etc., or offerings of them ".

p. 252, ll. 17, 32. The " mortar " is in fact a quern.

CHAPTER XXI

THE FIRST PLOUGHING

The evening before the First Ploughing a Buddhist ceremony, known as Blessing the Seed Rice took place. It was introduced by Rāma IV in accordance with his usual practice of making Buddhist additions to hitherto Brahmanical ceremonies. The Buddhist service, together with translations of the texts read, is described by Wells, op. cit., pp. 187–190.

p. 257, l. 25. As to the omens to be drawn from whichever commodity the oxen choose to partake of, Coedès (rev.) points out that the Siamese appear to have lost the exact meaning of the animals' choice, this being better preserved by the Cambodians (cf. L, p. 169).

p. 261, bottom line. There is no evidence for a Khmer ploughing ceremony ; it is not mentioned by Cheou Ta-Kouan (Coedès, rev.).

CHAPTER XXII

TEMPORARY KINGS

p. 269, l. 10 from bottom. Coedès (rev.) remarks that there is no evidence for Khmer temporary kings. However, I would suggest that it is possibly significant that Cheou Ta-Kouan stated that the king was *not* present at the burning of the padi ceremony.

CHAPTER XXIII

THE WHITE ELEPHANT

p. 276, l. 23. *For* Bakong *read* Bayon.

p. 282. Death of a White Elephant. The White Elephant of the seventh reign (pictured in his extreme youth in our Pl. XLIII) " died on 19th January, 1943. He was then just 18 years old. His carcase was handed to the animal welfare department, and his skeleton kept for educational purposes. Perhaps because of the war, perhaps because times and beliefs change, he was given no ceremonial funeral." [1]

CHAPTER XXIV

FEASTS OF LAMPS

p. 288, note 1. The sources do not include *NN* and *KM*, since the "*Còṅ Ṗariaṅ*" mentioned in them actually refers to *Lòy Braḥ Ṗraḥdīp*. It is mentioned in *Evidence of the People of Ayudhyā*, p. 250.

p. 289. In the *Còṅ Ṗariaṅ* 200 coloured lanterns were also erected around the palace walls (*BRB*, p. 12) and this would account for the " magnificent illumination " that so impressed La Loubère.

p. 292, note 1. *Lòy Braḥ Ṗraḥdīp* is also mentioned in *Evidence of the People of Ayudhyā*, p. 250, and under the name "*Còṅ Ṗariaṅ*" in *KM*. Coedès (rev.) drew attention to the description of a comparable ceremony among the Burmese, described by C. Duroiselle in *BEFEO*, IV, p. 415; and also mentions an evidently corresponding practice of the Môns of Lāṁbūn recorded in the *Jinakālamālinī*, *BEFEO*, XXV, p. 82, note 1.

CHAPTER XXV

MINOR BRAHMANICAL CEREMONIES

p. 297. *Snāna*. In its heyday this was scarcely a " minor " ceremony. King Rāma V in *BRB* gives a detailed order of procession for the third reign, the last period during which it was possible to carry out the celebrations in the traditional manner, because after that war elephants were too few in number. No document survives giving an order of procession for a previous reign. After the third reign the character of the ceremony was altered owing to Rāma IV trying to give

[1] *The Borneo Story*, London, 1957, p. 83.

this essentially Brahmanical ceremony a Buddhist purpose. But the rope uncoiling and coiling ritual remained unchanged until abolished in the fifth reign; some further details from *BRB* are here given.

The ritual was hedged about by certain taboos: thus no women were allowed to be present, or indeed anyone not concerned with the ceremony. Playfully mimicking the dance outside could lead to madness. The *Bṛdhipāśa* (*Vṛddhipāśa*) Brahmans performed the rites in honour of Viṣṇu on the lines I have described in connection with the Swinging: first the usual purificatory rites, then the honouring of the images on the *Bhadrapiṭha*, with reading of "Festival of Elephants" text and blowing of conches. Two gold dishes of popcorn and flowers for the king and two silver ones for officials were displayed, a custom which began with King Nārāyaṇa who was regularly present. Though since then no king ever attended, the custom was maintained to the end. It appears that the noose dance, accompanied by *binbādya* music was not performed by the Brahmans, but by an official of the elephant department who was skilled at it. He announced that he was Viṣṇu, when that deity changed his appearance to that of an elephant in order to teach elephant-hunting to four people who were going to catch the one-tusked elephant. So presumably imitative magic is concerned. No adequate description of the dance exists, and King Rāma V says that it had to be witnessed to be appreciated. It seems to have been lively and entertaining. In the Bangkok period the Brahmans were rewarded for carrying out the ritual with a *tamlung* of silver and white cloth for the image stands, also other material required for the rites.

There is mention of *vṛddhipāśa* treatises being known to the Sukhodaya king in the inscription of Nagara Jum, A.D. 1357. This inscription was published by Coedès,[1] and in connection with it he quoted from Tachard a passage showing that Brahmans were concerned with King Nārāyaṇa's elephant-catching, it seems in order to tame them with consecrated water.

CHAPTER XXVI

THE PROPITIATION OF SPIRITS

p. 302, l. 11 from bottom. *For* Shrine of the Pillar of the Lord of the Country *read* Shrine of the Spirit of the City Pillar. Chiengmai has

[1] G. Coedès, *Recueil des Inscriptions du Siam*, Part I, Bangkok, 1924, p. 88, and *JSS* xiii, pt. 3, p. 37.

a similar pillar, named Indakhila, housed in a special shrine which is illustrated by C. Notton on the plate facing p. 32 of his translation of the *Chronicle of Suvaṇṇa Khamdëng.* In the same work (pp. 57 sqq.) he gives details of the offerings made to the Chiengmai guardian deities.

My section on the Guardian Spirits of Cities did less than justice to the importance of securing the protection and goodwill of these spirits and other local *devatā* in connection with the state ceremonies, and indeed with most royal occasions. At least until very recent times it was the custom for an official to read out an address called *prakāśa devatā*, " appeal to the heavenly powers ", with appropriate variations, at the beginning of each such occasion. Prince Damrong collected a large number of these, dating from both the Bangkok and the Ayudhyā periods, which he published in two octavo volumes totalling 500 pages, *P̱rakāśa Kāra Rājabidhī*, Bangkok, 1913. The city guardian spirits, the spirits of the royal umbrella, as well as a host of atmospheric and local *devatā* are in each case invoked. K. Wells [1] has given an English translation of the *prakāśa* used at New Year and on the King's Birthday, which give an adequate idea of their contents. Furthermore, the Oath of Allegiance is essentially a *prakāśa*, appealing to the deities for protection against traitors, and is couched in very much the same terms. A somewhat unusual one I noticed in Prince Damrong's collection (Vol. II, pp. 202 sq.) is an appeal made for the recovery of a royal riding elephant, suffering from fever and off its feed for three days, with the promise of offerings to be made by the king if the request is granted. A sequel records that the elephant has recovered and mentions the candle and *pạị̱-śrī* offerings which were then made, coupled with a further appeal for the animal's continued well-being. Other types of occasion on which I have noticed in literature references to the guardian spirits being invoked include: prior to the launching of military campaigns, during the siege of Ayudhyā, and at the birth of a royal child. These varied examples will place the importance of the guardian genii in better perspective.

p. 307. Harvey in his *History of Burma*, p. 320, appends a note on *Myosade*, the Burmese name for human victims buried as guardian spirits. In addition to giving the Burmese evidence he refers to *ERE*, s.vv. " Bridge " and " Foundation, Foundation Rites " for examples showing that the practice has been world-wide. For the custom in Cambodia and Laos, see Mme. E. Porée Maspero, " Notes sur les particularités du culte chez les Cambodgiens ", *BEFEO*, XLIV, pt. 2, p. 639.

[1] Op. cit., pp. 184, 197.

CHAPTER XXVII

THE EXPULSION OF EVIL

p. 308. The General Expulsion of Evil at New Year. K. Wells [1] summarizes Rāma V's discussion of the popular belief in evil spirits, and he also mentions that the *Āṭānāṭiya Suṭra* is translated in *SBE*, Vol. IV, pp. 189–197. In addition to the sources already mentioned, there is a brief description in *Evidence of the People of Ayudhyā*, p. 251.

p. 309. The Expulsion of Disease. R. Lingat's source for his description of the cholera epidemic of 1820 is Prince Damrong's *History of the Second Reign*, pp. 279 sq. The ceremony for the expulsion of disease, performed in the cholera epidemics of 1811 and 1820, but thereafter abandoned, was known as *ābādhabināśa*. According to *BRB*, apart from the special features of the processions with Buddhist images, it had much in common with the yearly expulsion of evil, such as the closing of the city and palace gates, the drawing of the sacred thread around the buildings, the firing of guns and the recitation of the *Āṭānāṭiya Suṭra*.

p. 311. A Royal Exorcism. A Cambodian ceremony of royal exorcism is described by Leclère.[2] It probably had its parallel at the Siamese court.

CHAPTER XXVIII

GENERAL CONCLUSIONS

p. 315, l. 6. The word evolution is used here and elsewhere in this book (e.g. pp. 235, 247, 265) in a loose sense to mean change of any kind and not in its strict sense as meaning " a process of opening out or developing what is contained or implied in something". As correctly stated on page 317, line 7, we are frequently confronted with " a series of superimposed rites, the objects of which have often been forgotten or confused". As with Siamese architecture there is a joining or juxtaposition of elements from diverse sources. Change is thenceforward likely to be in the direction of degeneration. The adoption of the widespread institution of Temporary Kings (p. 265) is hardly likely to have been the result of local invention, and in the absence of any sign of moulding the borrowed institution in a specific direction, the later stages in the " evolution " really signify cultural loss.

[1] Op. cit., pp. 185 sq.
[2] L., pt. V, ch. VI.

p. 315, l. 3 from bottom. See Note referring to page 19, line 28, with regard to Buddhism at Lāṁbūn.

p. 316, l. 7. *For* 1656–84 *read* 1657–1688.

There is nothing in the main conclusions as formulated in this chapter that I now see any reason to alter, with the inevitable reminder that there was a change of regime in Siam the year after this book was published, and the Monarchy was Absolute no more. So our interest in the time when, as Coedès put it at the beginning of his review, " le salut même de l'Etat dépendait de la célébration ponctuelle des cérémonies royales " becomes more essentially historical. So far, that is, as our main subject matter is concerned. But this I already anticipated, while foreseeing a continuing function for Buddhist ceremonial. On my recent visits to Siam I have seen no reason to doubt the validity of the prophetic note on which I closed the book: " With the growth of education the change to a democratic form of government is certain to come sooner or later, and the beneficent influence of Buddhism manifested in every Ceremony of State will probably do much to mollify the dangers of the period of transition."

For Product Safety Concerns and Information please contact our EU representative GPSR@taylorandfrancis.com
Taylor & Francis Verlag GmbH, Kaufingerstraße 24, 80331 München, Germany

www.ingramcontent.com/pod-product-compliance
Lightning Source LLC
Chambersburg PA
CBHW050557270326
41926CB00012B/2094
* 9 7 8 1 1 3 8 9 9 6 1 6 8 *